D0954413

Madagascar
& Comoros

Gemma Pitcher, Patricia C Wright

Contents

Comoros
(p207)

Northern
Madagascar
(p141)

Western
Madagascar
(p125)

Eastern
Madagascar
(p164)

Antananarivo
(p58)

Central
Madagascar
(p80)

Southern
Madagascar
(p99)

Destination Madagascar & the Comoros

The first Europeans to reach Madagascar returned home with stories of baboons 2m tall and carnivorous trees that attacked humans. On reflection, these seem to be the only two species the giant island *hasn't* laid claim to at some point in its ecological history. After floating away from Africa 165 million years ago, Madagascar set about evolving a teeming mass of animals and plants unknown anywhere else on earth.

'A naturalist's promised land' was how one 18th-century visitor described Madagascar. With jumping rats, hissing cockroaches, moths as big as dinner plates and chameleons the size of matchsticks, not to mention something that looks like a teddy bear and sounds like a police car, it's easy to see what he meant.

Not that Madagascar's human inhabitants are exactly dull either. Rites of honour to the dead, sacred waterfalls, spirit caves and a complex web of beliefs and taboos bind them powerfully to the natural world and the ancestors they venerate.

The Comoros islands, scattered like pebbles in the ocean to the northwest of Madagascar, are just about as far off the world's radar as it's possible to be. Those travellers who do make it here will be rewarded with giant fruit bats flapping slowly across sunset skies, prehistoric fish swimming in turquoise seas, and wooden fishing boats bobbing in front of turreted stone mosques. The islands' crazy politics have earned them the nickname 'Cloud Coup-Coup Land', but the inhabitants are as warm and welcoming as their golden, sunlit beaches.

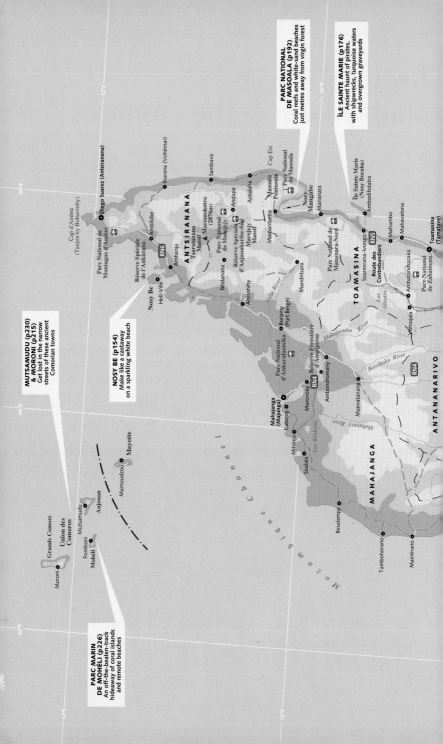

MUTSAMUDU (p230) & MORONI (p215)
Get lost in the narrow streets of these ancient Comorian towns

NOSY BE (p154)
Make like a castaway on a sparkling white beach

PARC MARIN DE MOHÉLI (p226)
An off-the-beaten-track hideaway of coral islands and remote beaches

PARC NATIONAL DE MASOALA (p192)
Coral reefs and white-sand beaches just metres away from virgin forest

ÎLE SAINTE MARIE (p176)
Ancient haunt of pirates, with shipwrecks, turquoise waters and overgrown graveyards

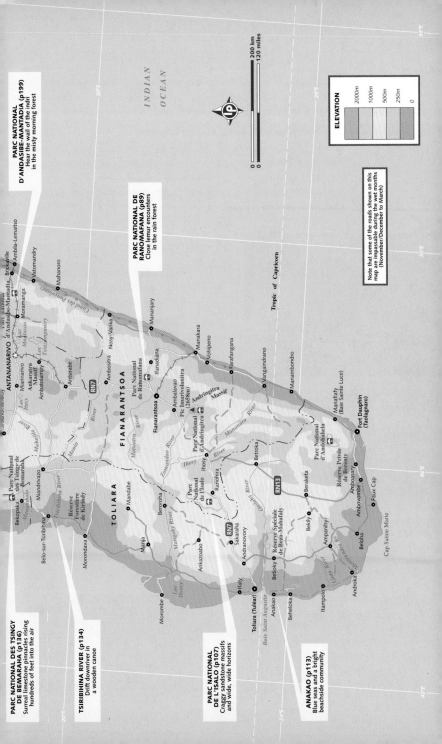

PARC NATIONAL DES TSINGY
DE BEMARAHA (p136)
Surreal limestone pinnacles rising
hundreds of feet into the air

TSIRIBIHINA RIVER (p134)
Drift downriver in
a wooden canoe

PARC NATIONAL DE L'ISALO (p107)
Craggy sandstone massifs
and wide, wide horizons

ANAKAO (p113)
Blue seas and a bright
beachside community

PARC NATIONAL
D'ANDASIBE-MANTADIA (p199)
Hear the wall of the indri
in the misty morning forest

PARC NATIONAL DE
RANOMAFANA (p89)
Close lemur encounters
in the rain forest

INDIAN
OCEAN

ELEVATION

| 2000m |
| 1000m |
| 500m |
| 250m |
| 0 |

Note that some of the roads shown on this
map are impassable during the wet months
(November/December to March)

200 km
120 miles

ANTANANARIVO

Tropic of Capricorn

Madagascar's national parks are rightly famous among wildlife aficionados worldwide. Lemurs are their best-known draw, but don't forget the weird and wonderful reptiles and birds – not to mention the unforgettable scenery.

At **Parc National de Ranomafana** (p89) wildlife watching in the cloud forest can be followed by a dip in a blissfully hot outdoor bath, while in **Parc National de Masoala** (p192), you can trek in the forest and snorkel over coral reefs all in the same day. **Parc National d'Andasibe-Mantadia** (p199), within easy reach of Antananarivo, is renowned for the eerie wail of the bearlike indri, Madagascar's largest lemur.

Encounter lizards as you clamber on the limestone pinnacles of Parc National des Tsingy de Bemaraha (p136)

CHRIS BARTON

KARL LEHMANN

Explore sacred waterfalls, rocky gorges and underground caves in Réserve Spéciale de l'Ankàrana (p152)

Hike past gigantic red-sandstone massifs, rising like statues from acres of undulating yellow grass in Parc National de l'Isalo (p107)

KARL LEHM

Madagascar's beaches are a spectacular addition to the forests and mountains for which the country is better known. The island's long coastline provides enough blue water, white sand and palm trees to keep the most insatiable beach addict happy for weeks. In the Comoros, the islands of **Parc Marin de Mohéli** (p226) rise dramatically from the sea and are a little-known paradise of coral reefs and hidden bays. Alternatively, don a snorkel and take to the water off **Mayotte** (p240) to watch sea turtles swimming – then return at night to see them lay their eggs on the shore.

DENNIS JONES

Hunt for shipwrecks and pirate graveyards, or just wander barefoot along miles of white sand on Île Sainte Marie (p176)

OLIVIER CIRENDINI

Discover a perfect slice of turquoise water next to a colourful fishing village in Anakao (p113)

Madagascar's range of things to do should satisfy everyone from hardened hikers to shopaholics – even trainspotters are catered for! In the Comoros, organised activities make way for hikes through the tangled green plantations of **Anjouan** (p229), or afternoons simply spent wandering the narrow stone streets of ancient Arab towns such as **Mutsamudu** (p230) and **Moroni** (p215).

MARGIE POLITZER

Shop for handmade paper in the medieval-looking, red-brick village of Ambalavao (p96)

Float downstream in a dugout canoe, watching birds, bathing in waterfalls and camping on sandbanks near the Tsiribihina River (p134)

CHRIS BARTON

Gaze out of the carriage window at misty gorges, remote villages and lush plantations on the way from Fianarantsoa to Manakara by train (p94)

OLIVIER CIR

Getting Started

One of the first Malagasy phrases you're likely to learn when you arrive in the country is '*mora mora*'. It means 'slowly, slowly' and pretty much sums up the attitude of the Malagasy to over-impatient or demanding travellers. There's no doubt that practical preparations help in creating the perfect trip to Madagascar, but the most useful piece of forward planning you can do is to get yourself into the mindset of the locals – what can't be changed isn't worth worrying about. Natural and man-made catastrophes are pretty common in Madagascar – bridges fall into rivers, cyclones destroy villages, buses break down for days on end and cargo boats capsize. The Malagasy give a Gallic shrug, a 'what can you do' grin, and make the best of it. The traveller who wishes to remain sane will be wise to do the same thing.

The second-most important thing you can do before setting off – especially if you're planning to travel independently in Madagascar – is to get yourself a French phrasebook and start learning. Almost no-one outside the most upmarket tourist hotels speaks a word of English, and that includes any fellow travellers you might be socialising with along the way. The gentle, charming Malagasy are a reserved lot – if you're used to travelling in Africa they can seem positively reticent. A phrase or two in a language they understand will go a long way towards breaking the ice.

See Climate (p247) for more information.

The Comorians are more forthcoming than the Malagasy, but certainly no more organised. In the Comoros, the phrase meaning 'slowly, slowly' is '*pole pole*', and it sums up the indolent, carefree feeling of the islands perfectly. Luckily, the Comoros' small size and good roads make them pretty easy to travel around, but you'd still be well advised to prepare yourself for some frustrating moments.

WHEN TO GO

Any time of year is fine for a visit to Madagascar except from January to March, when heavy rainfall in many areas of the country makes many roads muddy and impassable, and when the risk of cyclones (particularly in the east and northeast of the country) is high. In general, the best time to travel in most areas is April and October/November. The coolest time to travel anywhere in the country is during the winter months from May to October. During this time the Central Highlands (which include Antananarivo) can get bitingly cold and windy, with freezing showers, so bring enough warm and waterproof clothing, plus a decent sleeping bag if you're planning to camp.

During the rainy season between December and March/April, there is a risk of cyclones in the north and east of the country. Snorkelling and diving can be difficult, and some sailing trips aren't possible at this time due to rough seas. On the plus side, the rain makes parts of inland Madagascar particularly lush and green during this time. If you're planning to visit Fort Dauphin, be aware that it can have rain as late in the year as July.

The west and southwest get searingly hot during the summer, which can make moving around a struggle, particularly if you're travelling by *taxi-brousse* (bush taxi). By contrast, the winter months in these regions are pleasant, with blue skies, cooler temperatures and essentially no rain.

In the east and northeast be prepared for rain and overcast skies at any time, although rain showers don't usually last long during the winter months. The months with most rain in the northeast, the Masoala

Peninsula and around Maroantsetra, are from July to September. At this time the sea is too dangerous to travel by cargo boat.

Hotels and popular tourist attractions often get full, and prices go up, during the European holiday period from July to August, at Christmas and over Easter. The period between June and October is vanilla season on the east coast, so flights between towns such as Maroantsetra, Mananara and Antalaha are often full long in advance.

The Comoros are hot and sticky year-round. If you're visiting between October and April, be prepared for torrential monsoon rains. The coolest part of the year is between April and September. In July and August plane tickets to the Comoros are expensive and hard to come by, thanks to expat Comorians returning from Europe for their annual holiday. During the holy Muslim month of Ramadan (dates vary from year to year), shops open for only a couple of hours a day, and many restaurants, bars and discos are closed.

COSTS & MONEY

Madagascar is a pretty cheap travel destination by global standards, but transport in particular is getting more expensive due to the rising cost of fuel. If you're a couple staying in mid-range hotels, eating at fairly decent restaurants and travelling mostly by public transport, with the odd domestic flight, reckon on about €35 per person per day. If you're travelling alone, this could go up significantly as mostly you'll have to pay for double rooms in hotels. Most hotels offer significant discounts for children under 12. Budget travellers camping or sleeping in very cheap hotels, eating street meals and going everywhere by public transport can get by on about €17 per day.

Car hire, at around €85 per 4WD per day, is a significant cost of travel, as are hotel or tour-operator transfers, which can be essential if you're trying to get off the beaten track.

For both food and lodging, prices in Antananarivo and Nosy Be are a bit higher than elsewhere in the country.

The Comoros, and Mayotte in particular, can be a nasty shock for price-conscious travellers. Fixed exchange rates and imported goods make the islands some of the most expensive destinations in the Indian Ocean. Hotel rooms, however basic, rarely fall below €20, while private

LONELY PLANET INDEX

Madagascar
Litre of petrol €0.75

Litre of bottled water €1

THB beer €1

Souvenir T-shirt €12.25

Street snack €2.05

Comoros
Litre of petrol €0.70

Litre of bottled water U€0.80

Imported beer €1.25

Souvenir T-shirt €12.25

Street snack €4.05

DON'T LEAVE HOME WITHOUT...

- **Antimalarials** Most of Madagascar, and all of the Comoros, are a high-risk malaria area (p271).
- **Insect repellent** Better still, don't let the blighters bite you in the first place (p273).
- **Waterproofs and warm clothing** Much of Madagascar is colder and wetter than you think.
- **A decent tent with a groundsheet** Tents can be hired in Madagascar, but they're not always good quality.
- **Water purifiers** Better to treat your own water than lug litres along with you on hikes.
- **Modest clothing** Your skimpy little number won't be appreciated in the Muslim Comoros (p213).
- **Torch (flashlight)** You'll need it for night walks, cave explorations and unlit camping grounds, and during power cuts.
- **Earplugs** Taxi-brousse drivers love their radios and cheap hotels are usually noisy, too.
- **Tampons** Not easy to find in many places and often chauvinistically expensive.

TOP FIVE

LEMUR-WATCHING SPOTS

Let's face it, they're what you've come to see. Beady yellow eyes, shiny fur and treetop acrobatics are on all offer at:

- Parc National d'Andasibe-Mantadia (p199)
- Parc National de Ranomafana (p90)
- Réserve Spéciale de l'Ankàrana (p153)
- Réserve Privée de Berenty (p122)
- Parc Zoologique Ivoloina (p172)

TROPICAL BEACH PARADISES

After days slogging through the jungle, slipping on mud or wedged into a taxi-brousse, here are the perfect spots to kick back and indulge your inner sloth:

- Anakao, near Toliara (p113)
- Nosy Iranja, off Nosy Be (p163)
- Île aux Nattes, off Île Sainte Marie (p184)
- Lokaro Peninsula, near Fort Dauphin (p120)
- Itsandra Beach, near Moroni, Grande Comore (p219)

HIKES & TREKS

Madagascar is a walker's destination. Conditions and levels of difficulty vary, but most visitors will be strapping on their walking boots at some point. These are some of the most breathtaking walks on the island:

- Grotte des Portugais, Parc National de l'Isalo (p108)
- Grands Tsingy, Parc National des Tsingy de Bemaraha (p136)
- Peninsula circumambulation, Masoala Peninsula (p194)
- Ascent of Pic Imarivolanitra, Parc National d'Andringitra (p97)
- Mananara to Maroantsetra, northeast coast (p189)

taxi charters cost around €35. Meals at Comorian restaurants cost at least €7 for a main course, and in Mayotte the cost is usually even higher, with pizzas costing €12 not being unheard of!

TRAVEL LITERATURE

Most books are published in different editions by different publishers in different countries. As a result, a book might be a hard-cover rarity in one country, but readily available in paperback in another. Your local bookshop or library is best placed to advise you on the availability of the following recommendations.

Maverick in Madagascar, by Mark Eveleigh, is a quirky tale of what must have been a nightmarishly hard trip. The author travelled on foot down Madagascar's northwest coast and the infamous western 'Zone Rouge'.

Zoo Quest to Madagascar, by David Attenborough, is a marvellously dated account of the intrepid TV presenter's trip to Madagascar in the 1960s.

The Aye-Aye and I, by Gerald Durrell, is another golden oldie – the irrepressible Durrell took his team of long-suffering naturalists and film-makers to Madagascar to capture the island's rarest lemur.

The Coelacanth: A Fish Out of Time, by Samantha Weinberg, is a fascinating account of one fish-lover's lifelong quest to find the prehistoric coelacanth, finally caught off Anjouan in the Comoros. This book has lots of good background on the Comoros.

Madagascar, A World Out of Time, by Frans Lanting, has the world-famous wildlife photographer turning his magic lens to Madagascar for this glossy coffee-table book, with stunning and surreal results.

The Eighth Continent: Life, Death, and Discovery in the Lost World of Madagascar, by Peter Tyson, is a blend of scientific journalism, conservation politics and travelogue. The author accompanied four scientists on their journeys through Madagascar.

Mammals of Madagascar, by Nick Garbutt, is a recently published and comprehensive (read: heavy) full-colour guide to the various mammal species found on the island.

Muddling Through Madagascar, by Dervla Murphy, is the eccentric travel writer's account of an accident-prone trip to Madagascar with her 14-year-old daughter.

INTERNET RESOURCES

Internet sites on Madagascar and the Comoros are fairly numerous, but most are in French, and few are entirely up to date. The following have some or all of their content in English as well.

Angap (www.parcs-madagascar.com) The official website of Madagascar's national parks association has maps and information on each park and reserve in the country – plus a bizarre floating lemur.

BBC Country Profiles (http://news.bbc.co.uk/1/hi/world/africa/country_profiles) Comprehensive background information and the latest news headlines on both Madagascar and the Comoros.

Comoros Home Page (www.ksu.edu/sasw/comoros/comoros.html) Comprehensive, if slightly random, information and a long list of links, plus some photos.

Lonely Planet (www.lonelyplanet.com) General information on Madagascar and the Comoros, with links to traveller reports and useful websites.

Maison de Tourisme de Madagascar (www.tourisme-madagascar.com) Official site of Madagascar's tourist board; it has some useful maps but not much else.

World Factbook (www.cia.gov/cia/publications/factbook/geos/ma.html) Reams of rather dry statistical information on every aspect of the country. Pretty comprehensive, but it is a site run by the CIA...

HOW MUCH?

Madagascar
Cup of coffee €0.60

Seafood feast €10.60

Shared-taxi ride €0.75

50km bus trip €1.65

A zebu €163

Comoros
One dive €28.50

Seafood feast €12.25

Shared-taxi ride €0.80

Half-day canoe hire €14.65

A goat €20.35

Itineraries

CLASSIC ROUTES

ROUTE DU SUD

One month / Antananarivo to Toliara

The lovely smooth tarmac of the Route Nationale (RN) 7, commonly known as the Route du Sud, will whisk you from Antananarivo down to Toliara, stopping en route for some fantastic trekking opportunities.

Begin in **Antananarivo** (p58), with a few days adjusting to Malagasy life and taking in the sights. Then set off south for **Antsirabe** (p83), with its wide colonial streets and hordes of colourful rickshaws. Continue south to **Ambositra** (p87), the shopping capital of Madagascar. From here, you could opt for a side trip hiking around the **Zafimaniry villages** (p88) – allow at least three days if you want to get off the beaten track.

From Ambositra, head south to **Fianarantsoa** (p91), Madagascar's second-largest city, then on to **Ambalavao** (p96), one of the most beautiful towns in the highlands. Take a few days to hike among the spectacular granite valleys of **Parc National d'Andringitra** (p96). Spend a night relaxing in the peaceful atmosphere of Ambalavao, then head on through flatter scenery towards **Ranohira** (p106). This is the base for three or four days of trekking in **Parc National de l'Isalo** (p107), with its sandstone massifs and endless plains.

After some pretty hard travelling and trekking, you'll be overdue for a rest on the perfect beaches of **Anakao** (p113) or **Ifaty** (p110), near **Toliara** (p102), from where you can fly back to Antananarivo or travel on to Fort Dauphin (p116) or Morondava (p137).

The Route du Sud is 941km of tarmac, plied by numerous *taxi-brousse* (bush taxi) as far as Toliara. You can speed it up by leaving out some of the treks en route.

EAST COAST

One month / Antananarivo to Île Sainte Marie

A voyage to the east will take in everything from wailing lemurs to leaping whales, via pristine cloud forests and pirate graveyards. Unless you take your own car all the way, you'll need to be flexible enough to travel by *taxi-brousse* (bush taxi), canal boat and even dugout canoe!

Begin in **Antananarivo** (p58), spending a few days strolling along the cobbled streets. Then head east along the tarmac RN2 to the charming village of **Andasibe** (p201) and the eerie forests of **Parc National d'Andasibe-Mantadia** (p199), home of the legendary indri. Continue to **Brickaville** (p206), then rent a car or hitch to the tiny villages of **Ambila-Lemaitso** (p205) or **Manombato** (p205). From here, take to the French-built **Canal des Pangalanes** (p204), travelling up the waterways and lakes, stopping off at **Le Reserve d'Akanin'ny Nofy** (p205), or the tranquil fishing villages on the way north.

Chug onwards up to **Toamasina** (p167) to stroll on the esplanade or visit **Parc Zoologique Ivoloina** (p172). Continue north along the white beaches of **Mahavelona** (p174), **Mahambo** (p175) and **Fenoarivo-Atsinanana** (p175), or head straight to **Soanierana-Ivongo** (p175). From here catch a boat across to **Île Sainte Marie** (p176), with its turquoise seas and torrid history, and, should you need some serious R and R, splash out on one of the fabulous luxury hotels. The brave-hearted can continue north up the Vanilla Coast (p186).

The east coast route is around 500km of road, track, canal and sea! A shorter version leaves out the resorts north of Toamasina, and heads straight for Île Sainte Marie.

THE NORTH
Two weeks / Diego Suarez to Nosy Be

The north of Madagascar offers cloud forests, spectacular rock formations and white beaches, just waiting to be hiked in, climbed up or lazed upon.

Begin in colonial **Diego Suarez** (p144), Madagascar's northernmost town. Spend a few days hiking, sailing or rock climbing around the area (p148), then head out to sleepy **Joffreville** (p149) for a trek in the magical forest of **Parc National de Montagne d'Ambre** (p150). It's worth spending a night here at the beautiful forest camp site and gîte.

Return to Diego before setting out for the **Réserve Spéciale de l'Ankàrana** (p152), a wilderness of caves, pinnacles, gorges and canyons. You'll need at least three days to explore it fully, especially if you go to the less accessible, but more scenic, western side of the park.

At the end of your trip, you can either return to Diego once more or continue to **Ambilobe** (p154), from where it's easy enough to find onward transport to **Ambanja** (p154) and on to **Ankify** (p154). From here you can catch a ferry or smaller boat across to **Nosy Be** (p154), which is Madagascar's premier beach destination.

Once on the 'big island', head north from **Hell-Ville** (p158) to **Andilana** (p162) to avoid the tourist hordes and find the best beaches. Factor in a good few days to enjoy the coral reefs, white sand and palm trees of the outlying islands, such as **Nosy Iranja** (p163; the place to splurge on a luxury hotel), **Nosy Komba** (p162) or **Nosy Sakatia** (p163).

From Nosy Be you could continue by plane or boat to **Mahajanga** (p131) or the **Comoros** (p208).

The north route is around 250km, plus a bit more for Parc National de Montagne d'Ambre and Réserve Spéciale de l'Ankàrana. Flying between Diego and Nosy Be will save time.

ROADS LESS TRAVELLED

THE VANILLA COAST   One month / Île Sainte Marie to Diego Suarez

The crazy world of the Vanilla Coast is best explored by travellers with plenty of time and a well-developed sense of adventure. Those who do attempt this journey are sure not to regret it.

Begin in **Île Sainte Marie** (p176), with a few days on the beach to fortify you for the mission ahead. From here, fly or catch a cargo boat to **Mananara** (p187) for a trip to **Parc National de Mananara-Nord** (p186), or a night on **Aye-Aye Island** (p188). Fly, trek or catch another cargo boat northwards to **Maroantsetra** (p190), the base for visiting the lost world of **Nosy Mangabe** (p189) and its dramatic surrounding coastline. From here, it's on to the stunning **Masoala Peninsula** (p192). You can hike or mountain bike right around it or, less energetically, just spend a few days sea kayaking or snorkelling at **Cap Masoala** (p192) or **Tampolo** (p192). Return to Maroantsetra and fly across to **Antalaha** (p195), or trek all the way to **Cap Est** (p195).

Once in Antalaha, a good road leads to the dramatic beaches at **Sambava** (p196), with a side trip to charming **Andapa** (p197) and **Parc National de Marojejy** (p197) or **Réserve Spéciale d'Anjanaharibe-Sud** (p197). These are hard hiking areas, so factor in some recovery time, or opt for easier walks in the region of Andapa. From Sambava, you can fly or continue by taxi-brousse to Diego Suarez (p144).

This route is around 900km, much of it without proper roads. Between June and October rough seas make cargo boats dangerous, so you'll have to walk or fly some sections.

THE WILD WEST
Two weeks / Antsirabe to Morondava

Travel in Madagascar's harsh western region, home of the fiercely proud Sakalava people, can be daunting at first, but a number of organised tours (see p265) are available if you want to make things easier on yourself.

Begin in **Antsirabe** (p83), a genteel and civilised town in the Central Highlands and the best place to find a group if you're looking to do an organised tour. From here, drive to the hot little town of **Miandrivazo** (p134), the push-off point for canoe trips down the **Tsiribihina River** (p134). It takes around three days to drift down to the village of Antsiraraka, then three hours by 4WD to **Belo-sur-Tsiribihina** (p135).

From Belo, continue to **Morondava** (p137), or take the rough road to **Parc National des Tsingy de Bemaraha** (p136). Once there you can explore the Grands and Petits Tsingy, before the long day's drive back to Morondava, stopping to get those sunset photos at the impressive **Avenue du Baobab** (p139). Morondava itself is a laid-back seaside town that makes a good base for a visit to the **Réserve Forestière de Kirindy** (p139), home to the elusive fosa and the giant jumping rat, or a pirogue ride down the coast to the fishing village of **Belo-sur-Mer** (p140). From Morondava you can fly, sail or drive (if you're brave) down to Toliara (p102) in the south. Alternatively, you can fly or drive back to Antananarivo (p58).

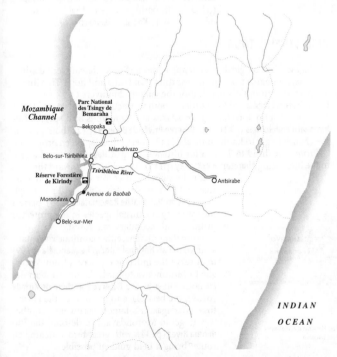

The wild west route is about 630km, encompassing tarmac, river and dirt roads. Leaving out Parc National des Tsingy de Bemaraha will reduce it to about a week.

TAILORED TRIPS

BEACH ODYSSEY

The dizzying variety of perfect beaches and coral-fringed islands of Madagascar and the Comoros means that unless you're prepared to take several internal flights or spend months travelling, you'll have to be selective.

Begin in **Mayotte** (p233), whose charms lie almost entirely underwater, with several diving companies available to help you discover them. Snorkel with sea turtles, then island-hop to the hidden bays and rocky islets of the **Parc Marin de Mohéli** (p226). Continue to **Grande Comore** (p210) to relax on the white sands of the beaches at Itsandra or Mitsamiouli. **Anjouan** (p227) offers less in the way of beaches than the other Comoros islands, but is still worth a visit for the chance to swim in the perfect bay of **Moya Plage** (p233).

A flight or perhaps a passing yacht can take you to **Nosy Be** (p154) and its outlying islands, which provide at least a week's worth of diving, sailing, fishing or simply lazing on beaches that are fit for the most discerning castaway.

The beach odyssey needn't end there – you can always head from Nosy Be to **Diego Suarez** (p144) and set off eastwards, ticking off the beaches at **Sambava** (p196), **Antalaha** (p195) and **Nosy Mangabe** (p189), with perhaps a spot of whale-watching on your way to **Île Sainte Marie** (p176).

BIODIVERSITY TOUR

Madagascar's ecological diversity provides a wide variety of very distinct habitats, home to a fascinating assortment of fauna and flora. This itinerary provides an initial snapshot of the islands' biodiversity.

Begin in **Fort Dauphin** (p116), bordered both by tracts of humid coastal forest and unique spiny forest, home to sifakas and numerous bird species. **Parc National d'Andohahela** (p121) and **Réserve Privée de Berenty** (p122) both provide the chance to get to know more about this perfectly adapted environment.

From here, head to Toliara for bird-watching at **Ifaty** (p110) and a visit to the interesting **Aboretum d'Antsokay** (p112). Travelling northward through

gradually hillier and cooler country, you'll arrive at Fianarantsoa, from where it's a rough drive to **Parc National de Ranomafana** (p89), perfect for watching nocturnal species in the protected primary and secondary rain forest.

From Ranomafana, either continue via Antananarivo to **Parc National d'Andasibe-Mantadia** (p199) to observe the indri, or cut across from Antsirabe to Morondava towards the dry western deciduous forest at the **Réserve Forestière de Kirindy** (p139), the best place to try and see the elusive fosa, Madagascar's largest carnivore. Another way to get to Morondava is to descend the **Tsiribihina River** (p134), with great bird-watching en route (bring a field guide if possible).

The Authors

GEMMA PITCHER
Coordinating Author

Gemma Pitcher spent her childhood in England reading books with titles such as 'Safari Adventure' and 'Across the Dark Continent'. These books prompted her to disappear to Africa at 17, travelling from Nairobi through six countries to Harare. She obtained a degree in English Literature and African History, and after a spell as a safari consultant, moved to Tanzania to become a travel writer. Her interest in the western Indian Ocean region led to two years in Zanzibar, travels along the Kenyan coast and dhow trips around the islands of Mozambique before setting off for Madagascar and the Comoros islands. She speaks fluent French and Swahili.

My Favourite Trip

Throughout my travels in Madagascar, I never tired of watching lemurs – from the minute *Microcebus* (mouse lemur) to the 90cm-tall indri. My favourite lemur-watching spots are Parc National d'Andasibe-Mantadia (p199), Parc National de Ranomafana (p89) and Aye-Aye Island (p188), near Mananara. But you can't spend a whole trip craning up into trees in a humid rain forest... As a self-confessed sea-and-sand addict, I consider the beaches at Anakao (p113), northern Nosy Be (p154) and Île Sainte Marie (p176) more than able to compete with anywhere on the globe for sheer perfection. I also love the independent Comoros islands (p208) for their super-friendly locals and unique version of Swahili culture, which is almost untouched by the outside world.

CONTRIBUTING AUTHORS

Patricia C Wright wrote the Environment chapter (p42) and the introduction to the Wildlife Guide (p49). She is Professor of Anthropology and Adjunct Professor of Ecology & Evolution at the State University of New York and Director of the Institute for the Conservation of Tropical Environments. In 1986 Dr Wright and colleagues discovered a new species of primate in Madagascar, the golden bamboo lemur. She assisted the Malagasy government in developing Parc National de Ranomafana. Dr Wright has received the Chevalier's Medal of Honor from the Malagasy government and an Officier Medal of Honor from the President of Madagascar for her conservation services.

David Andrew contributed the species information for the Wildlife Guide (p49). The founding editor of *Wingspan* and *Australian Birding* magazines, David was also the editor of *Wildlife Australia* magazine, and among other jobs has been a research assistant in Kakadu National Park, a birding guide for English comedian Bill Oddie and an editor of Lonely Planet guides. He also authored several *Watching Wildlife* guides for Lonely Planet.

Dr Caroline Evans wrote the Health chapter (p267). Having studied medicine at the University of London, Caroline completed general practice training at Cambridge. She is the medical adviser to Nomad Travel Clinic, a private travel-health clinic in London, and is also a GP specialising in travel medicine.

Snapshot

After nearly 27 years in power, Madagascar's veteran president Didier Ratsiraka was finally ousted in 2002 by yogurt baron Marc Ravalomanana. Since then, talk among Madagascar's political intelligentsia has revolved around little else than the self-made millionaire's chances of success in government. Discussion of the fate of the old president, currently living in France, is also rife. He was sentenced *in absentia* to 10 years' hard labour, a fate that many consider inadequate for a man convicted of embezzling US$8 million of public money. Other Malagasy, used to unquestioning respect for figures in authority, argue that Ratsiraka should have been granted immunity as an ex–head of state. In any case, the ex-president, reportedly ensconced in a Parisian palace by his friend Jacques Chirac, is unlikely to be extradited.

Sharp-suited, smooth-talking President Ravalomanana began his tenure by taking steps to fulfil one of his chief election promises – to repair Madagascar's ravaged roads. The new currency he introduced, the ariary, even features road builders on one of its banknotes, a move denounced by his opponents as political manipulation. Madagascar's taxi drivers, however, have a different beef – they grumble that the new, higher-denomination notes will make it even harder for them find small change for their customers.

Opponents of Ravalomanana also accuse him of violating human rights and abusing justice in his trails of those accused of taking part in the 2002 civil unrest that marked his disputed claim to the presidency. International human rights organisations have expressed concern over the new regime's methods of dealing with opposition, which have led to violent confrontations during protest meetings in major cities.

On the conservation front, environmentalists were jubilant when Ravalomanana announced that he would almost triple the amount of protected land on the island to 15 million acres by 2005, a move hailed by the World Wildlife Fund for Nature (WWF) as a 'gift to the earth'.

Foreign investors, cheered by news of a major hike in economic growth since the beginning of the new government's reign, were further wooed by a series of laws providing tax breaks for investors and allowing foreigners to own land on the island, presumably in the hope of encouraging tourism. The World Bank, too, showed its confidence in the new government with a US$30 million credit to help fight poverty. 'Madagascar is ready for take-off', Ravalomanana told a press conference. For the moment, most people share in his belief, and there is now a consensus of opinion that the country is further than expected down the road to economic recovery.

For the average citizen of Madagascar, however, nothing has yet changed, although most street traders, hawkers and rice farmers agree that things have returned to normal after the upheavals caused by the political crisis of 2002. Most remain optimistic as to the future of their country and firm in their support of Ravalomanana, who promises to use his entrepreneurial flair to fight poverty and hunger, which are still huge problems for the population.

Two commodities that are in the news as part of the predicted economic boom are vanilla and sapphires. The Malagasy are proud of their country's provision of half the world's supply of vanilla, with about 1000 tonnes a year being exported. The product is vital to the country's

FAST FACTS

Madagascar

Population: 16,979,700

GDP per capita: €711.10

Average annual income per capita: €218

Average life expectancy: 53

Annual rate of inflation: 18%

Degrees a chameleon can swivel its eyes: 180

Length of an aye-aye's tail: 45cm

economy and represents 10% of its gross domestic product (GDP). The price of vanilla has increased over 10 times in the last decade, with a corresponding increase in thefts, murders and vanilla-poaching on the fertile northeast coast. Most farmers realise that bust must follow boom, but are riding a new wave of prosperity in the meantime, with shiny mountain bikes and new fridges being delivered to the thatched huts of the vanilla growers.

Madagascar's sapphire-mining sector, only five years old, is largely unregulated. One politician recently told a local newspaper that just 20kg of sapphires could repay all the country's outstanding international debts. The new government is understandably keen to start controlling the mining industry in order to prevent the income from the sale of precious stones going to foreign buyers and smugglers, who presently lay claim to the best gems.

In the Comoros, talk, as usual, revolves around the torrid grappling for power among a group of fairly unscrupulous politicians. A recently signed peace accord between the three islands of the L'Union des Comores allowed for better definition of the role of the central government under President Azali Assoumani and the semi-autonomous islands of Anjouan and Mohéli. Assoumani is currently locked in a dispute with Grande Comore President Abdou Soule Elbak over the respective powers of their offices. Comorian politics, as always, is a struggle between individuals who use inter-island rivalry to secure their own powers. Market traders in Moroni complain that the feud between the federal and island governments has resulted in them being taxed twice, while employers claim the finance ministry has refused to listen to their grievances.

Gossip in the mosques reports tales of *agents provocateurs* from fundamentalist groups in the Middle East being sent on recruitment drives to the islands, but being promptly sent packing by the religiously moderate Comorians. Interest in world politics, though, is high, with most Comorians feeling sympathy for their Muslim co-religionists in the Middle East.

In Mayotte, most political discussion revolves around the chances of the island gaining the status of a French *département d'outre mer* (overseas territory) in the coming few years, a move sought by local leaders for its economic benefits. Attacks against Anjouannais and Grande Comorians living in Mayotte have also brought concern.

FAST FACTS

Comoros
Population: 636,900

Average annual income per capita: €318

Average life expectancy: 60

Annual rate of inflation: 5%

Fruit bat population: 1200

History
MADAGASCAR

ARRIVALS FROM ASIA...

Humankind is a relatively new arrival to the evolutionary party that is Madagascar's history. The first settlers – from whom the majority of the present-day population is descended – arrived just 2000 years ago from the distant shores of Indonesia and Malaysia. How these first Indonesian settlers reached Madagascar is a mystery, but anthropological and ethnographical clues – for example the distribution of Indonesian-style sailing boats found along the northern shores of the Indian Ocean – suggest Indonesians may well have colonised the island after migrating in a single voyage, stopping en route at various points in the Indian Ocean. Their coastal craft possibly worked their way along the shores of India, Arabia and East Africa, trading as they went, before finally arriving in Madagascar. Linguistic clues also support this theory, as elements of Sanskrit have been identified in the Malagasy language.

These first settlers brought with them the food crops of Southeast Asia, and even today the island's glassy tiers of paddy fields resemble the landscape of Southeast Asia than that of the much closer African mainland. This Asian way of life was tempered over the years by contact with the Arabic and African traders who plied the seas of the region with their cargoes of silks, spices and slaves. Gradually the Asian culture of the new settlers was subsumed into a series of geographically defined kingdoms, which in turn gave rise to the different tribes found in Madagascar today.

...& EUROPE

Marco Polo was the first European to report the existence of a 'great red island', and gave it the name Madagascar, possibly having confused it with Mogadishu in Somalia. Others posit that it is a corruption of the word Malagasy – the name used by the island's people to refer to themselves. Whatever its origins, the name Madagascar soon became widely accepted.

Arab cartographers, as usual way ahead of the Europeans, had long known the island as Gezirat Al-Komor, meaning 'island of the moon', a

Flags, lists of kings and queens, and the chance to listen to Madagascar's national anthem at www.worldstatesmen .org/Madagascar.htm.

THE VAZIMBA

The Vazimba, according to legend, were a mysterious race of 'white pygmies' who lived in the central highlands of Madagascar before being chased out by the Merina. They supposedly fled to the area around Parc National des Tsingy de Bemaraha (p136), where their spirits still inhabit caves and they are venerated in the same way as ancestors, with *fady* (taboos) and sacrifices. No-one knows for sure if the Vazimba really existed, but one theory is that the name refers to an earlier wave of Indonesian settlers who arrived before the ancestors of today's Malagasy.

TIMELINE **c2nd Century**

Madagascar is settled by Malay-Polynesians

1500

First Europeans arrive in Madagascar

name later transferred to the Comoros. It wasn't until 1500 that a Portuguese fleet under the command of one Diego Dias arrived, earning the dubious honour of being the first Europeans to set foot on Madagascar. The island's Portuguese name, Ilha de São Lourenço, lasted only briefly.

In the centuries following the island's 'discovery' by Europeans, Portuguese, Dutch and British settlers tried valiantly to establish permanent bases at various points around the coast, only to be defeated by disease and less-than-friendly locals, who suspected them of being slave traders.

More successful efforts, however, were made by distinctly nongovernmental organisations – for several decades from the end of the 17th century, bands of pirates from Britain, France, the USA and elsewhere made Madagascar one of their Indian Ocean bases. They used Île Sainte Marie, in the northeast, as a base to attack ships on the way to the Cape of Good Hope, buried copious amounts of treasure, and contributed generously to the local gene pool.

Check out www.met museum.org /toah/hd/madg_1/ hd_madg_1.htm for information on Merina history from the Metropolitan Museum of Art in New York.

THE NEW SUPER-TRIBES

As trade with the Europeans grew, several rival kingdoms began to gain dominance. In the west, the Menabe people occupied the area around Morondava, then, under their king Andriamisara I, moved eastward into the highlands and founded a capital on the banks of the Sakalava River. This river eventually gave its name to the modern-day Sakalava tribe.

Meanwhile, on the east coast, Ratsimilaho – son of an English pirate and a Malagasy princess – succeeded in unifying rival tribes into a single unit, known as the Betsimisaraka.

In central Madagascar, the most powerful group was known as the Merina. In the late 18th century, a certain Chief Ramboasalama assumed the throne of Ambohimanga (p76) and took the snappy name Andrianampoinimerinandriantsimitoviaminandriampanjaka, meaning The Hope of Imerina. With the help of European arms traders and military advisors, Andrianampoinimerina (as he was called for short) was able to unify the various Merina peoples into a powerful kingdom that soon came to dominate much of Madagascar.

THE GLORY DAYS OF THE MERINA
Good King Radama & Bad Queen Ranavalona

In 1810 Andrianampoinimerina was succeeded by his equally ambitious son Radama I. Radama developed a highly organised army and set about conquering Boina (the main Sakalava kingdom in northwestern Madagascar) and the Betsimisaraka peoples to the east. He then turned his attention to defeating the Betsileo to the south and the kingdom of Antakàrana in the far north, whose warrior princes preferred suicide or exile to surrender. Unable to take the Sakalava kingdom of Menabe by force, Radama prudently married Princess Rasalimo, daughter of the Menabe king, thereby fulfilling a vow made by his father that the Merina kingdom would have no frontier but the sea.

His empire building complete, Radama I set about courting European powers. In 1817 he entered into diplomatic relations with the British, beginning a period of British aid and influence which remained strong until well into the 19th century.

King Andrianampoinimerina gave his soldiers charms made from crocodile teeth filled with magic herbs to protect them from the bullets of their Sakalava enemies.

Late 1800s & Early 1900s	1895
The Merina became the dominant tribe in Madagascar	French forces capture Antananarivo in Madagascar, beating forces led by British mercenaries

With the British came the missionaries, notably the London Missionary Society (LMS), which arrived with a contingent of Welsh missionaries, many of whom died from fever almost as soon as they arrived. Undaunted, however, the survivors soon converted the Merina court to Christianity and set up several schools around the country. By 1835, the Bible had been printed in Malagasy.

Criminal suspects under Queen Ranavalona I were forced to drink a strong poison. If they vomited sufficiently profusely, they were declared innocent. Most died.

But in 1828, at the age of just 36, Radama died. His successor was his widow Ranavalona I, who may well have done away with him herself. To say that the new queen was a psychopath would be something of an understatement. She promptly set about reversing Radama's policies, declaring the Christian faith illegal and announcing her hatred of all Europeans. Those who refused to abandon their faith were hurled to their deaths from the cliffs outside the Rova in Antananarivo (p66).

Executions quickly became the queen's favourite hobby and, as her madness grew, she devised ever more creative ways of putting her subjects to death. Boiling water was poured over victims tied to stakes in pits, while some condemned prisoners were sawn in half or had their arms and legs chopped off and were sewn up into sacks for a lingering death. Some estimates suggest that the queen reduced the island's population by a quarter during her 33 years in power. She was said to be sexually insatiable and had a stream of lovers, many of who were put to death in their turn. One of the few Europeans she tolerated was a French engineer, Jean Laborde, who built her summer palace and began Madagascar's industrial revolution with his huge factory complex at Lac Mantasoa (p78).

Queen Ranavalona I was partial to coral silk crinolines, which she often wore with feathered bonnets.

Radama II

In 1861, Queen Ranavalona died, understandably unlamented by what remained of her subjects. She was succeeded by her son, Radama II, who thankfully abandoned most of his mother's policies, abolishing forced labour, reinstating freedom of religion and welcoming back the Euro-

---

SLAVERY

While east-coast European pirates traded in Malagasy slaves to supply the plantations of Réunion and Mauritius, slavery was widely practiced in Madagascar until the French declared it illegal at the end of the 19th century.

A Malagasy could acquire slave status as punishment for a crime or by being captured by a rival group. Once someone was a slave, the status was then inherited by their offspring. Queen Ranavalona was fond of taking shipwrecked European sailors as her personal slaves.

Today, slave ancestry remains a cause of discrimination in parts of Madagascar. Among the Merina and Betsileo, the descendants of slaves are relegated to the lowest social ranks and prevented from gaining lucrative government jobs, or making good marriages.

A modern form of slavery is present in the form of children from poor families, known as *mpanampy* (assistants), who are sold by their parents into domestic slavery at ages as young as ten. Girls must do domestic chores such as carrying water for their owners, while boys are often sold to farmers as zebu herders in exchange for a plot of land. These modern-day slaves are often mistreated or abused until they have raised enough money to buy their freedom. There are also reports of women and girls from Madagascar being trafficked to Réunion and Mauritius to become prostitutes.

1896	1912
Madagascar is officially declared a French colony	The Comoros formally become a French colony administered from Madagascar

peans. Christianity became the predominant religion of Madagascar and missionary activity began to expand.

After Radama II had been in power for a year, a mysterious plague struck Antananarivo, killing thousands of people. The malady was attributed to the ancestors' discontent over the new king's relations with foreign powers and the growing influence of outsiders in Madagascar. In May 1862, Radama II was assassinated, strangled by a silken cord to avoid the fady over the shedding of royal blood.

The Prime Minister & His Queens

The king's assassin, named Rainilaiarivony, promptly took the post of prime minister and married Radama's widow, who took the title Rasoherina I. Any ideas the queen might have had of emulating her powerful predecessor were quickly quashed when the prime minister issued an edict stating that she could act only with the consent of her ministers – effectively leaving the real power to her husband.

Rasoherina survived until 1868, and was succeeded by Ranavalona II, who died in 1883 and was succeeded by Ranavalona III. Prime Minister Rainilaiarivony married both succeeding queens and became the principal power behind the throne, building a magnificent residence for himself in Antananarivo (p67).

The Turn of the French

CONQUEST

As British interest in Madagascar began to wane, French influence on the island increased. In 1883 French warships attacked Madagascar, occupying the main ports and forcing the government to sign a treaty declaring it a French protectorate.

In 1894, the French demanded the capitulation of Queen Ranavalona III, accusing the Merina government of tyranny. When the queen rejected their demands, the French army launched an attack on Antananarivo. In September 1895, a British artillery officer, Major John Graves, led the Merina army out of Antananarivo against the invaders and was soundly defeated, despite heavy losses on the French side because of disease.

COLONIALISM

On 6 August 1896, Madagascar was officially declared a French colony. General Joseph Gallieni, the first governor general, attempted to destroy the power of the Merina by suppressing the Malagasy language and all British influence, declaring French the official language. In 1897 Queen Ranavalona III was sent into exile in Algeria and the Merina monarchy was abolished.

Slavery was also abolished, although it was replaced with an almost equally exploitative system of taxes, which resulted in forced labour for anyone who could not pay. Land was expropriated by foreign settlers, and a coffee-based import and export economy developed.

As the education system expanded, a new Malagasy elite began to emerge, and resentment of the colonial presence grew in all levels of society. Several nationalist movements evolved among the Merina and Betsileo tribes, with strikes and demonstrations becoming more frequent.

The Last Travels of Ida Pfeiffer, by Ida Pfeiffer, tells how Victorian traveller Ida Pfeiffer became caught up in a plot against Queen Ranavalona and only just escaped with her life. Plenty of gory detail about the queen's reign.

A History of Madagascar, by Mervyn Brown, is the most up-to-date and authoritative work on the islands' history.

1960	1974
Madagascar gains independence in a peaceful transition	Three of the Comoros islands vote for independence, but Mayotte votes to stay with France

WORLD WAR & NATIONALISM

For a good diving yarn intermixed with the story of Captain Kidd's time in Madagascar check out *Return to Treasure Island & the Search for Captain Kidd* by Barry Clifford & Paul Perry.

During WWII, the French in Madagascar came under the authority of the pro-Nazi Vichy government. Occupying British forces captured the town of Diego Suarez (p144) to prevent the Japanese from using it as a base. Antananarivo and other major towns also fell to the British but were handed back to the Free French (those that fought on the side of the Allies in WWII) of General de Gaulle in 1943.

Nationalist leader Jean Ralaimongo began the Malagasy independence movement in the 1930s, but his campaign was cut short by the outbreak of WWII. Post-war Madagascar experienced a nationalist backlash, with resentment towards the French culminating in a rebellion in March 1947. This rebellion, which was led by Joseph Raseta and Joseph Ravoahangy, was eventually subdued, but some estimates suggest that 80,000 Malagasy were killed in the struggle. Its leaders were then sent into exile.

In the 1950s, nationalist political parties were formed, the most notable being the Parti Social Démocrate (PSD) of Philibert Tsiranana.

INDEPENDENCE

When General de Gaulle returned to power in France in 1958, Madagascar made a peaceful transition to independence, and in 1960 Tsiranana was elected as the first president. Under Tsiranana, the French were permitted to retain control over trade and financial institutions and maintain military bases on the island. In effect, the *colons,* as the French were known (Tsiranana referred to them as 'the 19th tribe'), still ran the country.

The new government's continued ties with France, combined with a period of economic decline, contributed to Tsiranana's increasing unpopularity. In the wake of the brutal repression of a 1971 uprising in southern Madagascar, followed in 1972 by a massive antigovernment uprising in the capital, Tsiranana was forced to resign and hand over power to his army commander, General Gabriel Ramantsoa.

Tabataba (The Spreading of Rumours), directed by Raymond Rajaonarivelo, is a film set in a small village near Manakara during the bloody 1947 rebellion against French rule.

In February 1975, after several coup attempts, General Ramantsoa was forced to step down and was replaced by Colonel Richard Ratsimandrava, who was assassinated within a week of taking office, with a rebel group of army officers announcing a military takeover. The Merina blamed the murder on rebels from coastal tribes.

The military officers who had usurped power were quickly routed by officers loyal to Ramantsoa, and a new government headed by Admiral Didier Ratsiraka, a former foreign minister, came to power.

The 'Second Republic'

Madagascar was by this time suffering severely from the departure of many French expats, who took with them their skills, money and technology. Ratsiraka attempted radical political and social reforms in the late 1970s, severing all ties with France and courting favour with former Soviet-bloc nations. Following the example of Chinese leader Mao Tse-tung, Ratsiraka even compiled a 'red book' of government policies and theories.

In March 1989, Ratsiraka was dubiously 'elected' to his third seven-year term, sparking riots. The beginning of 1991 was marked by widespread demonstrations demanding the president's resignation. From

1975	1976
Didier Ratsiraka takes the reins as Malagasy president	The new president of the Comoros, Ali Soilih tries to turn the country into a secular, socialist republic

May 1991 to January 1992, the government, economy and transportation systems ground to a halt in general strikes and riots, and protests left dozens dead.

In late October 1991, an agreement was signed with opposition politicians in preparation for popular elections and the birth of the so-called 'third republic'. However, Ratsiraka still refused to step down. In July 1992, there was an attempted civilian coup, but the rebels failed to gain popular support and were forced to surrender.

The 'Third Republic'

Civil unrest leading up to the first round of elections culminated in the blockading of the capital and the bombing of a railway bridge between Toamasina and Antananarivo. For weeks, the capital was without petrol and transportation was disrupted.

The first round of elections, which remained remarkably peaceful, resulted in victory for opposition candidate Professor Albert Zafy, ending Ratsiraka's first 17 years in power.

Years of communist-style dictatorship and mismanagement made it difficult for Zafy's government to ignite the economy and gain the trust of the people. Zafy was accused of money laundering and dealings with drug traffickers.

The 70-year-old Zafy was unexpectedly impeached by his parliament in July 1996 for abuse of authority and exceeding his constitutional powers, which included trying to sack his prime minister. The first round of new presidential elections were called in November 1996 with 15 candidates, including Ratsiraka (who had been in exile in France for the previous 19 months).

To the surprise of everyone, including international monitors, Ratsiraka won the presidential elections in two rounds of balloting with 50.7% of the vote. Zafy, who came a close second with 49.3%, accused the opposition of vote rigging. Appealing for Madagascar to become a 'humanist and ecological republic', Ratsiraka took office once again in February 1997.

> Nationalist leader Jean Ralaimongo shared a room in Paris with the young Ho Chi Minh.

ONE COUNTRY, TWO PRESIDENTS

Marc Ravalomanana began his path to success by peddling around his hometown on a bicycle selling pots of home-made yogurt. By the time he entered the political arena with his campaign to become mayor of Antananarivo in 1999, his company Tiko was the biggest producer of dairy products in Madagascar and the newly minted millionaire was able to give away his yogurts to supporters on the streets. On election, he started a huge clean-up operation of the capital and won huge popularity.

In the run up to the 2001 elections, Ravalomanana announced his candidacy for the presidency of Madagascar under the banner of his party TIM (which stands in Malagasy for 'I ♥ Madagascar'). He campaigned on a platform of rapid economic development, promising to put his skills as a businessman to use in courting foreign investment, fighting poverty and repairing Madagascar's badly-maintained infrastructure. He also promised to stamp out government corruption, rife under Ratsiraka's government. His political role model was Franklin Roosevelt, and his slogan was 'Don't be afraid of anything – only believe in me'.

> Browse news stories about Madagascar with a humanitarian perspective at www.irinnews.org.

1995	1996
In the Comoros, Djohar is toppled in a coup led by Denard. Denard surrenders after intervention by French forces	Didier Ratsiraka makes a surprise return to the presidency in Madagascar

Mr Ravalomanana claimed outright victory in presidential elections in December 2001, but there was just one snag – so did Didier Ratsiraka. A bitter six-month struggle for power ensued, with both men insisting they were the rightfully elected leader of the country, and accusations of vote-rigging by both sides. As Ravalomanana swore himself in as president, Ratsiraka declared a state of emergency and imposed martial law. As protests by supporters of both sides grew violent, Ratsiraka and several of his provincial governors set up an alternative capital in Toamasina.

In 2002, while the country was still in a grip of a political crisis, thousands died in a flu epidemic that spread across five provinces.

The balance of power, however, swung towards Ravalomanana as sections of the military gradually went over to his side. Ratsiraka supporters blockaded the roads into the capital to prevent supplies of fuel and essential medicines from the country's ports reaching their rivals.

At the end of April 2002, the Malagasy High Constitutional Court declared Ravalomanana the outright winner of the disputed elections. Ratsiraka, however, still refused to accept that the game was over, ordering his partisans to blow up electricity pylons, plunging Antananarivo into darkness. But by August it was all over bar the shouting, with Ravalomanana's administration receiving endorsement from the UN, then winning a convincing majority in elections for the National Assembly. Ratsiraka left for exile in France, and was sentenced *in absentia* to 10 years' hard labour for embezzlement of public funds.

THE COMOROS

It is thought that the earliest inhabitants of the Comoros islands were the same Southeast Asians who first reached Madagascar. Unlike in Madagascar, however, traces of this Asian ancestry have been subsumed by the influence of African, Arab and Shirazi (Persian) immigrants. The Shirazis, who appeared in the Comoros in the 15th and 16th centuries, set up a series of Islamic sultanates and took part in Swahili networks of trade, architecture and culture that linked the independent states of the East African coast.

During the heyday of the Swahili civilisation, the Comoros became a major marketplace for trade goods such as spices, animal hides, weapons and precious metals. Many of the sailing dhows that landed in the harbours of the Comoros also brought men, women and children captured from as far away as Zambia on the African mainland. Some of these slaves escaped or managed to buy their freedom, remaining on the islands to add an African element to the Arabic origin of today's Comorians.

The only comprehensive history of the islands in English is Malyn Newitt's *The Comoro Islands: Struggle Against Dependency in the Indian Ocean*.

The first reliable European accounts of the Comoros came from the Portuguese travellers Diego Dias and Ferdinand Soares, but up until the mid-19th century, it was pirates from Madagascar rather than European explorers who caused the most disruption to Comorian life. Pirate raids were common, with some Comorian women preferring suicide to capture and slavery (see p222). During this time the number of sultans mushroomed at an alarming rate and at one stage there were no fewer than 12 sultans on the island of Grande Comore alone. Inter-sultanate squabbling and even war was a regular occurrence. This situation was exploited by the French, who began to take an interest in the island from the late 19th century. For the post-colonial history of the Comoros, see the Comoros chapter on p210.

2001	2002
Malagasy presidential election results disputed, Marc Ravalomanana declared winner after an eight-month showdown	Presidential elections are held in the Comoros. Azzali declares himself the winner. Name changes to L'Union des Comoros

The Culture

THE NATIONAL PSYCHE
Madagascar

On arrival in Madagascar, your first impression is likely to be of a reserved people, unfailingly polite but rather distant. The Malagasy concept of *Fihavanana*, which means 'conciliation' or 'brotherhood', is enshrined in society, meaning that confrontation is avoided and compromises are sought. If you've travelled in Africa, you may well be surprised by the seeming timidity of the Malagasy when compared to the more confident and ebullient Africans.

In fact, it quickly becomes apparent that regarding the Malagasy as Africans at all is a big no-no. As far as the citizens of 'La Grande Île' are concerned, they are just that – an island people, by implication far superior to the 'primitive' Africans. When the French invaded and colonised Madagascar, they used Senegalese troops in some of their military operations, so many Malagasy, regardless of their own skin colour, regard black Africans as nothing more than 'dangerous brutes'.

The colours of the Malagasy flag represent the red of royal blood, the white of the people and the green of the forest.

This fierce pride in the superiority of Malagasy culture is, if anything, on the increase in modern times. The new government of Marc Ravalomanana has declared its aim of breaking the French cultural influence on the country and restoring Malagasy language and traditions.

The reserve of the Malagasy in everyday conversation can be seen as arrogant or standoffish, but in fact it stems from a deeply held cultural belief that some subjects are simply not for discussion in polite company. It's considered tactless to air personal issues or problems, even with close friends. Likewise, searching or indiscreet questions are avoided at all costs.

Politeness in general is very important to the Malagasy, and impatience or pushy behaviour is regarded as shocking. Passengers arriving for a flight place their tickets in a neat row on the check-in desk before settling down patiently to wait for their turn. Similarly, customers in the bank arrange their papers in strict order along the counter while queuing, with no jostling or cheating tolerated.

The welcoming of strangers and the traditions of hospitality are sacred throughout Madagascar. Many areas have a version of the same legend about the villagers who refused a cup of water to a mysterious stranger, only to be punished by having their village immolated. Any household considers it a duty to offer food and water to a guest, no matter how poor they themselves are.

Sexually, Malagasy society is fairly liberated, with marriage being a pretty relaxed institution and divorce common. Children are seen as the primary purpose of marriage, and essential to happiness and security. The idea that some people might choose not to have children is greeted with embarrassed disbelief. Women are seen – by themselves, anyway – as the most dynamic force in Malagasy society, with wives regarded as the head of the domestic sphere, even if they also go out to work.

At www.ecpat.org you'll find information on sex-tourism issues in Madagascar, with international laws that apply.

The family is the central tenet of Malagasy life, including not only distant cousins but also departed ancestors. Even urban, modern Malagasy, who reject the belief that ancestors have magic powers, regard those who are no longer alive as full members of the family. At *Famadihana* (literally, 'the turning of the bones') exhumation ceremonies, it's not unusual to see people lining up for a family photograph with the shroud-wrapped bodies of dead family members laid out neatly in the foreground.

The Comoros

Comorians bear little resemblance to Malagasy on any level. For the most part they are outgoing, extroverted and emotional people, ready to discuss their problems, life stories or political opinions at the drop of a hat. A notable exception to this are the people living on Mayotte, who appear on first acquaintance to be extremely standoffish and surly. A succession of ever less competent governments has left Comorians with a healthy scepticism about politicians, and most rely on themselves to get ahead, with corruption and sharp business practice understandably rife.

Islam and family values are strictly enshrined, with life revolving around the mosque and religious events such as the fast of Ramadan. Society is strictly divided between the upper classes, defined as those who have made a *Grand Mariage* (an elaborate wedding ceremony) or completed the pilgrimage to Mecca. Comorians generally regard themselves as African, holding close ties with fellow Muslims in Kenya and Zanzibar. Mistrust is mainly reserved for the Malagasy, whose pirates hounded the islands for centuries. Resentments also run high between Comorians from the different islands, with occasional outbreaks of inter-ethnic violence.

Excellent articles on Comorian culture and literature can be found at www.comores-online .com/accueilgb.htm – even if it's all in French.

LIFESTYLE
Madagascar

The Malagasy home, as the centre of the extended family, ancestors included, is furnished with care and attention, regardless of how poor the householder may be. Custom dictates that furniture, doors and windows should all be astrologically aligned and placed in specific parts of the building.

In many areas, it's considered disgusting to have a toilet inside the house, or to defecate inside a building at all, even if it's a purpose-built latrine. This is a tradition that health workers in Madagascar are trying to change, as open-air toilets carry a higher risk of disease.

Personal adornment and fashion are hugely important to the Malagasy, partly due to the influence of the French colonists – men and women alike take great care with their appearance. Hats are the most beloved of all fashion items, whether they're worn cocked jauntily over one eye or with the brims demurely turned down to shade the face. It's not unusual to see swaggering young men sporting the sort of floral straw hat that Westerners associate with old ladies at garden parties!

It would be a mistake to think that Madagascar's catastrophic environmental degradation is due to a lack of concern for the natural world. In fact, Malagasy life is mostly still largely governed by the forces of nature. It's still common to find sacred offerings left at the base of baobab trees, beside forest waterfalls, or in front of royal tombs. Family outings, usually accompanied by a picnic, to a beautiful spot of family or tribal significance, are a popular leisure activity.

Alongside the landscape, concepts of time and date still have an influence on Malagasy lifestyle. One example of this is seen in the belief

If you see a young Malagasy man wearing a comb in his hair, he's advertising his search for a wife.

DON'T MAKE ME A BEGGAR

Resist the urge to hand out money or gifts to those cute children in the villages and towns of Madagascar. Rather than helping them, you will be teaching them to beg from every new traveller they see. If you want do something to aid those you meet, donate money to the local school or clinic instead.

FADY

Fady is the name given to a system of local taboos designed to respect the ancestors. Fady can take innumerable forms and varies widely from village to village. It may be fady to whistle on a particular stretch of beach, to walk past a sacred tree, to eat pork or to swim in a certain river.

Although foreigners and other outsiders are normally exempt from fady (or are excused for breaking them), they should be respected. The best thing to do is to ask locals for information, and to be particularly careful in the vicinity of tombs or burial sites.

---

in *vintana* (destiny), which influences the dates of parties held to mark circumcisions, marriages or reburials. Friday, which is associated with nobility, is considered a good day to hold a celebration.

Since independence, the influence of French culture has not been lost. Village ladies weave themselves chic raffia shopping bags that wouldn't look out of place on a Parisian street; in these they put long baguette loaves of bread. Teenage boys play *boules* in the dusty streets of rural towns, avoiding the Citroen 2CVs Renault 4s that buzz past. The French language continues to be widely spoken.

> In some Malagasy villages it's fady to talk about crocodiles.

The sight of aged, raddled European males with young and beautiful Malagasy girls on their arms is a common and sorry sight in the streets of tourist hotspots such as Nosy Be and Diego Suarez. In recent years, several arrests have been made on grounds related to sex tourism and the abuse of minors.

The Comoros

In the Comoros, Islamic culture has led to the adoption of many aspects of Arab dress and custom. Men wear long, white robes known in Swahili as *kanzus,* often accompanied by embroidered skullcaps called *kofias.* Homes are often extremely colourful, decorated with luridly patterned fabrics and elaborate gold-and-black plastic furniture. A picture of the holy mosque at Mecca nearly always has pride of place. The homes of those Comorians who've made the pilgrimage to Mecca usually feature a large photo of the pilgrim standing outside it.

Shoes are always left outside, as walking on the floor would render it unclean for prayer. Toilet paper is not used – instead a bucket of water or hosepipe is provided for the same purpose. Women cover their heads when walking outside the home.

The centre of local life is the village or town square, known as the *bangwe,* where men spend many hours sitting in the shade of trees, discussing religious or political matters, drinking strong Arabic coffee and playing dominos or traditional board games.

> Forty-five percent of the population of Madagascar is under 14.

POPULATION

Although the country shares one culture and language, the Malagasy people are officially divided into 18 tribes, whose boundaries are roughly based on old kingdoms. Tribal divisions are still evident between ancient enemies such as the Merina and the Sakalava.

Also important is the distinction between Merina highlanders and so-called *côtiers*. Literally, *côtiers* refers to those from the coast, but really means any non-Merina groups.

Thirty-one per cent of the population is urbanised.

The main ethnic groups are Merina 27%, Betsimisaraka 15%, Betsileo 12%, Tsimihety 7%, Sakalava 6%, Antaisaka 5% and Antandroy 5%, with a number of smaller groups making up the remainder.

LE GRAND MARIAGE

The major event in any Comorian village or town are the immense and overblown wedding ceremonies known as *Grands Mariages*. The most elaborate sometimes require three years of planning and can plunge the bridegroom into debt for the rest of his life.

Although revolutionist Ali Soilih and his juvenile delinquents tried to do away with the *Grand Mariage*, most Comorian men still aspire to one. Economic factors, however, have dictated that few these days can afford to foot the bill.

A *Grand Mariage* is almost always arranged between an older, wealthy man and a young bride, often selected when she is still just a child. Not only must the man pay for the elaborate two- to nine-day *toirab* (public festivities), which involves catering for the entire village. He must also present his fiancée with a huge dowry of gold jewellery, which she is entitled to keep in the event of a divorce.

All this entitles him to wear a special *m'ruma* (sash), which signifies his status as a *wandru wadzima* (*grand notable* in French). Only *grands notables* may participate in village councils held in the *bangwe* (village or town square).

If you hope to attend a *toirab*, your chances will be best in July and August. Just wait around looking curious about what's happening; you're sure to be invited, or in fact forced, to join in. Bring some kind of present (a small amount of money is best) and don't take photos unless invited.

In the Comoros, the main ethnic groupings (not usually emphasised) are Antalote, Cafre, Makoa, Oimatsaha and the Sakalava (who are the descendents of Malagasy pirates).

RELIGION

Half of Madagascar's population adheres to traditional beliefs, while half belong to the Roman Catholic and Protestant churches. A small proportion, mainly on the west coast, is Muslim. In recent years, Christian-revival meetings held in venues such as sports stadiums and town halls have become popular, with charismatic preachers and lots of singing and dancing. Even among Christians, there is generally great respect and reverence for traditional rituals.

Haiteny: The Traditional Poetry of Madagascar, by Leonard Fox, has translations of beautiful Merina poems charting love, revenge and sexuality.

Malagasy religion has been shaped by diverse influences. The funeral rites of many of the Malagasy tribes, for example, have Austronesian roots, while the status of cattle is thought to have African roots, and belief in *vintana* may originate with Islamic cosmology.

Traditional Malagasy culture is rooted in reverence and respect for its ancestors. Among most tribes, this is manifested in a complex system of fady and burial rites, the best known of which is the ceremonial exhumation and reburial known as *Famadihana*, see boxed text opposite.

The Comoros are overwhelmingly Muslim.

ARTS
Literature

Voices from Madagascar: An Anthology of Contemporary Francophone Literature, edited by Jacques Bourgeacq & Liliane Ramarosoa, contains Malagasy writing in French and English.

The earliest written literature dates from historical records produced in the mid-19th century. Modern Malagasy poetry and literature first began to flourish in the 1930s and 1940s. The best-known figure was the poet Jean-Joseph Rabearivelo, who committed suicide in 1947 at the age of 36 – reputedly after the colonial administration decided to send a group of basket-weavers to France to represent the colony instead of him. Modern-day literary figures include Jean Ndema, Rakotonaivo, Rainifihina Jessé and Emilson D Andriamalala. Nearly all their works are published in French or Malagasy.

The first written literature in the Comoros was in the form of folk tales and histories written by princes, sultans and aristocrats. It was originally laid down in Arabic. A lot of Comorian literature is unpublished and/or in Shimasiwa, but some writers to look out for are Aboubacar Said Salim, Said-Ahmed Sast and Abdou Salam Baco.

Over the Lip of the World: Among the Storytellers of Madagascar, by Colleen J McElroy, is a journey through Malagasy oral traditions and myths.

Oral Traditions

Hira gasy are popular music, dancing and storytelling spectacles held in the central highlands of Madagascar. Brightly clad troupes of 25 performers compete for prizes for the best costumes or the most exciting spectacle. An important part of *hira gasy* is *kabary*, in which an orator delivers a series of proverbs using allegory, double entendre, metaphor and simile. The speaker continues for as long as possible while avoiding direct contact with the subject at hand. Unfortunately, unless you have fluent Malagasy, you're unlikely to agree with the proverb that says: 'While listening to a *kabary* well spoken, one fails to notice the fleas that bite one'.

More visitor-friendly are the songs and acrobatic dances that follow the *kabary*. Dancers are dressed in oddly old-fashioned European-style gowns called *malabary,* and women also wear the traditional *lamba* (scarf). The themes are upbeat, extolling the virtues of honesty and encouraging young people to respect their parents. The competition winner is decided by the audience.

For information on how to see a *hira gasy,* see p73.

The Comoros, too, have a strong tradition of oral literature. Most Comorian literature derives from oral traditions, which have been passed down through the generations in the form of *hali* (folk tales). *Hali* are similar to fables and normally end with a moral.

Check out the latest from the Malagasy music scene at www.madanight.com. The site is mostly in French, but there's lots of articles and band interviews.

Music

Most traditional Malagasy music revolves around favourite dance rhythms: the Indonesian- and Kenyan-influenced *salegy* of the Sakalava tribe; the African *watsa watsa*; the *tsapika*, which originated in the south; and the *sigaoma*, which is similar to South African music.

Outside special occasions such as the Donia festival in Nosy Be (p156), traditional Malagasy music can be hard to find and is often relegated to

---

FAMADIHANA

On the crest of a hill a grove of pine trees whispers gently. In the shade, trestle tables are spread with sticky sweetmeats and bowls of steaming rice. A band plays a rollicking, upbeat tune as the stone door of a family tomb is opened. Old ladies wait at the entrance, faces dignified under their straw hats. Middle-aged men are getting stuck into lethal home-made rum, dancing jerkily to the rhythms of the band.

One by one the corpses are brought out of the tomb, wrapped in straw mats and danced above the heads of a joyful throng. The bodies are re-wrapped in pristine white burial *lambas* (scarves), sprayed with perfume and meticulously labelled by name with felt-tip pens. A period of quiet follows, with family members holding the bodies on their laps in silent communication, weeping but happy at the same time. The air is charged with emotion. Then the bodies are danced one more time around the tomb, a few traditional verses are read out and the stone sealed with mud for another seven years.

Famadihana ceremonies take place every year between June and September in the *hauts plateaux* (highlands) region from Antananarivo south to Ambositra. If you'd like to attend one, ask at your hotel or contact a local tour company (p84).

MALAGASY PROVERBS

■ He who refuses to buy a lid for the pot will eat badly cooked rice.

■ Other people's children cause your nostrils to flare.

■ Done in by his own trade like a water merchant in the rain.

---

rural areas. The music you'll hear blasting out of tinny radios and rocking the local discos is usually a cheesy blend of guitar rock, rough-and-ready rap and hip hop, and soulful ballads. Love songs with catchy choruses are the nation's favourite, and songstresses such as national treasure Poopy (yes, that's her real name) keep the syrup coming with a stream of identi-kit, but irritatingly catchy hits.

The Sapphire Sea, by John B Robinson, is a rollicking beach novel, charting the adventures of a gem dealer who finds the biggest sapphire in the world.

The most-widely played traditional wind instrument is the *kiloloka,* a whistle-like length of bamboo capable of only one note. Melodies are played by a group of musicians, in a manner similar to a bell ensemble. The tubular instrument you'll see on sale at tourist shops and craft markets is a *valiha,* which has 28 strings of varying lengths stretched around a tubular wooden sound box; it resembles a bassoon but is played more like a harp. It has fallen out of favour in Madagascar but is still played in Malaysia and Indonesia, which suggests that it was bought to Madagascar by the earliest settlers of the island.

Other well-known contemporary Malagasy pop groups and singers include Jaojoby, Tiana, Mahaleo, Dama (who was popular enough to get elected to parliament in 1993) and Jerry Marcos, a master of *salegy*. Malagasy groups that have toured internationally, mainly in France and the UK, include Njava and Tarika. The best place to see live performances is at the bigger venues in Tana – look in the newspapers on Friday for event details (p73).

The Comoros, having been part of Indian Ocean trade for over a thousand years, have absorbed cultural and musical influences from East Africa, the Middle East, Madagascar and southern India. There is a remarkably wide range of musical styles in the Comoros. Contemporary Comorian artists often mix traditional sounds with reggae or rap backbeats in collaboration with European producers. Traditional instruments include gongs, drums, tambourines, rattles, oboes, zithers and five-stringed lutes.

Architecture

Each region of Madagascar has its own architectural style and building materials. The Merina and Betsileo of the *hauts plateaux* live in distinctive red-brick houses that are warm on cold nights. The typical Merina home is a tall, narrow affair with small windows and brick pillars in the front supporting open verandas. The Betsileo areas dispense with the pillars and trim their houses with elaborately carved wood. Coastal homes are generally constructed of lighter local materials, including cactus and raffia palm.

The brass studs on traditional Comorian doors come from a design that originated in India to repel war elephants.

In the independent Comoros (but not Mayotte), Swahili architectural traditions are superbly preserved. The old Arab towns in Moroni (p215) and Mutsamudu (p230) are laid out haphazardly with mazelike narrow streets. Townhouses are tall and narrow, with internal balconies running around a central courtyard and an open cooking area at the back. Traditionally doors are elaborately carved with Islamic lettering or abstract motifs, sometimes inlaid with brass studs. Mosques, particularly those used in Friday prayers, are splendid, glittering, white affairs with high, elegant minarets and rows of galleries around the outside. They are often built using funds from Islamic organisations in the Middle East.

Textile Arts

Textiles have always played a huge part in Malagasy society, with some types of cloth even being imbued, it is believed, with supernatural powers. The Merina used cocoons collected from the wild silkworm to make highly valued textiles called *lamba mena* (red silk). The silks were woven in many colour and pattern combinations, and in the past had strong links with royal prestige, expressed by the colour red. Worn by the aristocracy in life and death, *lamba mena* were also used in burial and reburial ceremonies.

Modern textile arts are particularly strong in Madagascar. Ancestral materials such as *lamba mena* are combined with modern textiles such as lycra, or 'found objects' such as shells or even computer circuit boards. Ask at the Centre Culturel Albert Camus (p63) in Antananarivo for details of textile exhibitions.

Theatre & Dance

In addition to *hira gasy* (p33), the best place to see traditional dance performances is at the Donia, the arts festival held every year in Nosy Be (p156). The Centre Culturel Albert Camus in Antananarivo (p63) is the best place to see theatre and dance performances in the capital. In the provinces, the various branches of Alliance Française can usually provide information on local events.

In the Comoros, dancing forms an integral part of every Muslim festival. One of the most popular is the *mougodro,* a circular dance with African and Malagasy origins in which men, women and children all participate.

On Mayotte, the most popular dance is the *wadaha* (or *danse de pilon*) in which women and young girls dance in a circle around a mortar filled with rice, to the rhythm of drums, guitars and popular songs, simulating the pulverisation of the rice with pestles. It also serves as a pre-nuptial dance. Contact the Comité de Tourisme in Mayotte (p238) for details of performances.

The interesting film *Quand les Étoiles Rencontrent la Mer* (When the Stars Meet the Sea), directed by the Malagasy Raymond Rajaonarivelo, is the story of a young boy born during a solar eclipse.

A very weird but rather wonderful tale by the veteran US author William S Burroughs is *Ghost of Chance*. It's a surreal account of the founding of Libertalia, the pirate republic.

Food & Drink

The melting pot of Arabic, Chinese, French, African and Indian cultures in Madagascar and the Comoros has produced an exciting and often mouth-watering cuisine. Regional variations are common, with the very different fruits, vegetables and fish on offer in each area of the two countries dictating local tastes and recipes. The most interesting Malagasy food is only on offer in private homes, so if you're hoping to sample some of the unique local dishes you're probably best off making friends with some hospitable local cooks.

However, if you don't manage to inveigle your way into a Malagasy home, console yourself with the fact that the country's restaurants normally serve excellent French cuisine to suit all budgets, from simple zebu *steack frites* (steak and chips) to *paté de foie gras* (goose liver paté) and *magret de canard* (duck fillet). Staples such as pizza and pasta are easy to find, too. In the Comoros, restaurants are few and far between, but those that do exist serve up mouth-watering local dishes. You might find that portions in cheaper local restaurants tend to be smaller than those in Europe or the USA.

STAPLES & SPECIALITIES
Rice

Malagasy food is always based around fish, beef or chicken accompaniments to the staple diet of rice. If you don't like rice, then brace yourself as the average Malagasy considers a bowl of rice a perfectly valid meal in itself, and, in rural areas, rice is often only accompanied by a bowl of warm water with a couple of cabbage leaves floating in it (this 'sauce' is known as *ro*).

The growth of a rice plant is described in Malagasy using the same words as a woman becoming pregnant and giving birth.

Eating rice three times a day is so ingrained in Malagasy culture that people often say they won't be able to sleep if they have not eaten rice that day. Rice is accompanied by a stew made from *hen'omby* (boiled beef), *hen'andrano* (fish), *hen'akoho* (chicken or duck) or vegetables, with a few spices added to give it flavour. A common side dish is *brèdes* (boiled greens) in water.

The most usual alternative to rice is a steaming bowl of *mi sao* (fried noodles with vegetables or meat) or a satisfying *soupe chinoise* (clear noodle soup with fish, chicken or vegetables), both dishes that show the Asian origins of the Malagasy. Poorer rural communities supplement their rice diet with starchy roots such as manioc or corn. In the Comoros, cassava (*mhogo* in Swahili), replaces rice as the staple food. It looks like boiled potatoes and tastes like nothing at all.

Meat

Zebu cattle not only provide status, transport and a handy means of obtaining a wife in Madagascar, they are also well known for their excellent meat. Zebu beef in stews or zebu steak, if cooked well, is hailed by carnivorous types as particularly succulent and delicious. If the beef is of a lower quality it is often cut into small pieces, simmered until done, shredded, and then roasted until it is browned. Pork is sometimes available in Chinese restaurants, but it's *fady* (taboo) to eat pork in many parts of Madagascar, and entirely forbidden in the Muslim Comoros. Stringy chicken or goat is standard fare at *hotelys* (small roadside place that serves basic meals).

Fish

Near the coast of Madagascar, and everywhere in the Comoros, seafood fans are in for a treat – every menu features lobster, prawns or squid together with a fish of the day. Seafood prices are so low that all but those on the smallest of budgets can gorge on lobster without any difficulty. A delicious and unusual variation for crustacean fans are the bright orange, ready-boiled and salted freshwater crayfish on offer in the area around Ranomafana. If you take the Fianarantsoa–Manakara train in the dry season, you'll be able to buy these through the windows as a snack for the journey.

If you decide to buy your fish from the local fishermen while staying near the coast, take care to find out when the catch comes in – this varies from place to place and could decide whether your dinner is straight out of the ocean or has been hanging around sitting in the sun all day.

Fruit

Mangos, lychees, bananas, of all shapes and sizes, and even strawberries are available in various parts of Madagascar. Likewise fresh juice is on sale everywhere in Madagascar and the Comoros. Bear in mind that the juice in cheaper restaurants will be diluted with untreated water. For a delicious thirst quencher near the beach, split open a young coconut and drink the vitamin-packed juice inside.

A 2002 survey conducted by the Food and Agricultural Organization of the United Nations estimated that Madagascar had 11 million cattle, almost two million sheep and goats and 21 million chickens.

Breakfast

Rice is eaten for breakfast everywhere in Madagascar. If you're staying in a tourist hotel, you'll invariably be served bread, croissants and jam, sometimes with the option of eggs. Comorians prefer to start the day with *supu* – an oily meat broth with shreds of beef floating in it, plus the odd knuckle of cartilage. The general form is to buy this from the market and carry it home in a plastic bag.

Snacks

One of the first things you'll notice on arriving in Madagascar is the dizzying variety of patisserie. Presumably a legacy of the French, sticky cakes, croissants, pastries and meringues are on sale in even the most humble of cafés. In the bigger cities, the concoctions on offer at glitzier *salons de thé* (tea rooms) would rival the snootiest Parisian *boulangerie* (bakery). Baguettes (French bread sticks) can be bought everywhere in Madagascar and the Comoros.

Savoury snacks include the ubiquitous samosas (called *sambos* and nearly always filled with minced meat), small doughnuts called *mofo menakely* and *masikita* (skewers threaded with grilled beef). The odd, log-like thing you'll see sold in glass boxes on the pavements of Antananarivo and elsewhere is *koba,* a concoction made from peanuts, rice and sugar, wrapped tightly in banana leaves, baked and sold in slices. More pleasure for the sweet of tooth lies in Roberts chocolate, so good that even nonchocoholics may be converted.

President Ravomalanana's Tiko company ferries little pots of yogurt and sachets of flavoured milk to the remotest corners of the island. Homemade yogurt is also available in glass pots in even the humblest hotely.

DRINKS

As far as drinks go, most Malagasy like to accompany their meal of rice with a drink of – rice water. This brown, smoky-tasting concoction, known as *rano vola*, and often jokingly referred to as 'whisky malgache'

TRAVEL YOUR TASTEBUDS

Look out for these on your culinary travels in Madagascar:

Achards Hot pickled vegetable curry used as a relish.

Betsa-betsa Fermented sugar-cane juice.

Kitoza Dried beef strips charcoaled and often served with cornmeal mush for breakfast.

Punch coco Sickly but delicious alcoholic drink made from sweetened coconut milk.

Ravitoto Bitter tasting, dark-green cassava leaves and often added to pork dishes.

Tapia Small red berries that taste similar to dates.

We Dare You...

Only for the brave of heart and mouth:

Locusts When a locust storm attacks, the locals retaliate by catching and frying the crop-eating critters.

Pimente Malgache The hottest flavour of food.

Sakay Red-hot pepper mixed with ginger and garlic paste; thankfully served on the side, not in the food.

Toaka Gasy Illegal and dangerous home-brewed rum, served in plastic buckets.

is made from boiling water in the pot containing the burnt rice residue. An acquired taste.

Excellent coffee is usually served at the end of the meal in French restaurants, but if you drink it white, you'll have to learn to love condensed milk. In the Comoros, tea is spiced with lemongrass or ginger, and coffee is served syrupy and black in tiny Arabic-style cups.

The most popular local-brand Malagasy beers are Three Horses Beer (known as THB) and Gold, which is slightly stronger and more flavoursome. The most common import brand is Castle from South Africa.

Madagascar's speciality, however, is not beer but rum. Most bars and restaurants have an array of glass flasks behind the bar filled with *rhum arrangé* – rum in which a variety of fruits and spices have been left to steep. Nearly all of them have an alcohol content that will blow your socks off.

Madagascar has a small wine industry, started by the Swiss and centred around Fianarantsoa (see p95). Not much of it can stand up to better international wines, but a bottle makes a good present to take home. Imported French and South African wine is served in better restaurants in Madagascar but only in the most upmarket, Westernised restaurants in the Comoros. On Mayotte, all wine, beer and spirits are imported from France.

A tip: don't give out sweets to the children who beg for them – without access to dentists, their teeth will rot. Try giving them chewable fruit-flavoured vitamins instead.

CELEBRATIONS

Celebrating in Madagascar or the Comoros means eating big. Weddings, funerals, circumcisions, and reburials are preceded by days of boiling up food in cauldrons big enough to fall into. A Malagasy proverb says 'the food which is prepared has no master'. Extended family, friends and also passers-by are always invited to share the food, which is usually a stew made of chicken, several salads and, of course, a mountain of rice.

Those of a squeamish bent shouldn't turn up at the venue of a party the day before it's due – you're likely to be greeted by the sight of dozens of zebu cattle having their legs roped together and their throats slit before being butchered to feed the expected guests. At Malagasy parties, copious quantities of home-brewed rum are consumed, and helpless drunkenness is entirely expected.

WHERE TO EAT & DRINK

The least expensive places in Madagascar and the Comoros are street stalls (which are not found everywhere) and hotely, small informal restaurants serving basic meals. These are sometimes called *gargotes* in French and are found in every city and town. They are your best bet for fast food during the day, but they're rarely open much past 7.30pm. Standards of hygiene vary widely, but none would be likely to pass a food safety test in the Western world. For tips on how to avoid health problems with food, see p273.

One step up from these is the *salon de thé*, a tearoom that offers a variety of pastries, cakes, ice cream and other snacks, sometimes offering sandwiches and light meals as well. All serve tea and coffee. Most close at about 6pm; a few close at lunchtime, too.

The African Cookbook, by Bea Sandler, has some good recipes from Madagascar.

Lastly, the next step up from a *salon de thé* are restaurants, which range from modest to top-end establishments and serve French, Indian or Chinese cuisine with a few Malagasy dishes thrown in. Most offer a *menu du jour* (three-course set menu), or a *plat du jour* (daily special), sometimes just called a *speciale*. Most hotel dining rooms offer a set three or more course dinner known as a *table d'hôte*. Prices for these are usually around FMg40,000. For à la carte menus, the average price of a main course is FMg25,000.

VEGETARIANS & VEGANS

Vegetarians shouldn't have too much of a problem in Madagascar. French restaurants rarely cater for veggies, while small local hotelys are usually happy to whip up some noodles, soup or rice and greens. Protein could be a problem for vegans, as beans are not as widely available in Madagascar as they may be elsewhere.

In the Comoros, vegetable dishes are harder to find, but beans are back on the menu – there is a delicious red-bean-and-coconut stew (known as *maharagwe* in Swahili) which isn't to be missed. Fish-eating vegetarians should have no problems at all (p37). If you eat eggs, omelettes are available almost everywhere. Neither Malagasy nor Comorians find vegetarianism very difficult to understand and they are often more than happy to cater for special diets if you are polite and give them enough notice. Restaurants that are especially good for veggies are mentioned in our listings.

DOS & DON'TS

- Do bring a present (a small amount of money or a bottle of rum) if you're invited to a Malagasy celebration. Women should wear modest clothes.

- Do check before eating pork in rural Madagascar – in some places it's *fady* (taboo).

- Do hold your wrist with the opposite hand when passing food or drinks to a Malagasy – they will be impressed with your manners.

- Do offer to pay for food consumed in villages while trekking or visiting.

- Don't eat or pass food with your left hand in the Comoros – the left hand is considered unclean in Muslim societies.

- Don't drink alcohol in the street, public places or most hotel restaurants in the Comoros.

- Don't eat, drink or smoke in public in daylight hours during the fast of Ramadan in the Comoros.

ANTANANARIVO'S TOP FIVE

■ **Chez Mariette** (Map pp60-1; ☎ 22 216 02; 11 Lalana Joel Rakotomalala; ☯ dinner only with advance booking; 6-course meals FMg100,000) Traditional Malagasy royal banquet, cooked in the home of a chef with charisma.

■ **La Paillotte** (Map pp64-5; ☎ 032 02 201 26; Arabe Ramanantsoa; ☯ lunch & dinner; 2-course meal FMg10,000) Fun-and-friendly, no-frills African-style restaurant with a lively bar.

■ **La Varangue** (Map pp64-5; ☎ 22 273 97; varangue@simicro.mg; 17 Lalana Printsy Ratsimamanga; 3-course meals FMg80,000) A little-known and very classy small restaurant in the hotel of the same name, cosy and brimming with character. Reputedly the best French food in Madagascar.

■ **Patisserie Colbert** (Map pp64-5; Lalana Printsy Ratsimamanga; ☯ breakfast & lunch; lunch FMg20,000) A gilt and marble-decorated cake-lovers' paradise.

■ **Restaurant Sakamanga** (Map pp64-5; ☎ 22 358 09; Lalana Andrianary Ratianarivo; ☯ breakfast, lunch & dinner; mains FMg30,000) Bustling bistro with excellent food and reasonable prices – great atmosphere and popular with locals. The seafood spaghetti is exquisite.

HABITS & CUSTOMS

A true Malagasy or Comorian serves up a meal without any fancy preliminaries such as cocktails or hors d'oeuvres. Comorians politely say '*bismillah*' (thanks to Allah) before starting their meal. The food is heaped together on the plate and a spoon, rather than a knife or fork, is used to eat it. Many people in the Comoros prefer to use their hands to eat with. Meals in more traditional households are eaten sitting on mats on the floor. Cooking is done outside the house in an open courtyard.

In Madagascar heavier dishes with rich sauces are kept for Sunday, celebrations or holidays. Light dishes such as greens boiled in water or peas are served to aid digestion the day after a particularly heavy meal.

When drinking in Madagascar, it's customary to pour a little on the ground first as an offering to the ancestors.

EAT YOUR WORDS

Menus in Madagascar and the Comoros are almost exclusively in French, even in the cheapest roadside restaurants. Avoid the puzzled stare and Gallic shrug of even the snootiest waiters – brush up on your ordering skills by learning a bit of French foodie jargon. For further pronunciation guidelines, see p276.

Useful Phrases

For recipes and presentation tips check out: www.sas.upenn.edu /African_Studies/ Cookbook/ Madagascar.html.

Well done	*bien cuit*
bee-en kwee	
I don't eat...	*Je ne mange pas de...*
je-ne-monje-pa-de	
meat	*viande*
vee-ande	
fish	*poisson*
pwa-so	
seafood	*fruits de mer*
fwee-de-mair	
I'm vegetarian	*Je suis vegetarien(ne)*
je-swee-vejetair-ee-en	

Menu Decoder
archards – hot, pickled vegetable curry
grillades (*gree*-yard) – grilled meats
mi sao (mee-*sow*) – stir-fried noodles with meat or vegetables
poulet au gingembre (poolay oh *jan*-jombre) – chicken with ginger
ro – a leaf-based broth
soupe chinoise (soup-*sheen*-warse) – Chinese noodle soup
steack frîtes (steak *freet*) – steak and chips
zebu au poivre vert (zebu oh *pwav*-ra vair) – beef steak with green-pepper sauce

Food Glossary
BASICS
bread	*pain*	pan
butter	*beurre*	ber
eggs	*oeufs*	ur
pepper	*poivre*	*pwav*-ra
rice	*riz*	ree
salt	*sel*	sel
sugar	*sucre*	*soo*-cra

MEAT
beef	*boeuf*	berf
chicken	*poulet*	*poo*-lay
duck	*canard*	can-*ar*
pork	*porc*	porc
rare (steak)	*saignant*	say-*nyo*

SEAFOOD
lobster	*langouste*	long-*goost*
prawns	*crevettes*	crevettes

VEGETABLES
beans	*haricots*	*ah*-ri-co
onions	*oignons*	on-*ee*-on
potato	*pomme de terre*	pom-de-*tair*

Ma Cuisine Malgache (Karibo Safako), by Angeline Espagne-Ravo, contains the best collection of Malagasy recipes in French.

Environment Patricia C Wright

THE LAND

Madagascar split from the African land mass around 165 million years ago. As a result of continental drift it reached its present position about 100 million years ago. Later, approximately 88 million years ago, the eastern half of Madagascar broke off from the African mainland, moving northward to eventually become India. Since then, Madagascar has remained at its present size and shape, isolated from the rest of the world.

Madagascar is 1600km long and up to 570km wide, and is the world's fourth-largest island, after Greenland, Papua New Guinea and Borneo. The 5000km-long coastline is sprinkled with several small islands and coral atolls, including Nosy Be to the northwest and Île Sainte Marie to the east.

Madagascar can be divided geographically into three parallel north–south zones: the west consists of dry spiny desert or deciduous forest, the central plateau (known as the *haut plateaux)* has now been mostly deforested and the eastern zone is rain forest. The coasts are marked by alternating mangrove swamps and long, sweeping sandy beaches, with coral reefs offshore. The 2876m volcanic Maromokotro peak in the Tsaratanana massif is Madagascar's highest point, followed by the 2658m Pic Imarivolanitra (formerly known as Pic Boby) in Parc National d'Andringitra. All but the island's southern tip lies north of the Tropic of Capricorn.

Patricia C Wright is Professor of Anthropology at the State University of New York and Director of the Institute for the Conservation of Tropical Environments. In 1986 she and colleagues discovered a new species of lemur, the golden bamboo lemur.

Unlike the neighbouring Comoros islands, Madagascar is not the result of volcanic activity, but consists of an ancient crystalline bedrock base. Madagascar is tipping east very slowly, and the entire west coast contains mostly marine fossil deposits. Going east from the western shore, limestone is replaced by sandstone which rises into majestic formations in places such as Parc National de l'Isalo (p107). Sapphire deposits found in the southwest near de l'Isalo have recently resulted in the mushrooming of a large boom town with dealers and diggers easily seen from the highway.

Further east are deposits of minerals and semiprecious stones, such as jasper, agate, zircon, rose and smoky quartz, moonstone, tourmaline, morganite beryl and amethyst, although most stones and minerals are not found in commercially viable quantities. There are ancient volcanos at Parc National de Montagne d'Ambre (p150), the Ankaratra massif (p78) and Lac Itasy (p79), west of Antananarivo, which have produced fertile soil, good agricultural lands and picturesque places for locals to picnic. Northern and western Madagascar host impressive limestone karst formations – jagged, eroded limestone rocks which contain caves, potholes, underground rivers and forested canyons rich in wildlife such as crocodiles, lemurs, birds and bats. Karst is known locally as *tsingy*, and is protected within Madagascar's only World Heritage site, Parc National des Tsingy de Bemaraha (p136), as well as in the Réserve Spéciale de l'Ankàrana (p152).

Erosion – exacerbated by deforestation – is a serious problem, and has given rise to the description of Madagascar as the 'great red island'. In the most dramatic cases, the ground has slumped, leaving eroded landslides of red soil which now scar most of the highlands and has turned rivers red. When you fly over the country, you can see the red, silted waters of the rivers pouring the soil of Madagascar into the sea. Soil erosion is a major threat to freshwater fish, many of which are on the brink of extinction.

WILDLIFE

Madagascar's isolation for over 80 million years created an explosion of plants and animals found nowhere else on earth. The conservation of wildlife in Madagascar is a worldwide priority, the alternative being the loss of all these beautiful species. Over the last thousand years, many large animals, including 17 species of lemurs (some the size of gorillas), tortoises, hippopotami, giant aardvarks, the world's largest bird (the ostrich-like elephant bird) and two species of eagle, have become extinct.

In *The Eighth Continent: Life, Death and Discovery in the Lost World of Madagascar*, Peter Tyson follows the footsteps of five (eccentric) explorers and scientists, and their pioneering studies and expeditions of Madagascar.

Animals

MAMMALS

Madagascar's best-known mammals are the lemurs, of which there are nearly 50 species in five families. Sifakas *(Propithecus)* and indris *(Indri indri)* are well known for their leaping abilities. Mouse lemurs *(Microcebus)* are the world's smallest primate. The ring-tailed lemur *(Lemur catta)* is adapted to very dry areas and engages in territorial battles by waving their scent-marked, striped tails in the air. Aye-ayes *(Daubentonia)* extract grubs from bark with a long, bony finger. Fat-tailed dwarf lemurs *(Cheirogaleus)* hibernate for up to six months during the cold season. Black-and-white lemurs *(Varecia)* give loud territorial calls. The best places to view lemurs are the national parks of Ranomafana (p89), d'Andasibe-Mantadia (p199) and de Montagne d'Ambre (p150), and Kirindy reserve.

Tenrecs are primitive mammals and include the hedgehog-like spiny tenrecs *(Setifer, Echinops* and *Hemicentetes)* and shrew tenrecs *(Microgale)*. Rodents include giant jumping rats *(Hypogeomys antimena)*, red-forest rats *(Nesoymys)* and tuft-tailed forest mice *(Eilurus)*. There are six species of carnivore – all are mongooses and civets – including the ring-tailed mongoose *(Galidea elegans)*, the fanaloka *(Fossa fossana)* and the puma-like, lemur-eating fosa *(Cryptoprocta ferox)*.

For more information, see the Wildlife Guide (p49).

BIRDS

There are up to six native families of birds on Madagascar and 209 breeding species; of these 51% are endemic, the highest proportion of any country in the world. Eighty of the 120 native bird species are found only in the forest. Species include the diverse vanga shrikes; the noisy sickle-billed vanga *(Falculea palliata)* found in the west; the bright-blue vanga *(Cyanolanius madagascarinus)* in the eastern rain forests; and the helmeted vanga *(Euryceros prevostii)* found in the rain forests of the northwest. Couas are large, iridescent birds which prey on chameleons and geckos. The pitta-like ground roller *(Atelornis pittoides)* is another large iridescent rain-forest bird. The Madagascar crested ibis *(Lophotibis cristata)*, the Madagascar harrier hawk *(Polyboroides radiatus)* and the Hensti's goshawk *(Accipiter henstii)* all hunt in the rain forest. The Madagascar serpent eagle *(Eutriorchis astur)* and the Madagascar fish eagle *(Haliaeetus vociferoides)* are the largest living raptors. Possible sightings from the road may include the Madagascan red fody *(Foudia madagascariensis)*, the Madagascan kestrel *(Falco newtoni)* and the crested drongo *(Dicruruius forficatus)*.

Madagascar has the world's smallest chameleon – smaller than your thumb.

REPTILES & AMPHIBIANS

There are 346 reptile species on Madagascar, including most of the world's chameleons, ranging from the largest – Parson's chameleon *(Calumna parsonii)*, which grows to around 60cm – to the smallest – the dwarf chameleon (of the genus *Brookesia)*. Reptiles include the leaf-tailed gecko *(Uroplatus)*, the bright-green day gecko *(Phelsuma)*, the Madagascar boa *(Sanzinia)*, the leaf-nosed snake *(Langaha madagascariensis)*, the Nile crocodile *(Crocodylus niloticus)* and the radiated tortoise *(Geochelone radiata)*. Madagascar has over 200 species of frogs, including the bright-red tomato frog and iridescent brightly coloured Malagasy poison frogs *(Mantella)*.

For more information, see the Wildlife Guide (p49).

FISH

Most of the freshwater fish are endemic and include the colourful rainbow fish *(Bedotia* and *Rheocles)*, the often large cichlids *(Paratilapia)* and the swamp fish *(Pantanodon)*. Many of the freshwater fish are the most endangered group of animals on Madagascar.

Plants

The Malagasy plant community is one of the most diverse on earth with around 6000 species. Of Madagascar's 4220 tree species, a whopping 96% are endemic. Each of Madagascar's three north–south zones has its own ecosystem, each containing its own unique species of plants and animals.

The spiny desert can be easily seen at Réserve Privée de Berenty (p122) and Réserve Spéciale de Beza-Mahafaly (p115). It is distinguished by a wide array of plants that look like cactus, but are actually a separate family called the *Dideriaceae*. *Alluaudia procerans* stand 3m tall, with columnar pillars of spines that can erupt into tiny cloverlike leaves at the first drop of rain. White Verreaux's sifakas bound feet first between these plants, munching carefully on the new leaves, despite the abundant needle-like spines.

There are nine species of *Pachypodia*, including a tall species with large fragrant yellow-white blossoms, and the diminutive elephant foot species that nestle in cliff crevices on the sandstone massif at Parc National de l'Isalo (p107).

Madagascar has seven species of baobabs *(Adansonia)*. The baobab's bulbous thick trunk stores water, allowing them to survive the dry season. The large, bright flowers are filled with copious amounts of nectar, often sipped by the fork-marked lemurs *(Phaner furcifer)*. About 60 species of aloe occur in Madagascar and many dot the spiny desert landscape.

The eastern rain forests can be seen in the national parks of Ranomafana (p89), d'Andasibe-Mantadia (p199), de Montagne d'Ambre (p150) and de Marojejy (p197). These forests are filled with large tropical trees which provide the fruits, flowers and leaves that lemurs thrive on. Most trees flower from September to November with fruits abundant when the rains come from November to March. Throughout the forests are over 10 species of endemic bamboo, with three species of bamboo lemurs (primate pandas) to eat them.

Especially abundant in rain-forest swamps are tree-like screw pines *(Pandanus)*. Villagers harvest the leaves of the pines to weave mats, vests and hats. Within the oldest trees hang giant bird's nest ferns and clusters of parasitic mistletoe plants, home to tree frogs and day geckos.

The Duke University Primate Center website at www.duke.edu /web/primate has great photos and up-to-date natural-history facts about lemurs, including details on the release of black-and-white ruffed lemurs back to the wild in Madagascar.

In *Zoboomafoo Leapin' Lemurs,* Chris and Martin Kratt have created the first wildlife series created specifically for viewing by children. A leaping sifaka takes you on an adventure explaining why you should save the lemurs of Madagascar.

There are a thousand species of orchids in Madagascar, more than in all of Africa. Most orchids bloom from November to March, although a few bloom in July. More than 60 species of pitcher plants (*Nepenthes*) are found in the swampy areas of the rain forest, and can be seen in Ranomafana. These carnivorous plants produce nectar that attracts insects, with the downward-pointing hairs along the side of the pitcher trap eventually dissolving its prey.

The dry, deciduous forest can best be seen in the national park of d'Ankarafantsika and its d'Ampijoroa forest reserve (p133), and the Kirindy forest reserve (p139). This forest contains giant baobabs, but no palms or ferns. Travellers should not miss the majestic baobab alley (p139) on the way to Réserve Forestière de Kirindy, which has stands of thousand year-old baobabs.

NATIONAL PARKS

The environmental movement in Madagascar began in earnest in 1985, with an international conference of scientists, funding organisations and Malagasy government officials. Biologists knew Madagascar was an oasis of amazing creatures and plants, but devastation and the burning of Malagasy forests were threatening these treasures. Concerned international donors and the Malagasy government joined together to plan a major conservation program.

By 1989 Madagascar had the world's first country-wide Environmental Action Plan, which offered a blueprint for biodiversity action for the next 20 years. The first order of the day was to create a national park system, called the Association Nationale pour la Gestion des Aires Protégées (Angap, National Association for the Management of Protected Areas), and then set Angap to work on creating new parks and training new staff.

Much change has occurred – in 1985 there were two national parks in Madagascar and today there are over 14. During the first five years of the Environmental Action Plan, five sites were chosen as integrated conservation and development projects. The national parks were officially mapped and registered, and teams were trained to work in them. Meanwhile the people living in and around each park were courted with alternatives to forest destruction, such as bee-keeping, fish farming and tree farming.

In the late 1990s focus shifted from national parks to a more regional approach. This broader view started biological, botanical and anthropological surveys in vast stretches of wilderness connecting the parks, especially concentrating on the southern forest corridor between Ranomafana and d'Andringitra and the northern forest corridor connecting Mantadia with Zahamena. This included mapping with Geographic Information Systems (GIS) and setting up ecological monitoring.

In 2003, at the World's Park Conference, President Ravalomanana announced a bold plan to expand protected areas by three times. Currently only 10% of Madagascar is covered with natural vegetation and 3% of the country is protected in national parks, classified forests or natural reserves.

This initiative to triple protected areas is echoed by a move to recognise more Unesco World Heritage sites. Currently Parc National des Tsingy de Bemaraha (p136) is Madagascar's only World Heritage site, and in 2003, the government began a plan to nominate a cluster of eastern rain forests as another World Heritage site.

Common tenrec mothers can give birth to 25 infants at one time, the most of any mammal in the world.

Lords and Lemurs, by Alison Jolly, is a history of the Berenty reserve that skilfully weaves together the stories of the spiny desert Tandroy people, three generations of French plantation owners, lemurs and lemur-watchers.

NATIONAL PARKS & RESERVES HIGHLIGHTS

Parc National de Montagne d'Ambre (Amber Mountain; p150), in the north of Madagascar, is the closest national park to the equator. It's a lush rain forest on the top of a volcano overlooking the Indian Ocean's white-sand beaches. Bright orange and steel-grey crowned lemurs *(Eulemur coronatus)*, as well as svelte Sanford's lemurs *(Eulemur sanfordi)* are scattered throughout the trees, grunting like pigs and looking like stuffed toys. There is a spectacular waterfall at the end of one trail and the remnants of an old French botanical garden at the end of another (for more details, see p150).

Réserve Spéciale de l'Ankàrana (p152), nearby, is less accessible than Parc National de Montagne d'Ambre, but is a wonderland of old eroded limestone caves and canyons, containing living and fossil lemurs. When visiting, remember that the limestone is razor sharp, so proper footwear is a necessity. Beware of the streams inside the caves, which are clear and inviting, but can hide hungry crocodiles. One of the larger caves is the 'Cave of the Lone Barefoot Stranger' where some footprints went in, but none came out... The environment in l'Ankàrana is fragile and tourists are advised to tread softly and not remove any artefacts. Enjoy vistas of fishing eagles nesting on cliffs, the spectacular dry-forest bird life and ring-tailed mongooses playing at cave entrances. In the dry scrub forest look for brightly coloured chameleons lurching from branch to branch, stalking insect prey.

Masoala Peninsula (p192), in the northeast, is the only rain forest intact from mountaintop to sea level. Small fishing villages dot areas of the coast, and the blissfully blue Bay of Antongil links the forests of Masoala with the iridescent beaches of Mananara-Nord (see below). Whale-watching is possible in the bay. Established in 1997 Parc National Masoala is the largest national park in Madagascar at 210,000 hectares.

Réserve de Nosy Mangabe (p189) is an island covered with rain forest and the best place to observe aye-ayes, white-fronted brown lemurs and leaf-tailed geckos.

Parc National de Mananara-Nord (p186) is a Unesco biosphere reserve, which includes large areas of primary rain forest, coastal vegetation and coral reefs, and encompasses one of Madagascar's marine parks. The aye-aye and hairy-eared dwarf lemur are seen here, as well as tomato frogs and chameleons.

Parc National de Marojejy (p197) is crowned by a series of mountainous peaks covered by lush rain forest. Within the forest, sifakas leap from tree to tree like a flock of earth-bound angels. The sacred mountain is a challenge that few have crested. Don't miss the opportunity to stay overnight at one of the camp sites, where you can watch the helmeted vanga shrike and gaze down over the magnificent cliffs into the canyon. Iridescent green millipedes dot the trails and curl up like gleaming balls of malachite when disturbed.

The Institute for the Conservation of Tropical Environments (ICTE) at http://icte.bio.sunysb.edu, part of the Stony Brook University site, has photos of rain forest wildlife and natural history details, as well as information on research and tourist opportunities in southeastern Madagascar.

People & Wildlife

From the very beginning of Madagascar's environmental movement, the needs of the people living in and around the parks were incorporated into park management plans. Fifty per cent of park admission fees from tourists are returned to villagers that live around the parks. This money is used to build wells, buy vegetable seeds, help with tree nurseries, rebuild schools and build small dams to facilitate paddy rice, rather than hillside rice cultivation. By visiting a national park, you are economically helping village residents.

Biodiversity Research & Parks

Most of the research on the unique animals and plants of Madagascar occurs in national parks. In 2003 an international Malagasy research and training centre called Centre ValBio was inaugurated, adjacent to Parc National de Ranomafana (p89). It is mostly funded by universities from Europe and the USA, and researchers from all over the world visit to take advantage of its modern facilities. Stop in to have lunch, chat with the

Parc National d'Ankarafantsika (p133) is an easy ride from Mahajanga and contains western, dry deciduous forest where you'll find mongoose lemurs, sifakas and brown lemurs. A nest of the fishing eagle overhangs a nearby lake, where sacred crocodiles lie.

Parc National d'Andasibe-Mantadia (see p199) was the third national park formed in Madagascar and is easily reached from Antananarivo by car. The forest is spectacular with beautiful views of the diademed sifaka and the most musical prosimian, the indri. Early mornings are the best time to hear the indri's clarinet-like melodies, as each group echoes the others in a set of 'rounds'. The indris themselves, with their teddy bear ears, bunny-rabbit tails and furry long legs, are a sight to see. Be warned that these large lemurs are quite lazy, bedding down for the night right after lunch and sleeping until dawn, so viewing can be difficult. The calico diademed sifaka – bright orange, tan, brown and white in colour – is arguably the most beautiful of all mammals. As they bathe in the sun or leap between fruit trees, these beauties remind one of an acrobatic ballet. The black-and-white ruffed lemurs are also close by, but can only be found in the lower altitudes of this forest.

Parc National des Tsingy de Bemaraha (p136) is Madagascar's only World Heritage site. It contains limestone *tsingy* and forested canyons with sifakas, brown lemurs and fishing eagles.

Parc National de Ranomafana (p89) was only established after the 1986 discovery of a new lemur species, the golden bamboo lemur. With the additional rediscovery of the greater bamboo lemur, as well as the gentle grey bamboo lemur, Parc National de Ranomafana had the unique situation of having three 'primate pandas' living in harmony with nine other species of lemurs. Difficult to see forest birds, such as the pitta-like and short-legged ground rollers, the brown mesite, the crested ibis and the Hensti's goshawk, can also be viewed here. In this mountainous area the fragile forest protects the watershed of the region from siltation. The waters are important not only for farming and drinking, but the region also has a hydroelectric dam, which is its only source of electricity.

Parc National d'Andringitra (p96) contains the second-highest mountain range in Madagascar and good hiking trails. At the top of Pic Imarivolanitra are high-altitude ring-tailed lemurs, which are held sacred by the local people.

Parc National de l'Isalo (p107) is one of Madagascar's largest parks, with sandstone mountains reminiscent of the Grand Canyon in the USA. Verreaux's sifakas and other wildlife live in the forests within the canyons and groups of ring-tailed lemurs scamper along the cliffs.

Réserve Spéciale de Beza-Mahafaly (p115) protects spiny forest and gallery forest and provides a habitat for ring-tailed lemurs and sifakas.

Réserve Privée de Berenty (p122) contains gallery forest and spiny desert, with ring-tailed lemurs, brown lemurs and sifakas.

scientists, see a slide show of the staff's ongoing research and hear about the latest biodiversity findings.

ENVIRONMENTAL ISSUES

Madagascar's big environmental issues are deforestation and the consequent erosion caused by 'slash-and-burn' farming. Malagasy soils are old and fragile, and cannot survive the annual burning that occurs across the island, earning Madagascar the label 'the land of pyromaniacs'. Fire is also used in political protest, its meaning going far beyond agricultural use. You will see the effect of deforestation everywhere; much of it has occurred within the last thousand years. We know from the subfossil record that fires and the extinction of large animals occurred after the first human contact (around 1500 years ago). The impact of the present day farmer's lifestyle on the landscape is obvious and the impact of slash-and-burn techniques in particular are catastrophic. Within a decade of a forest being slashed and burned, it becomes irretrievable. The savannah wasteland is covered with an invasive, sun-loving grass, and almost no

Madagascar has no poisonous snakes that can bite and kill humans.

Madagascar Living Edens, by Andrew Young, is a series of breathtaking images of Madagascar's special wildlife. The predator-prey interactions gives this film the suspense of a thriller.

endemic plants or animals exist can exist in this kind of environment, which covers more than 80% of the island. People also have a tough time living on this fragile landscape, with no fertile soil and polluted water, so it is in everyone's best interest to help people and wildlife live in harmony.

The conservation efforts of the 1990s slowed the devastation of natural resources, and satellite photos suggest most park boundaries have been preserved from slash-and-burn methods. The government has seen that its future depends on preserving and marketing its natural resources – and this bodes well for Madagascar's future.

Wildlife Guide

The best time to see birds, insects and reptiles is October to December, when they breed. Lemurs are out and about at all times of year, and from April until June the infants and juveniles are particularly playful. January until March can be beautiful, but this is during the risky cyclone season, which is not a good time to travel.

Because of Madagascar's environmental problems, several species are endangered; however, you can see these animals in nearly all of Madagascar's protected areas. The helmeted vanga shrike is most often seen in Parc National Masoala (p192) and Parc National de Marojejy (p197). The white silky sifaka is also seen in Parc National de Marojejy. The critically endangered white-collared brown lemur can only be seen in Manombo Reserve on the southeastern coastal town of Farafangana. Blue-eyed black lemurs are not found in any reserve, but can only be found at the peninsula near Moramandia. Parc National d'Andasibe-Mantadia (p199) and Réserve Spéciale d'Analamazaotra (often referred to as Périnet; p200) are the best places to see and hear the majestic indri, Madagascar's largest lemur. Golden bamboo lemurs and greater bamboo lemurs can only be viewed in Parc National de Ranomafana (p89). Aye-ayes are widespread, but Réserve de Nosy Mangabe (p189) is the easiest place to arrange a night-time viewing.

Very few of the endemic species of mammal, reptile, amphibian and bird are found in any of the areas devoid of natural vegetation. This means that travellers shouldn't expect to see endemic wildlife on the *haut plateaux* (highlands), or other deforested regions.

A ring-tailed lemur mother carrying her young.
PHOTO BY CAROL POLICH

When threatened, the hedgehog tenrec rolls into a ball with its protective spines facing outwards.

PHOTO BY DAVID CURL

GREATER HEDGEHOG TENREC
Setifer setosus

As its name suggests, this spiny example of Madagascar's tenrecs is similar to the European hedgehog. Apart from the face and snout, its upper parts are covered in short spines: creamy white at the base, dark grey-brown in the middle and white at the tips, giving the animal an overall grey-brown appearance. The hedgehog tenrecs (of which there are two species) are nocturnal and although they can climb, they forage primarily along the ground where they sniff out food, including insects and their larvae, and fallen fruit. **Size:** 16–22cm, including a 1.5cm tail. **Distribution:** found throughout Madagascar, where it survives in many habitats, including human settlements, and is usually easy to see on nocturnal walks in major reserves (eg Parc National de Montagne d'Ambre and Réserve Privée de Berenty). **Status:** not endangered.

The colour of giant jumping rats vary from midbrown to dark brown on its back with white or creamy-coloured underparts.

PHOTO BY DAVID CURL

GIANT JUMPING RAT
Hypogeomys antimena

The giant jumping rat would more closely resemble other rats if not for its size and large, rabbitlike ears. Strictly nocturnal, it lives in family burrows occupied by a pair and their offspring. The rat moves on all fours or at a hop on its back legs as it forages for seeds and fallen fruit, which it holds and manipulates in the forepaws when it is eating. Pair-bonding rarely lasts more than a year as giant jumping rats often fall prey to fosas and ground boas. **Size:** Madagascar's largest rodent, reaching 54–58cm, including a 21–24cm tail. **Distribution:** restricted to a narrow zone of dry deciduous forest on the west coast. Apparently most active on moonless nights, it is regularly encountered at Réserve Forestière de Kirindy. **Status:** critically endangered.

The fanaloka is probably the island's most common large carnivore.

PHOTO BY NICK GARBUTT/
NATUREPL.COM

FANALOKA
Fossa fossana

This nocturnal, cat-sized hunter is also known as the Malagasy civet, the striped civet or simply the fossa (not to be confused with the fosa). Its dense fur is light brown, and marked with four uneven rows of black blotches along the flanks and back, with spots further scattered on the lower flanks and thighs. The thick, round tail is a similar colour, though not as densely spotted; underparts are cream and usually unmarked. The foxlike face is grey. (The small Indian civet, an introduced species, may also sometimes be seen at night.) **Size:** 61–70cm, including a 21–25cm tail. **Distribution:** found throughout rain forest in eastern and northern Madagascar, although encounters are rare and usually only at night. Guides at Parc National de Ranomafana leave food for fanalokas and they are regularly seen there. **Status:** vulnerable.

RING-TAILED MONGOOSE
Galidia elegans

Because of its diurnal behaviour, the ring-tailed mongoose is probably the easiest carnivore to spot in Madagascar. Both males and females are covered in short chestnut hair, which is greyer on the chest and narrow snout; the bushy tail (almost as long as the body) has four to six black bands. It's an agile

Three subspecies of the ring-tailed mongoose have been identified, each differing slightly in colour.

PHOTO BY DAVID CURL

climber, but it also hunts on the ground. Small family parties of up to five forage for a wide variety of small animals, including insects, frogs, reptiles, young birds, eggs, rodents and even small lemurs.

Size: 60–70cm, including a 27–32cm tail. **Distribution:** widely found in forests in the east, north and west, most commonly below 1500m. The eastern subspecies is seen at Parc National de Ranomafana, but there's a better chance of seeing the northern subspecies at Réserve Spéciale de l'Ankàrana. **Status:** not endangered.

MILNE-EDWARDS' SPORTIVE LEMUR
Lepilemur edwardsi

Long, powerful back legs enable the various species of sportive lemurs to make prodigious leaps from tree to tree, balanced by a long tail. This lemur is grey-brown above, sometimes with a dark stripe down the spine, but usually with richer patches on the shoulders, forelimbs

The Milne-Edwards' sportive lemur mainly feeds on leaves, although this species is also known to eat fruit, seeds and flowers.

PHOTO BY DAVID CURL

and upper thighs. Underparts are usually grey or creamy and the head is grey, darkening on the short muzzle. It is nocturnal, sleeping during the day in holes in trees and emerging after dark to feed.

Size: 54–57cm, including a 27–29cm tail. **Distribution:** dry deciduous forest in west and northwest Madagascar. **Status:** endangered by habitat loss and hunting; fosas are a major natural predator, pulling the lemurs from their sleeping quarters.

GREY BAMBOO LEMUR
Hapalemur griseus

The grey bamboo lemur is the most common of the three species of bamboo lemurs (also known as gentle lemurs). As the name suggests, these lemurs are often found where bamboo is present. It feeds on bamboo shoots, leaf bases and parts of the stem. The grey bamboo lemur's dense, woolly fur is

The grey bamboo lemur generally climbs in an upright posture, and is the smallest of the diurnal lemurs.

PHOTO BY DAVID CURL

entirely grey, highlighted with chestnut on the crown, shoulders and part of the back. The tail and the characteristic 'blunt' face are generally grey, and its underparts are a creamier shade of grey.

Size: 56–70cm, including a 32–40cm tail. **Distribution:** lives in rain forest with bamboo throughout the east coast, and at Parc National de Ranomafana or Parc National d'Andasibe-Mantadia; the western subspecies lives in dry deciduous forests and is difficult to see. **Status:** endangered.

The ring-tailed lemur's white face, ear tufts and throat highlight its staring red eyes – set in a black 'mask' – and snout.

PHOTO BY ANDREW MACCOLL

RING-TAILED LEMUR
Lemur catta

This unmistakable species is the most ground-dwelling of all lemurs and is active during daylight hours. Grey to grey-brown upper parts (darker on the neck and crown) contrast with a white or creamy belly and a black-and-white striped tail. It associates in larger groups than any other type of lemur (typically composed of 13 to 15 animals, but as many as 25 have been recorded), and walks on all fours with its distinctive tail held high as it forages for fruit, flowers, leaves and other vegetation.

Size: 95–110cm, including a 56–62cm tail. **Distribution:** throughout southern and south-west Madagascar in spiny forest, dry deciduous forest and gallery forest. Habituated troops are seen at Réserve Privée de Berenty; they can also be seen in Réserve Spéciale de Beha-Mahafaly. **Status:** endangered.

The black crown of the male crowned lemur is flanked and highlighted by rich russet fur that extends to the face.

PHOTO BY DENNIS JONES

CROWNED LEMUR
Eulemur coronatus

Apart from the black lemur, the crowned lemur is the most sexually dichromatic species (ie males and females have very different colouration). The male is grey-brown on the upper parts and tail (richer on the flanks and lower limbs) and creamy below; face, ears and snout are white or pale grey, highlighting the yellow-orange eyes and black tip to the nose. The female is grey on the upper parts and legs, paler to almost white on the face and ears, and has pale-grey to cream belly fur. Females lack the black crown stripe and have a paler chestnut crown.

Size: 75–85cm, including a 41–49cm tail. **Distribution:** dry and semidry deciduous forest at the northern tip of Madagascar. Habituated troops can be seen at Réserve Spéciale d'Ankàrana and there's a good chance of seeing wild troops in Parc National de Montagne d'Ambre. **Status:** endangered.

The red-bellied lemur lives in family parties of two to six, moving horizontally through the canopy by day or night as it feeds on a large variety of vegetation.

PHOTO BY ANDREW MACCOLL

RED-BELLIED LEMUR
Eulemur rubriventer

Both the male and the female red-bellied lemur have long, rich chestnut fur that is darker (and can be almost black) on the tail, but there are striking differences: the male has a slate-grey crown, face and snout; white 'teardrops' of bare skin under the eyes; and long fur around the ears making its head look square. Less square of head, and lacking a grey crown and often the teardrops, the female has white or creamy belly fur.

Size: 78–93cm, including a 43–53cm tail. **Distribution:** mid- to high-altitude rain forest (up to 2400m). Habituated troops are easily seen at Parc National de Ranomafana, especially in May and June. **Status:** endangered by continuing rain-forest destruction.

WHITE-FRONTED BROWN LEMUR
Eulemur fulvus albifrons

The white-fronted brown lemur is a subspecies of the brown lemur. Like most subspecies of this group it is sexually dichromatic; the male has pale-grey to creamy-white underparts and has mid- to dark-brown upperparts, often becoming redder towards the rear. The head is creamy white with fluffy cheeks, while the muzzle is black and the eyes are red-orange. The female has grey underparts and mid- to dark-brown upperparts, and is darker towards the rear. The head and muzzle are dark grey. This subspecies is arboreal and feeds on fruit and, to a lesser extent, leaves.

Size: 39–43cm, including a 50–55cm tail. **Distribution:** it inhabits rain forest in the northeast and can be seen at Réserve de Nosy Mangabe, Parc Zoologique d'Ivoloina and on the Masoala Peninsula. **Status:** endangered.

The white-fronted brown lemur usually forages in parties of five to seven individuals.

PHOTO BY OLIVIER CIRENDINI

BLACK LEMUR
Eulemur macaco

The black lemur is a large, tree-dwelling lemur with striking sexually dichromatic colouration. The male is all dark with penetrating yellow-orange eyes. Its fur colour varies from very dark brown to almost black, including the tufted ears and cheeks. The female black lemur varies considerably in colour: from golden brown to a rich shade of chestnut, sometimes paler on the flanks and legs; the face and snout are dark grey, paler on the upper part of the face; and the flamboyant ear and cheek tufts are white, shading to ginger on the cheeks.

Size: 90–110cm, including a 51–65cm tail. **Distribution:** restricted to rain forests around Ambanja in northwest Madagascar, also straying into adjacent plantations. Easily seen in Réserve Spéciale de Lokobe on Nosy Be, and on Nosy Komba, where local *fady* (taboos) protect these animals. **Status:** endangered.

The black lemur lives in parties of up to 15 individuals and is active during the day and at night depending on the season.

PHOTO BY DAVID CURL

RUFFED LEMUR
Varecia variegata

With its black-and-white fur, yellow eyes and extravagant ear tufts that merge with cheek fur to form a 'ruff' around the face this is an unmistakable lemur. There's variation within populations, but usually the ruffed lemur is white with a black face, crown, hands, feet, inner limbs, shoulders and tail. Social behaviour is complex: in some areas males and females appear to occupy exclusive territories, but in other areas mixed social groups have been observed.

Size: 110–120cm, including a 60–65cm tail. **Distribution:** restricted to lowland rain forest in eastern Madagascar, where it is best seen at Réserve de Nosy Mangabe. **Status:** endangered by heavy hunting, collection for the pet trade and rain-forest destruction.

Primarily active during the day, the ruffed lemur searches for fruit and nectar, dipping into blossoms with its comparatively long snout.

PHOTO BY DAVID CURL

Almost exclusively nocturnal, avahis live in small family groups numbering from two to four animals.

PHOTO BY CONNIE BRANSILVER

WESTERN AND EASTERN AVAHIS
Avahi occidentalis

Also known as woolly lemurs, the two species (western is pictured) of avahis are small, nocturnal lemurs. Their dense fur is grey above with a light dusting of brown and pale-grey below. Their tails are grey, becoming reddish towards the tip, and their face fur is pale grey, contrasting with the black muzzle and large orange eyes. Their diet consists mainly of a large variety of leaves and buds, and families huddle together during the day in dense foliage in the canopy.

Size: 56–65cm, including a 31–36cm tail. **Distribution:** restricted to dry deciduous forests in scattered parts of western and northwest Madagascar. Commonly seen at night at Station Forestière d'Ampijoroa. **Status:** endangered by a restricted range, habitat destruction and hunting.

Milne-Edwards' sifaka eats a wide variety of leaves, fruits and flowers.

PHOTO BY CONNIE BRANSILVER

MILNE-EDWARDS' SIFAKA
Propithecus edwardsi

This distinctive subspecies of the diademed sifaka is all dark (dark-brown to almost black), apart from its bare, dark-grey face with orange-red eyes and a pale saddle on the lower back and flanks, which are creamy white with red-brown edges that merge with the darker fur. This is a very large rain-forest lemur; it is diurnal and arboreal and lives in groups of three to nine. As in many lemur species, the female is dominant and is resident in the troop (the male often migrates between troops).

Size: 83–100cm, including a 41–47cm tail. **Distribution:** restricted to the southern half of the eastern rain forests, where it is found at midaltitudes. Well-habituated troops can be readily seen at Parc National de Ranomafana. **Status:** endangered by continuing habitat destruction.

Verreaux's sifaka defies gravity by leaping about between the trees of the spiny forest, apparently without injury.

PHOTO BY OLIVIER CIRENDINI

VERREAUX'S SIFAKA
Propithecus verreauxi verreauxi

This striking species is almost entirely clad in soft, thick white fur, except on the chest and belly, where the grey skin shows through; the dark-brown crown which extends to the nape; and the black mask and snout. When this mainly arboreal lemur crosses the ground to reach a tree, it adopts a most extraordinary posture, leaping sideways on its strong back legs while holding its forelegs above its head. This species is diurnal and clings vertically to tree trunks.

Size: 90–108cm, including a 50–60cm tail. **Distribution:** southern and southwest Madagascar. Western troops live in dry deciduous forest; southern populations live in gallery and spiny forest. It's easily sighted in Réserve Privée de Berenty. **Status:** endangered by habitat destruction; hunting is fady in some areas.

COQUEREL'S SIFAKA
Propithecus verreauxi coquereli

This subspecies of Verreaux's sif-aka has dense, white fur on its body and tail, offset with patches of deep maroon on the thighs, arms and chest. It is active during the day, commonly travelling in groups of four or five. Like all sifakas it is primarily arboreal, clinging verti-cally to tree trunks and branches

Brilliant yellow eyes stare from the black face; the ears of Coquerel's sifaka are also black.

PHOTO BY CONNIE BRANSILVER

between leaps through the canopy. Feeding mainly on mature leaves and buds during the dry season, this species switches to young leaves, flowers and fruits in the wetter months.

Size: 93–110cm, including a 50–60cm tail. **Distribution:** restricted to dry deciduous and semievergreen forest in Madagascar's north west. Troops can be seen fairly easily at Station Forestière d'Ampijoroa. **Status:** endangered by habitat destruction; hunted in some areas, although hunting is fady in other areas.

INDRI
Indri indri

Far-carrying eerie hoots that can travel up to 3km through the for-est usually announce the indri well before it is seen. The largest lemur in Madagascar and almost tail-less, the indri is a tree dweller that clings vertically to tree trunks, leaping up to 10m at a time through the can-opy on large, powerful back legs.

Large, rounded ears and rounded hindquarters give the indri a 'teddy-bear' appearance, although it is entirely black and white (the pattern varies throughout its range).

PHOTO BY CONNIE BRANSILVER

It is active strictly by day, travelling in small family groups of two to six foraging mainly for leaves and buds, although it also eats flowers and fruits.

Size: 64–90cm, including a 4–5cm tail. **Distribution:** northeast Madagascar, where it inhabits lowland and midaltitude rain forests, most commonly between sea level and 1000m. It has been habituated at Parc National d'Andasibe-Mantadia. **Status:** endangered.

AYE-AYE
Daubentonia madagascariensis

The nocturnal aye-aye is probably the most unusual of all lemurs, and is the subject of many a Malagasy fady. Both the male and the female have shaggy, dark grey-brown fur, with white flecks that give their coats a grizzled appearance. The underparts and face are paler – grey to creamy white; the snout is short

Search for aye-ayes in trees along the beaches of Nosy Mangabe.

PHOTO BY DAVID HARING

and pink, the ears are large and leathery and the eyes are bright orange. But most amazing are the aye-aye's long and leathery fingers – the mid-dle digit of each forehand is extremely long and slender for slipping into crevices and extracting insect larvae and other morsels.

Size: 74–90cm, including a 44–53cm tail. **Distribution:** the aye-aye is widely distributed in low- and midaltitude rain forests, dry deciduous forests and plantations. Sightings are never guaranteed, but a good place to look is at Réserve de Nosy Mangabe. **Status:** endangered.

When an insect is sighted by Parson's chameleon, it is caught by an elastic tongue that shoots out as long again as the chameleon's body length.
PHOTO BY PAUL GREENWAY

PARSON'S CHAMELEON
Calumna parsonii

The eyes of a chameleon can swivel independently of each other on raised cones to watch for enemies and prey simultaneously. Chameleons can change colour, but not as rapidly as some would believe; usually this is in response to a mate or rival. The male Parson's chameleon is usually turquoise, sometimes with yellow eyelids and yellow-rimmed jaws; some individuals have dark stripes or spots across the body. Males have a massive, helmetlike casque and two blunt 'horns'.

Size: one of the largest of all chameleons: males commonly surpass 40cm in length, and giant specimens reach 69cm. Females are much smaller. **Distribution:** endemic to mainland Madagascar and Île Sainte Marie, where it inhabits rain forests, typically in or near the canopy of narrow ravines. **Status:** not endangered.

Like other chameleons, the leaf chameleon can change colour, but this trait is not well-developed.
PHOTO BY DAVID HARING

LEAF CHAMELEONS
genus *Brookesia*

Aptly named, leaf (or stump-tailed) chameleons resemble a dead leaf in colour and size – even their short tail looks like a stalk. Leaf chameleons rely on subtle shades of brown, buff and ochre to work as camouflage. Some 24 species of the *Brookesia* genus are known; males lack ornate horns and crests – although some sport an angular snout – and their tail is only partly prehensile (adapted for grasping). All catch insects with a sticky, elastic tongue, but they hunt on the forest floor and only climb above the ground to sleep at night.

Size: the largest species grows to 10cm, but *Brookesia minima* of Nosy Be is possibly the smallest of all lizards – females measure only 33mm and males 28mm. **Distribution:** most species inhabit leaf litter and undergrowth in montane rain forests, although a few live in dry deciduous forest. **Status:** not endangered.

Fleshy pads on their toes give day geckos adhesion to vertical surfaces.
PHOTO BY DAVID CURL

DAY GECKOS
genus *Phelsuma*

Like most members of the widespread gecko family, day geckos have large eyes which they wipe clean with a broad, fleshy tongue. The 27 species are thought to have evolved in Madagascar, from where they spread to islands of the Indian Ocean as far-flung as the Andamans. Most geckos are coloured brilliant green, punctuated with spots of scarlet, orange, blue or even a rainbow-hued iridescence. Males bob their head and wave their tail as signals – probably to rivals in a show of dominance, or to attract prospective mates.

Size: the largest species, *Phelsuma grandis*, reaches 30cm or more in length. **Distribution:** day geckos reach their greatest diversity in Madagascar, where 19 species live in a variety of forested habitats. **Status:** not endangered.

Madagascar

OLIVIER CIRENDINI

Antananarivo

CONTENTS

The tongue-twisting name of Madagascar's capital means 'City of a Thousand', a reference to the thousand massed warriors of its founder, Andrianjaka. Today, a thousand Renault 4 taxis whine up and down the cobbled hills, belching blue exhaust fumes over the crowds of hurrying pedestrians. In spring, a thousand purple jacaranda trees blaze into life all over the city, raining nectar on to the heads of skipping children and strolling couples. A thousand terracotta mansions with wooden balconies and tiled roofs are stacked on to the hillsides, turning gold in the light of the setting sun. Beyond the city sprawl, a thousand paddy fields glint in the pale sunshine, forming endless chequered patterns of green and brown among the surrounding highlands.

If you're just off a plane from the West, Tana, as the city is always called, can be a bit of a shock to the system. Many travellers, put off by the pollution, the traffic and the crowds, set off hurriedly for the easier pace of the provinces. But for those who stay, Tana offers a glimpse into the edgy, urban side of Malagasy culture, often eclipsed by the spectacular natural attractions of the rest of the country. There's also the opportunity to embrace the blood-curdling and dramatic history of the Merina, Madagascar's royal tribe, and indulge in fine French cuisine, a legacy of the colonial era.

HIGHLIGHTS

- A morning stroll around **Lac Anosy** (p66), stopping to buy an armful of blooms at the daily flower market
- Sunset at the **Rova** (p66), the imposing palace of the bloodthirsty queen Ranovalona I
- An evening of gastronomic delight, with wine to match, at one of the city's fine **French restaurants** (p72)
- An entire day of self-pampering at the Hôtel Colbert's chic and hedonistic **spa** (p67)
- A weekend in the **countryside** (p75) surrounding the town, taking in lakes, views and sacred palaces

★
Antananarivo

■ HIGHEST POINT: 2643M   ■ PRINCIPAL TRIBE: MERINA

ANTANANARIVO

0   300 m
0   0.2 miles

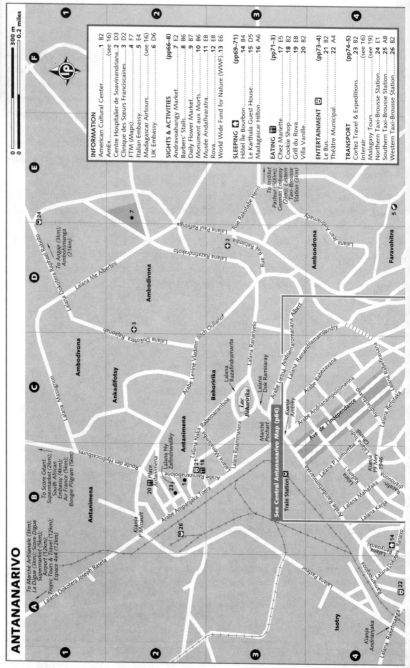

INFORMATION	
American Cultural Center........1	B2
AmEx......................................(see 16)	
Centre Hospitalier de Soavinandriana..2	D3
Clinique des Sœurs Franciscaines....3	D2
FTM (iMaps)..............................4	F7
Italian Embassy........................5	E4
Madagascar Airtours................(see 16)	
UK Embassy.............................6	D6

SIGHTS & ACTIVITIES	(pp66–8)
Andravoahangy Market............7	E2
Barbers' Stalls............................8	B6
Daily Flower Market..................9	B7
Monument aux Morts...............10	B6
Musée Andafivaratra.................11	E8
Rova...12	E8
World Wide Fund for Nature (WWF)..13	E6

SLEEPING ⌂	(pp69–71)
Hôtel Île Bourbon.....................14	B4
Le Karthala Guest House...........15	D5
Madagascar Hilton....................16	A6

EATING ⑪	(pp71–3)
Chez Mariette...........................17	E5
Cookie Shop.............................18	B2
Grill du Rova............................19	E8
Villa Vanille..............................20	B2

ENTERTAINMENT ▣	(pp73–4)
Le Bus.....................................21	B2
Théâtre Municipal....................22	A4

TRANSPORT	(pp74–5)
Cortez Travel & Expeditions......23	B2
Interair...................................(see 16)	
Malagasy Tours.......................(see 19)	
Northern Taxi-Brousse Station....24	E1
Southern Taxi-Brousse Station....25	A8
Western Taxi-Brousse Station.....26	B2

To Marché Artisanale (3km);
La Digue (3km); Score Digue
Supermarket (5km);
To Score Géant
Supermarket (2km);
South African
Embassy (4km);
Air France (5km);
Tropic Tours & Travel (12km);
Espace 4x4 (12km);
Boogie Pilgram (5km);

To Andap (3km);
Ambohimanga
(21km)

To Institut
Pasteur (500m);
German Embassy
(2km); Eastern
Taxi-Brousse
Station (3km)

See Central Antananarivo Map (p64)

Train Station

Ave de l'Indépendance

Antanimena

Ambodivona

Ankadifotsy

Behoririka

Ambondrona

Faravohitra

Isotry

Antanimena

Ambodivona

Lac
Behoririka

Marché
Pochard

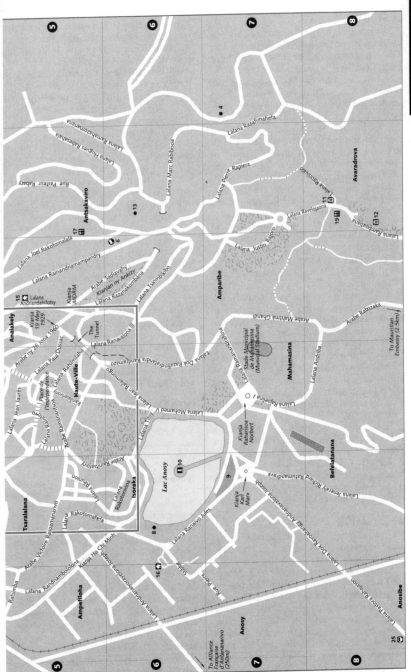

ANTANANARIVO

HISTORY

The area that is now Antananarivo was originally known as Analamanga (Blue Forest), and is believed to have been populated by the Vazimba – mysterious ancestors of today's Malagasy (see the boxed text on p22). In 1610 a king named Andrianjaka conquered the Vazimba villages, stationed a garrison of 1000 men to defend his new settlement, and renamed it Antananarivo. Andrianjaka then built his own *rova* (palace) on the highest of Antananarivo's hills, thus founding the Merina dynasty.

In the late 18th century, Andrianampoinimerina, the warrior king, moved his capital from Ambohimanga to Antananarivo, which became the most powerful of all the Merina kingdoms. For the next century, Antananarivo was the capital of the Merina kings and queens, and the base from which they carried out their conquest of the rest of Madagascar.

Tana was the seat of government during the colonial era, during which time it was known as Tananarive. The French gave the city centre its present form, building two great staircases and draining swamps and paddy fields to create the present-day area of Analakely. In May 1929 the city was the site of the first major demonstration against the colonialists, after which several nationalist figures, including Jean Ralaimongo, were arrested.

Antananarivo province is Madagascar's political and economic centre, and has a population of about four million, with the city centre's population at about 895,000. Madagascar's president, Marc Ravalomanana, hails from Tana and served as the city's mayor before his presidency.

ORIENTATION

Ivato airport lies 12km from Antananarivo, and the journey there or back can take up to 45 minutes during rush hour.

Central Antananarivo can be roughly divided into two sections: Haute-Ville (upper town) and Basse-Ville (lower town). The centre of Basse-Ville and the commercial district is the two-lane Avenue de L'Indépendance, which runs from the train station towards the Hôtel Le Glacier. From here, the road narrows and runs through the crowded main market area of Analakely, with a steep staircase leading to Place de L'Indépendance in the rather quieter Haute-Ville. Another staircase, directly opposite, leads to the busy district of Ambondrona, where several hotels are located. Narrow streets lead further uphill past several churches to the *rova* (queen's palace). Down the other side of the hill from Haute-Ville is Lac Anosy (Lake Anosy), which is accessed by vehicle through a tunnel.

Tana's outer districts go on for miles, and many neighbourhoods seem to be unknown even to taxi drivers, so allow yourself plenty of time if you're visiting somewhere in the suburbs.

Finding your way around Tana isn't easy – street signs are few and far between, and most streets have interchangeable French and Malagasy names, neither of which is generally known to locals. In this book, both Malagasy and French street names are used depending on which is most commonly used by locals.

Maps

Both Edicom and Carambole publish detailed maps of the city centre and suburbs that are widely available at bookshops from about FMg30,000 (p250). Neither map is entirely up to date, so you'll still have to ask around a lot.

INFORMATION
Bookshops

The best place to pick up English-language magazines (usually *Newsweek*), plus French periodicals, is from the street vendors in Place de L'Indépendance.

Espace Loisirs (Map pp64-5; ☎ 032 07 034 84; Lalana Ratsimilaho) Has the same kind of stock as Librairie de Madagascar below, plus a small selection of English-language books and newspapers.

Librairie de Madagascar (Map pp64-5; ☎ 22 224 54; 38 Avenue de L'Indépendance) Sells maps, guidebooks (in French) and dictionaries (French-English and Malagasy-English).

Cultural Centres

Alliance Française d'Antananarivo (☎ 22 208 56, 22 211 07; aftana@dts.mg; Lalana Seimad, Andavamamba) Offers French- and Malagasy-language courses and sponsors various cultural events.

American Cultural Center (Map pp60-1; ☎ 22 209 56; fax 22 345 39; Arabe Rainizanabolone) Occasional lectures, concerts and exhibitions.

Centre Culturel Albert Camus (CCAC; Map pp64–5; ☎ 22 213 75, 22 236 47; ccac@wanadoo.mg; 14 Avenue de L'Indépendance; ☺ 10am–1pm & 2–6pm Tue–Sat) The centre has a library and an exhibition hall showing photographic and other displays. It also sponsors an extensive programme of concerts, dance, film and other events.

Cercle Germano-Malagasy (Map pp64–5; ☎ 22 330 92, 22 214 42; cgm@malagasy.com; Araben'ny 26 Jona 1960; ☺ 8am–5.30pm Mon–Sat) Offers a library with German magazines and newspapers, as well as German-language classes, Internet access, a café, concerts and German films.

Emergency

Ambulance (☎ 22 200 40)
Espace Medical 24-hour clinic (☎ 22 265 66)
Fire (☎ 18)
Police (☎ 17)

Internet Access

There are now email facilities in most of Madagascar's major towns, but surfing the Net is usually cheaper in Tana. All the following places charge FMg150 per minute:

Cyber-Paositra Place de L'Indépendance (Map pp64–5; ☎ 22 296 76; paositra@dts.mg; ☺ 8am–noon & 2–6pm); Araben'ny 26 Jona 1960 (Map pp64–5; ☎ 22 296 76; paositra@dts.mg; ☺ 8am–noon & 2–6pm) Both Tana's main post offices have good Internet centres.

Outcool Web Bar (Map pp64–5; Lalana Andrianary Ratianarivo; ☺ 9am–11pm Mon–Sat, 3–9pm Sun) Has a bar, and does discounts for longer surfing times.

Teknet Group (Map pp64–5; ☎ 22 313 59; Arabe

Ramanantsoa; ☺ 8am–10pm Mon–Sat, 3–8pm Sun) Also has fax and printing services, and soft drinks.

Laundry

Most hotels have a laundry service, although when the weather is bad, it often takes two days for clothes to dry.

Net-a-Sec (Avenue de L'Indépendance) Diagonally opposite Pressing Palace, this place also does dry cleaning.

Pressing Palace (☎ 22 256 63; Hotel Palace, 8 Avenue de L'Indépendance; ☺ 8am–noon & 2–6pm Mon–Sat) The best place for express service.

Media

Look out for the English publication *Madagascar News* on sale at bookshops. It has bar and restaurant listings for Tana, as well as general articles. If you can read French, pick up a free copy of the magazine *Sortir à Tana*, which has details of clubs, bars, restaurants and events.

Medical Services

The daily newspapers list out-of-hours doctors, as well as the location and telephone numbers of dentists, duty chemists, and other hospitals.

Centre Hospitalier de Soavinandriana (Hôpital Militaire d'Antananarivo; Map pp60–1; ☎ 22 397 51; Rue Moss, Soavinandriana; ☺ 24hr) Has X-ray equipment and stocks most basic drugs and medicines. The hospital employs several French doctors. Requires payment in advance.

ANTANANARIVO IN...

Two days

Start your day with croissants in the *salon de thé* (tea room) of the **Hôtel Colbert**. Visit the **Musée de l'Art et de Archéologie**, then stop for a *steack frites* (steak and chips) at Kudéta restaurant. Thus fortified, you'll be ready for the steep walk up to the **Rova** and the **Musée Andafivaratra**. At sunset, have a drink on the terrace of **Grill du Rova**, accompanied by traditional Malagasy music. In the evening, treat yourself to a gastronomic dinner at **Le Rossini**.

The next morning, walk round **Lac Anosy**, stopping to admire the **flower market** and **barbers' stalls**, then squeeze your way in to the market of **Analakely**, which sells everything from cream cakes to raffia hats. After lunch at a local **hotely** (local restaurant serving basic meals), visit an art exhibition at the **Centre Culturel Albert Camus**, then have a traditional Malagasy dinner at **Chez Mariette**.

Four Days

Follow the two-day itinerary, then head out to the **royal palace** at Ambohimanga for a taste of Merina history. Catch a *taxi-brousse* (bush taxi) back into town for a cosy dinner at the **Hôtel Sakamanga**.

The next day, spend the morning shopping at the **Marché Artisanale** in La Digue, then relax your weary muscles with a massage in the Hôtel Colbert spa.

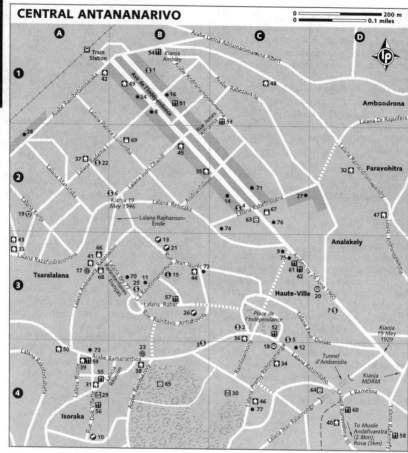

CENTRAL ANTANANARIVO

Clinique des Sœurs Franciscaines (Clinique et Maternité St-Français; Map pp60-1; ☎ 22 610 46; Lalana Dokotera Rajaonah, Ankadifotsy) Has X-ray equipment and is well run and relatively clean. Requires payment in advance of treatment.

Espace Médical (☎ 032 07 871 12; 65 Bis Lalana Pasteur Rabary) A private clinic just east of the city, with laboratory and X-ray capabilities and several French-trained doctors.

Institut Pasteur (☎ 22 401 64, 22 401 65; lpm@pasteur.mg; Ambatofotsikely Avaradoha; ☼ 9am-5pm Mon-Fri) The best place for lab tests.

Pharmacie Metropole (Map pp64-5; ☎ 22 200 25; Lalana Ratsimilaho; ☼ 8am-noon Mon-Sat) Antananarivo has many good, well-stocked pharmacies. One of the best and most convenient is this one near the Hôtel Colbert.

Money

The bureau de change at Ivato airport does better rates than many of the banks in Tana, so you have nothing to gain by waiting to change money until you get into the city.

Banks are generally only open on weekdays, and are closed on the afternoon before a public holiday (as well as on the holiday itself). Some have ATMs (see the list following), but most of these only work until about 8pm Monday to Saturday. The ATM at the Hilton Hotel is open 24 hours. **Socimad Bureau de Change** (Map pp64-5; Lalana Radama I; ☼ 8am-noon & 2-5pm Mon-Fri, 8-11.15am Sat) changes cash and travellers cheques, and does advances on Visa cards. Some hotels, including the Hôtel Tana

Plaza, change cash and travellers cheques for their guests.

Some useful banking addresses include the following:

Bank of Africa (BOA) Place de L'Indépendance (Map pp64-5; 8am-noon & 2-3.30pm); Avenue de L'Indépendance (Map pp64-5; 8am-noon & 2-3.30pm) Changes travellers cheques (no commission) and gives cash advances on MasterCard, which takes at least an hour.

BFV-SG Arabe Ramanantsoa (Map pp64-5; 8-11am & 2-4pm) This branch in Haute-Ville has an ATM; Avenue de L'Indépendance (Map pp64-5; 8-11am & 2-4pm) Both branches change travellers cheques (AmEx only) and do advances on Visa cards.

BMOI (Map pp64-5; Place de L'Indépendance; 8am-3.35pm) Changes travellers cheques and has an ATM that accepts Visa cards.

BNI-CL Kianja 19 Mey 1946 (Map pp64-5; 8am-4pm); Araben'ny 26 Jona 1960 (Map pp64-5; 8am-4pm) Changes travellers cheques and does advances on Visa cards. The branch on Araben'ny 26 Jona 1960 has an ATM.

Madagascar Airtours (Map pp60-1; 22 623 24; fax 22 641 90; airtours@dts.mg; Rue Pierre Stibbe, Anosy) The place to report lost or stolen travellers cheques. It's in the Madagascar Hilton.

UCB Lalana des 77 Parlementaires Français (Map pp64-5; 8am-4pm); Galerie Zoom shopping centre (La Digue; 8am-4pm) Changes travellers cheques and gives fairly rapid cash advances on both Visa and MasterCard.

Post & Telephone

There are public telephones for domestic and international calls at both post offices as well as plenty dotted around town. You can buy phonecards to use in them from any shop or kiosk.

Paositra (main post office; Map pp64-5; Lalana Ratsimilaho, Haute-Ville; 7am-5pm Mon-Fri, 8am-11am Sat) Near the Hôtel Colbert; poste restante is sent here.

Post office (Araben'ny 26 Jona 1960, Basse-Ville) Closed on Saturday.

Tourist Information

Maison de Tourisme de Madagascar (Map pp64-5; 22 351 78; www.tourisme-madagascar.com; 3 Lalana Elysée Ravelomanantsoa; 8.30am-noon & 2-7pm Mon-Fri) Has friendly but fairly clueless staff, and very limited printed information, but might be worth a visit if you have a specific question.

Travel Agencies

For listings of agencies offering trips within Madagascar, see p265. If you're travelling outside the country the following agencies sell air tickets and package holidays:

Dodo Travel & Tours (Map pp64-5; 22 690 36; www.dodotraveltour.com; Lalana Elysée Ravelomanantsoa)

Transcontinents (Map pp64-5; 22 223 98; transco@dts.mg; 10 Avenue de L'Indépendance) This company also has a branch in the Hôtel Colbert, see p71.

Tropic Tours & Travel (☎ 22 580 75; tropic@tropic-tours.net; Rte de l'Aéroport, Ivato)

DANGERS & ANNOYANCES

Antananarivo is safer than many developing world capitals, and if you take standard precautions, you shouldn't have any difficulties. It is not safe to take public transport at night, especially between the town and the airport. At night, take a taxi if you go out. If you do walk, go in a group, and remember that in much of the city there are no streetlights. During the day, keep a sharp eye out for pickpockets in markets, on public transport or in other crowded areas.

Perhaps a more likely annoyance is the headache or throat irritation you may experience for the first few days in Tana, particularly if you are prone to respiratory allergies or asthma. This is due in part to the altitude and in part to the city's polluted air.

Scams

Several readers have reported encountering freelance 'guides' in Tana, who promise to arrange transport or trips in other parts of the country. Once payment is made, however, the guide fails to deliver the promised services. The only way to avoid this is to book trips in advance with official tour operators (p69) or deal with local guides *in situ* once you arrive at your chosen destination.

SIGHTS & ACTIVITIES

If your knees can withstand the long flights of stairs and steep, sloping streets, central Tana is a good place to explore on foot. By simply walking around the Haute-Ville or the streets around Avenue de L'Indépendance, you'll come across plenty of little cameos of Malagasy life – ladies selling embroidered tablecloths spread out on the pavements, men hawking rubber stamps from improvised stalls on the steps, or taxi drivers sharing a hunk of peanut cake bought from a roadside kiosk. Most of the attractive old buildings are in Haute-Ville, which is quieter and easier to stroll around than the hectic, exhaust-fume-ridden Basse-Ville. Look out for the **President's Palace** (Map pp64–5), near the Hôtel Colbert, with its sentry boxes painted red and green to match the Malagasy flag. The current president lives in a townhouse just a few streets away.

Lac Anosy
Map pp64–5

Antananarivo's lake lies in the southern part of town, an easy downhill walk from Haute-Ville. In the early morning you may see flocks of white cattle egrets roosting in the nearby trees. The lake is at its most beautiful in October, when the jacaranda trees are covered in purple blossom. On an island, connected to the shore by a causeway, stands a large white angel on a plinth, the Monument aux Morts (Monument to the Dead), a WWI memorial erected by the French. There's a daily flower market just opposite the end of the causeway, and a neat little row of barbers' stalls on the southern shore. On sunny weekend afternoons, the paths around the lake fill up with strolling couples and families.

Markets

In central Tana, the main market is found in the 'pavilions' at **Analakely** (Map pp64–5), opposite the bottom of the stairs leading up to Haute-Ville. It's a packed, teeming place, selling every fruit, vegetable, fish or meat product you could imagine, and a few things you couldn't – jellied cow lips in oil, anyone? There's another, smaller market called **Marché Communal de Petit Vitesse** (pp64–5) on the tracks west of the old train station, which sells more or less the same goods as the one at Analakely. However, if the planned re-opening of the railway goes ahead, this market is likely to be relocated.

One of the city's best markets is the colourful **flower market** (Map pp60–1), which is held daily on the southeastern edge of Lac Anosy. For crafts, the **Marché Artisanale** is Tana's best-known market. It takes place on a bend in the road about 2km south of the Score Digue supermarket in the suburb of La Digue. There's another, smaller, craft market at **Andravoahangy** (Map pp60–1), about 1.5km northeast of the northern end of Avenue de L'Indépendance.

The Rova
Map pp60–1

The Rova (Palais de la Reine; Lalana Ramboatiana; admission FMg25,000; h10am-5pm Tue-Sun) is the imposing structure that crowns the highest hill overlooking Lac Anosy. Gutted in a fire in 1995, it has now been partially restored and is once again open to the public.

The Rova is a great place to spend an hour or two, with stunning views on all sides, and a chilling atmosphere that captures the bloody history of the Merina kings and queens. Young freelance guides hang around the entrance and offer their services – they speak good English and are full of anecdotes about the palace, so are worth paying for – about FMg10,000 per person is a fair price. While you are inside the palace, remember that it is considered *fady* (taboo) to point your finger directly at the royal tombs or the palace itself.

To get to the Rova from the centre of Antananarivo, it's a stiff 4km walk, or an easy taxi ride (FMg10,000).

Musée Andafivaratra   Map pp60–1

Housed in a magnificent pink baroque palace, a few hundred metres downhill from the Rova, the Musée Andafivaratra is filled with furniture, portraits and memorabilia from the age of the Merina kings and queens. The building was the former home of Prime Minister Rainilaiarivony – literally the power behind the throne of the three queens he married in succession. A half hour or so spent in the museum is the perfect way to end a visit to the Rova and bring the characters you've been hearing about to life – the evil queen Ranavalona I, dumpy in a coral silk crinoline, scowls out from her oil painting, while Jean Laborde,

the French adventurer presumed to be her lover, glowers from beneath his beard in the black-and-white photograph next to it. There's also a huge gilt throne, the Merina crown jewels, coats of chain mail and, surprisingly, tiny military uniforms belonging to former monarchs. Explanations to the exhibits are in English, as well as French. You can visit the museum using the same entry ticket as the Rova; opening hours are the same, too.

Musée de l'Art et de l'Archéologie   Map pp64–5

Smaller than the Musée Andafivaratra, but still worth popping into, the **Musée de l'Art et de l'Archéologie** (☎ 22 210 47; Lalana Dok Villette; admission by donation; ⏲ 10am-4pm Mon-Fri, 1-4pm Sat) has displays of grave decorations from the south (known as *aloalo*), an extensive exhibition of musical instruments and a few talismans and objects used for sorcery.

Gyms & Pools

If you're looking to stretch your muscles while in Tana, the Madagascar Hilton (p71) has a 25m pool (admission FMg25,000; ⏲ Mon-Fri summer only). There is also a gym, a fitness centre and tennis courts. For a more hedonistic experience, try the **Balneoforme Colbert** (Map pp64-5; ☎ 22 625 71; Hôtel Colbert, Lalana Printsy

---

A FINE PLACE TO RULE

The gate of the Rova (pronounced 'roova') is protected by a carved eagle (the symbol of military force) and a phallus (the symbol of circumcision and thus nobility). Inside the gate are royal tombs in the form of wooden huts. The French moved the remains of Merina kings and queens from the Rova when they took over the city in 1845, an act that is still considered to be a profanation by the Malagasy. Today the remains are back, and the townspeople still visit them to ask for blessings.

Beside the imposing stone structure of the queen's palace is a replica of a Malagasy palace in the old style. This was built to resemble the palace of King Andrianampoinimerina, who founded the Merina kingdom. It looks like a black wood hut, with a tiny, raised doorway. The royal bed is situated in the sacred northwest corner of the hut. The simple furniture inside is aligned according to astrological rules. The king supposedly hid in the rafters when visitors arrived, signalling whether the guest was welcome by dropping pebbles on to his wife's head.

The queen's palace, known as Manjakamiadana (A Fine Place to Rule), was designed by a Scottish missionary named James Cameron for Queen Ranavalona I. The outer structure, built in 1867 for Ranavalona II, was made of stone, with a wooden roof and interior (these were destroyed in the fire and have not yet been restored). Crows wheel around between the satellite aerials that flank the towers of the palace – the birds were considered sacred by the Merina royal family, having apparently warned one king of an impending attack. The best time to visit the Rova is at sunset, when you can enjoy the spectacular colours of the sky and the city spread out below.

Ratsimamanga, Ivato; ⊗ 1-9pm Mon-Sat, 10am-6pm Sun). It has a fantastic spa with a mosaic swimming pool and Turkish bath, plus a variety of stunningly decorated treatment rooms offering different types of massage. It's not cheap (FMg75,000 for the pool and sauna alone), but is worth it, especially if you've just arrived in Tana after some hard trekking in one of the national parks.

WALKING TOUR

Tana offers numerous opportunities for interesting walks, but this one takes in many of the city's major sights. For details of longer walks in and around Tana, get hold of the useful booklet *Cheminements Touristiques et Culturels D'Antananarivo*, published by the Mission de Coopération et d'Action Culturelle, which outlines seven walks, accompanied by very detailed historical information and maps. It's available at Espace Loisirs bookshop in Haute-Ville (p62).

To begin your tour hail a taxi to the starting point – the magnificent **Rova** (**1**; p66). The palace is open to the public, but is currently undergoing restoration after being gutted by fire in 1995. Afterwards, walk a few hundred metres downhill to the **Musée Andafivaratra**, (**2**; p67) housed in the magnificent palace of the former Prime Minister. From here, wend your way past the **Église d'Ambonimanpamarinana (3)**, which was built on the site where Queen Ranavalona would throw Christian martyrs from the cliffs, through the lanes to Lalana Ratsimilaho, the main artery of the lively Haute-Ville.

Stroll around the pretty garden in the centre of Place de L'Indépendance, then head down Lalana Rainilaiarivony to have a look at the **President's Palace (4)**, before continuing down Arabe Ramanantsoa and then Arabe Rainitsarovy (watch out for white cattle egrets in the trees on the left) to **Lac Anosy (5)**. Turn right and circumambulate the lake, passing rows of **barbers' shops (6)** on the southern side, then end your tour with a look at the **flower market (7)** and a stroll over the causeway to the **Monument aux Morts (8)** in the centre. From here, you can once again see the Rova, sitting on top of the tallest hill overlooking the lake like a tiny crown perched on the head of a glowering queen.

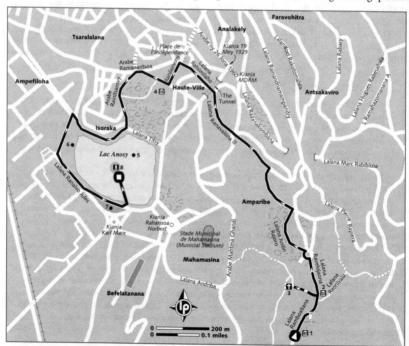

COURSES

Alliance Française d'Antananarivo (☎ 22 208 56, 22 211 07; aftana@dts.mg; Lalana Seimad, Andavamamba) sometimes runs Malagasy-language courses, as well as providing French lessons.

The **Centre Culturel Albert Camus** (CCAC; Map pp64-5; ☎ 22 213 75, 22 236 47; ccac@wanadoo.mg; 14 Avenue de L'Indépendance; ⏲ 10am-1pm & 2-6pm Tue-Sat) offers French courses only.

TOURS

Tany Mena Tours (Map pp64-5; ☎ 22 326 27; tany menatours@simicro.mg; Avenue de L'Indépendance) organise very interesting walks and day trips in Tana and the surrounding area, led by experts such as historians or anthropologists. Some of the guides are English-speaking. A day's guided tour of Tana, taking in the palace of Ambohimanga, costs FMg200,000. Tany Mena Tours also has cars for hire and offers trips further afield, all with a cultural emphasis.

For a list of companies that arrange tours around Madagascar, see p265.

SLEEPING

Antananarivo has an excellent selection of accommodation for all budgets, but the best places tend to be booked solid during peak season – Christmas, June to August and French school holidays – so it's a good idea to make bookings in advance. Only the top-range hotels have lifts, and many of the lower-priced places have very steep stairs. Not many establishments could be viewed as child-friendly – things like babysitting and highchairs are only available in the very upmarket hotels.

Prices for mid-range and top-end hotels are sometimes quoted in euros, but you can always pay the equivalent in Malagasy francs, and sometimes in US dollars, too.

Budget

Moonlight Hotel (Map pp64-5; ☎ 22 268 70; Lalana Rainandriamapandry; s without/with bathroom FMg45,000/70,000, d FMg70,000/80,000) The Moonlight is one of the cheapest and most-comfortable options in Tana, and is well known for its big breakfasts, friendly staff and lovely views from the 2nd-floor balcony. There aren't many restaurants in the surrounding area, so you'll have to take a taxi across town in the evenings if you stay here. This place is often full so book in advance.

Chez Francis (Map pp64-5; ☎ 22 613 65; Lalana Rainandriamapandry; r FMg90,000) Another good choice just up the hill from the Moonlight. Clean, good-sized rooms have their own shower and basin, but toilets are shared. Some rooms also have balconies with good views of Tana. There's a snack bar next door, and a 3rd-floor restaurant – order in advance for evening meals.

Le Karthala Guest House (Map pp60-1; ☎ 22 248 95; fax 22 272 67; Lalana Andriandahifotsy; d with breakfast FMg100,000) A very friendly, family-run B&B with a pretty garden courtyard. Rooms are large and very well furnished, with bathrooms. Malagasy meals (FMg25,000) are available with advance notice in the evenings. A family room for five people is also available. Airport transfers cost FMg100,000.

Snack Bar Jim (Map pp64-5; ☎ 22 374 37; gusth@netclub.mg; Arabe Ramanantsoa; d with shower FMg70,000) A small, very Malagasy snack bar with a few clean rooms available several storeys above the bar, high on the rooftop. There's fantastic views of the Avenue de L'Indépendance far below, and the owners are friendly. Rooms have internal showers, but toilets are shared.

Hôtel Le Jean Laborde (Map pp64-5; ☎ 22 330 45; labordehotel@hotmail.com; 3 Lalana Russie; r without/with bathroom FMg75,000/170,000) This place has a cosy French restaurant and bar, much frequented by middle-aged expats, and offers noisy but comfortable rooms off the bar or bigger, better-decorated rooms at the back.

Hôtel Raphia (Map pp64-5; ☎ 22 253 13; raphia@ blueline.mg; Lalana Ranavalona III; r without/with bathroom FMg96,000/126,000) This hotel was much praised by readers, but when we visited the bed was saggy, the bathroom water brown and the staff vague in the extreme. However, the décor is bright and the rooms clean – perhaps you'll have better luck.

Mid-Range

Hôtel-Restaurant Shanghai (Map pp64-5; ☎ 22 314 72; shanghai@malagasy.com; 4 Lalana Rainitovo; d/tw with bathroom & phone FMg115,000/122,500) A popular Chinese-run hotel, whose well-kept rooms have full-sized bathtubs and there's plenty of hot water (bliss during a cold, blustery Tana winter!). In summer, there's a pretty garden courtyard and balconies. The restaurant does very reasonable Chinese food (mains FMg25,000).

THE AUTHOR'S CHOICE

Hôtel Isoraka (Map pp64-5; ☎ 22 658 54; fax 22 658 54; 11 Arabe Ramanantsoa; s/d/tr FMg55,000/75,000/85,000) The best value of the budget hotels, offering a convenient location in Haute-Ville, decent rooms (those at the back are quieter) and powerful shared showers. The friendly young staff can organise airport transfers for FMg60,000. Snacks and soft drinks are available, as is car hire at FMg500,000 per day. This place is deservedly popular, so ring ahead to be sure you get a room.

Hôtel Sakamanga (Map pp64-5; ☎ 22 358 09; saka@malagasy.com; Lalana Andrianary Ratianarivo; d FMg145,000-200,000) Unquestionably the most attractive of the mid-range options – the Sakamanga's rooms have bright bedspreads, yellow-painted walls and wooden floors. Rooms in the upper price range have little sitting areas, too. There are a number of pretty outdoor sitting areas and a cosy, highly rated restaurant (p72). The busy reception has a noticeboard for visitors, and is the best place to meet fellow travellers. The reception staff can also organise trips elsewhere in the country, although reports of these vary. Make reservations as far in advance as possible, as the Sakamanga is almost always full.

Bed & Breakfast Résidence Lapasoa (Map pp64-5; ☎ 22 611 40; dina.lapasoa@malagasy.com; Lalana Dok Villette; s/d with breakfast FMg225,000/240,000) Another beautifully decorated place – the big sunny rooms have wooden floors, TVs, minibars and four-poster beds. There's a very friendly, family atmosphere and it's in a great location in the heart of Isoraka, just next to the Musée de l'Art et de l'Archéologie. The Lapasoa is also a good place to get information on the best-quality arts and crafts in the city.

La Varangue (Map pp64-5; ☎ 22 273 97; varangue@simicro.mg; 17 Lalana Printsy Ratsimamanga; r with TV, phone, minibar & safe FMg320,000-385,000) A little-known and very classy small hotel and restaurant, cosy and brimming with character, La Varangue is down a steep lane to the left of the President's Palace. Rooms come in two categories – the cheaper ones have modern décor, the more expensive ones are beautifully furnished with rustic-looking furniture and rich gold-brown fabrics. Many also have balconies with good views over Tana. There's a lovely bar, dining room and terrace. The restaurant menu changes monthly, and mostly features French cuisine (mains FMg40,000). Definitely the best choice in the top-end category – book ahead to make sure you get a room.

Hôtel Anjary (Map pp64-5; ☎ 22 244 09; anjary@dts.mg; 89 Lalana Razafindranovona; d/tw with TV & phone FMg150,000/175,000; 🛇) A big, comfortable and good-value business-style hotel, which is in a rather dubious part of Basse-Ville. The rooms are spick and span, with safes, and there's a snack bar and Indian restaurant (no alcohol is served), plus an inhouse travel desk. There's even a sauna and massage centre on the top floor! Visa cards are accepted.

Hôtel White Palace (Map pp64-5; ☎ 22 669 98; whitepalace@dts.mg; Lalana Razafindranovona; d/studio with TV, phone & fridge FMg138,000/228,000; 🛇) Just around the corner from the Hôtel Anjary, this is another good-value option, with clean, nicely decorated rooms and studios, basement parking and English-speaking receptionists who can arrange car hire. Rooms with air-conditioning are available at higher prices. Book in advance to arrange airport transfers.

Hôtel Île Bourbon (Map pp60-1; ☎ 22 279 42; 12 Lalana Benyowski; r FMg100,000) A dark, but quiet and friendly place, recommended by travellers. There's live music in the restaurant in the evenings, and Réunnionaise cuisine to go with it. It's sometimes full, so you may need to book in advance.

Hôtel Indri (Map pp64-5; ☎ 22 209 22; indri@dts.mg; 15 Lalana Radama I; s FMg75,000-135,000, d FMg105,000-165,000) A faded, pink edifice among the exhaust fumes of Basse-Ville. The rooms are spacious and well maintained, with horrid nylon carpets, but full-sized bathtubs. Some also have TV. The better, more expensive rooms are located in the main building, which is a bit quieter. There's a bar and small outside terrace (breakfast is FMg20,000). All in all, it's a bit chilly and characterless, but comfortable.

Karibotel (Map pp64-5; ☎ 22 665 54; karibotel@dts.mg; 26 Avenue de L'Indépendance; r with TV & phone FMg250,000) Entirely without character – a business hotel that could be anywhere in the world. The restaurant, however, serves half-decent Malagasy cuisine, and it's quiet.

Top End

Hôtel Colbert (Map pp64-5; ☎ 22 202 02; www.madagascar-guide.com/colbert; Lalana Printsy Ratsimamanga; r with TV, safe, phone & minibar €74-89; 🗙 P) An Antananarivo institution, the slightly eccentric Colbert is smaller, plusher, less expensive and more intimate than its main competitor, the Hilton. As a rule, the rooms aren't up to the standard of the rest of the hotel, being sparsely decorated and sombre. The lobby, however, has a marble floor and is satisfyingly glitzy, and the lounge bar, patronised by cigar-puffing businessmen, is very cosy and old fashioned. For the best décor, go down a couple of floors in the lift to the stunning spa (which has reduced rates for guests). The Colbert also has a small casino, two bars, a patisserie, two restaurants and a business centre. Dinner in the formal La Taverne restaurant requires a shirt and tie. The reception staff speak impeccable English and are a mine of information on anything and everything in Tana.

Le Royal Palissandre (Map pp64-5; ☎ 22 326 14; hotelpalissandre@simicro.mg; Lalana Rainandriamapandry; s/d with minibar, TV, phone & safe €77/97) A glitzy, upmarket hotel perched near the top of the steps in the Faravohitra section of town, with a terrace looking over the scurrying Analakely pavilions below. The spacious bedrooms feature balconies, green-marble baths and central heating. The restaurant has a log fire and serves dishes such as foie gras and escalope de veau for around FMg55,000.

Madagascar Hilton (Map pp60-1; ☎ 22 260 60; sales_madagascar@hilton.com; Rue Pierre Stibbe, Anosy; s/d with minibar, safe, TV & phone €180/204; 🗙 P) In a skyscraper just south of Lac Anosy, the Hilton offers everything you might imagine – smallish but comfortable rooms, a business centre, boutique, travel desk, gym, several bars, two restaurants and a nightclub. There's also a pool, gym and tennis court for the energetic.

Hôtel du Louvre (Map pp64-5; ☎ 22 390 00; www.hotel-du-louvre.com; 4 Place de L'Indépendance; s/d with TV & Internet €53/60; 🗙 🖳) A new and very convenient hotel above the Shoprite Supermarket, with wooden floors and Malagasy paintings on the walls. The Saint Germain restaurant has an outdoor courtyard and rather Parisian-looking coloured umbrellas.

The following three places along Avenue de L'Indépendance are all under the same management. All are comfortable and reasonably good value, but all favour an anodyne fake-pine-and-pastel-style décor and are much like a million other business hotels the world over. All accept credit cards.

Hôtel de France (Map pp64-5; ☎ 22 213 04; www.siceh-hotels.com in French; 34 Avenue de L'Indépendance; r with TV, safe & phone €58; 🗙) Popular with package tours, and has a good French restaurant called Ô! Poivre Vert and an ice-cream parlour.

Hôtel Tana Plaza (Map pp64-5; ☎ 22 218 65; www.siceh-hotels.com in French; 2 Avenue de L'Indépendance; r with TV, safe & phone €53; 🗙) Has money-exchange and luggage-holding facilities for its guests, plus a travel desk and multilingual staff.

Palace Hotel (Map pp64-5; ☎ 22 256 63; www.siceh-hotels.com in French; 8 Avenue de L'Indépendance; d/studio with TV, safe & phone €55/80; 🗙) More geared towards longer stays – studios have a kitchenette.

EATING & DRINKING

In addition to the hotel dining rooms mentioned above, Tana is well served for restaurants – the whole city is covered in eateries, from cheap and cheerful local *hotelys* (local restaurant serving basic meals) to sumptuous *salons de thé* (tea rooms) and sublime French temples of *gastronomie*.

Food Stalls & Hotely

The best place to find cheap hotelys and stalls serving plates of rice and zebu, bowls of *soupe chinoise* (Chinese noodle soup) or piles of *mi sao* (stir-fried noodles with meat or vegetables) is along the western end of Arabe Ramanantsoa or around the market at Analakely. Get there early – many of the smaller hotelys have run out of food by about 8pm. Convenient hotelys in the city centre include:

Snack Bar Jim (Map pp64-5; Arabe Ramanantsoa; rice dishes FMg7000; 🕑 breakfast, lunch & dinner) Serves patisserie, steak and delicious rice dishes.

Tropique Snack (Map pp64-5; Araben'ny 26 Jona 1960; soupe chinoise FMg7500; 🕑 breakfast & lunch) Does great fresh juices.

Restaurant Betoko (Map pp64-5; Araben'ny 26 Jona 1960; yoghurts FMg2000; 🕑 breakfast & lunch) Located near the bottom of the steps up to Haute-Ville.

Cafés & Salons de Thé

Tana's many gleaming and upmarket *salons de thé* serve French pastries, elaborate cakes, coffee, tea and hot chocolate, breakfasts and in many cases, wonderful ice cream.

Cookie Shop (Map pp60-1; ☎ 032 07 142 99; Arabe Rainizanabolone; cookies FMg500; ☺ breakfast & lunch Mon-Sat) Near the American cultural centre, the Cookie Shop is good if you prefer your calories American style. It serves up cookies, milkshakes and flavoured coffees to homesick Peace Corps volunteers.

Buffet du Jardin (Map pp60-1; ☎ 22 338 87; Place de L'Indépendance; ☺ 24hr) The only option for the 24-hour snacking is this place, which has the air of a disreputable Parisian bar and does sandwiches, snacks and beer at all hours of the day and night.

Among the better places to indulge are **Blanche Neige** (Map pp64-5; ☎ 22 206 59; 15 Avenue de L'Indépendance; ice creams FMg10,000; ☺ Tue-Sun) and **Honey Salon de Thé** (Map pp64-5; ☎ 22 621 67; 13 Avenue de L'Indépendance; cakes FMg5000; ☺ Wed-Mon). Neither is open in the evening, or at lunchtime. The **Patisserie Colbert** (Map pp64-5; Lalana Printsy Ratsimamanga; ☺ breakfast & lunch), in the Hôtel Colbert, is also a cake-lovers paradise.

Restaurants

MALAGASY & THE INDIAN OCEAN

Chez Mariette (Map pp60-1; ☎ 22 216 02; 11 Lalana Joel Rakotomalala; 6-course meals FMg100,000; ☺ dinner only with advance booking) In her 43 years as a chef, Mariette Andrianjaka has cooked for personages as diverse as François Mitterand, Prince Albert of Monaco and Paloma Picasso. These days she entertains guests to a *table d'hôte* (fixed menu) in her magnificent 19th-century villa, preparing meals based on the banquets once served to the kings and queens of Madagascar. These might include fillet of carp, eel or goose, exquisitely cooked and accompanied by myriad vegetable and rice dishes. At the end of the meal, Mariette herself will sally forth from the kitchen in her chef's hat and ruby earrings to explain how she did it. Groups of four or more are preferred, and you need to ring ahead to book.

Restaurant Sakamanga (Map pp64-5; ☎ 22 358 09; Lalana Andrianary Ratianarivo; mains FMg30,000; ☺ breakfast, lunch & dinner) A comforting yellow glow emanates every evening from the windows of the Sakamanga, which is usually packed

with appreciative locals and expats tucking into a meal or sampling the huge selection of rums available at the bar. Bistro-style food such as pasta (the seafood spaghetti is exquisite), grilled giant prawns or *steack frites* (steak and chips) is complemented by daily Malagasy specials chalked up on a blackboard. Reserve a table on Friday or Saturday nights if you're in a group.

Grill du Rova (Map pp60-1; ☎ 22 627 24; Lalana Ramboatiana, Avaradrova; mains FMg25,000; ☺ lunch & dinner Mon-Sat, lunch Sun) A very stylish and well-established restaurant/cabaret just downhill from the Rova. The menu serves French and Malagasy dishes, while the cabaret showcases Malagasy jazz and traditional music. There are performances every Sunday and Friday at sunset, and musical soirees on the first and third Wednesday of each month.

Villa Vanille (Map pp60-1; ☎ 22 205 15; Place Antanimena; mains FMg40,000; ☺ lunch & dinner) Another classy establishment, in an old colonial villa, with nightly musical performances from bands from the whole Indian Ocean region. The cooking is similarly eclectic, with dishes from Mauritius and Réunion, as well as Madagascar.

La Paillotte (Map pp64-5; ☎ 032 02 201 26; Arabe Ramanantsoa; 2-course meals FMg10,000; ☺ lunch & dinner) A fun and friendly, no-frills African-style restaurant with a lively bar, on the 1st floor above Snack Bar Jim. The choice of dishes is slim – you usually get grilled fish or chicken in sauce, followed by fruit – and the service can be pretty vague.

Caf'Art (Map pp64-5; ☎ 033 11 435 03; Lalana Ranavalona III; mains FMg20,000; ☺ lunch & dinner) A friendly little bistro serving Malagasy food and pizza in a garden courtyard.

FRENCH

La Varangue (Map pp64-5; ☎ 22 273 97; varangue @simicro.mg; 17 Lalana Printsy Ratsimamanga; mains FMg40,000) A little-known and very classy small restaurant in the hotel of the same name. It's cosy and brimming with character. The restaurant menu changes monthly, and mostly features French cuisine, with a few local touches. Reputedly the best French food in Madagascar.

Le Rossini (Map pp64-5; ☎ 22 342 44; Arabe Ramanantsoa; mains FMg40,000; ☺ lunch & dinner) A new addition to the eating scene and widely regarded as one of the best French restaurants in the city. A cosy dining room with a very rarefied atmosphere serves cuisine from the Perigoudines region in southwest France. Try the profiteroles – they're out of this world.

Kudéta (Map pp64-5; ☎ 22 281 54; 15 Lalana Réunion; grills FMg29,000; ☺ breakfast, lunch & dinner) A very stylish bar/restaurant run by Residence Lapasoa and with the same chic ethnic décor. It's always packed with fashionable young expats, so book ahead on Friday or Saturday nights.

Le Petit Verdot (Map pp64-5; ☎ 22 392 34; Lalana Rahamefy; mains FMg35,000; ☺ lunch & dinner Mon-Fri, lunch Sat & Sun) A little French bistro, the atmosphere here is homely, and the food is rustic French, simple but well-cooked. There's a daily special for FMg29,000 and a very good selection of wines and cheeses.

La Boussole (Map pp64-5; ☎ 22 358 10; 21 Lalana Dok Villette; mains FMg30,000-40,000; ☺ lunch & dinner Mon-Fri, dinner Sat & Sun) This attractive, lively restaurant/bar has funky décor and live bands on Thursdays. The restaurant serves *magret de canard* (duck fillet), as well as other French dishes and the bar does snacks and burgers.

Le Chalet des Roses (Map pp64-5; ☎ 22 642 33; 13 Lalana Rabar; grills FMg28,000; ☺ lunch & dinner Mon-Sat, dinner Sun) A sunny, pretty bistro serving pizza, pasta and salads.

ITALIAN & CHINESE

Nerone (Map pp64-5; ☎ 22 231 18; Lalana Ranavalona III; pasta dishes FMg35,000; ☺ lunch & dinner Mon-Sat, dinner Sun) A very high-quality Italian restaurant, with exquisite pasta and good wine.

The two best Chinese restaurants in town are **Dun Huang** (Map pp64-5; ☎ 22 669 65; 1 Rue James Adrianisa; dishes FMg30,000; ☺ lunch & dinner) and the more upmarket **Grand Orient** (Map pp64-5; ☎ 22 202 88; Kianja Ambiky; mains FMg40,000; ☺ Mon-Sat), which combines Chinese and Malagasy cooking.

Self-Catering

Antananarivo has several well-stocked supermarkets, selling a wide range of imported products. The most convenient are the two Shoprite supermarkets, one in **Haute-Ville** (Map pp64-5), underneath Hôtel du Lourve, and the other in **Analakely** (Map pp64-5) in Basse-Ville, just off Avenue de L'Indépendance. Both are also open on Sunday mornings. If you really need an even bigger supermarket, head for Cora or Score Digue to the north of town. You can pick up cheaper vegetables, meat and fish at the **daily market** (Map pp64-5) by the pavilions at Analakely.

ENTERTAINMENT

To find out what is going on and where, buy one of the three national daily newspapers, *Midi Madagasikara*, *Madagascar Tribune* and *L'Express de Madagascar*, all of which have advertisements for up-and-coming events, particularly in the Friday issue.

Music & Theatre

Centre Culturel Albert Camus (CCAC; Map pp64-5; ☎ 22 213 75, 22 236 47; ccac@wanadoo.mg; 14 Avenue de L'Indépendance; ☺ 10am-1pm & 2-6pm Tue-Sat) This is Antananarivo's foremost cultural venue. It holds regular concerts and theatre performances, art exhibitions and film screenings.

Théâtre Municipal (Map pp60-1; 4 Rue Hector Berlioz) This old theatre, in the Isotry district southwest of the train station, holds Malagasy theatre and dance performances, as well as some concerts.

Théâtre de Verdure Antsahamanitra (Map pp64-5; Lac Anosy) On the northeastern edge of the lake, the amphitheatre here often has pop concerts, known as *spectacles*, that often feature numerous artists from the Malagasy 'hit parade'. Check posters and the newspapers for details. Tickets are generally very cheap.

Grill du Rova (Map pp60-1; ☎ 22 627 24; Avaradrova) This restaurant has traditional Malagasy music recitals – see p72 for details.

Hôtel Le Glacier (Map pp64-5; ☎ 22 202 60; Araben'ny 26 Jona 1960) Has reggae and traditional music performances on Friday, Saturday and Sunday nights.

Hira Gasy

The traditional Malagasy performance of acrobatics, music and speeches, *hira gasy* (p33) is held most Sunday afternoons in the villages around Antananarivo. Check newspapers for details.

Nightclubs

Tana has a fair selection of nightclubs, all of which generally play a mixture of American hip-hop, Malagasy chart hits, and French soft-rock anthems. Many are packed with prostitutes so guys, more than girls, can expect a lot of hassle.

Le Pandora Station (Map pp64-5; ☎ 22 377 48; just off Lalana Ratsimilaho; admission FMg25,000) Le

Pandora Station is an exception to the action mentioned above and is relaxed and popular. It also serves pizzas and snacks.

Le Bus (Map pp60–1; ☎ 22 691 00; Arabe Raini-zanabolone; admission FMg22,000) Another good, chilled-out option.

SHOPPING

Marché Artisanale de La Digue (La Digue; ☿ daily) The most popular place to pick up art and crafts is the Marché Artisanale in the suburb of La Digue about 3km out of town towards Ivato airport. Here artisans and middlemen from the *hauts plateaux* (highlands) region, principally Ambositra, come to sell their products, which include embroidered table-cloths, brightly coloured raffia baskets and wooden carvings. Bargaining is expected. A taxi (around FMg20,000) is by far the easiest way to get here and back with your purchases.

You will also find arts, crafts, T-shirts, coffee and spices in the souvenir shops in central Tana. Some of the best are:

Baobab Company (Map pp64–5; ☎ 22 691 08; Lalana Andrianary Ratianarivo) Has T-shirts and clothes; there's another branch on Lalana Rainandriamapandry.

Le Flamant Rose (Map pp64–5; ☎ 22 557 76; off Avenue de L'Indépendance; ☿ 9am-6pm) Raffia items and embroidery.

Les Jocondes Galerie (Map pp64–5; ☎ 22 384 68; Lalana Andrianary Ratianarivo; ☿ 9am-5pm) Wooden sculptures.

TAF le Gourmet (Map pp64–5; ☎ 22 215 42; Lalana Patrice Lumumba) Sells coffee, tea and chocolate.

GETTING THERE & AWAY
Air

For details of international flights from Ivato international airport, see p256. For details of Air Madagascar's domestic flight network, see p259. The following is a list of domestic and international airline offices in Tana.

Air Austral/Air Mauritius (Map pp64–5; ☎ 22 359 90; www.airaustral.com in French; Lalana des 77 Parlemen-taires Français)

Air France (☎ 23 230 23; fax 23 230 41; Tour Zital, Rte des Hydrocarbures, Ankorondrano)

Air Madagascar (Map pp64–5; ☎ 22 222 22; www.airmadagascar.mg; 31 Avenue de L'Indépendance)

Corsair (Map pp64–5; ☎ 22 633 36; www.corsair.fr; 1 Rue Rainitovo Antsahavola)

Interair (Map pp60–1; ☎ 22 224 06; fax 2262421; Galerie Marchande, Rue Pierre Stibbe, Anosy) In the Madagascar Hilton.

Car & Motorcycle

Car-rental agencies in Tana all handle rentals for use throughout the country, and drivers are generally obligatory. Rates shown don't include petrol.

Budget (Map pp64–5; ☎ 22 317 08; 26 Avenue de L'Indépendance; per day from FMg375,000)

Espace 4x4 (☎ 22 441 84; espace4x4@dts.mg; Ivato; per day from FMg450,000)

Hertz (Map pp64–5; ☎ 22 229 61; somada@simicro .mg; 17 Lalana Rabefiraisana, Analakely; per day from FMg396,000)

You can also hire cars through several of the hotels in Tana (p69 for listings), or through most of the tour operators listed on p265. Also see p262 for general information on car rentals and rates.

Taxi-Brousse

Taxis-brousse leave from Tana to almost everywhere in Madagascar, departing about every hour to Antsirabe, Fianarantsoa and Toamasina. There's also daily connections to Mahajanga and Toliara. For more details on these journeys, see the individual town entries in the specific destination chapter.

There are four main *gares routières* (bus stations), which all have a chaotic plethora of minibuses, cars and coaches.

Eastern taxi-brousse station (Gare Routière de l'Est; Map pp60–1) At Ampasampito, in the suburbs about 3.5km to the northeast of the town centre. Taxis-brousse and *taxis-be* (literally, 'big taxis') to Lac Mantasoa (FMg5000) and Moramanga (FMg13,000). A taxi from the centre to the station costs from FMg10,000.

Northern taxi-brousse station (Gare Routière du Nord; Map pp60–1) In Ambodivona, about 2km northeast of the city centre, this station has transport to Toamasina (from FMg35,000), Mahajanga (FMg60,000 for a minibus) and Diego Suarez (FMg165,000). To get here take the Malakia No 4 bus or a taxi.

Southern taxi-brousse station (Gare Routière du Sud; Map pp60–1; Lalana Pastora Rahajason) At Anosibe about 1.5km southwest of Lac Anosy. Provides transport to all points south, as well as to some points on the east and west coasts. There are regular departures to Antsirabe (FMg15,000), Fianarantsoa (FMg45,000), Morondava (FMg65,000), Manakara (FMg70,000), Toliara (FMg90,000) and Fort Dauphin (FMg150,000). To get there take the Fima No 10 bus or a taxi (FMg5000).

Western taxi-brousse station (Gare Routière de l'Ouest; Map pp60–1) About 400m to the northwest of the southern taxi-brousse station. Has taxis-brousse to Ivato (FMg1500) and the airport.

Train

There are no trains presently operating from Antananarivo. There are, however, plans to reopen the line from Tana to Toamasina via Andasibe in 2004, so it's worth inquiring at the station when you arrive.

GETTING AROUND

Most restaurants and hotels are within a short distance of each other, so it's usually no problem to walk, except at night, when it's best to take a taxi. For places in the suburbs, a taxi is the best option.

To/From the Airport

Ivato airport is 12km from the city centre. Taxis to or from Ivato airport cost between FMg60,000 and FMg80,000 depending on the time and your powers of bargaining! A taxi-brousse from the village of Ivato, just outside the airport, costs FMg1500, but don't do this at night – it's not safe. The taxi-brousse station in Ivato is about 2km from the airport, and the taxis-brousse come into the western taxi-brousse station (see opposite).

Bus

There are a few large buses and many minibuses available for getting around Antananarivo and the outlying suburbs; fares range from FMg500 to FMg1500. Most buses and minibuses around the city begin and end of Avenue de L'Indépendance and Araben'ny 26 Jona 1960 in the centre of town. Buses are usually packed, so try to avoid the peak periods from around 7am to 8.30am and 5pm to 6.30pm; they'll only stop at official bus stops. As in any crowded setting, beware of pickpockets in the crush. Given the traffic and narrow, steep roads, it is often quicker to walk to places nearby. It's generally much easier to take a taxi, especially if you don't know the area in which your destination is located.

Car & Motorcycle

Hiring a car to drive yourself around Antananarivo's traffic chaos is very nerve-wracking, and it's unlikely to be worth the hassle because of the relatively high risk of damage to the vehicle through minor accidents or vandalism.

For a listing of some rental agencies in the capital, see opposite.

Taxi

At times there appears to be more taxis than people on the streets of Antananarivo, so you will never have much difficultly finding one, even late at night. The ubiquitous Citroëns Deux Chevaux (2CVs) and Renault 4s tend to be less expensive than other sedans. Taxis caught outside the more upmarket hotels are the most expensive. Taxis don't have meters, so agree on the price before you climb in. Fares in town range from FMg5000 to FMg15,000, often depending on whether the journey is downhill or uphill! Fares at night are more expensive.

AROUND ANTANANARIVO

The highlands around Antananarivo are often ignored, but there are several rewarding day trips you can do that offer spectacular views and an insight into the history and culture of the Merina people.

IVATO

About 14km from Antananarivo is Ivato, where the international airport is located. If you're killing time between flights, pay a visit to the newly revamped **Croq Farm** (☎ 22 234 10; Ivato; admission FMg25,000; ☺ 9am-5pm), which offers the chance to see various species of lemur, chameleons, and even the rare fossa, Madagascar's biggest predator, alongside the enormous crocodiles. You can buy meat to feed the crocs, or let the crocs feed you by dining on crocodile steak in the restaurant. A taxi from the croc farm to the airport costs about FMg40,000 return.

Sleeping & Eating

If you want to avoid paying taxi fares to and from the city, there are some modest hotels in and around Ivato.

Le Manoir Rouge (☎ 22 441 04; www.madatana .com in French; dm/d FMg25,000/50,000, d with bathroom FMg75,000) Barely 1km from the airport, this comfortable backpacker-type place has a clean, sunny feel about it, with wooden furniture and brightly painted bathrooms. Meals are available, and you can camp for FMg10,000.

AROUND ANTANANARIVO

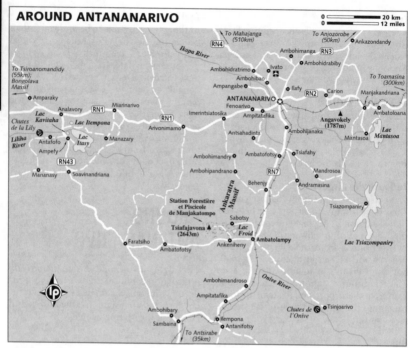

Ivato Hotel (☎ 22 743 05; ivatotel@dts.mg; d/tr FMg95,000/125,000) This hotel is quite unassuming from the outside, but the rooms inside are big, bright, clean and modern. The restaurant serves Chinese and Malagasy food.

Auberge du Cheval Blanc (☎ 22 446 46; cheval blanc@dts.mg; r with bathroom FMg110,000) The rooms here are quite simple, but clean and tiled, with raffia on the walls. There's a restaurant and a pretty garden, and it takes credit cards (5% fee).

All the above places do free transfers from the airport if you book.

Chez Daniel and Sahondra (Villa Soahmahatony; ☎ 033 11 033 37; soamahatony@wanadoo.mg; d FMg75,000) A worthwhile option if you plan on staying in the area longer, this friendly B&B is about a 1½-hour drive away from the airport, and can arrange visits to nearby silk workshops.

Getting There & Away

A charter taxi from the airport to Ivato will cost about FMg10,000. A taxi between Ivato village and Antananarivo costs FMg40,000.

Minibuses into Antananarivo leave every 20 minutes from the Ivato taxi-brousse station and cost around FMg1500.

AMBOHIMANGA

Ambohimanga ('blue hill' or 'beautiful hill') was the original capital of the Merina royal family. Even after the seat of government was shifted to Antananarivo for political reasons, Ambohimanga remained a sacred site, and was off-limits to foreigners for many years.

The entrance to Ambohimanga village is marked by a large traditional gateway, one of the seven gateways to the eyrie-like hilltop. To one side is a large, flat, round stone. At the first sign of threat to the village, the stone would be rolled by up to 40 slaves to seal off the gate.

Sights

A few hundred metres uphill from Ambohimanga village is the **Rova**, the fortress-palace of the all-powerful Merina king Andrianampoinimerina. These days it's an excellent **museum** (admission FMg35,000, plus guide tip; 9am-5pm) with very well-informed English-speaking guides – you tip them whatever you like, but at least FMg10,000 is reasonable.

Slaves were once sacrificed on the rock inside the entrance to the palace, and the many pilgrims who come to ask the blessings of the royal ancestors sometimes still slaughter animals in the same spot. The fortress was constructed using cement made from egg whites – 16 million eggs were required to build the outer wall alone. Inside the wall stands the wooden summer palace of the queens of Madagascar, constructed by the French engineer Jean Laborde in 1870. It's been beautifully restored and painted in blue and red, and has original European-style furniture inside. The dining room is lined with mirrors, which allowed the queen to check that her guests weren't poisoning her food.

Next door is the older, pre-colonial king's palace, dating from 1788. The central pole is made from a single trunk of sacred palissandre wood, which was apparently carried from the east coast by 2000 slaves, 100 of who died in the process. The top of the pole is carved to show a symbolic pair of women's breasts, a sign of the king's polygamy and thus power. Behind the palace are the baths, where the king performed his royal ablutions once a year, in the company of his 12 wives and diverse honoured guests. Afterwards his bathwater was considered sacred and was delivered to waiting supplicants.

Follow the stairs up past the palace compound to the left for amazing views back towards Tana.

Sleeping & Eating

Ambohimanga is best visited as a day trip from the capital, as accommodation options in the village are limited.

Restaurant d'Ambohimanga Rova (3-course lunch FMg30,000) Next to the Rova, this restaurant has good views over the countryside. There are also occasional rehearsals and displays of Malagasy dancing, which are often accompanied by live music.

Getting There & Away

Ambohimanga is 21km north of Antananarivo. Taxis-brousse leave throughout the day from the eastern taxi-brousse station (FMg2000, one hour). From the village, you'll need to walk 1km up the hill to the Rova. Charter taxis from Antananarivo cost around FMg150,000 for the return trip, including waiting time.

ILAFY

Ilafy was founded around the turn of the 17th century on a sacred hilltop and was used as the country residence of the Merina royal family. The residence – which is a two-storey wooden building with three rooms per floor – was redesigned in the 1830s to its present form by Ranavalona I. It is now an **ethnographic museum** (admission FMg15,000; 9am-noon & 2-5pm Tue-Sun) displaying a small collection of artefacts,

---

THE MERINA

The region surrounding Antananarivo is known as Imerina ('land of the Merina tribe'). Today the Merina tend to be among the most well-educated of the Malagasy tribes. They are also among the most Christianised. Traditionally, the Merina work as administrators, shopkeepers, teachers and traders.

The first Merina kingdoms were established around the 16th century, and by the late 19th century, the Merina were the dominant tribe in Madagascar. Their position was enhanced by the choice of Antananarivo as the seat of the French colonial government, and by the establishment of an education system there.

The Merina have a three-caste system, which is largely based on skin colour. The *andriana*, or nobles (who are generally fairer-skinned and with more pronounced Asian rather than African features), comprise the upper third, while the *hova*, or commoners, comprise the middle third. The remainder – descendants of former slaves – are the *andevo* (workers), although this term is generally avoided.

The Merina place great importance on *Famadihana* – the second burial ceremony, or 'turning of the bones'. For more information about this ritual, see p33.

including model tombs, hunting and fishing tools, modern wooden carvings and information about magic and religious rituals.

Ilafy lies 12km from Antananarivo just east of the road leading to Ambohimanga. To get there from Antananarivo, either take a taxi or find a taxi-brousse headed for Ambohimanga from the eastern taxi-brousse station. Some taxis aren't able to make it up the steep dirt road to the museum, so you may need to walk the last stretch.

LAC MANTASOA

This 2000-hectare artificial lake, which was built in 1837, is a good place for fishing, sailing and picnicking, and has become a popular weekend retreat for Antananarivo residents.

In 1833, three years before the surrounding land was flooded, the Frenchman Jean Laborde built a country palace for Queen Ranavalona I, as well as carpentry and gunsmith shops, a munitions factory, an iron forge and a foundry. The primary aim was to supply the monarch with swords, arms and ammunition. Most of this now lies underwater, and **Jean Laborde's home** was closed for renovation at the time of research. However, his **grave** in the local cemetery can still be seen, along with the closed **munitions factory**.

It's best to bring your own food as there are limited supplies in Mantasoa village.

Le Chalet Suisse (☎ 42 660 20; d FMg120,000) and the four-star **L'Ermitage** (☎ 42 660 54; d FMg200,000), about 6km past the village, both do set dinners for FMg55,000 and breakfast for FMg20,000. Four kilometres past L'Ermitage, by the lake, is the more upmarket **Le Riverside** (☎ 42 660 85).

Camping is possible near Chalet Suisse if you ask for permission, or you can camp at the Centre de Loisirs in the village.

Mantasoa village lies about 60km east of Antananarivo, about an hour south of the RN2. The lake and the hotels are around 3km southeast of Mantasoa village; follow the main path through the village.

Direct taxis-brousse go from Antananarivo's eastern taxi-brousse station to Mantasoa village (about FMg4000). Start early from Antananarivo for a day trip, and leave the lake by about 2pm.

AMBATOLAMPY & AROUND

Ambatolampy lies on both the RN7 and the railway line, 68km south of Antananarivo. The surrounding area, including the forestry station at **Manjakatompo** (admission FMg25,000) is a good place to do some walking and bird-watching among the picturesque forests and hills of the Ankaratra massif.

About 2km south of the town centre and 1km east of the main road is the **Musée de la Nature** (☎ 42 492 64; admission FMg25,000; 🕑 8am-5pm), which has an extensive collection of butterflies and insects.

Manja Ranch (☎ 42 492 34; r FMg50,000, bungalows with bathroom FMg100,000) Has pretty rooms and a peaceful setting just south of town near the museum. You can camp for free here with your own tent, but you must eat at the restaurant (approximately FMg30,000). The ranch is about 1km east of the main road and is signposted. There are sometimes horses for hire to explore the surrounding area.

Au Rendezvous des Pecheurs (☎ 42 492 04; d/tw FMg75,000/100,000) Has shabby rooms but a decent restaurant, with a set dinner for FMg55,000.

Camping is possible at Manjakatompo with your own tent and supplies.

Taxis-brousse run several times daily between Ambatolampy and the southern taxi-brousse station in Antananarivo. To get to Manjakatompo, there are occasional taxis-brousse from Ambatolampy to Ankeniheny, 1km from the station entrance. To get there in your own vehicle, you'll need a 4WD.

ANTSAHADINTA

Antsahadinta (Forest of Leeches), founded by King Andriamangarira in 1725, is one of the most remote and best preserved of the hilltop villages around Antananarivo. The *rova*, or royal precincts, contain several terraced **tombs** and a well-maintained garden. As you enter the settlement, the large tomb on your right belongs to Queen Rabodozafimanjaka, one of King Andrianampoinimerina's 12 wives. Accused of disloyalty, she had to undergo an ordeal with tanguin, a strong poison, and no-one today is certain whether she survived it.

There is a small **museum** near the tomb that explains the story in more detail (in French only).

Antsahadinta is 14km southwest of Antananarivo. As the road is in bad condition and public transport is scarce, the best options are to walk or hire a vehicle. To get here, go left at Ampitatafika (not to be confused with Ampitatafika between Antsirabe and Ambatolampy) soon after crossing the Ikopa River and head southwest following the only road. When you reach the turn-off, you'll see a signpost saying 'Antsahadinta 1.7km' which leads up to the wooded sacred hill. From here, the road is good.

LAC ITASY & AROUND

Lac Itasy (45 sq km) was formed when the valley surrounding it was blocked by lava flow about 8000 years ago. Although the area has been completely deforested and none of the original vegetation remains, the volcanic domes that rise above the landscape have a certain beauty of their own. Recently the **World Wide Fund for Nature** (WWF; Map pp64–5) declared Itasy to be a site of interest, and a large area of land has been allocated for research into bird species.

There are good possibilities for hiking around the lakeshore (except in the boggy south), but both crocodiles and bilharzia make swimming a bad idea. The crater lake of **Lac Andranotoraha**, about 5km south of Ampefy, is also reputed to contain a Loch Ness–style monster!

About 5km north of Ampefy, in the village of **Antafofo**, the Liliha River plunges more than 20m. In French, the falls are known as the **Chutes de la Lily**.

In Ampefy, you can stay at **Hôtel Kavitaha** (☎ 22 358 01; d FMg175,000, compulsory half-board per person FMg105,000), above Lac Kavitaha, which has reasonably good rooms, a terrace and a restaurant. There is also a simple local guesthouse in the village.

Lac Itasy lies near the village of Ampefy, 120km west of Antananarivo and south of Analavory (which lies along the RN1). To get here, take a taxi-brousse headed for Tsiroanomandidy from Antananarivo and get off in Analavory. From there, wait for another taxi-brousse heading south, or hitch or walk south along the RN43 for about 7km to Ampefy.

Central Madagascar

CENTRAL MADAGASCAR

CONTENTS

Central Madagascar encompasses the rolling hills, bright green paddy fields and medieval-style villages of the beautiful *hauts plateaux* (highlands) region, which stretches from Antsirabe south to Fianarantsoa. It's a fascinating area, with hot springs, interesting architecture, amazing views and endless opportunities for trekking. The climate in the *hauts plateaux* is cool, with crisp air and clear blue skies during much of the year, and freezing nights in winter. The region is historically the centre of rice production in Madagascar, with glassy, terraced paddy fields stretching for miles in every direction. Together with the Indonesian features of many of the Betsileo and Merina people, who inhabit central Madagascar, this gives the region a rather Southeast Asian feel.

CENTRAL MADAGASCAR

HIGHLIGHTS

- Wallowing in hot springs or tracking lemurs in **Parc National de Ranomafana** (p89)
- Trekking among the spectacular mountain scenery of **Parc National d'Andringitra** (p96)
- Visiting local artisans in the villages around **Ambositra** (p87)
- Attending an **Famadihana** (exhumation; p83) ceremony in one of the local villages
- Chugging through the countryside on a **train ride** (p94) from Fianarantsoa

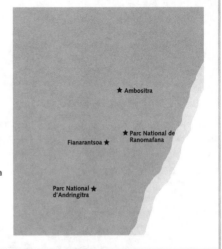

- HIGHEST POINT: 2643M
- PRINCIPAL TRIBES: MERINA, BETSILEO

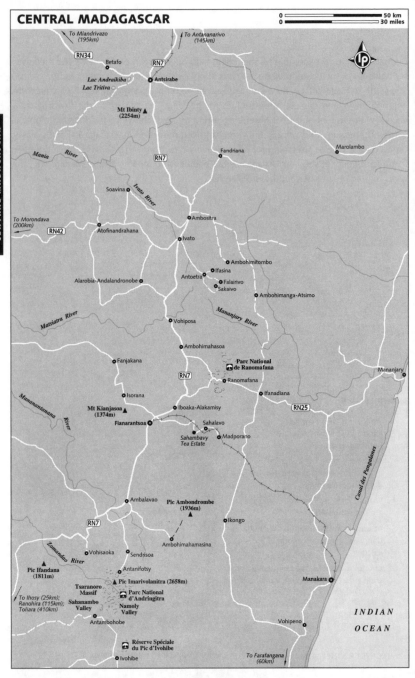

CENTRAL MADAGASCAR

0 — 50 km
0 — 30 miles

To Miandrivazo (195km)

To Antananarivo (145km)

RN34

Betafo

RN7

Antsirabe

Lac Andraikiba
Lac Tritiva

Mt Ibinty (2254m)

Fandriana

Marolambo

Mania River

RN7

Soavina

Ivato River

To Morondava (200km)

RN42

Atofinandrahana

Ambositra

Ivato

Ambohimitombo

Ifasina

Antoetra
Falairivo

Sakaivo

Ambohimanga-Atsimo

Alarobia-Andalandronobe

Mananjary River

Matsiatra River

Vohiposa

Ambohimahasoa

Fanjakana

Parc National de Ranomafana

RN7

Ranomafana

Mananjary

Isorana

Ifanadiana

RN25

Mt Kianjasoa (1374m)

Iboaka-Alakamisy

Manananiananana River

Fianarantsoa

Sahalavo

Sahambavy Tea Estate

Madporano

Ambalavao

Pic Ambondrombe (1936m)

RN7

Ikongo

Ambohimahamasina

Zomandao River

Vohisaoka

Sendrisoa

Pic Ifandana (1811m)

Antanifotsy

Pic Imarivolanitra (2658m)

To Ihosy (25km);
Ranohira (115km);
Toliara (410km)

Tsaranoro Massif

Parc National d'Andringitra

Sahanambo Valley

Namoly Valley

Manakara

Antambohobe

INDIAN OCEAN

Réserve Spéciale du Pic d'Ivohibe

Vohipeno

Ivohibe

To Farafangana (60km)

Canal des Pangalanes

Getting There & Around

Central Madagascar is easily reached from Antananarivo (Tana), with Antsirabe located only a couple of hours drive from the capital. Once in the region, you can get around fairly easily in *taxis-brousse* (bush taxis), which mostly take the form of minibuses. From Fianarantsoa, a passenger train goes to Manakara on the east coast (p94).

ANTSIRABE

pop 159,000

Norwegian missionaries founded Antsirabe (ant-sira-*bay*) as a health retreat, attracted by its cool, highland climate and therapeutic springs. It later became popular with French colonials as a spa town and hill station to escape the bustle of Tana. Today Antsirabe is a sophisticated and relaxed town, which retains a genteel, 19th-century feel. There are wide, palm-lined boulevards, elegant facades, and a legion of brightly coloured *pousse-pousses* (rickshaws) to ferry you around. The Norwegian missionaries are still here, and they now run the hospital.

Orientation

North of the cathedral is an area of long wide boulevards and colonial-era buildings, plus banks, the post office and several hotels and restaurants. The dusty and bustling lower-lying part of the town contains the southern taxi-brousse station and the market.

Information

INTERNET ACCESS

Cyber Paositra (Cnr Avenue de L'Indépendance & Grand Avenue; per min FMg150; ⏰ 8am-6pm Mon-Sat), at the post office, is your best option.

MONEY

Banks that will change money include the Bank of Africa, on the eastern side of Rue Jean Ralaimongo, BNI-CL next door, and BFV-SG, which is opposite. There's a BMOI ATM near the Petit Marché (market), too.

POST & TELEPHONE

The post office is near the train station, and there is a cardphone nearby.

TRAVEL AGENCIES

Voyages Bourdon (☎ 44 484 60) can assist you with booking Air Madagascar flights for other parts of Madagascar (there are no flights to or from Antsirabe). It can also arrange car rental.

Sights & Activities

LAC RANOMAFANA & THERMAL BATHS

The **thermal baths** (Centre National de Crénothérapie et de Thermoclimatisme; admission FMg2500; ⏰ 7am-1pm Mon-Sat), near Lac Ranomafana, have changed little since their construction during the colonial era. The baths and pool are very dirty and not maintained – those in the town of Ranomafana (p89) are better for bathing. **Lac Ranomafana** itself, below the Hôtel des Thermes, was mainly created for ornamental purposes, although it also helps prevent the escape of thermal gases. You can walk or cycle around the lake, but it's too dirty for swimming.

FAMADIHANA

Famadihana (literally, the 'turning of the bones') is the name given to the traditional exhumations of dead ancestors by the Betsileo and Merina people. *Famadihana* are joyous and intense occasions, which occur in each family roughly every seven years. Amid feasting, drinking, music and dancing, the bodies of the dead are disinterred from the family tomb, wrapped in bamboo mats, and carried and danced around the tomb. The bodies are then re-shrouded and reburied.

Famadihana ceremonies occur in the region around Antsirabe between July and September only. Local tour operators or *pousse-pousse* men can help you find one and arrange an invitation. If you receive an invite, it's polite to bring a bottle of rum as a gift for the host family, and to ask before taking pictures. Foreigners are generally warmly welcomed, and most people find that the experience, far from being morbid, is moving and fascinating. For more information, see p33.

Tours

Antsirabe is the best place to pick up a tour down the Tsiribihina River (p134), most of which are combined with a trip to Parc National des Tsingy de Bemaraha (p136). You can also organise trips from here to Parc National de Ranomafana (p89) or to the Zafimaniry villages, near Ambositra (p88).

CENTRAL MADAGASCAR

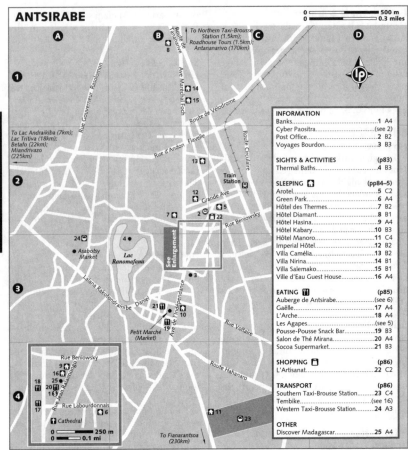

Discover Madagascar (☎ 033 12 232 08; discover mad@yahoo.com; Rue Jean Ralaimongo) In the Hôtel Baobab, this establishment has been highly recommended by readers. Guide Désiré speaks impeccable English and does Tsiribihina River descents, trips to Tsingy de Bemaraha, bike hire and more.

Hôtel Kabary (☎ 032 04 350 31; kabary@simicro.mg) Can arrange excursions to sights around Antsirabe, *Famadihana* ceremonies and Tsiribihina River descents.

L'Arche (☎ 032 12 591 52; robinsoncruso20032000@ yahoo.fr; Avenue Maréchal Foch) Guides Laza and Robinson Crusoe (yes, that's his real name) are based in the restaurant and do trips down the Tsiribihina River and to Tsingy de Bemaraha, together or separately. They can also organise car hire. Laza speaks better English than Robinson.

Roadhouse Tours (☎ 44 492 26; www.madagascar -info.de; Mahazoarivo Avaratra) A German-run outfit

that does Tsiribihina River descents, hikes around the Zafimaniry villages near Ambositra, and excursions to elsewhere in the country.

Sleeping
BUDGET

Green Park (☎ 032 07 535 81; Rue Labourdonnais; camping per tent FMg15,000, d/tr FMg70,000/80,000) This place has a beautiful garden and picnic ground. There's also three excellent round rooms, very prettily decorated, all with bathrooms, hot water and balconies. Green Park is the best-value accommodation in Antsirabe – book ahead to make sure you get a room.

Hôtel Kabary (☎ 0320435031; kabary110@yahoo.fr; d/tw FMg55,000/65,000) One of the few real backpacker hotels in Madagascar. The convivial bar does meals (mains FMg25,000) and has music every evening from 6pm. The hotel also organises excursions (see opposite) and hires cars and bikes. It's also the best place in town to find a group for tours. Contact in advance to book the shuttle bus from Antananarivo (€10).

Hôtel Manoro (☎ 44 480 47; r without/with bathroom FMg51,000/56,000) A little place, Manoro has noisy but clean rooms, and is your best choice if you want to be close to the southern taxi-brousse station.

Hôtel Diamant (☎ 44 488 40; diamant@madawel .com; Rte de Tananarive; d/tr FMg49,000/74,000; 🖳) A big Chinese-style edifice in the exhaust-fume-ridden northern part of town. The rooms, though, are peaceful, wood-floored and good value. The restaurant (Chinese dishes FMg25,000), café and disco on site are all very tacky, but civilised.

Ville d'Eau Guest House (☎ 44 499 70; intcorn @simicro.mg; 80 Rue Jean Ralaimongo; r without/with bathroom FMg64,000/74,000) Next to Salon de Thé Mirina, this is fairly overpriced, but clean and central. Not much French is spoken.

MID-RANGE & TOP END

Hôtel Hasina (☎ 44 485 56; Avenue de L'Indépendance; d/tw FMg100,000/105,000) Located behind the Courts furniture shop, this is a modern, friendly and efficient place with big, well-decorated rooms, some with balconies.

Villa Camélia (☎ 44 488 44; tw/d FMg95,000/115,000) A very genteel little guesthouse with a small, shady garden and an attractive restaurant with a log fire and outdoor terrace. Rooms come in various shapes, sizes and prices.

Villa Salemako (☎ 44 495 88; Ave Maréchal Foch; r without/with bathroom FMg95,000/100,000) An interestingly decorated villa, but it has an old-fashioned, rather stuffy feel – all lace tablecloths and dark wood. Rooms are huge and palatial, some with chaises longue.

Villa Nirina (☎ 44 486 69; Ave Maréchal Foch; r with breakfast FMg95,000) Family-run and friendly, but the rooms here are small and overpriced. Excursions can be arranged.

Arotel (☎ 44 485 74; arotel.inn@dts.mg; r with phone & bathroom FMg189,000; 🌂 P 🕿) A modern business hotel, opposite the post office. Rooms are big, drab and spotless. There's a restaurant (mains FMg35,000), a snack bar,

a small pool (FMg5000 for nonresidents) and a tennis court.

Imperial Hôtel (☎ 44 860 93; imperialhotel@dts.mg; Grand Ave; r with bathroom, TV & phone FMg148,000) Plush but tacky, with fairly luxurious rooms that have TV and a bathroom. There's a whole floor of pinball machines and a Chinese restaurant.

Hôtel des Thermes (☎ 44 487 61; sht@wanadoo.mg; r with TV, phone & bathroom FMg213,000; P) The facade of this old colonial hotel is elegant and imposing, with wonderful views over Lac Ranomafana. Unfortunately the interior is a mess of orange-and-brown 1970s décor, with fake wood and leather furniture and repulsive nylon carpets. It's best admired from the outside.

Eating

In the lower end of town, and in the area just south of the cathedral, are numerous places serving inexpensive Malagasy food and other meals.

Pousse-Pousse Snack Bar (rice dishes FMg7000; 🕑 lunch & dinner Thu-Tue) Near the market, this is one of the better places for inexpensive eating.

Hôtel Kabary (☎ 032 04 350 31; mains FMg25,000) For down-to-earth French food.

L'Arche (☎ 032 02 479 25; mains FMg20,000, 🕑 lunch & dinner Mon-Sat) Serves homely French food and has live music in the evenings.

Gaëlle (mains FMg10,000) Diagonally opposite the cathedral, this place is popular and dishes up French classics.

Auberge de Antsirabe (☎ 033 12 127 78; pizzas FMg30,000; 🕑 lunch & dinner Tue-Sat, lunch Sun) Has a log fire, stone-flagged walls and a cosy atmosphere, with pizza and pasta on the menu.

Salon de Thé Mirina (Rue Jean Ralaimongo; 🕑 breakfast & lunch Tue-Sun) The place to try for breakfast, pastries, ice cream and snacks.

Les Agapes (☎ 44 485 74; arotel.inn@dts.mg) Antsirabe's most expensive resturant is Les Agapes at the Arotel hotel. There is not much atmosphere to be found here, but the meals are good.

The best-stocked supermarket is Socoa, behind the Petit Marché.

Entertainment

Reggae and traditional Malagasy music can be heard at Hôtel Kabary and L'Arche restaurant several evenings a week.

CENTRAL MADAGASCAR

Shopping

There are several shops in town selling carvings and Antaimoro paper. One to try is **L'Artisanat** (Avenue de L'Indépendance), which is near the post office. You will also possibly be approached in the street to buy gemstones – not a good idea unless you're an expert.

Getting There & Away

Antsirabe lies 170km south of Tana. There are three taxi-brousse stations: the northern one for transport to Tana (FMg20,000, four hours) and all points north; one in the southern end of town for transport to Ambositra (FMg15,000, two hours), Fianarantsoa (FMg40,000, five hours), Miandrivazo (FMg40,000, five hours) and Morondava (FMg80,000, 15 hours); and another one on the western edge of town for transport to nearby villages, including Betafo.

Getting Around

BICYCLE

Antsirabe's long wide avenues and the relatively flat surrounding area means it is ideal for cycling. The best place to rent mountain bikes is **Tembike** (☎ 033 12 591 33; tembike@yahoo.com; 80 Rue Jean Ralaimongo; half-day/full-day FMg20,000/35,000), in the Ville d'Eau Guest House. Bikes come with puncture kits and maps. You can also hire bikes at Hôtel Kabary for FMg30,000 per day; see p84.

BUS & TAXI

Antsirabe can be easily negotiated on foot, but there are also a few taxis that can be chartered for getting around town and to destinations in the surrounding area, or you can take the bus.

CAR

Car rental can be arranged through **Voyages Bourdon** (☎ 44 484 60) and a guide called **Omega** (☎ 032 04 912 46), who can be found at L'Arche restaurant. Prices are around FMg250,000 per day for a 2WD vehicle, not including petrol.

POUSSE-POUSSE

The *pousse-pousse*, or rickshaw, is the main form of local transport in Antsirabe. The standard fare for town rides is about FMg3000.

POUSSE! POUSSE!

Brightly painted and sporting racy names like 'Air France' and 'Zidane', *pousse-pousses* (literally, 'push-push') are the Malagasy version of the rickshaws found in Asia. Hundreds of them fill the wide avenues of Antsirabe and cluster like oversized prams in front of the post office and the market. Passengers and freight vary – from haughty teenage girls, reclining like queens, to newly slaughtered cows, heads lolling and hoofs protruding.

When it rains, the price doubles and a sheet of plastic is pulled over the *pousse-pousse* as a makeshift hood. Most *pousse-pousse* men – who are also sources of information about almost anything in Antsirabe – rent their vehicles, and have to make a certain number of rides a day just to break even. In pursuit of their goal, they hound pedestrians relentlessly with whistles, hisses and cries of 'pousse!'. For more information, see p263.

AROUND ANTSIRABE
Lac Andraikiba & Lac Tritiva

In the hills west of Antsirabe are two volcanic lakes, both easily reached as day trips from town. **Lac Andraikiba**, the larger of the two, lies 7km west of Antsirabe just off the Morondava road (RN34). In the 19th century, it was a favourite retreat of Queen Ranavalona II; today it is dirty with local sewage, although it's possible to walk around the shores of the lake. According to tradition, Lac Andraikiba is haunted by the ghost of a pregnant girl who drowned during a swimming competition with another girl for the prize of marriage to a Merina potentate. Villagers say that each day at dawn she may be seen resting for a few minutes on a rock by the lakeshore.

The turquoise **Lac Tritiva**, which lies in the hills about 18km southwest of Antsirabe, is smaller and more picturesque than Lac Andraikiba, and makes a better excursion. It is said that the lake's water level inexplicably falls during the rainy season and rises in the dry season. An easy walk circles the lake. To enter the area around Lac Tritiva you'll need to pay a FMg10,000 fee, which will also get you a couple of kids to guide you (while trying to sell you polished stones).

As with Lac Andraikiba, a tragic legend surrounds Lac Tritiva. The waters are supposedly haunted by two star-crossed lovers who leapt from the cliff's edge when they were refused permission to marry. Their spirit is said to live on in two intertwined thorn trees above the lake. In accordance with local *fady* (taboos), you shouldn't bring pork to the region and should not swim in the lake.

Camping is possible at both lakes; village accommodation can also be arranged.

It's possible to visit both lakes in a combined day trip, although you'll need to get an early start if you will be walking part of the way or travelling via taxi-brousse. Bicycling is the best option for Lac Andraikiba, but you'll need to be fit to cycle to Lac Tritiva and back. For information on bicycle rentals and tours, see opposite. Apart from a small kiosk, there are no facilities en route, so carry food and water with you. Alternatively, taxis-brousse go from Antsirabe to Talatakely, on the northeastern side of Lac Andraikiba; the lake is 1km south of the main road.

Betafo

The Merina town of Betafo, whose name means 'many roofs', lies 22km west of Antsirabe. As well as the roofs in question, the village has numerous arcades and intricate wrought-iron trimmings, plus amazing views over the surrounding rice paddies. There's an imposing **Catholic church** behind the taxi-brousse station with some modern stained glass inside.

The interesting old town is dominated by the crater lake, **Lac Tatamarina**. A short circular road at the northern end of the lake passes a **cemetery** with tombs of local kings.

From the lake, a 5km return walk takes you through often-muddy fields to the **Chutes d'Antafofo** – a two-tiered, 20m waterfall slicing through basalt rock.

There are no hotels in Betafo, but basic meals are available.

Buses and taxis-brousse to Betafo leave Antsirabe throughout the day from the western taxi-brousse station. Riding a mountain bike is also a good way to get here as the road to Betafo is flat and paved and in relatively good condition; see opposite for information about bicycle hire.

AMBOSITRA
pop 28,000

The vibrant and pretty town of Ambositra (am-*boo*-sh-tr) is also the arts-and-crafts capital of Madagascar. In between the tall red-brick Betsileo houses that line the streets are over 25 artisans' shops, selling woodcarvings, raffia baskets, polished stones, *marqueterie* (coloured wood collages) and paintings. The souvenirs here are cheaper than those in Tana, and the atmosphere in the shops less pressurised.

Orientation & Information

Coming into town from the north, Rue du Commerce (the main road) passes the market area before it forks. To the left, it continues through a congested area towards the banks and the southern taxi-brousse station. The right fork leads to the quieter upper part of town, with a church and the post office.

BNI-CL in the town centre changes cash and travellers cheques and does advances on Visa cards.

Sights & Activities

There are many good walks from Ambositra through the nearby villages, where you can see the artisans at work in their homes, working the wood with homemade tools or spreading brightly dyed raffia out in the sun to dry. At the western edge of town is a **Benedictine monastery**, where the monks and nuns sell postcards, cheese and jam in a small **shop** (☉ until 6pm).

Tours

For visits to the Zafimaniry villages or local beauty spots contact the **Maison des Guides** (☎ 47 714 48; guides per day FMg80,000), a guide co-operative which has a small office next to the Grand Hôtel.

Alternatively, ask at the Grand Hôtel or Prestige Hotel for François Nirina, a highly respected young guide, who organises trips around Ambositra and may also be able to hire out mountain bikes and arrange adventurous tours further afield.

Sleeping & Eating

Hôtel Mania (☎ 47 710 21; d/tw FMg85,000/95,000; set meals FMg40,000) Ambositra's most upmarket option is tucked away in the northern part of town. It has big, clean rooms, a leafy courtyard and spotless marble bathrooms.

Motel Violette (☎ 47 610 84; Rue du Commerce; d/tw FMg90,000/110,000) A comfortable setup in the northern end of town, near the taxi-brousse station. Rooms have good bathrooms and views.

Grand Hôtel (☎ 47 712 62; Rue du Commerce; dm/d FMg25,000/50,000) This pink-painted, rustic inn has a wooden interior and quaint, little, old-fashioned rooms with chintzy screens around the washbasins. The restaurant (mains FMg20,000) has gingham tablecloths, a log fire (when wood is available) and elderly waiting staff. Simple but interesting.

Prestige Hôtel (☎ 47 711 35; Rue du Commerce; camping FMg10,000, s/d FMg35,000/50,000; dishes FMg15,000) A simple and very good-value hotel. There's a wide choice of rooms, with or without bathroom, but all with very comfortable beds, and a lovely little garden with a nice view.

Le Relais des Tropiques (☎ 47 711 26; ambositra_net@yahoo.fr; d/f FMg70,000/100,000; set dinner FMg35,000) Le Relais des Tropiques is a centrally located guesthouse with large, bare rooms, one of which has a log fire. The restaurant serves Malagasy food.

La Source (☎ 47 711 96; d/tr FMg50,000/75,000) The rooms at this little guesthouse are quite basic, but the views are the best in town. Try to get room No 1 or 2 – both have balconies.

Hotely Tanamasoandro (Hotely Gasy; ☎ 47 713 65; r FMg35,000) A local restaurant, which has some very basic rooms behind it. Portions are huge and the interior is a strange mix of Malagasy and Scottish themes, but it's very attractive.

L'Oasis (mains FMg11,000) For Chinese food, basic groceries and fresh bread, head to this place, just north of the southern taxi-brousse station.

Getting There & Away

Transport to points north, including Antsirabe (FMg15,000, two hours) and Antananarivo (FMg35,000, five hours), departs from the far northern end of town, about 2km north of the fork and down a small staircase from Rue du Commerce, where you'll find a whole lot of taxis-brousse lined up on the side of the road. Departures for Fianarantsoa (FMg25,000, four hours) and other points south are from the southern taxi-brousse station, just south of L'Oasis restaurant.

ANTOETRA & AROUND

East of Ambositra is a cluster of villages inhabited by the **Zafimaniry people**, a subgroup of the Betsileo known for their woodcarving. Many of their homes are works of art, with shutters and walls carved into geometric designs. The main village is Antoetra, which is linked with other villages higher on the massif by a good system of walking tracks.

Sadly, Antoetra and the villages closest to it have been spoiled by deforestation and tourism – you can expect bare hillsides, mud and very persistent souvenir sellers. A visit to this region is really only enjoyable if you do a trek of at least three days, which will allow you to get far enough off the beaten track to experience village life, watch skilled woodcarvers at work and enjoy the surrounding hills and forests.

All tours must start in Antoetra, where you'll need to pay a 'community fee' of FMg10,000 at the mayor's office in the centre of the village. The best villages to visit are **Sakaivo** (five hours from Antoetra), **Falairivo**, the highest of the villages (two hours from Sakaivo), and **Antetezandrota** (one hour from Sakaivo).

For all the villages, except Antoetra, you will need to visit with a guide, who can help you communicate with the locals and instruct you in local fady. Guides can be arranged in Ambositra (p87) or Antsirabe (p83). Expect to pay around FMg80,000 per day for an English-speaking guide, less for a French speaker.

The best times to visit are the months of May, June and September. During the rainy season the paths get very muddy and some become impassable.

Sleeping & Eating

There is no lodging in Antoetra, but you can usually arrange camping. Get permission first from the mayor. **Camping** (FMg5000) or basic **hut accommodation** (FMg25,000) can also normally be arranged at the other villages.

You will need to be self-sufficient with food and water as nothing is available in the villages, although tours from Ambositra sometimes include basic meals. Only a few basics are available in Antoetra.

Getting There & Away

Antoetra lies about 40km southeast of Ambositra. Taxis-brousse travel weekly (departing at 6am on Wednesday) between the two towns (FMg15,000, two hours).

None of the other villages are served by taxis-brousse, but they can all be reached from Antoetra via the network of walking trails.

RANOMAFANA

Ranomafana (Hot Water) served for a long time as a thermal bath centre and was a popular spot during the colonial era. It's easy to see why – nestled in the hills next to the rushing Namorona River, it's a pretty and friendly village, well worth a morning or afternoon's visit on either side of a trip to nearby Parc National de Ranomafana.

Sights & Activities

The **thermal baths**, for which the town is named, are across a bridge, behind the now defunct Hôtel Station Thermale. The baths – which are a bit dingy, but cleaner than the ones at Antsirabe and in a beautiful setting – are supposed to cure various ailments, including rheumatism, asthma, stomach ailments and sterility. Just below the baths is a deliciously warm **swimming pool**, in which you can float on your back while admiring the forested hills all around.

On the road out of the village, about 400m towards the park is the grandly titled **Environmental Interpretation Centre** (admission free; ☉ daily), which has explanations of the forest biodiversity in French and English, plus a small gift shop.

Sleeping & Eating

Hôtel Domaine Nature (☎ 75 750 25; desmada@ malagasy.com; r FMg195,000; dinner FMg45,000; P) This very charming hotel, 4km out of the village on the road to the park, has rustic bungalows on stilts and fantastic views of the forest and waterfalls. Be warned, however, there are a lot of steps to climb.

Hôtel Manja (r without/with bathroom FMg60,000/160,000; mains FMg12,000) The bungalows here are good value, but the rooms with bathrooms are overpriced. The restaurant serves tasty, inexpensive Malagasy meals. This is a good option if you are arriving late at night off the taxi-brousse from Manakara or Mananjary – it's easy to spot in the dark, and there's always someone around to let you in. It's about 500m before town as you arrive from the east.

Centrest (☎ 75 513 47; d FMg225,000; mains FMg18,000) Ranomafana's most upmarket option is often full with tour groups. Rooms are spotless, huge and very comfortable. The hotel has a private reserve at Mahakajy, 9km away, which has chameleons and 80 species of orchid. English is spoken.

Ihary Hotel (☎ 75 523 02; d/f with bathroom FMg100,000/175,000; mains FMg17,000) The exterior of this new hotel is painted a garish ice-cream pink, but the wooden bungalows next to the river are more tasteful and pretty comfortable.

Palmerie (dm/s/d FMg25,000/35,000/40,000) This pretty blue-and-white-painted guesthouse is in the centre of the village, and has simple but clean rooms that are ideal for budget travellers.

Hôtel Ravinala (d/tr FMg65,000/90,000), opposite the museum, and **Hotel Rianala Annexe** (r FMg30,000), next door, are both local guesthouses with clean and simple rooms.

Getting There & Away

Taxis-brousse go daily from Ranomafana to Fianarantsoa (FMg15,000, three hours) and Manakara or Mananjary (FMg50,000, six hours). If you're arriving from either place, let the driver know if you want to get off at the park entrance rather than in the village. In both directions, you'll need to wait for a vehicle with an empty seat – at weekends and holidays this can take ages. Taxis-brousse from Manakara generally arrive in Ranomafana in the middle of the night.

Chartering a taxi from Fianarantsoa for a day visit to Ranomafana costs about FMg250,000.

PARC NATIONAL DE RANOMAFANA

Parc National de Ranomafana consists of 40,000 hectares of cloud forest, spread out over rolling hills and punctuated by small streams that plummet down through the dense vegetation to the rushing Namorona river. The park was set up in 1986 to protect two species of rare lemur – the golden bamboo lemur and the greater bamboo lemur. Today Ranomafana is one of Madagascar's most popular parks, excellent for forest walks and lemur-spotting, and one of the best-developed for travellers. Nonetheless, only a small section of the park is accessible to visitors.

Information

The park entrance, the Angap reception, the camp site and the Hotel Restaurant Raviniala are all in the tiny village of Ambodiamontana, about 7km west of Ranomafana.

Permits cost FMg50,000 per person for three days, and are available at the park entrance. Fifty per cent of this park fee goes to local people for use in community projects. Guide prices start at FMg30,000 per guide for a two-hour circuit, and go up to FMg120,000 for a multiday trek. Be warned – some guides ask for more than their official fee, so check the prices carefully with the Angap office before paying.

The best time to visit is during the drier July to November season. However, the park can get very crowded during this time, particularly in July and early August. Temperatures range from 20°C to 25°C during the day, and from about 10°C to 20°C at night.

Wildlife

Parc National de Ranomafana is home to 29 mammal species, including 12 species of lemur. On a typical day's walk, you are likely to see red-bellied lemurs, diademed sifakas and red-fronted lemurs. With luck,

---

TAVY

Tavy is the Malagasy term for the type of slash-and-burn agriculture in which pieces of land are set on fire each year in order to clear them for crops and grazing.

Tavy promotes erosion, destroys precious forests and results in grasses growing back with fewer nutrients. It's a vicious circle – farmers are forced to practice tavy in the short term, but as the land degenerates they have to look elsewhere for land or grazing areas, and thus start the tavy process again.

The only way to halt tavy practices is to introduce more efficient farming methods, that allow the land to yield higher harvests and last longer. Organisations are working with the government to educate farmers in these methods – which can be as simple as spacing rice plants differently in the fields or transplanting them at different times – but it's a slow process, as tavy practices are viewed by many impoverished Malagasy as an economic necessity.

---

you may also see a golden bamboo lemur. This species was first discovered in 1986; Ranomafana is one of its two known habitats.

Even rarer is the broad-nosed gentle lemur, which was thought to be extinct until it was rediscovered in Ranomafana in 1972; it was observed again in the late 1980s, and is very occasionally seen by visitors to the park.

Night visits to the park involve a trip to a clearing where bait is set to attract woolly, mouse and sportive lemurs, as well as the striped civet (Fossa fossana). Baiting wildlife for tourist observation is a controversial practice, and for some visitors the whole experience can seem rather contrived and artificial.

Not to be confused with the Fossa fossana, the much larger fosa (Cryptoprocta ferox), a puma-like creature and the largest of Madagascar's predators, is the bane of local farmers, who blame it for night raids on stock and other mischief. The fosa is rarely sighted.

The park's bird life is also rich, with more than 100 species. Of these, 68 species are endemic to Madagascar. The forests abound with geckos, chameleons and frogs.

Although most visitors come for the animals, the plant life is just as impressive, with orchids, tree ferns, palms, mosses and stands of giant bamboo.

Hiking

There are three major walking trails that go through the park. The short **Ala Mando trail** (Petit Circuit) takes a leisurely two hours up and back and heads as far as the lookout at Bellevue, with lemur-spotting along the way. The **night walk** follows the same route, ending up in the 'Place du Nuit' to see the nocturnal lemurs and the civet. The three-to four-hour **Moyen Circuit** goes a bit further in its search for lemurs.

There are various other walking trails upstream from the Namorona River bridge, but you will need special permission from the Angap office to visit these areas.

Sleeping & Eating

At the entrance to the park is the basic **Hotel Restaurant Raviniala** (camping/dm FMg10,000/25,000; mains FMg20,000). Camping within the park is only possible with special permission.

Tents can be hired at the park entrance for FMg10,000.

For details on accommodation options in Ranomafana village, see p89.

Getting There & Away

The park entrance is 7km west of Ranomafana village on the main road. It's possible to visit the park on a day trip from Fianarantsoa using public transport if you start early; ask the driver to drop you off at the park entrance. Angap runs a shuttle bus (FMg5000 each way) from Ranomafana village to the park at 7am and 4.30pm daily, or you can hitch. For details on tour operators who can organise day excursions, see p92.

FIANARANTSOA

pop 138,000

Fianarantsoa (often shortened to simply Fianar) was founded in 1830 when Queen Ranavalona I decided to build an intermediate capital between Tana and the remote southern provinces. Today it's Madagascar's second city and intellectual capital, but for most visitors the town itself is a disappointment – it's dirty and crowded, with a downbeat atmosphere. There are, however, some good walks around Fianar, which lies at the heart of one of Madagascar's most fertile agricultural areas, renowned for its production of wine and tea.

Orientation

Fianarantsoa is divided into three parts. Basse-Ville (Lower Town), to the north, is a busy, chaotic area with the main post office and the train and taxi-brousse stations. Up from Basse-Ville is Nouvelle Ville (New Town), the business area with the banks and several hotels. Further south and uphill is Haute-Ville (Upper Town), which has cobbled streets, a more peaceful atmosphere, numerous church spires and wide views across Lac Anosy and the surrounding rice paddies.

Information

CULTURAL CENTRES

Alliance Franco-Malgache (☎ 75 515 71; affianar@dts.mg) holds a cabaret concert on the last Friday of every month. It also organises a guided two-hour walk around the city on the second Sunday of the month; meet at 2pm outside the Ambozontany cathedral.

INTERNET ACCESS

The main post office has **Internet access** (per min FMg500; 🕒 7am-9pm Mon-Sat). Internet connection is also possible at Chez Dom restaurant (p93).

MONEY

All the **banks** (🕒 8-11am & 2-4pm Mon-Sat) can be found along the same street in Nouvelle-Ville.

POST & TELEPHONE

The main post and telecom offices are opposite the train station. There's another post office branch in Nouvelle-Ville.

TOURIST INFORMATION

Angap (☎ 75 512 74; angapfnr@dts.mg; Nouvelle Route d'Antananarivo) can provide information and permits for the parks near Fianarantsoa. Permits can also be purchased at the parks themselves.

Sights & Activities

The oldest and most attractive part of town is **Haute-Ville** (known as Tanana Ambony in Malagasy). A stroll (or climb) around the cobbled streets in this part of town gives great views of the surrounding countryside. In the centre of Haute-Ville, and dominating the skyline, is the imposing **Ambozontany cathedral**, which dates back to 1890.

The largest market is the weekly **Zoma**, where you'll find everything from beef sausages to party hats. It's held on Friday along Araben'ny Fahaleovantena.

In hot weather, head for the large **pool** (nonresidents FMg10,000) at the Hôtel Tonbontsoa. There's also a **sauna** (per hr FMg40,000).

Tours

Several hotels and tour operators can organise excursions to nearby places of interest, including Parc National de Ranomafana, Ambalavao, the Sahambavy Tea Estate, as well as hikes to the many picturesque Betsileo villages surrounding Fianarantsoa. It's also possible to arrange excursions further afield, including to Toliara on the west coast.

Tsara Guest House, Hôtel Cotsoyannis and some other hotels in Fianarantsoa will hold your luggage while you visit Parc National de Ranomafana or go trekking.

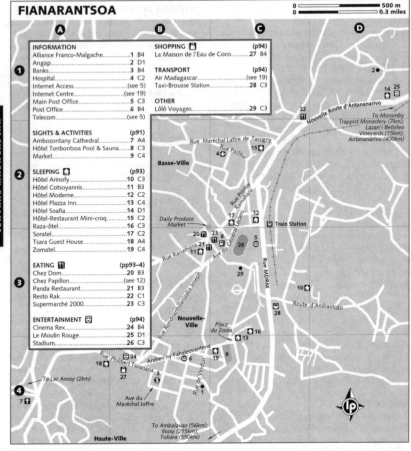

FIANARANTSOA

0 ———— 500 m
0 ———— 0.3 miles

INFORMATION
Alliance Franco-Malgache.................1 B4
Angap...2 D1
Banks...3 B4
Hospital..4 C2
Internet Access........................(see 5)
Internet Centre......................(see 19)
Main Post Office.............................5 C3
Post Office.....................................6 B4
Telecom....................................(see 5)

SIGHTS & ACTIVITIES   (p91)
Ambozontany Cathedral..................7 A4
Hôtel Tonbontsoa Pool & Sauna.......8 C3
Market...9 C4

SLEEPING 🏠   (p93)
Hôtel Arinofy...............................10 C3
Hôtel Cotsoyannis.........................11 B3
Hôtel Moderne.............................12 C2
Hôtel Plazza Inn...........................13 C4
Hôtel Soafia................................14 D1
Hôtel-Restaurant Mini-croq...........15 C2
Raza-ôtel.....................................16 C3
Soratel...17 C3
Tsara Guest House........................18 A4
Zomatel.......................................19 C4

EATING 🍴   (pp93–4)
Chez Dom....................................20 B3
Chez Papillon..........................(see 12)
Panda Restaurant.........................21 B3
Resto Rak....................................22 C1
Supermarché 2000........................23 C3

ENTERTAINMENT 🎭   (p94)
Cinema Rex..................................24 B4
Le Moulin Rouge...........................25 D1
Stadium.......................................26 C3

SHOPPING 🛍   (p94)
La Maison de l'Eau de Coco...........27 B4

TRANSPORT   (p94)
Air Madagascar.......................(see 19)
Taxi-Brousse Station.....................28 C3

OTHER
Lôlô Voyages................................29 C3

Rue Maréchal Lattre de Tassigny
Rue Pasteur
Basse-Ville

Nouvelle Route d'Antananarivo

To Moromby
Trappist Monastery (7km);
Lazan'i Betsileo
Vineyards (15km);
Antananarivo (400km)

Daily Produce Market
Train Station

Rue Ranamana
Ave du Général Leclerc
Rue MDRM

Nouvelle-Ville
Place du Zoma
Route d'Andrainiato

Rond-point Raniazaka Joseph

Araben'ny Fahaleovantena
Rue Philibert Tsiranana
Rue de Verdun

To Lac Anosy (2km)

Ave du Maréchal Joffre

To Ambalavao (56km);
Ihosy (215km);
Toliara (550km)

Haute-Ville

The Ranomafana treks advertised in Fianarantsoa focus on the Tanala villages in the area surrounding Parc National de Ranomafana. These multiday treks can be tough-going, especially in the rainy season when you will spend a lot of time slogging through rice paddies and dense patches of forest. You will need good shoes and long trousers to dissuade the leeches.

Places that organise treks and excursions include:

Chez Dom (☎ 75 512 33; Rue Ranamana) Ask for Angelo and Tina, both English-speaking guides who use this restaurant as their base. They do tours to Ranomafana (FMg350,000 per car) and Andringitra (FMg300,000 per person per day), hikes in the local area and trips up the Canal des Pangalanes starting from Manakara.

Hôtel Arinofy (☎ 75 506 38) This hotel organises treks and homestays in the Betsileo villages around Fianarantsoa.
Lôlô Voyages (☎ 75 519 80; lolovoyages@dts.mg) This recommended guide specialises in treks and hikes in the Tanala villages around Parc National de Ranomafana. He also can arrange excursions to nearby attractions, pirogue excursions on the Matsiatra River (FMg325,000 for two days), and vehicle transport and multiday excursions between Fianarantsoa and Tana, with stops at points of interest along the way.

Tsara Guest House (☎ 75 502 06; www.tsaraguest .com; Rue Philibert Tsiranana) This excellent guesthouse offers a wide variety of excursions, including trekking in Parc National de Ranomafana, day hikes through villages around Fianarantsoa and pirogue excursions on the Matsiatra River. It can also hire out 4WDs, with driver, for FMg500,000 per day.

Sleeping

BUDGET

Raza-ôtel (☎ 75 519 15; d/tr FMg51,000/71,000; mains FMg20,000) A very charming and nicely decorated family-run guesthouse that's down a small road to the left of the Hôtel Plazza Inn. There are just four rustic rooms, a cosy restaurant and a tiny bar. All very convivial, but order in advance for evening meals if you're not staying there – the restaurant closes early when there aren't any customers.

Hôtel Arinofy (☎ 75 506 38; camping/s/d FMg10,000/50,000/67,000) Northeast of the taxi-brousse station in a quiet area, this is a friendly local guesthouse that also organises community tourism in the villages around Fianarantsoa. It has a variety of rooms at different prices and will also allow camping. The restaurant serves Malagasy dishes (FMg18,000).

Hôtel Moderne (Chez Papillon; ☎ 76 608 15; Rue MDRM; s/d with bathroom FMg60,000/70,000) A good-value option, although it's in the hectic area opposite the train station. Rooms are small but cosy, and the downstairs restaurant has excellent French food and good service, but a rather dull atmosphere. It's very convenient if you have to get up early for the train.

Hôtel-Restaurant Mini-croq (☎ 75 505 87; d without/with bathroom FMg55,000/76,500; mains FMg20,000) Clean, and recommended by readers, but it's in a very scurrilous area north of the train station. There's a Chinese restaurant, too.

MID-RANGE & TOP END

Tsara Guest House (☎ 75 502 06; www.tsaraguest.com; Rue Philibert Tsiranana; d without/with bathroom FMg100,000/280,000; mains FMg34,000) Wildly popular, this orange-painted converted church enjoys a reputation as one of the best guesthouses in Madagascar. If you're a budget traveller, consider a splurge here. The décor is excellent – a roaring fire and bright-red walls in the reception area, a glass-walled restaurant serving delicious food, and a charming outdoor terrace with great views. Some of the cheaper rooms are rather plain, but the more expensive ones are positively luxurious, and by any standards the Tsara is a very good bet. Staff speak English, and the hotel organises excursions in the surrounding area and further afield. Advance bookings are recommended.

Hôtel Cotsoyannis (☎ 75 514 72; cotso@malagasy.com; d FMg91,000; mains FMg26,000) 'Le Cotso' has rustic, simple and attractive rooms and a garden courtyard. There's also a cosy restaurant with a log fire and good pizzas and crepes, which are its speciality. It also runs Camp Catta, a rock-climbing hotel just outside Parc National d'Andringitra on the Tsaranoro Massif (see p98).

Hôtel Soafia (☎ 75 503 53; soafia@simicro.mg; Nouvelle Route d'Antananarivo; s/d with TV, phone & fridge FMg95,000/135,000; mains FMg25,000; ✷ P) Surely a contender for the weirdest hotel in Madagascar – an enormous Chinese-style palace, fitted out like a kitsch 1970s theme park, plastic pagodas and all. There's an enormous swimming pool, a vast, empty restaurant, a travel agency, a 'dance club' and an arcade of shops. Labyrinthine corridors lead to rooms fitted out haphazardly with gilt trimmings, some with bathrooms you could play football in. The prices are reasonable for the facilities, so lovers of the surreal might want to stay here for sheer novelty value.

Zomatel (☎ 75 507 97; www.zomatel-madagascar.com; Araben'ny Fahaleovantena; s/d/f with TV, phone & fridge FMg95,000/150,000/225,000; ✷ ▢) A big, new and very modern Western-style business hotel with a *salon de thé* (tea room), Internet centre and pizzeria in the same complex. It's also where you'll find the Air Madagascar office.

Hôtel Plazza Inn (☎ 75 512 72; Place du Zoma; s/d with TV & phone FMg115,000/120,000) The same kind of place as the Zomatel – lacking in atmosphere, but with comfortable rooms that have all the trimmings.

Soratel (☎ 75 516 66; www.soratel.com; Avenue du Général Leclerc; d/tr with TV & phone FMg120,000/145,000) More of the same – big rooms, faintly Chinese décor and nylon carpets. There's a snack bar on the ground floor.

Eating

The best hotel restaurants in town for French cuisine are those at the Tsara Guest House and Chez Papillon. Hôtel Soafia has a huge choice of Chinese dishes, and Hôtel Cotsoyannis is famed for its wood-fired pizzas and crepes. Some others to try in town include:

Chez Dom (☎ 75 512 33; Rue Ranamana; mains FMg18,000; ◷ lunch & dinner; ▢) A smoky backpacker café with Internet access and freelance guides available for excursions and treks. The bar specialises in local rum.

CENTRAL MADAGASCAR

Panda Restaurant (☎ 75 505 69; Rue Ranamana; mains FMg20,000; ⊙ lunch & dinner Mon-Sat) There's no real need for the copulating pandas painted on the wall, but the food is very good. Wild duck is a speciality.

Resto Rak (Nouvelle Route d'Antananarivo; mains FMg10,000) The best Malagasy establishment in the Basse-Ville does simple rice dishes and noodles with beef or chicken.

Supermarché 2000, in Basse-Ville, is the best-stocked place for self-caterers.

Entertainment

Alliance Franco-Malgache (☎ 75 515 71; affianar@dts.mg) In Nouvelle-Ville, this cultural centre (see p91) has regular exhibitions, films, plays and concerts.

Cinema Rex (admission FMg2500) This cinema shows films of the French and usually gangster variety.

On Sunday afternoon, spirited games of football (soccer) are played at the **stadium** (off Avenue du Général Leclerc), near the train station. There are also occasional beer festivals here, attended enthusiastically by university students from as far away as Tana. Look out for posters around town.

For nightlife, try Le Moulin Rouge at the northeastern end of town, or the casino and 'dance club' at Hôtel Soafia.

Shopping

La Maison d'Eau de Coco (☎ 75 511 42) This place sells crafts, postcards and perfumed soaps in aid of underprivileged children and adults.

Getting There & Away
AIR

Air Madagascar (☎ 75 507 97; Araben'ny Fahaleovantena) flies once weekly between Fianarantsoa and Tana (FMg750,000, one hour). The booking agent is in the complex behind the Zomatel.

TAXI-BROUSSE & MINIBUS

Frequent taxis-brousse connect Fianarantsoa with Ambositra (FMg20,000, four hours), Antsirabe (FMg30,000, about seven hours) and Antananarivo (FMg40,000, nine to 10 hours).

Minibuses also go daily to Ambalavao (FMg10,000, two hours), Ihosy (FMg25,000, four hours), Ranohira (FMg35,000, seven hours) and on to Toliara (FMg75,000, 11

hours). Departures from Fianarantsoa are at around 5pm, arriving in Toliara at about 4am the next day. If you're heading east there are vehicles daily between Fianarantsoa and Ranomafana (FMg15,000, three hours), Mananjary (FMg40,000, eight hours) and Manakara (FMg50,000, 10 hours). It's no longer possible to go from Fianarantsoa to Fort Dauphin (Taolagnaro) as the road is impassable – you have to go to Toliara instead.

TRAIN

Fianarantsoa is connected to Manakara on the eastern coast by Madagascar's only functioning passenger train service, the FCE (Fianarantsoa – Côte Est). The train leaves Fianar early each morning and chugs on lines built in the 1930s through plantations and past hills and waterfalls, reaching Manakara around seven hours later. It takes about an hour longer in the other direction as the train has to go uphill. Despite its antiquity and unreliability, the train is still an economic lifeline for the people of the inland villages, who use it to transport their cargos of bananas and coffee to be sold and exported.

Departures from Fianarantsoa are scheduled for Tuesday, Wednesday, Thursday, Saturday and Sunday at 7am, and from Manakara on Monday, Wednesday, Thursday, Friday and Sunday at 7am, although there are frequent delays and cancellations. Tickets cost FMg55,000/45,000 in 1st/2nd class.

No advance reservations are taken – simply arrive at the station about an hour before departure. The only actual difference between 1st and 2nd class is that the seats and windows are bigger, and it's less crowded. First class is generally only used by tourists, while 2nd class is packed with a noisy and friendly crowd of Malagasy, all leaning out of the windows at each tiny station to haggle with hordes of vendors balancing baskets of bananas, crayfish or fresh bread on their heads.

For the best views of the cliffs, misty valleys and waterfalls en route, sit on the north side of the train (ie the left side when going from Fianarantsoa to Manakara). However, the most impressive waterfall is on the right as you go towards Manakara, just after Madporano, about two hours from

Fianarantsoa. Bring water, and, if you're making the journey in winter, plenty of warm clothes – it's often freezing early in the morning, when some of the best views can be hidden by fog.

For a more detailed history of the railway and the regions through which it passes, pick up a booklet called *The FCE: A Traveler's Guide* by Karen Schoonmaker Freudenberger. It's sold in English or French for FMg25,000 at the station or at the reception of the Zomatel hotel.

Getting Around

Taxis charge FMg5000 per person for rides within Fianarantsoa. Villages and destinations in the surrounding area are served by *buxi* (minivans), which have route numbers marked in their front window. The fare to all destinations is FMg500; departures are from the taxi-brousse station.

THE BETSILEO

The Betsileo, Madagascar's third-largest tribe, inhabit the *hauts plateaux* (highlands) area around Fianarantsoa and Ambalavao. They only began viewing themselves as a nation after being invaded and conquered by the Merina in the early 19th century.

The Betsileo are renowned throughout Madagascar for their rice-cultivation techniques – they manage three harvests a year instead of the usual two, and their lands are marked by beautiful terracing and vivid shades of green in the rice paddy fields. Betsileo herdsmen are famous for their trilby hats and the blankets they wear slung in a debonair fashion around their shoulders. Betsileo houses are distinctively tall and square, constructed from bricks as red as the earth of the roads.

As well as the *Famadihana* (reburial ceremony), which was adopted from the Merina after the unification of Madagascar, an important Betsileo belief centres on *hasina*, a force that is believed to flow from the land through the ancestors into the society of the living. Skilled traditional practitioners are thought to be able to manipulate *hasina* to achieve cures and other positive effects. The reverse of *hasina* is *hery*, which can result in illness and misfortune.

AROUND FIANARANTSOA

The area around Fianarantsoa is considerably more attractive than the town itself and is well worth visiting. Most villages, vineyards and tea estates can be easily visited on your own – just ask around to find out which *buxi* to jump on. If you'd prefer an organised tour, contact the places listed on p92.

Vineyards

Wine production in the area around Fianarantsoa began in the 1970s, with technical expertise and funding from a Swiss corporation. Today, Fianarantsoa is Madagascar's wine-making centre. Several of the largest vineyards lie northwest of town along the route to Isorana, or northeast along the road to Ambositra.

The most popular and accessible vineyard is **Lazan'i Betsileo** (☎ 75 516 24), about 15km north of Fianarantsoa. If you're visiting on your own, ring in advance.

About 7km outside Fianarantsoa is the **Maromby Trappist monastery** (admission FMg1000), where you can observe the wine-making process and taste the wine. To get here, take *buxi* No 24 (FMg500) towards Vohipeno and ask the driver to drop you off at the junction, from where the monastery is about a 2km walk.

Sahambavy Tea Estate

The **Sahambavy Tea Estate** (admission FMg25,000; ⊙ 7.30am-3.30pm Mon-Fri) produces high-quality tea for export and a lesser-grade for local consumption. It lies near the village of Ampaidranovato about 15km east of Fianarantsoa, and along the rail line towards Manakara. A visit includes a tour of the tea-processing factory and ends with a tea-tasting.

Organised day excursions can be arranged in Fianarantsoa for about FMg200,000, including the entry fee. To visit on your own, take a taxi-brousse heading towards Sahalavo to the signposted turn-off, from where you will need to walk about 1km. Alternatively, take the train to Sahambavy station (the second stop after Fianar) and walk about 500m from there.

Lake Hôtel (☎ 75 518 73; d FMg125,000; set dinners FMg40,000), a good Chinese establishment near the station, is the only place to stay. The lake in question isn't clean enough for swimming.

AMBALAVAO

pop 25,000

Ambalavao (New Valley) is one of the most beautiful towns in the *hauts plateaux*. The brightly painted buildings of the main street look a bit like gingerbread houses with their steeply tiled roofs and carved, weathered wooden balconies. Outside, ladies sit in the clear highland sunlight, spinning silk or kneading dough, little raffia hats perched on their heads and blankets around their shoulders. Every Tuesday and Wednesday, the town plays host to the largest zebu market in the country, with tough, wizened herdsmen walking from as far away as Toliara to sell their cattle.

The World Wide Fund for Nature (WWF) and the **Parc National d'Andringitra office** (☎ 75 340 81) is on the northern edge of town, opposite Ambalavao's only petrol station. The office can provide information on the park, and assist with transport and guides.

For gifts made from wild silk and the chance to visit a silk workshop, look for a shop called Nathocéane in the main street.

Sights

FABRIQUE DE PAPIER ANTAIMORO

The **Fabrique de Papier Antaimoro** (Antaimoro Paper Factory; ☎ 75 340 01; admission free; ⏰ 7.30-11.30am & 1-5pm) lies behind the Hotel Aux Bougainvillées. You can see the ladies of the factory making paper from scratch. They start with the bark of the *avoha* bush, which is first boiled in water to form a pulp, then it is pounded, spread out over cotton cloth on wooden frames and left in the sun to dry. Once it's almost dry, fresh flowers are pressed into it. It is then left to dry again, after which the paper is removed from the frames and made into cards, envelopes and picture frames, all of which are for sale.

ANJAHA RESERVE

This village **reserve** (admission FMg25,000), about 7km from Ambalavao, features a semi-tame colony of ring-tailed lemurs and some Betsileo tombs in a small patch of forest. You can make a day's walk of it, or catch a taxi-brousse towards Ihosy and ask to be dropped at the office of the reserve. Guides cost FMg15,000.

Sleeping & Eating

Hôtel Aux Bougainvillées (☎ 75 340 01; ragon@wanadoo.mg; r without/with toilet FMg70,000/106,000; mains FMg30,000) The best place to stay is this one, which is on the grounds of the paper factory. The rooms are comfortable and clean, but only the more expensive have hot water. There's a decent restaurant, which is popular at lunchtime with tour groups. The lackadaisical staff, though, profess to know nothing about anything in the region. If you need information, look for one of the two guides, Adrien and Fidy, who are based at the hotel part-time.

Getting There & Away

Ambalavao lies 56km south of Fianarantsoa. The town has direct taxi-brousse connections with Fianarantsoa (FMg10,000, 1½ hours), Ihosy (FMg25,000, two hours) and Ilakaka (FMg30,000, five hours). For destinations further north, you'll have go to Fianarantsoa first.

PARC NATIONAL D'ANDRINGITRA

The beautiful Parc National d'Andringitra (an-*dring*-itr) is a walker's paradise. It has spectacular views of huge granite peaks towering above the Namoly and Sahanambo Valleys, 100km of well-developed hiking trails, and the opportunity to climb Pic Imarivolanitra (formerly known as Pic Boby) – at 2658m it's Madagascar's second-highest peak. The roads into the park are no less spectacular, surrounded on all sides by the glittering mud and symmetrical patterns of thousands of paddy fields.

The areas around the northern part of the park (where the main tourism area is located) are primarily inhabited by the rice-cultivating Betsileo, while the largest group in the south is the cattle-herding Bara. Andringitra is administered in partnership with the local communities, who can be visited in the villages bordering the park – ask your guide to arrange a trip, or inquire at the WWF *gîte* near the park entrance.

Information

The **WWF/Angap office** (☎ 75 340 81) in Ambalavao can provide information on the park and on weather conditions, verify camping ground availability, and help find guides.

The main entrance to the park, and the most common starting point for treks, is in the Namoly Valley on Andringitra's eastern side. There is another entrance at the Sahanambo Valley on the park's western border.

When visiting the park, you will need to be self-sufficient with both food and water. It's also important to respect local fady, which are taken seriously in this area. There is a fady that pork should not be consumed in the valley or near the sacred waterfalls, and another that no boats should cross the Zomandao River. Your guide can help you with others. Andringitra is a 'pack it in – pack it out' park, so you'll need to take all rubbish from your visit out with you.

Technical mountain-climbing equipment, rock-climbing equipment and hang-gliding are not permitted in the park.

Temperatures in Andringitra range from -7°C at night during the winter months of June and July to daytime highs of 25°C in December and January. You will definitely need extra warm clothing and a good sleeping bag if camping during the winter. Afternoon mists are common, and you should be prepared for bad weather at any time of year. The park is officially closed in January and February when heavy rains make access difficult.

Permits (FMg50,000 for three days) can be arranged at both the Namoly Valley and Sahanambo Valley entrances.

Guide/porter fees range from FMg25,000/ 10,000 per day for a four-hour circuit to FMg45,000/30,000 per day on the Pic Imarivolanitra ascent. Local guides – which should be arranged at one of the two entrance gates, rather than in Ambalavao – are required for most trails, and recommended for all. If you need assistance carrying your gear, you will need to hire a local porter in either Namoly or Sahanambo.

Wildlife

Fourteen lemur species have been identified in Andringitra – more than in any other park in Madagascar – but sightings by visitors are rare since most of their habitat is outside the tourism zone. Among Andringitra's lemur species is an ecotype of *Lemur catta* (ring-tailed lemur) adapted to living in the mountains, which has been sighted on the upper reaches of Pic Imarivolanitra. The park's rich flora includes over 30 species of orchid, which bloom mainly in February and March.

Hiking

Andringitra's 100km of trails traverse a variety of habitats and offer fantastic trekking. There are four main circuits catering to various abilities. One of the most popular is the climb to the summit of Pic Imarivolanitra (2658m). There is now a natural trail up the mountain, which makes the summit accessible to most visitors with no technical climbing skills, although you'll need a reasonable degree of fitness for the hike. The circuit takes about 12 hours; so it's best to allow at least two days from start to finish. There is a beautiful camping ground for overnight stays about 3.5km before the summit.

Other circuits include the easy Asaramanitra (6km, about four hours) and the scenic Diavolana (13km, six to seven hours). The best route for lemur-spotting is Imaitso (14km, about eight hours) which goes through the eastern forests. Pocket maps and details of the various routes are available from the WWF office in Ambalavao.

Sleeping

Camping grounds (camping per person FMg10,000) The park has four wilderness camping grounds, all with running water and flush toilets. Tents can be rented from some of the local guides.

WWF gîte (dm/d FMg30,000/60,000) The *gîte*, in Namoly, is outside the park boundaries about 6km from the start of the trails. Once hotel facilities are available in the valley, the *gîte* will no longer be open to the public. Check availability with the WWF office in Ambalavao before setting out.

Soa Camp (☎ 22 530 70; www.boogie-pilgrim.net; full board per person €54) A tented camp, with great views, run by tour operator Boogie Pilgrim. It's located in the village of Ambodifotsy on the southern side of the park.

For information on accommodation on the park's west side, see Tsaranoro Massif on p98.

Getting There & Away

The Namoly Valley entrance lies east of Andringitra, about 100km south of Fianarantsoa. Allow about 2½ hours from Fianarantsoa in a private vehicle. The road is in good condition and negotiable with 2WD at most times of year.

The Sahanambo Valley entrance to the west of the park is about 110km from

Fianarantsoa and four hours in a private vehicle.

Taxis-brousse go to Namoly from the western side of the market in Ambalavao on Thursday. On other days you can find transport to the village of Sendrisoa, 17km before Namoly, then walk in. For Sahanambo, you'll have to get a taxi-brousse to Vohisaoka, 15km before the entrance. Alternatively, you can charter a vehicle in Ambalavao for the very scenic drive up to the park (about FMg300,000 per day).

TSARANORO MASSIF

Just outside the western boundary of Parc National d'Andringitra is the Tsaranoro massif. It has an approximately 800m-high sheer rock face considered by rock climbers to be one of the most challenging in the world.

Camp Catta (☎ 75 505 68; www.campcatta.com; tent/bungalow per person FMg35,000/80,000), on the western edge of the park, is run by the Hôtel Cotsoyannis in Fianarantsoa, and specialises in rock climbing.

Southern Madagascar

CONTENTS

With its arid deserts, surreal spiny forests and fabulous beaches, the south is the best-known and most-visited region of Madagascar. It's also the poorest area of a poor country – the baking sun and lack of rainfall make life particularly hard for the famously tough tribes who inhabit Madagascar's southern provinces. Many people live off the little charcoal they can sell on the dusty roadsides.

The south is the driest, hottest and wildest area of the country, with the most interesting plant life. Flora found here includes stands of weirdly squat baobabs and the famous spiny forest, a fantastical landscape of golden earth and silver trees. On the cooler and wetter southeastern side of Madagascar you'll find carnivorous pitcher plants and triangular palms, along with spiky, symmetrical sisal plantations.

Among the many peoples of the region are the Bara, who consider cattle-herding the only noble activity; the Vezo, a semi-nomadic people of the sea; and the Mahalefy, who are famous for their carved tomb decorations. Toughest of all are the Antandroy, known as 'people of thorns' after the cacti that grow in their deserts.

Despite the fact that southern Madagascar sees the most tourism, travelling outside the better-known areas such as Parc National de l'Isalo and Toliara can be hard going. Road conditions can be terrible and hotels very basic. If you want to explore off the beaten track, you'll need time, resources and a certain level of resistance to discomfort.

HIGHLIGHTS

- Trekking through the spectacular rock formations of the **Parc National de l'Isalo** (p107)
- Diving in the turquoise waters off **Anakao** (p113) or **Ifaty** (p110)
- Walking in the bizarre spiny forest in **Parc National d'Andohahela** (p121)
- Camping by the beaches or in the rain forests of the **Lokaro Peninsula** (p120)

★ Parc National de l'Isalo

★ Ifaty

★ Anakao

Parc National d'Andohahela ★

★ Lokaro Peninsula

| ▪ HIGHEST POINT: 1964M | ▪ PRINCIPAL TRIBES: ANTAISAKA, ANTANDROY, BARA, MAHALEFY, VEZO |

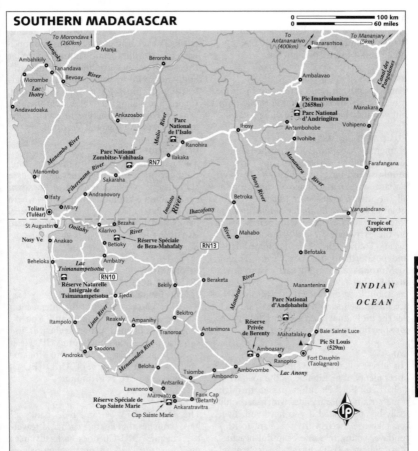

SOUTHERN MADAGASCAR

Getting There & Away

The quickest and easiest options for arriving in Southern Madagascar are a flight on Air Madagascar or a road trip down the so-called 'Route du Sud' – the Route Nationale 7 (RN7) from Antananarivo.

AIR

Air Madagascar flies daily from Antananarivo to Toliara (FMg965,000, one hour) and Fort Dauphin (FMg965,000, about two hours).

BUS & TAXI-BROUSSE

The RN7 between Antananarivo and Toliara is well-served by minibuses and some larger coaches. The total journey time between the two towns is around 24 hours; but most people do the journey in stages, taking in attractions such as the beautiful Parc National de l'Isalo on the way. Off the RN7, the roads are very poorly maintained and public transport is scarce – it's very difficult to get down to Fort Dauphin on public transport from northern towns such as Fianarantsoa.

Getting Around

Once you've arrived, transport in southern Madagascar is tricky. Many of the roads, particularly the route between Fort Dauphin (Taolagnaro) and Toliara, are in a very bad state and only negotiable by 4WD vehicles.

SOUTHERN MADAGASCAR

AIR
Air Madagascar has flights between Fort Dauphin and Toliara (FMg680,000, one hour) about three times a week.

BICYCLE
There are currently no mountain bikes for hire officially in Toliara and Fort Dauphin, but you may be able to hire one privately.

BUS & TAXI-BROUSSE
Numerous *taxis-brousse* (bush taxis – any kind of public passenger truck, car or minibus) and buses ply the route between Toliara and Antananarivo, stopping at all the major towns. Off this route, possibilities are more limited. *Camions-brousse* (Mercedes lorries fitted with bench seats) do the extremely rough 30-hour trip between Toliara and Fort Dauphin daily, and go north up the coast from Toliara to Morondava. Around each major town *taxis-bé* (big taxis) serve the outlying villages, but long-distance routes off the RN7 are rarely well served by public transport. See the individual town sections, following, for specific details.

CAR
For lovers of 4WD adventures, the south offers plenty of possibilities – the road from Toliara to Fort Dauphin passes through some striking countryside, which can only really be appreciated if you have your own car. Likewise the trip from Toliara to Morondava, taking in some beautiful beaches, is possible in a 4WD during the dry season. You can hire 4WD vehicles in Toliara (p104) and Fort Dauphin (p117), or rent one in Antananarivo (p69) and drive it south.

Motorcycles are available for hire in Toliara – see p104 for details.

TOLIARA (TULÉAR)
pop 102,000

Toliara, often still known by its French name of Tuléar, is the largest town in southern Madagascar. It's a hot, dusty place, bustling with brightly coloured *poussepousse* rickshaws, which slips into heat-drenched torpor between midday and 3pm. French expats are very much in evidence, as are the numerous Indian traders, who run most of the town's shops and businesses.

Most of Toliara's buildings are fairly nondescript, in keeping with its setting against a backdrop of mangroves and mudflats. Most visitors set off almost at once for the superb beaches around Ifaty to the north and Anakao to the south, which offer endless opportunities for diving, snorkelling, surfing and sailing. Off the beach, the area around Toliara has nature reserves, spiny forests, lakes and unspoilt Vezo villages.

Orientation
Toliara's airport lies 7km to the east, along the busy main road from the taxi-brousse station. Blvd Gallieni leads into the town centre about a kilometre to the west, where the market and most of the businesses, banks and hotels are located. From here Ave de France leads down past the post office to the port.

Information
INTERNET ACCESS
Prilimite Ganivala Internet (☎ 94 419 92; ⊙ 8am-noon & 3-6pm; per min FMg750), at the intersection of Blvd Philibert Tsiranana and Rue du Marché, has English-format keyboards and can also put digital photos onto CD. Flash Video, opposite Glace des As, and Mohammedi Net, near the Bank of Africa (BOA), are the same price as Prilimite.

MONEY
The BNI-CL, BFV-SG and BOA banks all have branches that change cash and travellers cheques. BNI-CL does cash advances on Visa cards; BOA can advance money on MasterCard. Socimad, next to the mosque, changes cash and travellers cheques for slightly better rates than the bank, and does advances on Visa cards.

POST & TELEPHONE
The post office and the Telecom are both on Blvd Gallieni; the Telecom has cardphones.

TOURIST INFORMATION
Angap (☎ 94 435 70; Rue Lucciardi), just west of the market, can provide general information on national parks in southern Madagascar.

Sights
A few blocks southwest of the market, the **Musée Regional de l'Université de Toliara** (admission FMg10,000; ⊙ 8-11.30am & 2.30-5.30pm Mon-Fri)

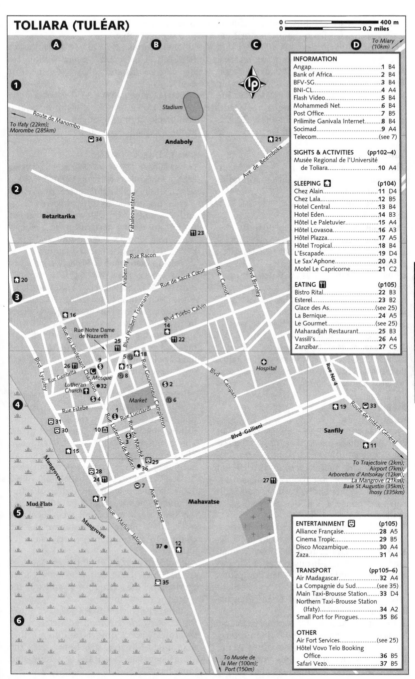

TOLIARA (TULÉAR)

0 — 400 m
0 — 0.2 miles

To Miary (10km)

INFORMATION	
Angap	1 B4
Bank of Africa	2 B4
BFV-SG	3 B4
BNI-CL	4 A4
Flash Video	5 B4
Mohammedi Net	6 B4
Post Office	7 B5
Prilimite Ganivala Internet	8 B4
Socimad	9 A4
Telecom	(see 7)

SIGHTS & ACTIVITIES	(pp102–4)
Musée Regional de l'Université de Toliara	10 A4

SLEEPING	(p104)
Chez Alain	11 D4
Chez Lala	12 B5
Hotel Central	13 B4
Hotel Eden	14 B3
Hôtel Le Paletuvier	15 A4
Hôtel Lovasoa	16 A3
Hôtel Plazza	17 A5
Hôtel Tropical	18 B4
L'Escapade	19 D4
Le Sax'Aphone	20 A3
Motel Le Capricorne	21 C2

EATING	(p105)
Bistro Rital	22 B3
Esterel	23 B2
Glace des As	(see 25)
La Bernique	24 A5
Le Gourmet	(see 25)
Maharadjah Restaurant	25 B3
Vassil's	26 A4
Zanzibar	27 C5

ENTERTAINMENT	(p105)
Alliance Française	28 A5
Cinema Tropic	29 B5
Disco Mozambique	30 A4
Zaza	31 A4

TRANSPORT	(pp105–6)
Air Madagascar	32 A4
La Compagnie du Sud	(see 35)
Main Taxi-Brousse Station	33 D4
Northern Taxi-Brousse Station (Ifaty)	34 A2
Small Port for Pirogues	35 B6

OTHER	
Air Fort Services	(see 25)
Hôtel Vovo Telo Booking Office	36 B5
Safari Vezo	37 B5

Route de Manombo

To Ifaty (22km); Morombe (285km)

Stadium

Andaboly

Ave de Belemboka

Betaritarika

Fahalecovantena

Rue Racon

Rue de Sacré Coeur

Araben'ny

Rue Philibert Tsiranana

Blvd Tsiebo Calvin

Rue Carriol

Blvd Branley

Rue Notre Dame de Nazareth

Rue du Lieutenant

Rue Gambetta

Rue Flacourt

Mosque

Lutheran Church

Rue Estebe

Blvd Lyautey

Market

Rue Luccardt

Rue Gouverneur Campistron

Blvd Camain

Hospital

Rue No 4

Route de Interêt Général

Sanfily

Blvd Gallieni

Mangroves

Mud Flats

Mangroves

Rue Lieutenant de Briditel

Rue du Marché

Rue Martux Jalop

Ave de France

Mahavatse

To Trajectoire (2km); Airport (7km); Arboretum d'Antsokay (12km); La Mangrove (21km); Baie St Augustin (35km); Ihosy (335km)

To Musée de la Mer (100m); Port (150m)

SOUTHERN MADAGASCAR

has a few dusty exhibits on local culture, as well as an egg from the pre-historic elephant bird, *Aepyornis* (p124).

Only really worth a visit for real fish fanatics, the **Musée de la Mer** (Ocean Museum; admission FMg25,000; ☾ 8am-noon & 3-5pm Mon-Fri, 8am-noon Sat) has displays of pickled sea life, coral and shells, including a coelacanth (p229) It's near the end of the road that leads to the port.

Tours

The following places can organise excursions to attractions in the surrounding area and further afield.

Air Fort Services (☎ 94 426 79) Inside Maharadjah Restaurant. Rents 4WDs.

Chez Alain (☎ 94 415 27; www.chez-alain.net in French; Sans Fil) Located down a small lane near the main taxi-brousse station; staff can help with excursions in the surrounding area.

Motel Le Capricorne (☎ 94 426 20; capric@dts.mg; Ave de Belemboka) More expensive than the others, but reliable; visits to Réserve Privée de Berenty west of Fort Dauphin can be arranged here.

Safari Vezo (☎ 94 413 81; Ave de France) Organises boat transfers and excursions to Anakao and Nosy Ve.

Trajectoire (☎ 94 433 00; www.trajectoire.it; Rte de l'Aéroport) Specialises in motorcycle and quad hire and off the beaten track biking, trekking and camping excursions in southern Madagascar. No car hire.

Sleeping
BUDGET

Chez Lala (☎ 94 434 17; vivianelala@hotmail.com; Ave de France; r without/with bathroom FMg40,000/50,000; mains FMg20,000; ☒) Tiled, almost luxurious rooms in the main block, or smaller but still very comfortable rooms in the garden. This is a very friendly, sociable and well-run guesthouse. It's also very popular, so book ahead.

Chez Alain (☎ 94 415 27; www.chez-alain.net in French; Sans Fil; r without/with hot water FMg70,000/100,000) A Toliara institution, down a small lane near the taxi-brousse station. It has simple but comfortable wooden bungalows in a garden, a lively bar and an excellent restaurant. Helpful staff can organise excursions and car hire.

L'Escapade (☎ 94 411 82; escapade@wanadoo.mg; Blvd Gallieni; r with bathroom FMg75,000) On a busy road round the corner from Chez Alain, L'Escapade has simple and comfortable rooms with fans, but no nets. The breezy

blue and white upstairs restaurant has a TV and snooker table.

Hotel Central (☎ 94 428 84; r with bathroom FMg75,000) This good budget option has big, cool rooms and is handy for the town centre.

Hôtel Lovasoa (☎ 94 418 39; r without/with bathroom FMg30,000/50,000) Very cheap and fairly acceptable rooms with fans but no nets around a shady courtyard.

MID-RANGE & TOP END

Le Sax'Aphone (☎ 94 440 88; http://saxaphone.org; Besakoa; r without/with bathroom FMg75,000/95,000) A very friendly and slightly eccentric French-run B&B with rooms in the owner's house and a couple of bungalows in the garden. Lots of interesting decoration from all over the world. There's a restaurant and piano bar, and a very cute rescued lemur.

Motel Le Capricorne (☎ 94 426 20; capric@dts.mg; Ave de Belemboka; s/d FMg165,0000/180,000; mains FMg35,000; ☒) Located about 1.5km northeast of the town centre, Le Capricorne is Toliara's most upmarket option and frequently used by package tours. It's very comfortable, with a whitewashed courtyard restaurant that makes a welcome refuge from the heat of the day. The helpful, English-speaking staff organise excursions and transfers to Ifaty and Anakao.

Hotel Eden (☎ 94 415 66; eden.hotel@wanadoo.mg; d/tw FMg128,000/120,000; ☒) A new, modern and well-run tourist hotel in the centre of town painted an attractive shade of leaf green. The rooms have a TV, minibar and safe. There's no restaurant, but there's a breakfast bar. This hotel offers free airport transfers.

Hôtel Tropical (☎ 94 438 31; r FMg100,000-130,000; ☒) This place was in the middle of refurbishment when we passed, but it looks like it'll be a very smart and well-decorated small hotel. There's no restaurant as yet, and room prices may go up when it's finished.

Hôtel Plazza (☎ 032 02 492 14; r without/with sea view FMg130,000/170,000; ☒) A gloomy edifice overlooking the mangrove swamps at the western edge of town.

Hôtel Le Paletuvier (☎ 94 440 39; d FMg130,000-170,000; ☒ ▣) A few hundred metres north of Hôtel Plazza, this is another rather abandoned-looking big hotel, but the rooms here are clean and spacious, and some have TV.

Eating

Toliara's large French population means some good French cuisine is available in town.

Chez Alain (mains FMg25,000) Try the great seafood.

Le Sax'Aphone (mains FMg28,000) This spot has a piano player and regular live jazz evenings.

Esterel (☎ 032 02 650 52; Voirie; mains FMg28,000; ⊗ lunch & dinner Mon-Sat) Esterel offers seafood, pizza and amazing chocolate pudding in a beautiful lamp-lit courtyard.

Bistro Rital (Cortomaltese; ☎ 94 433 15; Blvd Campan; mains FMg25,000; ⊗ lunch & dinner Mon-Fri, dinner Sat & Sun) This place has reasonable-quality Italian food.

Vassili's (☎ 94 432 83; Rue Gambetta; mains FMg22,000; ⊗ lunch & dinner) Vassili's does authentic Greek dishes.

Zanzibar (Chez Jeff; ☎ 032 02 650 60; pizza dishes FMg30,000; ⊗ dinner Wed-Sat & Mon) This place has wood-fired pizzas, big salads and 30 different kinds of rum.

The cheapest places to eat are the food stalls near the market. A few steps up and also inexpensive are several *salons de thé* (tea rooms) in the centre of town, including Maharajah Restaurant, and Glace des As, next door. Both do breakfast, sandwiches, milk shakes and ice creams. The other side of Maharajah is Le Gourmet, which does Malagasy rice dishes.

Entertainment

Alliance Française (Blvd Lyautey) has schedules of cultural events and French newspapers and magazines. French and occasional subtitled English films are shown at **Cinema Tropic** (admission FMg2500).

Popular drinking hangouts in town include **La Bernique** (☎ 032 02 606 55; Blvd Gallieni; tapas FMg5000; ⊗ Mon-Sat) or the bar at Chez Alain (above).

The main nightclubs in town are **Zaza** (Blvd Lyautey) and **Disco Mozambique** (Blvd Lyautey), which get going about midnight. Young Malagasy girls and middle-aged *vazaha* (European) men are the main customers at both, but the environment is generally OK.

Getting There & Away

AIR

Air Madagascar (☎ 94 415 85, 94 422 33) has an office northwest of the market. It flies from Antananarivo to Toliara (FMg965,000, one hour) daily, from Toliara to Fort Dauphin (FMg680,000, one hour) about three times a week, heading occasionally to Morondava (FMg680,000, 1½ hours) via Morombe (FMg425,000, one hour).

BOAT

For scheduled boat transfers from Toliara to points south such as St Augustin, Anakao or Beheloka, contact **La Compagnie du Sud** (☎ 94 437 21; www.compagniedusud.com in French), which does speedboat transfers from FMg100,000 per person. Departures can be cancelled, however, if there isn't enough demand. It has an office in the pirogue port south of the post office.

You can also find pirogues (local cargo boats) at this port that run along the coast to the north and south. Allow plenty of time (three to four days to Morombe), and bring water and food.

HITCHING

It's relatively easy to hitch a lift from Toliara to Antananarivo as many tourist vehicles and supply trucks from Antananarivo return to the capital empty. Expect to pay a bit more than the taxi-brousse fare. The best places to ask are the major hotels.

TAXI-BROUSSE

The main taxi-brousse station, which handles transport to Antananarivo, Fianarantsoa and Fort Dauphin, is in the far eastern part of town along the main road.

Taxis-brousse leave from 6.30am every day towards Antananarivo, arriving in Fianarantsoa around 5pm, and in Antananarivo at about 5am the next day. Some sample taxi-brousse fares include: Ranohira, FMg40,000; Ihosy, FMg45,000; Fianarantsoa, FMg60,000; and Antananarivo, FMg100,000. Fares on smaller and slightly faster minibuses are from FMg5000 higher. Vehicles to Antananarivo usually fill up quickly, so get to the station early or book a seat the afternoon before.

To get to Fort Dauphin (FMg80,000), via Betioky, Ampanihy and Ambovombe, a *camion-brousse* leaves daily, taking 30 to 60 hours depending on breakdowns and road conditions.

Transport along the sand road north to Ifaty (FMg15,000, one to three hours) and Manombo departs from the northern taxi-brousse station on Route de Manombo. There are a few trucks daily to both destinations, generally departing between 6am and early afternoon.

A taxi-brousse leaves for Morondava a few times weekly (FMg100,000, two days). The road is very rough, and you will need to change vehicles in Beyoay and overnight in Manja on the way.

Taxis-brousse also connect Toliara with St Augustin (FMg10,000, two hours) via a good tarmac road every day except Thursday and Sunday. Departures are at noon from Toliara and 2am (!) from St Augustin. There's a taxi-brousse every Thursday to Beheloka and Itampolo (12 hours).

Getting Around
TO/FROM THE AIRPORT
A taxi between Ankorangia airport and the centre of town costs a standard FMg25,000. Many hotels in Toliara and Ifaty do airport transfers.

CAR & MOTORCYCLE
Most tour companies listed on p104 hire 4WD cars for excursions around Toliara. Prices start at FMg500,000 per day without fuel. **Trajectoire** (☎ 94 433 00; www.trajectoire.it; Rte de l'Aéroport) hires out motorcycles from FMg275,000 per day without petrol, and quad bikes from FMg450,000 per day.

POUSSE-POUSSE
Standard rates for *pousse-pousse* (rickshaw) rides start at about FMg3000.

TAXI
For rides within town, taxis charge a standard rate of FMg5000 per person.

EAST OF TOLIARA
Ihosy
The sleepy town of Ihosy (*ee*-oosh) is the traditional capital of the Bara tribe. Unlike most other Malagasy groups, the Bara practise polygamy. Cattle often have a higher profile than wives in the hearts of Bara men, who believe a man's worth is judged by the number of zebu he owns (p110). Ihosy is most attractive in October when the jacarandas are in bloom. There's no particular reason to stop here, but you may find yourself overnighting while on the taxi-brousse journey between north and south Madagascar.

The Bank of Africa beside the central market changes money.

Electricity in Ihosy often works only from 5.30pm to midnight.

If you need accommodation, try **Hôtel Nirina** (r FMg50,000), which is near the taxi-brousse station, **Zahamotel** (r FMg90,000), 2km east of town, or **Relais Bara** (r FMg100,000), near the roundabout, which has hot water.

Ihosy is a transport junction where the RN13 from Fort Dauphin meets the RN7, which connects Antananarivo and Toliara. Taxis-brousse regularly ply the good 216km road between Ihosy and Fianarantsoa (FMg25,000, four to five hours), and between Ihosy and Toliara (FMg40,000, five to six hours).

Daily taxis-brousse travel along the very rough road to Fort Dauphin (FMg150,000, 36 hours), via Ambovombe.

Ranohira
The small, dusty town of Ranohira serves as a base for exploration of Parc National de l'Isalo. Acres of waving yellow grass stretch away on all sides of the town, punctuated by towering rock massifs. At sunset or sunrise, the whole vista is lit up with an unearthly red and pink glow.

Angap (☻ 7am-5pm Mon-Fri, 7am-noon & 2-5pm Sat & Sun) is down the road towards Chez Momo, 100m from the centre of town.

ACTIVITIES
The focus of activity in Ranohira is trekking in the nearby Parc National de l'Isalo. The best trekking option for budget travellers is undoubtedly **Momo Trek** (☎ 75 801 77). Debonair Momo runs an extremely efficient operation involving porters, equipment (tents, mattresses, sleeping bags and even pillows) and food from his base in the village. You choose your route and your menu, and Momo will organise everything else, including the appointment of one of the Angap guides. The only extras you pay for are your park permit (FMg50,000 for three days), camp site fee (FMg25,000) and drinks.

Prices vary according to the size of the group – a two-day, three-night trek will cost FMg315,000 per person for two people, FMg360,000 for four or more. Such is Momo's popularity that you'll usually have no trouble in finding other trekkers to bring the costs down.

Alternatively you can arrange a trek yourself; basic supplies are available in the village and several of the Angap guides can hire out tents and equipment. See p108 for details of guide fees.

SLEEPING & EATING

Le Relais de la Reine (in Antananarivo ☎ 22 336 23; www.3dmadagascar.com/relaisdelareine; standard/luxury d €60/68; set dinner €9) About 9km southwest of Ranohira, this is one of the most beautifully situated hotels in Madagascar. Its stylishly plain rooms and small pool are sculpted around natural rock formations, with a beautifully decorated bar, restaurant and sun terrace in the main building. There's also an equestrian centre on site for sunset gallops across the plains (€15 per hour). The hotel organises treks and car excursions in the surrounding area. It doesn't accept credit cards.

Isalo Ranch (BP 3, 313 Ranohira; d without/with bathroom FMg75,000/125,000, tr FMg90,000/140,000; set meal FMg40,000) A friendly mid-range place with lovely views and bright, cheerful and tastefully decorated bungalows dotted around a garden. It's 5km south of Ranohira – the taxis-brousse from Ilakaka can drop you off.

Motel Isalo (☎ 75 801 79, in Antananarivo ☎ 22 330 82; r FMg150,000; mains FMg30,000) A quiet place about 2km east of Ranohira on the north side of the main road, with rows of stone bungalows and great views. The comfortable rooms have attractive mosaic bathrooms.

Hôtel Berny (☎ 75 801 66; d without/with bathroom FMg51,000/90,000, larger rooms FMg100,000) A good option in the centre of the village, Berny is stone-clad with a cosy log fire and TV in the restaurant. It has big rooms and bathrooms, lots of hot water, and is ideal for the end of an exhausting trek.

Hôtel l'Orchidée de l'Isalo (☎ 75 801 78; d FMg91,000-71,000) A very comfortable option with a big restaurant, marble floors, stone walls and gleaming bathrooms.

Chez Momo (☎ 75 801 77; camping/bungalow FMg7500/46,000) The base for Momo's trekking operation has a convivial bar and dining room and basic bungalows with outside showers – more comfortable rooms are under construction.

GETTING THERE & AWAY

For travel from Ranohira to Ilakaka, the best option is to catch a passing taxi-brousse, hitch, or take a *taxi-ville* (FMg7500). From there, taxis-brousse leave every morning and afternoon to Toliara and Ambalavao (FMg30,000, six hours), and sometimes continue to Fianarantsoa. You may also be lucky enough to find a taxi-brousse travelling between Toliara and Antananarivo with an empty seat. One or two direct taxis-brousse each morning connect Ranohira with Ihosy, 91km to the east (FMg15,000, two hours). You could also ask around in the hotels to see if any empty tourist vehicles are going back to Antananarivo – Chez Momo (see above) is a good place to start.

Public transport from Toliara generally arrives in Ranohira between 10am and 1pm, while vehicles from the north usually arrive before 10am.

Parc National de l'Isalo

Parc National de l'Isalo (ish-*ah*-loo) covers 81,540 hectares of the eroded Jurassic sandstone massif of the same name. It's a savagely beautiful place of extraordinary, otherworldly landscapes. Its golden plains are punctuated by great craggy pinnacles of terracotta rock, valleys, waterfalls and canyons. You won't be alone in admiring Isalo's beauty, however – it's one of Madagascar's most popular parks, with 20,000 tourists visiting in 2001. If you want to get away from other visitors, you'll need to do a trek further afield, which could mean several days of walking. Alternatively, some of the park can be explored by car.

Numerous local *fady* (taboos) are in effect in l'Isalo and should be respected while trekking. One tradition requires the placing of a stone on existing cairns to ask for the fulfilment of wishes and safe travel. It's said that if your wish comes true, you should return to the cairns to say thank you. Isalo's rocky cliffs and ridges often shelter concealed Sakalava tombs – remember that it's fady to point at tombs with your finger outstretched. The best time to visit l'Isalo is in the dry season between April and October.

Just outside the park, between Isalo Ranch (above) and La Relais de la Reine (above) is **La Maison d'Isalo** (admission free; ◷ 8am-6pm) an impressive ecological museum that's especially good for children, with photos, poems and paintings illustrating the area's biodiversity.

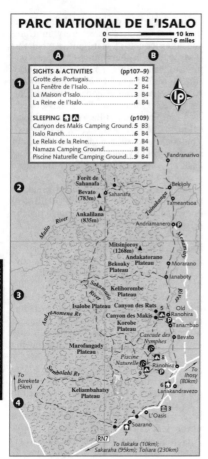

PARC NATIONAL DE L'ISALO

0 ————— 10 km
0 ————— 6 miles

SIGHTS & ACTIVITIES	(pp107–9)
Grotte des Portugais	1 B2
La Fenêtre de l'Isalo	2 B4
La Maison d'Isalo	3 B4
La Reine de l'Isalo	4 B4

SLEEPING	(p109)
Canyon des Makis Camping Ground	5 B3
Isalo Ranch	6 B4
Le Relais de la Reine	7 B4
Namaza Camping Ground	8 B4
Piscine Naturelle Camping Ground	9 B4

INFORMATION

Park permits cost FMg50,000 for three days and are available from **Angap** (7am-5pm Mon-Fri, 7am-noon & 2-5pm Sat & Sun) in the nearby village of Ranohira; staff speak English.

Official guides are required in the park, and can also be arranged at Angap – their names and competence levels are on display. Many speak English, and some speak German and Italian. Guide fees vary depending on the length and routing of your hike, but range from about FMg60,000 to FMg100,000 per group (up to four people) per day.

WILDLIFE

Although animal life isn't the park's most prominent feature, there are some interest-

ing lemur species to watch out for, including grey mouse, ring-tailed and brown lemurs, and Verreaux sifaka. The best place for lemur spotting is the aptly named Canyon des Makis. There are also over 50 bird species, including the endemic Benson's rock thrush, a small grey bird with a reddish breast.

Most vegetated areas of the park are covered with dry grassland or sparse, low deciduous woodland. Near streams and in the lush pockets of rain forest in the deeper canyons, there are ferns, pandanus, and feathery palm trees. At ground level in drier areas, look for the yellow flowering *Pachypodium rosulatum* (especially beautiful in September and October), which resembles a miniature, almost spherical baobab tree, and is often called 'elephant's foot'.

Unfortunately, fires are an ongoing problem and large swathes of l'Isalo are subject to intentional (illegal) or accidental burning. Poaching and hunting are also rampant, much to the detriment of the local ecology.

HIKING

There are several trails to follow in the park, all starting and finishing at Ranohira. A map of all the current routes is on display at **Angap** (7am-5pm Mon-Fri, 7am-noon & 2-5pm Sat & Sun) in Ranohira. On all of the hikes, carry plenty of water, or purification tablets for streams and rivers. There's little shade on Isalo's wide plains, so bring a hat and sunscreen. You will need to be self-sufficient with food. All distances quoted in this section are from Ranohira.

Piscine Naturelle is a beautiful natural swimming pool, fed by a waterfall. It's 6km one-way on foot (about 90 minutes), or 3km by car and then 3km on foot. There's a well-kept camping ground at Piscine Naturelle; both this and the pool itself can get very busy in high season. Climb the rock formations about 1km away for great sunset views.

Other popular day visits are the two canyons known as **Canyon des Makis** and **Canyon des Rats**, 9km one-way on foot (about two hours), or 16km by car, and then 1km on foot. In Canyon des Makis you will have a good chance of seeing sifakas or ring-tailed lemurs leaping through the trees. You can do the canyons and Piscine Naturelle in a day if you have access to a car to drive you some of the way between them. A good but hard one-day walk is from the Canyon des Makis to Piscine Naturelle, along a steep ridge then down the other side and across a wide plain with spectacular views.

You can hike (or scramble) from the peaceful camping ground near the dried-up river **Namaza** through deep gorges full of thick vegetation to a high waterfall called **Cascade des Nymphes**. The gorges in this area are excellent for bird-watching, and there's a good chance of seeing ring-tailed lemurs. If camping at Namaza, try not to use too much firewood.

The **Grotte des Portugais** at the far northern end of the park is a cave about 30m long and 3m high filled with animal droppings. The surrounding views are wonderful, and this part of the park sees far fewer visitors than the south. In the nearby **Forêt de Sahanafa** are natural water sources and four species of lemur, nocturnal and diurnal.

Trekking to the Grotte des Portugais is more of an expedition than visiting other park attractions as there is no direct access from Ranohira over the massif. The trip begins with a 33km walk along the front range of l'Isalo to the villages of Tameantsoa and Bekijoly. From Bekijoly, a track heads 19km west to the cave. The return trip from Ranohira takes five days on foot, or three by car and foot.

Alternatively, if you have your own transport, you can drive to the village of Andriamanero, 20km north of Ranohira, from where it's a two- to three-day trek to Grotte des Portugais and back.

CAR CIRCUITS

If you prefer to explore l'Isalo by vehicle, Angap has a half-day car circuit starting near the Maison d'Isalo and ending up at the canyons, passing several of Isalo's most striking geological formations and offering the chance to see the traditional life of the cattle-raising Bara tribe who live on the park's borders. The guide fee for this circuit is FMg75,000 per car.

The rock formation known as the **La Reine de l'Isalo** (Queen of Isalo) lies 10km south-west of Ranohira. As you are heading south, look for the rock about 10m from the road on the left. The stone is said to resemble a seated queen, and appears to some people to move as they pass by.

La Fenêtre de l'Isalo is a natural rock 'window' that lies southwest of Ranohira about 4km from Soarano. It is covered with green and orange lichen, and affords vistas over the plain. It's best viewed from below in the afternoon sun.

SLEEPING

There are several camp sites in and near the park – including those near Canyon des Makis, Piscine Naturelle and Namaza. They have varying facilities, but the best equipped, at Piscine Naturelle, has showers, toilets, sheltered dining tables and a big cooking area.

You can also camp at Isalo Ranch (p107), and at Chez Momo (p107) in Ranohira. Camping elsewhere in the park is possible if you are going on a longer trek, but you'll need to obtain permission from the Angap office. For other accommodation options, see p107.

GETTING THERE & AWAY

The beginning of various hikes in the Parc National de l'Isalo can be reached from Ranohira on foot or in a vehicle. See p107 for details of public transport to and from Ranohira.

Ilakaka

When sapphires were first discovered near Ilakaka several years ago, it grew from a tiny village to a sprawling and edgy Wild West boom town. Today, Asian gem dealers with briefcases handcuffed to their wrists, shiny suits and guns in their pockets mingle with sweat-stained miners and nonchalant prostitutes in the ramshackle main street. On the town's outskirts, eagles and kites wheel over the red earth scars of the open sapphire mines. South of Ilakaka is a gigantic casino surrounded on all sides by dusty plains.

Ilakaka is also a major taxi-brousse hub, and you may end up waiting some time here; if you need to stay there are a few motels in the centre of town.

Parc National Zombitse-Vohibasia

The 36,852-hectare Parc National Zombitse-Vohibasia protects a variety of flora and fauna, including various species of sunbird, greenbul, coua and vanga. It is also home to eight species of lemur.

ZEBU

Together with the lemur, the chameleon and the *ravinala* (travellers' palm), the zebu (Malagasy cow) is one of the most identifiable symbols of Madagascar. Zebu indicate wealth and status, and are sacrificed during ceremonies, yoked in pairs to wooden-wheeled *charettes* (carts) or chased in herds around rice fields to break up the earth for planting. Zebu are herded (and rustled) in vast numbers by the Bara and other southern tribes. According to tradition, a young Bara man must prove himself by stealing zebu in order to be considered a desirable marriage partner. Being imprisoned for zebu-rustling only enhances his appeal in the eyes of his prospective bride and her family.

Zebu have large wobbling humps on their backs and flaps of loose skin dangling lugubriously from their throats. The flap of skin increases surface area and thereby allows better regulation of heat, and the hump stores fat in case of famine. These physical advantages make zebu particularly hardy and well-adapted to their often harsh living conditions.

Zombitse, the most accessible section, extends across the main road northeast of the small town of Sakaraha, 75km from Ilakaka. There are two walking circuits in Zombitse, with several more under development here and in the other parts of the park. Permits (FMg50,000 for three days), guides (FMg15,000) and information can be obtained at the Angap offices in Sakaraha or Toliara. There's a camp site (FMg10,000) at Zombitse, but no facilities; bring all the drinking water you will need.

NORTH OF TOLIARA
Ifaty

Ifaty is the general name given to three dusty fishing villages – Ifaty, Mangily and Madio Rano – between which are strung a series of beach hotels. Ifaty is more visited than Anakao to the south of Toliara, and the beach is narrower and rockier. However diving, especially for sharks, is better here than further south.

Inland, the terrain is parched and dry with several salt flats, and a spiny forest

with good bird-watching east of the beach. In July and August, you may see migrating whales pass nearby through the Mozambique Channel.

There is nowhere in Ifaty to change money.

ACTIVITIES

The 35m coral reef running offshore along the coastline offers decent diving. While some sections of the reef are dead or damaged, it attracts a wide variety of fish. Most notable are the various shark species, which are best viewed near a break in the reef known as the Northern Pass. At both the full moon and the new moon, Ifaty experiences sharp tidal variations, so diving trips and other activities must be timed accordingly.

Dive prices are fairly standard, averaging about FMg250,000 for a *baptême* (first-time dive); FMg200,000 per dive without your own equipment; FMg250,000 for a night dive, and around FMg2,000,000 for a three- to four-day open-water PADI or CMAS certification course. Snorkelling costs FMg60,000. Most places also offer multidive or lodging and diving packages. The main dive centres and water sports operators are listed here; some are closed in May.

Bamboo Club (☎ 032 04 00 427; www.bamboo-club .com in French) At the northern end of Mangily village; offers PADI open-water certification courses, as well as fishing, water-skiing and windsurfing.

Lakana Vezo (☎ 032 04 858 60) Offers dive certification and various dive packages, plus windsurfing and fishing.

Le Grand Bleu (☎ 032 02 621 38; hotelvovotelo@ simicro.mg) Located next door to Hotel Vovo Telo but is not part of its setup. It's very highly recommended by readers and arranges standard diving packages and try dives for beginners. English-speaking.

Nautilus (☎ 032 07 418 74; fax 94 413 80) Offers certification courses and various dive packages, as well as fishing and water sports.

SLEEPING & EATING

Many hotels in Ifaty have a booking and information office in Toliara. During the July to August high season, it's worth making reservations in advance.

Ifaty's hotels are spread out over several kilometres of beach and most are about 1km to 1.5km in from the road, so if you're arriving by taxi-brousse and want to shop around, plan on a lot of hot walking. This is just a selection of what's on offer.

Hôtel Le Paradisier (☎ 94 429 14; www.paradisier .com in French; r/ste €57/84; set dinner €11) This is the most upmarket hotel in the whole Toliara area. It's beautiful two-storey bungalows, with straw roofs and patchwork quilts, overlook a good beach. Bird-watching, watersports, and whale watching in season are all on offer. There's an elegant glass-fronted dining room, and a pool was planned when we visited.

Nautilus (☎ 94 418 78; fax 94 413 80; s/d FMg220,000/ 250,000; ✦) A dive centre with futuristic white Perspex rooms shaped like Nautilus shells. Only French is spoken.

Lakana Vezo (☎ 94 426 20; d/ste with breakfast FMg180,000/230,000) Owned by the Hotel Capricorn, the prices of this upmarket hotel may well go up by the time you visit. For now, however, it's excellent value. It has big and well-decorated rooms with fans, and there is access to a good beach. There is also a diving and watersports centre on site.

La Voile Rouge (☎ 032 04 311 42; lavoilerouge@ wanadoo.mg; r without/with bathroom FMg75,000/90,000) A friendly budget beach hangout with lots of character. Right on the beach, with a lagoon nearby for swimming at low tide. A camp site is planned.

Hôtel Vovo Telo (☎ 032 02 621 38; hotelvovotelo@ simicro.mg; r FMg110,000-150,000; mains FMg30,000) This small but lively and friendly mid-range hotel and restaurant, right in Mangily village, has hammocks, excellent French food, horse riding and diving next door. There's a booking office opposite the post office in Toliara.

Bamboo Club (☎ 032 04 00 427; www.bamboo-club .com; r FMg170,000; mains FMg30,000; Ⓟ) It's a bit resorty, but well set up and comfortable with bungalows on the beach, a swimming pool, and a dive school on site. The terrace restaurant serves good Indian Ocean specialities. The booking office is in Glace des As (p105) in Toliara.

La Mira (☎ 032 02 621 44; lamiramadio@caramail .com; r without/with sea view FMg200,000/250,000; mains FMg45,000) An upmarket place 2km from Mangily in the village of Madio Rano. The rooms have high ceilings and terraces, and the food is superb, but the beach is a bit rocky.

For cheap accommodation in Mangily village, try **Chez Suzie** (d FMg45,000) or **Chez Alex**

(FMg50,000) which also has some rooms on the beach. If you'd prefer self-catering, try **Espadon Club** (☎ 032 02 36 38), which was about to open when we passed through.

GETTING THERE & AWAY

Ifaty village lies 22km north of Toliara along a rough, sandy road. Several taxis-brousse leave daily from the northern taxi-brousse station in Toliara, usually between 6am and early afternoon; the trip costs FMg15,000 and takes one to two hours. You can get out at Ifaty, Mangily or Madio Rano villages, or along the road in between, although many of the hotels are a long way from the road – just tell the driver where you'd like to be dropped. Transfers provided by the hotels for their clients cost around FMg100,000 per person, while taxis in Toliara charge around FMg150,000.

Travel to Andavadoaka and points north can also be done by boat (see following).

Andavadoaka

The tiny beach-side village of Andavadoaka lies about two-thirds of the way along the coast between Ifaty and Morombe. A reef runs offshore and diving is possible, though it is not as good as at Ifaty. The area's main attractions are its relative remoteness, its quiet beaches and its laid-back pace.

Coco Beach (FMg100,000) has simple, brightly painted bungalows and basic but inexpensive meals. **Laguna Blu Resort** (www.lagunablu resort.com in Italian; r FMg340,000) is a big Italian package-tour resort with an on-site dive centre.

Access is possible via boat from both Ifaty and Morombe. From Ifaty, allow about five hours with a speedboat run by a tour operator, or several days via local pirogue. Boat access is sometimes restricted during the rainy months of January and February.

There is no regular taxi-brousse service from either Morombe or Ifaty. If driving with your own vehicle, inquire first about road conditions.

Morombe

Morombe (Vast Beach) is a coastal town about halfway between Toliara and Morondava. As road access is difficult, it is seldom visited by tourists, and it's less appealing as a destination than the villages to the north and south of it, but it makes a useful stop if you're driving.

For inexpensive lodging try the basic **Hôtel Le Dattier** (r FMg25,000). **Hôtel Croix du Sud** (r FMg65,000) is more comfortable, with hot water. The best in town is probably **Hôtel Baobab** (r FMg80,000) with sea-view bungalows – staff can help arrange excursions in the area. Hôtel Croix du Sud and Hôtel Baobab both have restaurants.

Air Madagascar flights link Morombe a few times weekly with Morondava (FMg425,000) and Toliara (FMg425,000).

By land, Morombe lies about 285km north of Toliara along a rough and sandy road. There are usually several vehicles weekly direct to Morombe from both Toliara (FMg50,000) and Morondava (FMg60,000); allow about 18 hours from Toliara and 12 hours from Morondava. You can also try to find a pirogue to take you from either Ifaty or Morondava, a journey of several days, for which you'll need all your food and water.

SOUTH OF TOLIARA

Strung along the coast south of Toliara are a series of fairly unspoilt Vezo fishing villages, interspersed with some of the most beautifully wide and white beaches in Madagascar. Anakao, Nosy Ve and, further south, Beheloka and Itampolo are less touristy than the beach resorts to the north, if a little harder to get to. The tide doesn't go out as far in the southern beaches, making swimming possible for most of the day.

If you're just heading to the southern beaches such as Anakao or Beheloka for a few days, your best bet is to take a boat transfer from Toliara (p105).

To travel by road through the spectacularly arid landscapes between Toliara and Fort Dauphin you will need either a good 4WD vehicle or the willingness to put discomfort (and any sightseeing) aside and spend two to three days squashed into the back of a lorry. There are two routes: most travellers and all public transport follow the inland RN10 via Betioky and Ampanihy. Simple accommodation is available in both places.

During the dry season between May and late October it is possible, and often faster, to take the coastal route via Beheloka, Itampolo and Saodona. You will need your own 4WD for this as there is no regular taxi-brousse traffic, and you'll have to ford at least two rivers (which is impossible in the rainy season).

If you are travelling to Fort Dauphin by *camion-brousse*, a few things are worth noting. Firstly, the vehicles that pass the towns en route are often full, so if you're planning on doing the journey in stages, you could spend a lot of time waiting for a seat. Secondly, there's nowhere along the way to pick up provisions, so stock up on some basics in either Toliara or Fort Dauphin. If you will be riding in the back of the truck, bring along a scarf and pullover for the dust by day and the cool wind by night.

Arboretum d'Antsokay

This interesting private garden, also known as **Auberge de la Table** (☎ 032 02 600 15; admission FMg25,000; r with bathroom FMg50,000; mains FMg25,000; ⊙ 7am-8.30pm) established by a Swiss botanist, has close to 1000 species of plants endemic to the region. It's a must if you're interested in the flora of southern Madagascar. An English-speaking guide is included in the price. Simple bungalows are available if you want to stay the night, and the restaurant specialises in goat's cheese.

The arboretum lies about 17km southeast of Toliara, just a few hundred metres from the main road. To get here, catch any bus or taxi-brousse from the centre of Toliara heading towards Befety and ask to be dropped off, or charter a taxi. You can also walk from the junction to St Augustin (2km).

St Augustin

In March 1645, a bold company of English puritans landed in the bay at St Augustin, fuelled by travellers' reports of 'the fruitfulness of the soyle and the benignity of the ayre' and eager to start a colony like those that had just been established in Virginia. Sadly for the puritans, the soil proved infertile and if the air was benign, the locals weren't – they had learnt to equate foreigners with slavery. Disease and starvation took its toll, and only 12 of the 140 settlers ever returned to England. Baie St Augustin was left to become a haunt of pirates.

Today, St Augustin, with its little church spire showing white against the cliffs behind it, still has a lost, end-of-the-world feel. There's a lagoon for swimming, and several good hikes are possible from the village; 4km to the north are the **Grottes de**

Sarondrano, two caves filled with clear, blue fresh water. Nearby are several springs and a natural swimming pool – ask in the village for someone to show you the way and instruct you as to local fady.

In St Augustin village there are two local hotels, **Chez Glover** (r FMg20,000) and **Longo Mamy** (☎ 032 04 344 64; r FMg25,000). Both have simple bungalows and electricity from generators, but Longo Mamy is a bit smarter and more comfortable. Meals can be arranged at both. Inquire at Longo Mamy about excursions to the rivers, springs and caves around the village.

About 10km from Toliara on the way to St Augustin is **La Mangrove** (☎ 94 415 27; www .chez-alain.net; d/tr FMg90,000/120,000; meals FMg45,000), run by Chez Alain (p105). There's no beach, but the jetty is a relaxing spot for sunset drinks. Camping is possible and there are some good walks in the area – you can spot lemurs in a nearby cave.

St Augustin lies about 35km south of Toliara along a good road; the two towns are connected Monday to Saturday by taxi-brousse (FMg5000). Boat transfers can be arranged from Toliara (p105, FMg10,000, two hours).

Anakao & Nosy Ve

The small but fairly prosperous Vezo fishing villages of Anakao A and Anakao B are blessed with a ravishing crescent of white-sand beach, a slice of turquoise water and a fringe of dark-green vegetation. The various guesthouses on either side of the villages are the perfect place to recover from a hard journey, do a bit of diving or admire the hundreds of brightly painted canoes which set out fishing every day. Very serious divers, however, consider the diving slightly better at Ifaty to the north, especially for seeing sharks.

Most of Anakao's dive sites are around the nearby island of Nosy Ve, a former haunt of pirates. Today, it is visited mainly by those interested in exploring the offshore reef, and by fishermen from Anakao. There's a Marine Reserve fee (FMg10,000) to visit the island. Offshore about 7km south of Anakao is the island of **Nosy Satrana**, with some additional dive sites.

In between the second Anakao village and **La Reserve** is a headland with a big **Vezo cemetery**. *Aepyornis* egg-shell fragments can

be seen on the dunes around here (p124). Should you find any, remember it's illegal to collect them.

There is nowhere to change money in Anakao, so be sure you have cash – either euros or Malagasy francs.

TOURS

The tour companies listed on p104 and p105 offer trips to Anakao, starting from about FMg100,000 per person. For diving, boat transfers or whale watching, try **Safari Vezo** (☎ 94 413 81; Ave de France, Toliara), although travellers have reported a few logistical problems while using this company.

SLEEPING & EATING

Anakao villages and the surrounding beaches have several very relaxed and well-run beach hotels, some of which have booking offices in Toliara.

Budget

Longo Vezo (☎ 94 437 64; longovezo@simicro.mg; d/tr FMg90,000/120,000) The seven well-decorated bungalows here are discreetly hidden among the sand dunes, with bucket showers, verandas and solar powered electricity. Guests dine together in the evenings, so there's a relaxed and sociable atmosphere. There's also a dive centre on site, with CMAS certified instruction. Dives cost FMg225,000, while level one courses cost FMg2,000,000. Snorkelling or 4WD day trips can be organised for non-divers. It's relaxed, low-key and definitely one of the best options in Anakao. Book through the office at the pirogue port in Toliara.

Tranou Mena (Maison Rouge; r FMg70,000) South of the first village, this simple local hotel is brightly painted and charming. The rooms are a bit too basic for the price, however.

Chez Emile (☎ 032 04 023 76; r FMg40,000) Right behind the village, Chez Emile's cheap and basic rooms are breezy and quiet, and quite a long way inland among the dunes. The beach restaurant, with a view of the fishing boats, is the best place to eat cheap traditionally prepared seafood,. They're clean, have bucket showers and outside long-drop toilets; and some have electricity.

Chez Clovis (r FMg25,000) Basic rooms in a local house right in among the bustle of the village. The rooms are clean, but there are no bathrooms to speak of and only long-drop loos. Meals can be arranged.

SOUTHERN MADAGASCAR

Mid-range

La Reserve (☎ 94 437 17, 032 02 141 55; quad@dts.mg; r with bathroom FMg110,000; mains FMg38,000) Well worth the effort, around the headland from Anakao, about 45 minutes' walk or a quick pirogue ride along the beach. The beach here stretches unbroken and deserted for miles. La Reserve has the prime position, and is comfortable, well run and friendly, too. Guests and the French proprietors dine together in the evenings. The clean and new wooden bungalows are on stilts, with solar-powered electricity and amazing views. This is the beach, and the hotel, to head for if you want to surf in the area. The staff can also organise 4WD trips along the coast.

Chez Monica (☎ 032 02 275 20; d/tr FMg100,000/ 120,000) Next door to Longo Vezo, this relaxed, rustic and low-key place has a cool flotsam-decorated dining room and bar. The bungalows have outside bathrooms with bucket showers, hammocks, and little terraces. Diving can be organised here if you have your own equipment. It also has an office in the pirogue port in Toliara.

Safari Vezo (☎ 032 02 638 96, 94 413 81; d/tr FMg120,000/160,000) Nearer to the village, this long-established place is more bustling and lively than the hotels to the north. The bungalows are strung out for miles along the beach, with terraces and bucket showers. The restaurant has a maritime theme, draped in fishing nets with gingham tablecloths, and a menu that's big on seafood. Diving can be organised here, too (p104).

Le Prince Anakao (☎ 94 439 57; anakao@simicro .mg; s/tw/d FMg120,000/150,000/175,000) This hotel is more of a resort than its two neighbours, but the bungalows are very smart, with modern bathrooms. Cheaper rooms are available in the second row back from the beach. The hotel has an office at the pirogue port in Toliara. It's about a 15-minute walk from here to the village of Anakao.

GETTING THERE & AWAY

Anakao lies about 22km south of St Augustin. **Safari Vezo** (above) and **Compagnie du Sud** (☎ 94 437 21; www.compagniedusud.com in French) offer transfers via motorboat from Toliara for about FMg100,000 per person. If you are booking a hotel in advance, most provide transfers for around the same price. Alternatively, ask around at the pirogue port in Toliara for local transport, or get the taxi-brousse to St Augustin and try to find a pirogue from there (FMg25,000).

Beheloka

This low-key fishing village makes a convenient and relaxing stop if you are following the coastal route south from Toliara. The diving in Beheloka is reputed to be excellent, but no dive centre currently exists, although there is talk of one starting soon. For information and bookings check with Chez Alain (p105). **Chez Bernard** (La Canne à Sucre; ☎ 94 415 27; www.chez-alain.net; camping/d/tr FMg15,000/75,000/100,000; set dinner FMg45,000) provides simple but decent bungalows.

Taxis-brousse go to Beheloka from Toliara on Thursday (FMg50,000, 12 hours). With your own vehicle, head southeast from Toliara along the RN7 for 70km to Andranovory, then turn south on to the RN10 towards Betioky and Ambatry. About 8km south of Ambatry, turn right onto a track heading west about 75km to Beheloka. Allow up to 12 hours from Toliara. **Compagnie du Sud** (☎ 94 437 21; www.compagniedusud.com in French) offers boat transfers from Toliara to Beheloka for FMg150,000 per person, provided there is enough demand.

Parc National de Tsimanampetsotsa

The centrepiece of this 43,200-hectare park is the large, shallow **Lac Tsimanampetsotsa** with the nearby **Grotte de Mitaho** on the northeastern edge. The waters of the lake are eerily white and opaque, inhabited only by a species of blind white fish. The park supports more than 70 bird species, including thousands of pink flamingos, as well as a large population of ring-tailed lemurs. There's a FMg50,000 permit fee to visit the park.

There are two camping grounds in the reserve but you will need to be completely self-sufficient with food and water. Angap in Antananarivo or Beheloka can provide guides and hire camping equipment. Several hotels in Anakao arrange day trips to the park by 4WD.

The northern part of the lake begins 7km inland from the coast and about 10km southeast of Beheloka. There is a very rough track from Beheloka to the lake and cave. It's also possible to reach the lake by hiring a pirogue or boat down the coast from Anakao to the village of Etoetse, and then hiking inland.

Réserve Spéciale de Beza-Mahafaly

This little-visited reserve consists of two 'parcels' of land, one of sand and one of spiny forest, located 3km apart. During the dry season, the rivers are just trickles, but when it rains, they can flood and inundate the entire area. Lemur species found at the reserve include ring-tailed, fat-tailed dwarf, mouse and sportive lemurs and Verreaux sifakas, many of which are easily seen. Among other mammals is the rare large-eared tenrec. For information regarding the reserve, visit the Angap office in Toliara.

Accommodation is available in Betioky, the nearest major town to the reserve. For camping, you'll need to be self-sufficient with food. To get to Beza-Mahafaly without your own transport, you need to get to Betioky (easy by taxis-brousse from Toliara) and then walk or take a zebu cart the 17km to the reserve.

Itampolo

Itampolo is a lobster fishing village 95km south of Beheloka, another relaxing stop on the hard 4WD trip towards Fort Dauphin or a boat ride south from Anakao. Another Chez Alain enterprise, **Hôtel Sud-Sud** (☎ 94 415 27; www.chez-alain.net; camping FMg15,000, d without/with bathroom FMg75,000/120,000; set dinner FMg45,000) provides accommodation overlooking the bay.

Taxis-brousse (FMg60,000, 15 hours) go to Itampolo on Thursday and return on Saturday. It's also possible to reach Itampolo from Beheloka on the sand road along the coast (about 100km); allow at least two hours by 4WD.

To continue south from Itampolo along the coastal road, travel about 45km along a rough track to the Linta River, which you will need to drive through (only possible during the dry season). From Saodona, on the river's eastern bank, there is a poor track for about 85km to the northeast, where you join the RN10 at Ampanihy. Allow almost a full day for the stretch from Saodona to Ampanihy, and check the state of the road and river before setting out.

Ampanihy

Ampanihy (Place of Many Bats), famed for its mohair carpets, has a few amenities and is a good place to break the journey between Toliara and Fort Dauphin. Nearby are impressive stands of **spiny forest** and several good walking trails, as well as many Mahafaly tombs. For walks, it's best to go with a guide; ask at your hotel.

About 20km northwest of Ampanihy, near the village of Reakaly, is an enormous **baobab**, considered to be one of the largest and oldest still standing. There are no taxis in town, but it is easy to arrange a lift out to the tree.

Hôtel Relais d'Ampanihy (d FMg70,000) is the best place to stay the night, with decent rooms and a restaurant.

Ampanihy lies about 285km from Toliara and 225km from Ambovombe. Most days there is a direct vehicle from Ampanihy to Toliara. There is also frequent transport between Ampanihy and Betioky. Vehicles from Toliara to Fort Dauphin are often full when they pass through Ampanihy, so heading east you may need to wait a day or two for a lift.

TOMB ART

The Mahafaly and Antandroy people of southern Madagascar are renowned for their impressive tombs, the most colourful and skilfully decorated on the island. Tombs, which are constructed by the community, can take up to a year to complete. The huge monoliths, some of which can be 15 sq metres, are painted with scenes from the life of the deceased, and frequently adorned by *aloalo* – wooden posts carved with curved geometric figures. These can be family scenes or events from daily life, such as games, transport, work or sex. Carving aloalo has become an art form in itself, and representations of aloalo can be found in interiors (not to mention tourists' T-shirts) all over Madagascar.

Each stage in a tomb's construction is marked by ceremonies and the sacrifice of zebu, and the finished tombs are also adorned with zebu skulls, corresponding to the number of cattle sacrificed upon that person's death. Very important figures in Mahafaly or Antandroy society may merit as many as 100 bovine victims, but the majority of the tombs are adorned with 10 or fewer. Sadly, many of the tombs in southern Madagascar have been desecrated and robbed in the past, and are now off-limits to visitors, but some are still visible by the side of the road as you drive around the region.

The road is particularly bad between Ampanihy and Tranoroa to the east; the 40km trip can take over three hours. If you have your own vehicle, it's often faster to turn northeast at Tranoroa towards Bekitro, from where there is a track heading southeast to Antanimora on the RN13 (which rejoins the RN10 at Ambovombe).

FORT DAUPHIN (TAOLAGNARO)
pop 39,000

Fort Dauphin (its rarely used Malagasy name is Taolagnaro) is a dusty, windy and isolated town with a beautiful location along a curved sandy bay dotted with half-sunk shipwrecks. Thanks largely to the early efforts of a local hotel owner called Jean de

Heaulme, Fort Dauphin has become a popular tourist destination despite its difficulty of access. A number of excellent ecotourism projects, however, make it relatively easy to get off the beaten track and enjoy the lush, semi-tropical landscapes, stands of spiny forest and wild beaches of this corner of Madagascar.

Fort Dauphin was one of the original French territories in Madagascar. In 1643 the Société Française de l'Orient founded a settlement on a peninsula 35km to the south of the present-day town. The colonists constructed Fort Flacourt and named the surrounding settlement Fort Dauphin, after the six-year-old prince who was to become Louis XIV. The colony survived until 1674

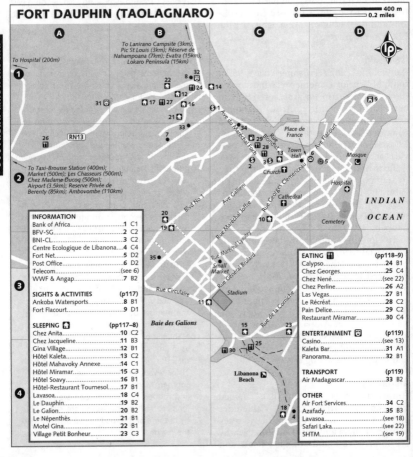

FORT DAUPHIN (TAOLAGNARO)

To Lanirano Campsite (3km);
Pic St Louis (3km); Réserve de
Nahampoana (7km); Evatra (15km);
Lokaro Peninsula (15km)

To Hospital (200m)

To Taxi-Brousse Station (400m);
Market (500m); Les Chasseurs (500m);
Chez Madame Ducoq (500m);
Airport (3.5km); Réserve Privée de
Berenty (85km); Ambovombe (110km)

Place de France

Town Hall

Mosque

Church

Cathedral

Hospital

INDIAN OCEAN

Cemetery

Blvd No 1

Baie des Galions

Small Market

Stadium

Rue Circulaire

Libanona Beach

INFORMATION	
Bank of Africa	1 C1
BFV-SG	2 C2
BNI-CL	3 C2
Centre Ecologique de Libanona	4 C4
Fort Net	5 D2
Post Office	6 D2
Telecom	(see 6)
WWF & Angap	7 B2

SIGHTS & ACTIVITIES	(p117)
Ankoba Watersports	8 B1
Fort Flacourt	9 D1

SLEEPING	(pp117–8)
Chez Anita	10 C2
Chez Jacqueline	11 B3
Gina Village	12 B1
Hôtel Kaleta	13 C2
Hôtel Mahavoky Annexe	14 C1
Hôtel Miramar	15 C3
Hôtel Soavy	16 B1
Hôtel-Restaurant Tournesol	17 B1
Lavasoa	18 C4
Le Dauphin	19 B2
Le Galion	20 B2
Le Népenthès	21 B1
Motel Gina	22 B1
Village Petit Bonheur	23 C3

EATING	(pp118–9)
Calypso	24 B1
Chez Georges	25 C4
Chez Nené	(see 22)
Chez Perline	26 A2
Las Vegas	27 B1
Le Récréat	28 C2
Pain Delice	29 C2
Restaurant Miramar	30 C4

ENTERTAINMENT	(p119)
Casino	(see 13)
Kaleta Bar	31 A1
Panorama	32 B1

TRANSPORT	(p119)
Air Madagascar	33 B2

OTHER	
Air Fort Services	34 C2
Azafady	35 B3
Lavasoa	(see 18)
Safari Laka	(see 22)
SHTM	(see 19)

0 — 400 m
0 — 0.2 miles

when, facing war with the local inhabitants and constant attacks of disease, it was abandoned. Some years later, the French returned in the form of slave traders who used Fort Dauphin as a port. At the end of the 19th century it was incorporated into the united French colony of Madagascar.

Fort Dauphin enjoys one of the sunniest and least humid climates on the east coast, although winds can be strong at any time of year, particularly between September and December. June and July tend to be rainy, with the short dry season beginning around August or September.

Information

INTERNET ACCESS

The **Fort Net** (per min FMg600) Internet café is around the corner from the post office.

MONEY

BOA (Ave du Maréchal Foch), **BFV-SG** (Ave du Maréchal Foch) and **BNI-CL** (Ave Flacourt) all change cash and travellers cheques. BOA also gives advances on MasterCard and BFV-SG gives advances on Visa cards.

POST & TELEPHONE

The post office and Telecom are both on Ave Flacourt.

TOURIST INFORMATION

The **Centre Ecologique Libanona** (☎ 92 217 54; www.andrewleestrust.org.uk) was established to help educate locals and visiting scientists about environmental issues. The centre is located in Libanona on the cliff overlooking Libanona beach.

WWF & Angap office (☎ 92 212 68), up a hill about 1km west of Ave du Maréchal Foch, has information about Parc National d'Andohahela.

Sights & Activities

On Fort Dauphin's northeastern tip is **Fort Flacourt** (admission FMg10,000; ⏰ 8-11am & 2-5pm Mon-Sat, 2-6pm Sun) built by the French in 1643. Today, little remains but a few cannons. To see what is left, and to admire the view, you can negotiate a 'fee' with a soldier at the gate who will show you around. Photos of the fort are permitted, but not of the barracks.

The cleanest and prettiest beach in Fort Dauphin itself is at **Libanona**, on the southwestern side of the peninsula. The beach along **Baie des Galions** to the north of Libanona is the place for surfing and windsurfing (late August to May only). To hire surfboards or windsurfers call in to **Ankoba Watersports** (☎ 92 215 15; ankoba@fortnet.net), near **Panorama** (p119), who can also help organise diving and fishing trips. From late June or early July until about mid-September, dolphins and humpback whales are visible offshore from the beaches around Fort Dauphin.

Tours

Several places in town that can organise tours throughout the region, including to Cap Sainte Marie and Berenty reserve. For most excursions, it's best to get a group together yourself if you are interested in cutting costs.

Air Fort Services (☎ 92 212 34; air.fort@dts.mg; Ave du Maréchal Foch) This company, which also has an office in Toliara, rents 4WD vehicles for FMg500,000 per day, arranges a variety of excursions in the southeast, and runs Réserve de Nahampoana (p120).

Azafady (☎ 92 212 65; www.madagascar.co.uk) Azafady isn't a tour operator but a volunteer organisation working on various community tourism projects around Fort Dauphin. It runs several well-equipped camping grounds in village, beach and forest sites in the area and can provide transport, camping equipment and guides to independent travellers who want to experience local life and nature while helping village communities. If you're interested in staying longer in Madagascar, ask the staff about volunteering opportunities.

Lavasoa (☎ 92 21 175; http://lavasoa.free.fr in French) This quality operator located at the Lavasoa hotel in Libanona offers trips to little-known spots throughout the region. Boat and 4WD rental can also be arranged. It has a camp site on the Lokaro Peninsula and offers boat transfers there from town for FMg250,000 per person.

Safari Laka (☎ 92 212 66) A reliable outfit based at Motel Gina with a variety of excursions to the surrounding area, including a good day trip to Evatra and the Lokaro Peninsula.

SHTM (☎ 92 212 38; fax 92 211 32) A upmarket tour company based at Le Dauphin catering mainly for package holidays. SHTM is the only option for visiting Réserve Privée de Berenty.

Sleeping

Fort Dauphin's hotels seem to have suffered more than elsewhere during the tourism crisis of 2002 – many have closed, and those that remain are often run-down and half-empty. Provided the tourists continue to return, new establishments may well have opened by the time you read this, and the old ones been given a lick of paint.

BUDGET

Chez Jacqueline (☎ 92 211 26; r with bathroom FMg50,000) Jacqueline has cute little blue bungalows, and is handy for Libanona beach. The rooms are small, breezy and have hot water.

Hôtel-Restaurant Tournesol (☎ 92 216 71; r with bathroom FMg85,000) Very clean, bright and good-value bungalows sit behind an attractive restaurant.

Chez Anita (☎ 92 213 22; bungalows FMg47,000-52,000) Rather ramshackle, but still comfortable, bungalows are arranged around a tiny garden. Some triple bungalows are also available for FMg67,000. Chez Anita is on a small street near the cathedral.

Le Népenthès (☎ 92 210 61; off Ave du Maréchal Foch; d/tr FMg75,000/130,000) A bit scruffy, but the chalet-style bungalows with wooden roofs are clean and tidy with hot water. It has a boat for hire to go to Evatra.

Hôtel Mahavoky Annexe (☎ 92 213 97; Ave du Maréchal Foch; r FMg55,000-60,000) The most basic option in town, with great views of the bay and the shipwrecks.

The camp site at Lanirano, about 3km outside Fort Dauphin, has latrines and a shower. Check with Azafady (p117) for the latest prices and availability.

MID-RANGE & TOP END

Lavasoa (☎ 92 211 75; http://lavasoa.free.fr in French; d/studio FMg200,000/250,000) This family friendly French-run guesthouse has beautifully designed bungalows in a superb location on a cliff overlooking Libanona beach. All are wooden-floored and brightly painted, with great views; some rooms have a mezzanine floor. The hotel runs a tour company (p117) and also a Pirate Camp on the Lokaro Peninsula. Book in advance as this place is very popular. There's a small cafeteria on site.

Village Petit Bonheur (☎ 92 212 60; villagepetit bonheur@fortnet.net; d/f with balcony FMg100,000/250,000; mains FMg25,000) Friendly management, beautiful sea views and big, new tiled rooms make this another excellent option near Libanona beach. The hotel also has a studio with TV and fridge for longer rentals. The owner rents out 4WD vehicles for FMg4,000,000 to go to Toliara, not including driver (FMg25,000) and petrol.

Motel Gina (☎ 92 212 66; r low/high season FMg180,000/220,000, smaller r FMg160,000) Big wooden slatted bungalows, each sleeping three to four people, have full bathtubs, stone inner walls and thatch roofs, and are set in a leafy garden. **Gina Village** (☎ 92 215 30; FMg94,000), across the road and under the same management, has similar brick-and-thatch bungalows, but is a bit simpler.

Le Dauphin (☎ 92 212 38; fax 92 211 32; d FMg150,000) Traditionally the most upmarket hotel in Fort Dauphin, this is the flagship of the de Heaulme hotel empire and the headquarters of SHTM tours, who book tours to the Berenty reserve. It's clean, bright and comfortable rather than mega-luxurious. Its sister hotel Le Galion, just across the street, is more or less of the same standard but looked rather sad and empty when we passed.

Hôtel Miramar (☎ 92 212 38; fax 92 217 50; d/tr FMg200,000/250,000) The third de Heaulme hotel in town is actually the nicest by far – it's got a good position overlooking Libanona beach, a sunny courtyard and better-maintained rooms than the other two.

Hôtel Soavy (☎ 92 213 59; d FMg200,000, smaller r FMg71,000) The best rooms here are big, airy and new, painted in bright colours and with TV. Smaller rooms are more simple, but just as clean and bright. The most basic of all, without hot water, are FMg45,000.

Eating & Drinking

Chez Georges (☎ 033 12 515 14; mains FMg25,000; ☽ breakfast, lunch & dinner) A very laid-back surf-style wooden shack on the beach. Grilled shrimp kebabs and dressed crab are specialities. It's recommended by readers as the ideal place for lunch and a cold beer. Get there early for dinner – it closes at 8.30pm if there aren't any customers.

Restaurant Miramar (mains FMg30,000; ☽ lunch & dinner) Nominally Fort Dauphin's most upmarket restaurant, the Miramar (not to be confused with Hotel Miramar up the road) has a rather limited menu of steak and fish (nothing at all for vegetarians). The outside terrace has wide views of the sea and sky, and is the perfect place for a sundowner, although it can get very windy.

Les Chasseurs (mains FMg15,000-20,000; ☽ lunch & dinner) Near the taxi-brousse station, this friendly local establishment has seafood, grills and pizzas. It's popular with volunteers and expats.

Calypso (☎ 92 216 61; mains FMg20,000; ☷ lunch & dinner) This new, Western-style place is live-ly, lit-up and busy in the evenings, with a well-decorated wooden bar and a restaur-ant serving pizzas and seafood. There are regular live music performances.

Las Vegas (mains FMg20,000; ☷ lunch & dinner) A popular local place with decent snacks and seafood early in the evenings, and Malagasy music and dancing later on. There's a caba-ret every Friday night.

Panorama (☎ 92 246 56; mains FMg20,000; ☷ lunch & dinner) Better known as a disco, the restaur-ant at the Panorama has some excellent dishes, including oysters (order in advance), steak thermidor and occasional lobster.

Several of the hotels in town also have decent restaurants, including Chez Néné at Motel Gina, Chez Anita and Village Petit Bonheur, which specialises in Malagasy dishes.

There are a few cheap hotelys in the market and near the taxi-brousse station. Chez Madame Ducoq and Chez Perline are two of the better ones, serving salads and yoghurt alongside the usual rice dishes. Pain Delice, near the BFV-SG, is a *salon de thé* with good yogurts and snacks, and a beach view.

Entertainment

For nightlife, try the disco at the **Panorama** (admission FMg7500). It plays a mix of Malagasy and Western music and is busiest on Fri-day and Saturday nights. Las Vegas (above) and Calypso (above) have regular Malagasy music and reggae concerts. Kaleta Bar, near the market, has a TV, pool tables and table football (*foosball*). There's a casino at Hôtel Kaleta.

Getting There & Away

AIR

Air Madagascar flies daily between Fort Dau-phin and Antananarivo (FMg962,000, two hours), and several times weekly between Fort Dauphin and Toliara (FMg681,000, one hour). Smaller Twin Otter planes also sometimes fly up the east coast from Fort Dauphin to Farafangana, Manakara and Mananjary; all flights to these destinations cost FMg680,000.

Air Madagascar (☎ 92 211 22) is just off Ave du Maréchal Foch, on a hill up from the Bank of Africa.

CAR

Cars are available for hire to do the trip to Toliara at Village Petit Bonheur, near Liba-nona beach, which has 4WD vehicles for around FMg4,000,000 (plus petrol) for the total trip. Drivers are FMg25,000 extra.

TAXI-BROUSSE

Fort Dauphin's taxi-brousse station is in Tanambao, in the northwestern part of town along the road leading to the airport. Roads from Fort Dauphin are rough in all directions, except for the short sealed stretch to Ambovombe.

Taxis-brousse travel from Fort Dauphin to Toliara (FMg80,000, two days) daily. This is a very rough trip, so it's best to break up the journey and spend some time explor-ing the various towns and nature reserves along the way. Taxis-brousse stop at Am-boasary (FMg12,500, two hours); Am-panihy (FMg60,000, one day); and Betioky (FMg80,000, two days).

To Ihosy (FMg175,000, 36 hours), Fian-arantsoa (FMg190,000, about 60 hours, dry season only) and Antananarivo (FMg200,000, three days), the route goes via Ambovombe and then north along the RN13. Heading towards Ihosy and Fianarantsoa, it's not feasible to break the trip until Ihosy, as it is difficult to get onward transport from the smaller villages along the way. The roads are abysmal and facilities almost non-existent, so this isn't a trip for the faint-hearted.

Getting Around

TO/FROM THE AIRPORT

The airport is 4km west of town. Taxis to/from the centre cost FMg20,000.

CAR & MOTORCYCLE

You'll need a 4WD to visit most attractions around Fort Dauphin. Rental prices average about FMg700,000 per day plus tax and fuel, and usually include a driver and unlimited kilometres. Places that rent 4WDs include Air Fort Services and Lavasoa hotel (p117). There are currently no official places to rent motorcycles or mountain bikes in Fort Dauphin.

TAXI

Taxis within town, including to the taxi-brousse station, cost FMg2000 to FMg5000 per person.

AROUND FORT DAUPHIN

The tour operators listed on p117 can arrange trips to the following places and other places close to Fort Dauphin. You can organise trips yourself by taxi-brousse to destinations along the sealed Fort Dauphin–Ambovombe road. Elsewhere, the roads are sandy and/or muddy and public transport is infrequent, so hiking, pirogues or a tour may be your only option.

Pic St Louis

The summit of the Pic St Louis (529m), which you can see around 3km north of Fort Dauphin, offers good views of the town and coast. From the base, allow two to three hours for the ascent and an hour and a half for the descent. A dawn climb is ideal, before the going gets too hot or windy. You'll need a guide to show you the way – ask in town or contact one of the tour agencies (p117).

Réserve de Nahampoana

This small **forest reserve** (admission FMg50,000; ☼ sunrise-sunset) offers a short walking circuit to see lemurs, tortoises, crocodiles, birds and a variety of endemic plants to southern Madagascar. It's a good place to visit if you want to see (and stroke) tame lemurs and don't have the time or the money to visit the Reserve Privée de Berenty. You can walk to a little waterfall, or do a boat trip on the river.

Nahampoana also makes a peaceful place to stay if you don't want to be in amongst the noise and dust of Fort Dauphin itself. There are **rooms** (r without bathroom FMg150,000) and a small restaurant (mains FMg25,000). If you stay the night you can do walks in the forest after dark to see the tiny *Microcebus* (mouse lemur).

The reserve is 7km north of Fort Dauphin. Visits can be organised with **Air Fort Services** (p117) or other travel agencies for about FMg100,000 including the entry fee, or you can charter a taxi or a pirogue.

Evatra & Lokaro Peninsula

Lokaro Peninsula is a beautiful and unspoilt area of inland waterways, green hills, barrier beaches and natural swimming holes. It lies about 15km northeast of Fort Dauphin along the coast, or about 40km by road.

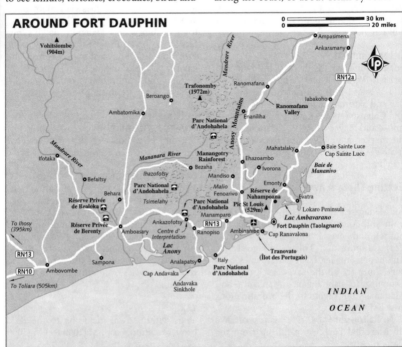

AROUND FORT DAUPHIN

0 ———— 30 km
0 ———— 20 miles

The sun sets on Antananarivo (p58)

The Rova (p66), Antananarivo

Woodcarver's workshop, Ambositra (p87)

Fianarantsoa train station (p94)

Avenue du Baobab (p139), near Morondava

Secluded cove near Lokaro Peninsula (p120)

Piscine Naturelle (p108), Parc National de l'Isalo

Spiny forest, Réserve Privée de Berenty (p122)

Day excursions offered by travel agencies in Fort Dauphin cost about FMg235,000 per person for a group of three. Most begin with a 3km drive from Fort Dauphin to the shore of Lac Lanirano, then continue by boat to Lake Ambavarano. On the northeastern end of this lake is the tiny fishing village of Evatra, from where it is about 20 minutes on foot over the hills to a good beach. Once at Evatra, you can arrange a pirogue to visit nearby Lokaro Island, or just stay and explore the peninsula itself, which has numerous opportunities for swimming, canoeing, snorkelling and walking. To reach the Lokaro area by road, you'll need a 4WD; allow about two hours from Fort Dauphin.

To reach Lokaro independently, either follow the above route, hiring a pirogue from locals, or else head northeast on foot from the customs post at the harbour in Fort Dauphin along the eastern beach for about 15km. On foot, it will take a full day; you will need to be self-sufficient with food and water. Don't do this walk on your own, as there is a risk of muggings along this beach. Alternatively, take a tent and camp in any number of the beautiful spots en route.

Once on the peninsula, options include **Pirate Camp** (bungalows FMg100,000), run by Lavasoa in Fort Dauphin, which also has a camp site and hires equipment; or the Azafady camp site, whose profits go to benefit the local community. Azafady can facilitate the pirogue journey, food and equipment if you want to stay here, or you can arrange things yourself and just use the site. Contact Azafady in Fort Dauphin for the latest prices.

Baie Sainte Luce

Baie Sainte Luce was the original site of the first French colony in Madagascar, established in 1642. It was abandoned by the settlers when they built Fort Dauphin a year later. It's a relaxing spot with a slice of well-preserved humid coastal rain forest running almost all the way down to a curved sandy beach. It's often possible to see lemurs in the forest.

The Azafady camp site here is right on the edge of the forest, and guides from the village of Sainte Luce are available to show you the lemurs, flying foxes and crocodiles

that inhabit the area. Consult the list pinned up at the camp site for details of possible excursions and prices. It's best to contact Azafady in Fort Dauphin (p117) to let the villagers know you're coming and check the camp site is available.

If you have a vehicle, drive 35km north of Fort Dauphin to the village of Mahatalaky (three hours by taxi-brousse) then continue 4km further and turn right; from there, it's 10km down to the camp site. There are no taxis-brousse on the last stretch. Alternatively, ask Azafady about transport – you can even fly in on a charter plane (FMg700,000 per plane, 20 minutes)! SHTM in Fort Dauphin may also have bungalows available on the beach – ask at the Hotel Dauphin (p118) for details.

PARC NATIONAL D'ANDOHAHELA

This 76,020-hectare park protects some of the last remnants of rain forest in southern Madagascar, as well as spiny forest and 13 species of lemurs. It also boasts over 120 species of birds, as well as a variety of amphibians and reptiles, including crocodiles. Its boundaries encompass the Trafonomby, Andohahela and Vohidagoro mountains, the last of which is the source of numerous rivers, and an important catchment area for the surrounding region.

The park is divided into four 'parcels' or areas: Tsimelahy, in a transitional zone where you will see a variety of vegetation including *Pachypodium* and baobab; Malio, made up of low-altitude rain forest; and Mangatsiaka and Ihazofotsy, both characterised by spiny forest. Each section has a trail walking; walks range from two to six hours' and take in pools and waterfalls.

The whole park is still fairly undeveloped and wild, but for self-sufficient campers it offers the chance to immerse yourself in the landscape of the area without the rather contrived atmosphere and high prices of the Reserve Privée de Berenty.

Drop into Angap (p117) in Fort Dauphin before your visit to the park, as facilities are still being developed and some notice may be needed to organise porters and guides.

The park's well-organised interpretation centre lies along the RN13 at Ankazofotsy, about 40km west of Fort Dauphin. You can buy entry permits (FMg50,000 for three days) and hire guides here. Guides speak English as well as French, and cost FMg30,000 to FMg50,000 depending on the circuit. You can combine the various circuits for longer trips. Porters are available.

Camp sites in each parcel, which cost FMg20,000 (except for the less developed camp site at Malio which costs FMg10,000). Cooking and washing facilities are available, but you will need to be self-sufficient with equipment and food.

All taxis-brousse heading west from Fort Dauphin towards Amboasary pass the interpretation centre (about FMg10,00). From here, you will need to walk into the park unless you have your own vehicle.

Tsimelahy is about 13km northwest of the interpretation centre, and is possible to visit on a long day trip. For Malio, which is about 15km northeast of the interpretation centre (4WD vehicles only), an overnight stay is best. Ihazofotsy begins about 30km northwest of the interpretation centre and can only be reached on foot or by zebu cart. To visit this part of the park you will need to stay at least one night.

RÉSERVE PRIVÉE DE BERENTY

Berenty, together with its small companion reserve of Bealoka, 7km to the north, contains nearly one-third of the remaining tamarind (or kily) gallery forest in Madagascar, nestled between the arms of a former oxbow lake on the Mandrare River.

Berenty was established in 1936 by sisal planter Henri de Heaulme in order to preserve the gallery forest. Together with the surrounding sisal plantation, the reserve is now managed by his son, Jean de Heaulme. In the decades since its founding, the reserve's relative ease of access has attracted numerous researchers, and in 1985 the WWF awarded Jean de Heaulme the Getty prize for nature conservation. Berenty was first opened to tourists in the early 1980s and has since become one of Madagascar's most visited reserves. It's a very colonial, slightly surreal place at first sight, with the endless, spiky rows of the de Heaulme sisal plantation stretching away on all sides, and neat white picket fences neatly dividing the bright-red roads that surround the bungalows.

Berenty is a controversial place. Some of the reserve's early practices – feeding lemurs bananas, sweeping leaf debris off forest tracks – led to environmental problems, and many visitors complain that the whole experience is contrived, ecologically unsound and overpriced. However, some of Berenty's early practices have been stopped, and teams have begun to remove non-endemic plant invaders such as sisal, raketa and the rubber vine from the forests.

For adventurous and mobile visitors with enough time to visit Madagascar's other, wilder parks (for example Andohahela nearby), Berenty will most probably be a disappointment. But for visitors with little time or limited mobility, Berenty offers a chance to experience the magic of the forest, observe lemurs up-close (Berenty's photo opportunities are second to none), and get an insight into the Antandroy culture of the region with a visit to the excellent **anthropological museum** on site.

Information

Berenty can only be visited on a tour organised by **SHTM** (☎ 92 212 38; fax 92 211 32; Fort Dauphin). If you are coming from Toliara, you can make arrangements through **Motel Le Capricorn** (☎ 94 426 20; capric@dts.mg).

Berenty costs €48 per room per night, plus a compulsory transfer cost of €176 for one or two people, or €78 per person for a group of three or more. For a two-night stay, the transfer costs go up to €208 for one or two people and €92 per person in a group.

The trails are easy to follow and guides are not required. In fact, one of Berenty's main attractions is the chance to wander in the forest by yourself. However, a good guide can help you with spotting wildlife, particularly on night walks in the spiny desert.

Wildlife

The Berenty forest contains over 115 plant species, providing habitat for a variety of wildlife. The 200-hectare forest, which is dominated by the tamarind, is enclosed by spiny desert, sisal plantations and the Mandrare River.

Most visitors come to see the lemurs, of which the ring-tailed are the most prominent. Many animals still have memories of unrestrained banana-feeding by tourists, and in the compound it's not unusual to see visitors being besieged by hopeful animals.

One of the best times to visit Berenty is late September/October, just after the young are born. In late September, the baby ring-tailed lemurs are clinging to their mother's undercarriage, but after a couple of weeks, they climb onto her back and cling as she goes about her daily business. Males are normally relegated to the sidelines and, except during breeding season in April or May, are largely exempted from the ring-tailed lemurs social life.

Berenty's other stars are the Verreaux sifakas, graceful white lemurs that line up carefully along the patches of open ground around the bungalows before crossing with wild and comical two-footed leaps. Also present in the forest are troupes of red-fronted brown lemurs, which scamper along the ground uttering soft grunting calls rather like furry pigs. This species was transplanted to Berenty from western Madagascar. At night, walking in the moonlit, silvery spiny forest, you might see two species of nocturnal lemur: the sportive lemur (*Lepilemur*) and the grey mouse lemur, whose eyes flash red in the beams of the torch.

Berenty is also good for bird-watching, with 83 bird species, nine of which are birds of prey. The most abundant is the Madagascan buzzard *(Buteo brachypterous)*. Others to watch for are the Madagascan coucal, the Madagascan paradise flycatcher, six species of vanga and four species of coua.

There are 26 species of reptile, including two species of chameleon, the radiated tortoise and the rare Madagascan spider tortoise.

The best times for walks along the forest paths are between about 5am and 6am, in the late afternoon, and just after dark. Although the sifakas and ring-tailed lemurs are habituated to visitors, you'll find the nocturnal lemurs and smaller creatures are still skittish.

Sleeping & Eating
Clean but extremely overpriced bungalows of differing standards all cost €48. Some are new and modern with hot water, and some are old and horrid with cold water. Set meals cost about FMg50,000. The food is average, and there is nothing whatsoever for vegetarians – try to warn SHTM (p117) in advance if you have any special dietary requirements. In high season the reserve can get very busy, so it's best to book in advance.

Getting There & Away
Berenty is situated about 80km west of Fort Dauphin and approximately 10km northwest of Amboasary. There's no way of getting there apart from on the expensive compulsory transfers organised by SHTM in Fort Dauphin. If you arrive in your own vehicle, you are most likely to be refused entry.

AMBOVOMBE
pop 57,500

Driving into the dusty and not particularly interesting town of Ambovombe will gladden the hearts of those who've arrived overland from Toliara – the town is connected to Fort Dauphin by 110km of relatively good sealed road. On Monday, the town holds a zebu market, the biggest in the south, from dawn until midmorning.

Few travellers stay in Ambovombe because the area is easily accessible from Fort Dauphin. If you do want to overnight here, try the clean **Hôtel L'Oasis** (☎ 92 700 16; d FMg50,000).

Taxis-brousse run frequently along the good sealed road between Ambovombe and Fort Dauphin (FMg10,000, three to four hours). All traffic towards Toliara also passes through Ambovombe, so finding a lift westward is generally not difficult. Ambovombe is the junction for the rugged trip along the RN13 to and from Ihosy.

RÉSERVE SPÉCIALE DE CAP SAINTE MARIE & FAUX CAP
Cap Sainte Marie (known in Malagasy as Tanjon'ny Vohimena) is the stark and wind-swept southernmost tip of Madagascar. To protect 14 species of bird and two rare species of tortoise, the surrounding area has been set aside as a special reserve. There's the chance to walk on beaches strewn with *Aepyornis* egg-shell fragments. Between July and November, you may be able to spot some migrating whales offshore.

There is little human development at the cape other than a religious statue, a lighthouse, and the former lighthouse keeper's house. At the village of Marovato, about 35km southwest of Tsiombe and about 15km northeast of Cap Sainte Marie, is a small Angap station marking the entrance to the reserve area. Guides can be arranged here for FMg50,000.

East of Cap Sainte Marie along the coast is Faux Cap (Betanty), which offers good views, but little else. There is no direct road access between the two points. **Tsiombe**, 30km north on the RN10, is the closest major town to Faux Cap and a good place to break the taxi-brousse journey between Ampanihy and Fort Dauphin.

There is no accommodation at Cap Sainte Marie. Camping is allowed, but because of the strong winds, it is usually not feasible unless you set up your tent next to or inside the lighthouse keeper's house. There's no charge, but you will need to request permission at the Angap office in Marovato. You'll also need to be self-sufficient with equipment, water and food.

Most travellers visit Cap Sainte Marie as an excursion from Lavanono, 37km to the west (about a two-hour journey by 4WD). The best accommodation option in Lavanono is **Hôtel Sorona** (gigi.lavanono@wanadoo.fr; r FMg120,000; meals FMg20,000).

Hôtel Le Cactus (d FMg36,000; meals FMg20,000), in a beautiful location overlooking the beach at Faux Cap, has basic and (if it's raining) somewhat leaky bungalows with bucket shower.

Cap Sainte Marie, just over 200km from Fort Dauphin, is difficult to reach unless you take a tour, have access to a mountain bike or a good 4WD, or have plenty of time at your disposal. Tours are best arranged in Fort Dauphin (p117). Allow about half a day between Fort Dauphin and Tsiombe if travelling by 4WD and another few hours from Tsiombe to Lavanono.

To reach the region on your own, take a taxi-brousse as far as Beloha, from where

---

THE ELEPHANT BIRD

The *Aepyornis*, commonly known as the elephant bird, was a gigantic flightless bird that inhabited southern Madagascar as recently as two or three centuries ago. Various species of *Aepyornis* existed, some standing 3m high and weighing over 300kg, some merely the size of today's ostriches. French travellers to the region in the 16th century reported local people using eggshells more than 30cm long as water vessels.

It is believed that early travellers' accounts of the elephant bird inspired the author of *Tales of the Arabian Nights* to invent the giant, eagle-like *roc* of Sinbad the Sailor, which was able to pick up an elephant in its vast talons.

No-one is sure why the birds disappeared – it is possible they may have been hunted to extinction by humans, or fallen victim to a climate change which transformed their swampy habitat into desert. Today complete *Aepyornis* eggshells can be seen in various museums in Madagascar, and fragments of shell still litter the beaches of Faux Cap. Tempting as it may be to pocket one as a souvenir, remember that it's illegal to take the shells or shell fragments out of the country.

---

there is very sporadic transport south to Lavanono. From Lavanono you will need to walk (about 30km) southeast to Cap Sainte-Marie. Cap Sainte Marie is also accessible on foot from Marovato. Alternatively, take a taxi-brousse to Tsiombe, from where it is a hot 30km walk to Faux Cap. Once off the RN10, there is no regular public transport on any of these routes. Between May and November you may be lucky and get a lift with a lobster truck.

Western Madagascar

CONTENTS

Geographically, the western side of Madagascar offers the traveller a unique dry, deciduous type of forest, towering limestone pinnacles known as tsingy (karst), and stands of bizarrely shaped baobab trees. Increasing numbers of visitors come to the region to wander in the forests of the Réserve Forestière de Kirindy and Parc National d'Ankarafantsika, float down the Tsiribihina River, or climb the tsingy in Parc National des Tsingy de Bemaraha.

The western part of Madagascar has traditionally been the area of the island with the strongest African influence. The language of the dark-skinned western peoples contains many words taken from African languages. The dominant tribe in the area is the Sakalava, who venerate the relics not of their own personal ancestors but of their ancient royal families. This belief, plus the use of spirit mediums to communicate with dead royalty, also has an African base.

Although temperatures here can climb considerably higher than those on the east coast, particularly during the April-to-December dry season, low humidity levels make the climate in the west fairly comfortable. Swimming in the sea off the west coast, however, can be a bizarre experience because of the brownish-red colour of the water. This is due to deforestation and erosion, which cause lateritic soils to be washed into the region's rivers and eventually out to sea.

WESTERN MADAGASCAR

HIGHLIGHTS

- Drifting down the **Tsiribihina River** (p134) in a wooden pirogue (dugout canoe) and camping on sandbanks at night

- Climbing among the soaring stone pinnacles of **Parc National des Tsingy de Bemaraha** (p136)

- Giant jumping rats and copulating tortoises in the **Réserve Forestière de Kirindy** (p139) and the **Parc National d'Ankarafantsika** (p133)

- Sunset among the giant trees of **Avenue du Baobab** (p139) outside Morondava

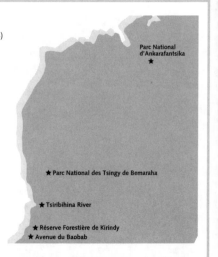

Parc National d'Ankarafantsika ★

★ Parc National des Tsingy de Bemaraha

★ Tsiribihina River

★ Réserve Forestière de Kirindy
★ Avenue du Baobab

| ■ HIGHEST POINT: 850M | ■ PRINCIPAL TRIBE: SAKALAVA |

WESTERN MADAGASCAR

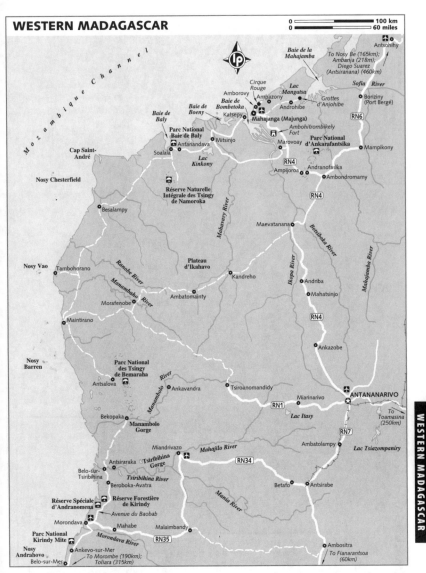

0   100 km
0   60 miles

To Nosy Be (165km); Ambanja (218km); Diego Suarez (Antsiranana) (460km)

Antsohihy

Baie de la Mahajamba

Sofia River

Cirque Rouge

Lac Mangatsa

Grottes d'Anjohibe

Borizny (Port Bergé)

RN6

Amborovy
Ampazony
Androhibe

Baie de Bombetoka

Katsepy

Mahajanga (Majunga)

Ambohitrombikely Fort

Baie de Boeny

Amboromalandy

Baie de Baly

Parc National Baie de Baly

Antanandava

Mitsinjo

Marovoay

Parc National d'Ankarafantsika

Mampikony

Soalala

Lac Kinkony

Andranofasika

Ampijoroa

Ambondromamy

RN4

Cap Saint-André

Nosy Chesterfield

Réserve Naturelle Intégrale des Tsingy de Namoroka

Mahavavy River

RN4

Maevatanana

Besalampy

Plateau d'Ikahavo

Nosy Vao
Tambohorano

Ramohe River

Manambaho River

Kandreho

Andriba

Ikopa River

Betsiboka River

Mahajamba River

RN4

Mahatsinjo

Ambatomainty

Morafenobe

Maintirano

Ankazobe

Nosy Barren

Parc National des Tsingy de Bemaraha

Manambolo River

Antsalova

Ankavandra

Tsiroanomandidy

Miarinarivo

ANTANANARIVO

RN1

To Toamasina (250km)

Bekopaka

Manambolo Gorge

Lac Itasy

RN7

Miandrivazo

Mahajilo River

Ambatolampy

Lac Tsiazompaniry

Antsiraraka
Tsiribihina Gorge

Tsiribihina River

Belo-sur-Tsiribihina

Beroboka-Avatra

RN34

Mania River

Betafo
Antsirabe

Réserve Spéciale d'Andranomena

Réserve Forestière de Kirindy

Morondava

Avenue du Baobab

Mahabe

Malaimbandy

RN35

Parc National Kirindy Mite

Morondava River

Ambositra

To Fianarantsoa (60km)

Nosy Andrahovo

Belo-sur-Mer

Ankevo-sur-Mer
To Morombe (190km); Toliara (315km)

WESTERN MADAGASCAR

MAHAJANGA (MAJUNGA)

pop 135,000

Mahajanga is a sprawling and somnolent port town with a palm-lined seaside promenade, wide avenues, shady arcades and walls draped with gorgeous bougainvillea. Mahajanga is sometimes also known as Majunga.

With its large Muslim and Indian populations, and its historical connections with Africa, Mahajanga is one of the country's more cosmopolitan centres, similar in atmosphere to many places on the East African coast. The ladies here wrap themselves in the brightly coloured cotton wraps seen in the Comoros, Zanzibar and Mombasa,

MAHAJANGA (MAJUNGA)

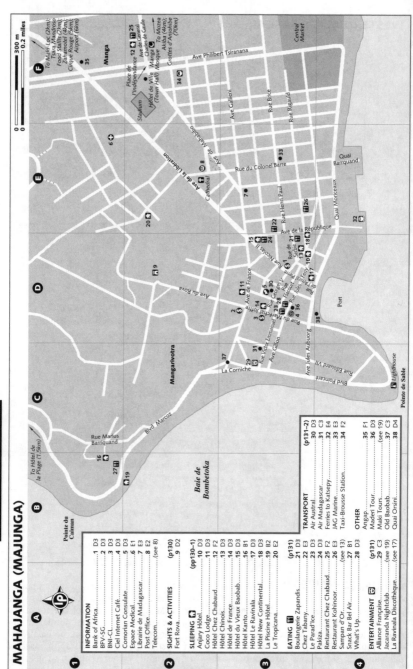

and a few Swahili-style carved doorways can be found amid the crumbling buildings in the older part of town.

North and south of Mahajanga are white-sand beaches, although some are not suitable for swimming due to sharks and strong currents.

History

Mahajanga became established in the 18th century as a trade crossroads between Madagascar, the East African coast and the Middle East. Swahili and Indian traders settled in the town, resulting in a thriving commerce in cattle, slaves, arms and spices from the Orient and the Middle East.

When the Sakalava people were eventually overcome by the Merina king Radama I, Mahajanga's inhabitants resisted, rioting and setting one section of the town on fire. Because of the capital's strategic location, in 1895 the French selected it as the base of operations for their expeditionary forces, which turned Madagascar into a French protectorate.

Orientation

Most hotels and restaurants are in the older part of town, as far as Rue du Colonel Barre in the east, with the port to the south and the bay to the west. Running beside the bay is a palm-lined promenade known as La Corniche.

At the intersection of Ave de France and La Corniche is an enormous baobab tree, thought to be well over 700 years old. It is considered *fady* (taboo) to touch it.

Information

BOOKSHOPS

Librairie de Madagascar (Ave Gallieni) sells the FTM map of the Mahajanga region, a street map of the town and French-language books, magazines and newspapers.

INTERNET ACCESS

For Internet access try **Ciel Internet Café** (Rue Jules Ferry; per min FMg300; ☯ 7.30am-8pm Mon-Fri).

MEDICAL SERVICES

Espace Medical (☎ 62 241 75; ☯ 24hr) is the best place for medical treatment.

MONEY

BNI-CL (Rue du Maréchal Joffre), opposite the Hôtel de France, **Bank of Africa** (BOA; Cnr of Rue Georges V & Rue Nicolas II) and **BFV-SG** (Rue du Maréchal Joffre) all change money.

SAKALAVA

We walked in convoy with three Sakalava men who were driving some cattle to be sold. They were tall and dark-skinned with hard features and athletes' bodies. Their black curls, stacked high on their crowns, made them look taller still. Their leader balanced a rifle of indeterminable vintage (and efficiency) across his shoulder and the other two carried assegais (clubs); all had coup-coups (machetes) in the wide belts that secured their lambas (scarves).

Our companions walked ahead, silent and aloof. Warriors like these had made the Sakalava the most powerful tribe in Madagascar and even the highly organised Hova guard of the Merina had never been able to subdue them. It was only the Sakalava's own fiery independence and clannishness that could sap the power of their greatest kings. Their aloofness, and the wild tracts of land across which they were dispersed, has historically made the Sakalava an unknown quantity. Ruling them was always, as the Merina proverb says, like carrying mud: if you hold it lightly in your open palms it spills over, and if you close your hand firmly it slips through your fingers.

An extract from Maverick in Madagascar *by Mark Eveleigh, published by Lonely Planet.*

Menabe & Boina

During most of the 17th century, the Menabe clan of the Sakalava tribe were ruled by Andriandahifatsy, the 'White King', whose ambition was to create a grand Sakalava kingdom that would take in all of Madagascar. He conquered the lands surrounding his own using firearms acquired from traders. Upon his death, a quarrel between his two sons resulted in the splitting of Sakalava into the Menabe in the south and the Boina in the north. Today, Menabe refers to the region surrounding Morondava, as well as to the Menabe people, and continues to be the seat of the southern Sakalava. Mahajanga is the most important town for the Boina or northern Sakalava.

POST & TELEPHONE
The main post office and Telecom buildings are on Rue du Colonel Barre, opposite the cathedral. There are cardphones in town.

Sights & Activities
The **Mozea Akiba** (Akiba Museum; ☎ 62 236 85; University of Mahajanga; admission FMg10,000; 🕑 9-11am & 3-5pm Tue-Fri, 3-5pm Sat & Sun) has a few small displays including photographs and explanations (some are in English) about the Grottes d'Anjohibe, the Parc National d'Ankarafantsika and Cirque Rouge. There are also some preserved fish and dinosaur bones.

Fort Rova (Ave du Rova), at the end of Rue du Maréchal Joffre, was built in 1824 by King Radama I and extensively damaged during the French–Malagasy wars of the late 19th century. The Rova offers good views over the city and bay.

There's a 50m **swimming pool** (nonguests per day FMg10,000) at La Piscine Hôtel (see below).

Tours
Several hotels and tour operators can assist you with arrangements for excursions to nearby attractions such as Cirque Rouge (FMg225,000), Grottes d'Anjohibe (FMg1,200,000), Ampijoroa (FMg425,000) and Katsepy (FMg1,100,000). Prices quoted are per person per day for a group of four. Car hire can be organised for around FMg600,000 per day. Try the following places if you'd like to organise a tour:

Maderi Tour (☎ 62 032 34; www.maderi-tour.com in French; Rue Jules Ferry) Catamaran sailing trips as far as Nosy Be, plus 4WD excursions.

Maki-Loc (☎ 62 231 21; makicd@dts.mg; Route de l'Aéroport) Car and quad hire, excursions.

Maki Tours (☎ 032 400 3400; makitours@wanadoo.mg; La Piscine Hôtel) 4WD trips and longer holidays.

Sleeping
BUDGET
Hôtel Kanto (☎ 62 229 78; Rue Marrius Barriquand; d with fan/air-con & bathroom FMg67,000/82,000; 🔀) A good-value and peaceful option up a hill behind La Piscine Hôtel. There's a view of the sea from the garden terrace, and the rooms (no net) are simple but clean. The restaurant (open Monday to Saturday) has Malagasy dishes from FMg10,000 to FMg20,000. A few cheaper rooms with shared bathroom are available.

Hôtel Chinois (☎ 62 223 79; Rue Georges V; r FMg60,000) Clean and reasonably comfortable rooms above the Sampan d'Or Chinese restaurant. No hot water in the bathrooms.

Hôtel de la Plage (Chez Karon; ☎ 62 226 94; r with bathroom FMg80,000) A once-popular beach hotel about 2km out of town that suffers these days from the lack of a beach (it's been eroded away almost entirely). The rooms are basic, but have fans and nets. No hot water in the bathrooms. Fishing excursions can be arranged here.

Hôtel Chez Chabaud (☎ 62 233 27; off Ave de Général Charles de Gaulle; d/tw FMg75,000/110,000) This hotel opposite the well-regarded restaurant of the same name has a few cleanish rooms (with fan), but a rather seedy lobby.

MID-RANGE & TOP END
Anjary Hôtel (☎ 62 237 98; anjary@dts.mg; Rue Georges V; d FMg150,000; 🔀) The rooms here are the cleanest and newest for the price in town. Each has TV and phone, and some have balconies. There's a snack bar, but no restaurant.

Coco Lodge (☎ 62 230 23; www.coco-lodge.com in French; Ave de France; d/tr with bathroom, TV & phone FMg178,000/228,000; 🔀 🔲 P) A very chic and well-designed little hotel, with pretty pink buildings built around a small pool and bar. There's also a casino on site.

Le Tropicana (☎ 6222069; www.hotel-majunga.com; Rue Administrateur; d with TV FMg200,000; 🔀 P) A set of rustic bungalows in a lush garden, full of character and often full of guests too, so reserve in advance. The restaurant has French dishes from about FMg30,000 and a good selection of wines.

La Piscine Hôtel (☎ 62 241 72/3/4; piscinehotel@ dts.mg; Blvd Marcoz; d FMg400,000; 🔀 P 🔲) Mahajanga's most upmarket hotel is chiefly famous for its fantastic 50m swimming pool. There are also great sea views, a terrace restaurant, a casino and a nightclub. The rooms have satellite TV and telephone. Cheaper rooms with a view of the 'garden' (read: road) are also available. The hotel has its own tour company for excursions.

Hôtel de France (☎ 62 237 81; h.france@dts.mg; Rue du Maréchal Joffre; s/d with TV, phone & minibar FMg275,000/ 300,000; 🔀) An upmarket hotel much used by tour groups, comfortable but rather corporate looking. There's a bar, restaurant, snack bar and casino. The blue-and-yellow restaurant has mains from FMg25,000 and a selection of Malagasy dishes.

Zahamotel (☎ 62 293 50; zahamotel.mjn@dts.mg; Amborovy; d low/high season with breakfast FMg275,000/ 400,000; ⊠ 🛖 ℗) A big, fairly tacky hotel in the village of Amborovy near the airport. There's ping-pong tables a playground, but the beach isn't much. Excursions and car hire can be arranged.

Hôtel du Vieux Baobab (☎ 62 220 35; fax 62 223 20; Ave de la République; s/d FMg112,000/152,000; ⊠) A Muslim-run hotel (so no pork or alcohol on the premises) with noisy and slightly shabby but comfortable-enough rooms (singles have fan, doubles air-con). There's a fish tank and payphone in the lobby.

Hôtel New Continental (☎ 62 225 70; nazir@dts .mg; Ave de la République; d with fan/air-con FMg140,000/ 150,000; ⊠) Another bog-standard mid-range hotel, all plastic and glass, with slightly tired but adequate rooms with TV and telephone, but no nets. Espace Tours, based here, can arrange trips in the region.

Hôtel Le Ravinala (☎ 62 229 68; Rue de L'Amiral Pierre; d with TV & phone FMg127,000; ⊠) There are some good-value rooms here if you don't mind a disco in the same building!

Eating

The least expensive places to eat are the tiny food stalls set up in the late afternoon along La Corniche. For more cheap eats, head to the suburb of Tsara Mandroso, on Route de l'Aéroport, where hundreds of brightly coloured shops and cafés are packed together along the side of the road.

Le Parad'Ice (☎ 62 231 34; Rue du Maréchal Joffre; mains FMg20,000; ☽ 7am-2pm & 5-9pm Mon-Sat, 5-9pm Sun) Has burgers, grills, sandwiches, plus a bar.

Restaurant Chez Chabaud (☎ 62 233 27; off Ave de Général Charles de Gaulle; ☽ lunch & dinner Mon-Sat, dinner Sun; mains FMg30,000) For good French cuisine, try here on the eastern edge of town, near the Manga Mosque. Portions are small, but the restaurant is cosy and the food is good.

Chez Tabany (Ave de la République; ☽ breakfast, lunch & dinner) This tiny place has mostly Western dishes from FMg22,000.

Sampan d'Or (☎ 62 223 79; Rue Georges V; mains FMg22,000) The best place for Chinese food.

Boulangerie Zapandis (Rue de Serbie; ☽ Fri-Wed) Good for patisséries, juice and coffee.

Also inexpensive, and good value, are the numerous cafés in town. **Pakiza** (Ave de la République; ☽ breakfast, lunch & dinner) and **What's Up** (Rue Flacourt; ☽ breakfast & dinner) both have samosas,

snacks, fresh juice and ice creams. **Restaurant Kohinoor** (Rue Rigauld; ☽ breakfast, lunch & dinner) and **Snack Bar Bel Air** (Blvd Marcoz; ☽ breakfast, lunch & dinner) have a good selection of local dishes from FMg10,000.

Entertainment

Mahajanga's main socialising spot is the seafront promenade, La Corniche, which fills up at sunset with people out for a stroll.

Alliance Française (☎ 62 225 52; afmajunga@dts .mg; Cnr La Corniche & Rue Victor Emmanuel) Has a program of films, exhibitions and concerts.

Popular nightspots in town include **Jacaranda Nightclub** (admission FMg10,000; ☽ Thu-Sat) at La Piscine Hôtel and **La Ravinala Discothèque** (admission FMg10,000) at Hôtel Le Ravinala.

Getting There & Away
AIR
Air Madagascar (☎ 62 224 21; Rue Victor Emmanuel) flies several times weekly to Nosy Be (FMg682,000), Antananarivo (FMg470,000) and Diego Suarez (FMg820,000).

Air Austral (☎ 62 223 91; Rue Georges V) flies twice weekly between Mahajanga and Dzaoudzi (Mayotte) for €200 one way.

BOAT
Cargo boats operate fairly often between Mahajanga and Nosy Be, although most are uncomfortable and very slow. There are also less frequent boats between Mahajanga and Diego Suarez.

A far better option is the MSL ferry **Jean Pierre Calloch** (☎ 62 226 86), which leaves weekly for Nosy Be, taking around 20 hours. See p157 for more details.

TAXI-BROUSSE
The *taxi-brousse* (bush taxi) station is east of town along the two-laned Ave Philibert Tsiranana. Vehicles go daily to Antananarivo (FMg80,000, 12 to 15 hours).

Transport north to Diego Suarez departs at least three times a week (FMg225,000, 36 hours); the best company to take you on this route is Sonatra. The road is rough – particularly the 218km between Antsohihy and Ambanja – and, apart from Antsohihy, there are few good places to break the trip. If you do decide to disembark en route, you may need to wait several days for onward transport. For Nosy Be, you will need to change vehicles in Ambanja.

In the dry season it's possible to go as far south as Soalala, Besalampy and perhaps even Maintirano, but the trip is long and difficult, and transport is scarce. To continue further south towards Morondava, you will need to either take one of Air Madagascar's small plane flights or backtrack via Antsirabe.

Getting Around
TO/FROM THE AIRPORT
The airport lies 6km northeast of town. Taxis into town charge about FMg20,000. You can catch a taxi-brousse from the road outside the airport to the taxi-brousse station in town for FMg1000.

CAR
Hôtel New Continental (p131), **Maki-Loc** (p130) and **Zahamotel** (p131) rent out 4WD vehicles for about FMg600,000 per day.

POUSSE-POUSSE
Pousse-pousse (rickshaw) rides cost from about FMg2000.

TAXI
Shared-taxis around town charge FMg3000 per ride. The standard rate for charter taxis is FMg5000 (FMg10,000 to Mozea Akiba).

WEST OF MAHAJANGA
Katsepy
Katsepy (kah-*tsep*) is a small fishing village across the estuary from Mahajanga, with a couple of swimmable beaches.

Chez Mme Chabaud (☎ 62 233 27; d FMg100,000; mains FMg20,000), under the same management as Restaurant Chez Chabaud in Mahajanga, is the place to stay and eat.

A ferry (one hour, FMg2500) runs to Katsepy twice daily from the ferry dock at the base of Ave de la République, departing Mahajanga at 7.30am (8am on Sunday) and 3pm, and departing Katsepy at 9am and 4.30pm. Ferries do not run on Monday afternoon.

Lac Kinkony
Lac Kinkony is a semiprotected wildlife reserve (15,000 hectares) about 75km southwest of Mahajanga. Its main attraction is its bird life, which includes myriad water birds, birds of prey and migratory species.

There are no facilities, so you will need to be self-sufficient. There is no regular public transport to the lake. It is sometimes possible to arrange a lift from Katsepy. If not, you can take a taxi-brousse heading towards the village of Soalala and asked to be dropped at the point nearest the lake.

EAST OF MAHAJANGA
Grottes d'Anjohibe
Some of the most impressive caverns in Madagascar are the remote Zohin' Andranoboka (Big Caves), which are sometimes referred to as the Grottes d'Anjohibe (Anjohibe Caves), after a nearby village.

Beneath two small hills wind a series of subterranean rooms and galleries adorned with stalactites, stalagmites and other cave decorations, although many have been damaged by visitors. The most extensive section of cave stretches over 5km.

The route to the Grottes d'Anjohibe is passable only between April and October. With a 4WD vehicle, follow the main road southeast from Mahajanga for 10km, then turn northeast on a seasonal track, which leads 63km to the caves.

Sporadic taxis-brousse go as far as Androhibe, about 15km before the caves, from where you will need to walk. Guides can be arranged at Androhibe or at Anjohibe. A guided day trip from Mahajanga will cost about FMg1,200,000 per person.

Cirque Rouge
The Cirque Rouge is a natural amphitheatre of eroded rock tinted in rainbow hues, including many shades of red. At one end is a stand of *ravinala* palms surrounding a freshwater spring. The best time to visit is from May to November.

A charter taxi will cost from FMg50,000 to FMg60,000 for the return trip from Mahajanga. Otherwise, it is a 45-minute walk from Amborovy village via a ravine heading inland from the coast. If you want to ask your taxi to drop you off and pick you up later, two hours should be plenty of time.

Lac Mangatsa
The tiny Lac Mangatsa (also known as Lac Sacré) is about 50km northeast of Mahajanga, near the sea. Locals come here to give thanks or to petition the help of the Boina royal ancestors, reincarnated in the form of the immense *tilapia* fish (freshwater perch) that inhabit the lake's clear waters.

Strict fady prohibits fishing and bathing, but feeding the fish is allowed. The surrounding green belt harbours wildflowers and interesting lizards, chameleons and spiders, all of which are also protected by fady. The best time to visit is from May to October.

There is no public transport to the lake; you will need to walk, take your own vehicle or charter a taxi. From the airport, go west 1km along the sealed road, then turn right on to a rough track and continue for 11km northeast to the lake. Local fady are taken seriously here, and it's best to visit with a guide. Organised tours from Mahajanga cost about FMg400,000/220,000 per person for a day/half-day trip.

SOUTH OF MAHAJANGA
Ambohitrombikely Fort
Southeast of Mahajanga, in the midst of a very dense forest, lie the ruins of the 19th-century Ambohitrombikely fort, built by the Merina. The surrounding area is littered with cannons, cannonballs, cooking utensils and other implements.

To get here, take a taxi-brousse or private vehicle along the road towards Marovoay, and then arrange a guide locally. There is a small display about the fort at the Mozea Akiba in Mahajanga.

Parc National d'Ankarafantsika
Probably the most interesting trip out of Mahajanga is to Parc National d'Ankarafantsika (130,026 hectares), which contains the only fully protected example of dry western deciduous forest in Madagascar. At the park headquarters (in the area known as Station Forestière d'Ampijoroa) is a fascinating breeding centre for two threatened tortoise species, the flat-tailed tortoise *(Pyxis planicauda)* and the very rare ploughshare tortoise *(Geochelone yniphora)*, as well as the only Malagasy endemic turtle, the *rere (Erymnochelys madagascariensis)*. This centre is jointly run by the Malagasy government and the Durrell Wildlife Trust.

INFORMATION
The driest time to visit d'Ankarafantsika is between May and November, but October and November can get very hot. Wildlife viewing is often better during the early part of the December-to-April wet season, when rainfall is still relatively light.

SURVIVAL OF THE FITTEST

The ploughshare tortoise is currently being reintroduced to its native habitat around Soalala, southwest of Mahajanga. The tortoise's vulnerability comes in part from its unusual mating habits – in order to mate with the female, the male tortoise must become aroused by fighting with other males. Males fight by locking together the front of their shells, which are shaped like a plough, before trying to tip each other over. If no other males are available to fight with, the male is unable to copulate and thus numbers drop, leading to even fewer males and a further decline in population. More details on the ploughshare's bizarre sexual habits can be found in the book *The Aye-Aye and I* by Gerald Durrell.

Park permits cost FMg50,000 for three days; these can be bought at the **Angap** (☎ 62 226 56) office in Mahajanga or at the Angap office in Ampijoroa. Guides (compulsory) can also be arranged at Ampijoroa – they cost between FMg25,000 and FMg40,000, depending on the circuit you do.

Tours to the park can be arranged through the operators listed on p130, or you can visit in your own by taxi-brousse. To appreciate the site fully you'll need at least two days. Night walks are usually very rewarding – bring a good torch.

WILDLIFE
Parc National d'Ankarafantsika is home to eight lemur species, many easily seen, including Coquerel's sifaka and the recently discovered *Microcebus ravelobensis*. You're also likely to see brown lemurs and four nocturnal species: sportive, woolly, grey mouse and fat-tailed dwarf lemurs. More elusive is the rare mongoose lemur, which is observed almost exclusively here. The best chances of seeing one are at the onset of the wet season, when this lemur is active during the day. Other mammals include two species of tenrecs and the grey long-tailed mouse *(Macrotarsomys ingens)*, which is found only in Ankarafantsika's higher elevations.

Ankarafantsika is also one of Madagascar's finest bird-watching venues, with 129 species recorded, including the rare Madagascan fish eagle and the raucous sickle-bill vanga. There are over 70 species of reptiles, including small iguanas, a rare species of leaf-tailed gecko *(Uroplatus guentheri)* and the rhinoceros chameleon *(Chamaeleo rhinoceratus)* – the male sports a large bulblike proboscis.

Vegetation consists of low and scrubby deciduous forest with pockets of such dryland plants as aloe and *Pachypodium* (or 'elephant's foot') plus baobabs and orchids.

SLEEPING & EATING

There is a **camping ground** (per tent FMg20,000), with showers and water points, and a **gîte** (per person FMg85,000) at the park headquarters in Ampijoroa; camping is also possible within the forest. Tents and mattresses can be hired from the Angap office. Meals and drinks can be arranged with advance notice.

Andranofasika village, 4km away in the direction of Ambondromamy, has several simple local *hotelys* (restaurants).

GETTING THERE & AWAY

The entrance to the park lies just off the RN4 about 114km southeast of Mahajanga and 455km from Antananarivo. To get there, catch a taxi-brousse towards Andranofasika, which depart Mahajanga early in the morning. Ask to be dropped off at Ampijoroa, 4km before Andranofasika, where you'll find the park headquarters and visitor centre.

MAHAJANGA TO NOSY BE

For those with time and fortitude, it's possible to travel the 624km stretch between Mahajanga and Nosy Be by road and boat. For the first 153km from Mahajanga to **Ambondromamy**, past the Parc National d'Ankarafantsika, the road is fairly good. It then gradually deteriorates from Ambondromamy northeast into **Mampikony**. Taxis-brousse often stop overnight in **Boriziny** (Port Bergé), which has a couple of simple hotels.

From Boriziny, a marginally better road takes you further north to **Antsohihy**, the main town in the area, with an airport, and a large missionary and educational presence. Allow anywhere from 20 to 35 hours between Mahajanga and Antsohihy.

If you've had enough of bumping around in a taxi-brousse, there are a few weekly flights connecting Antsohihy with Nosy Be, Antananarivo and Mahajanga; the Air Madagascar office is at Hôtel Biaina.

From Antsohihy north to **Ambanja**, the road is rough and quite impassable in the wet season. It can take 10 to 15 hours or more for the 218km stretch. Once in Ambanja, it's easy to find taxis-brousse to Ankify or Antsahampano, for boats to Nosy Be.

MIANDRIVAZO

Miandrivazo (Mee-an-dree-vaaz), which lies along the main road (RN 34) between Antsirabe and Morondava, enjoys the dubious honour of being the hottest place in Madagascar. Apart from this, it's on the travelling radar primarily as the starting point for boat trips along the Tsiribihina River to Belo-sur-Tsiribihina on the coast.

Unless you're starting the Tsiribihina River trip from here, it's probably best not to break your journey in Miandrivazo, as it is sometimes difficult to find reasonably priced road transport on to Morondava.

Chez La Reine Rasalimo (☎ 95 924 38; d/tr with fan FMg91,000/110,000) is the upmarket option in town. It has cool and spacious bungalows and a restaurant, and runs its own trips down the river (FMg600,000 for a three-day trip).

Slightly more downmarket but still perfectly adequate are **Hôtel Coin d'Or** (d with fan & net FMg65,000), which has great food, and **La Gîte de Tsiribihina** (d/tr with net FMg66,000/81,000), both in the village.

Air Madagascar flies weekly to Miandrivazo from Mahajanga (FMg682,000), Morondava (FMg306,000) and Antananarivo (FMg425,000).

Taxis-brousse run daily to Miandrivazo from Antananarivo (10 hours), Antsirabe (six hours) and Morondava (eight hours). Road condition is good. Taxis coming from Antananarivo reach Miandrivazo at night.

TSIRIBIHINA RIVER

Increasing numbers of visitors to Madagascar are opting to spend a leisurely three or four days drifting down the Tsiribihina (Tsi-ree-been) River in a traditional wooden pirogue. The canoes are poled and paddled by local *piroguiers* along the 146km route, passing beautiful and varied scenery, including the striking Tsiribihina Gorge, stretches of deciduous forest and fishing villages. The trip begins in Miandrivazo and ends at different points according to the time of year and the type of boat you're in. Most dry-season tours stop in the village of Antsiraraka.

As you drift along in the heat haze, you might catch the flash of a malachite kingfisher from among the reeds, hear the stentorian breathing of a herd of zebu being driven down to drink, or wave to the shrieking pot-bellied toddlers racing along the riverbank. If you're lucky, there's also wildlife to be seen – bats clinging to the cliffs, occasional crocodiles sunning themselves on the banks, or lemurs staring out from the swaying top branches of the forest. Lunch is taken in the shade of giant trees on the banks or next to cascading waterfalls, and camp is made each night on the flat white sandbanks in the shallows.

Bring along a hat and/or umbrella, sun cream, mosquito repellent, rain protection, plenty of drinking water, and a bird book if you can get hold of one – the bird-watching along the river is fantastic and not many guides know all the species. The main time for river descents is from April to November. During the rainy season, nights are spent in villages rather than on the sandbanks.

Tours

Organising a trip yourself works out marginally cheaper than going through a tour operator, but many travellers prefer to pay the extra for the sake of a French- or English-speaking guide, a reliable boat and someone to cook.

If you arrange a trip yourself, plan on spending about FMg400,000 to FMg500,000 per person for a three- or four-day trip (two days in the rainy season). Find out in advance what is included; standard items are the boat, a *piroguier* and food. If you're making your own arrangements keep in mind that many boat captains only speak Malagasy. For anything you organise yourself, you will need to supply your own tent.

Trips can be organised through agencies abroad, or in Antananarivo or Antsirabe. Some tour operators also offer more comfortable descents of the river in motorised boats known as *chalands*. See p138 and p84 for details of operators.

Miandrivazo and Antsirabe are generally the easiest places to organise river descents. A standard tour operator's trip includes a guide and *piroguiers*, boats, food and water, tents, transport to and from the river, and the first and last night's hotel accommoda-

---

MASONJOANY

In many areas of western and northern Madagascar, you will see women with their faces painted white. This facial mask, known as *masonjoany*, is supposed to protect skin from the sun, make it softer and more supple and remove blemishes. It's applied during the day and usually removed at night.

Masonjoany is made by grinding a branch from a tree of the same name against a stone with a small amount of water to form a paste. The *masonjoany* tradition persists in the Comoros, where the paste is made from ground sandalwood and coloured a startling canary yellow.

---

tion. Bargain hard, discuss your menu in advance, and try to examine the camping equipment before you pay. Organised tours cost from about FMg700,000 per person for a three-day trip with a group of four people, all-inclusive except for transport to Miandrivazo, which costs extra. Many trips combine the river descent with a trip to the Parc National des Tsingy de Bemaraha, which should cost about FMg1,600,000 per person for a group of five people. Most tour operators need at least three to four days' notice. It will work out to be less expensive if you get your own group together first. Antsirabe is probably the best place to do this.

Getting There & Away

Tour operators in Morondava or Antananarivo can arrange vehicle transfer to Miandrivazo (about FMg500,000 plus fuel one way from Antananarivo). Alternatively, you can fly or take a taxi-brousse (see opposite).

Most dry-season boat descents stop about 5km from the village of Antsiraraka, from where it's a rough three hours by 4WD to the ferry crossing into Belo-sur-Tsiribihina.

BELO-SUR-TSIRIBIHINA
pop 20,500

Belo-sur-Tsiribihina, lost in the marshes and mangroves of the Tsiribihina delta, is the finishing point for most trips down the Tsiribihina River, and a starting point for excursions to Parc National des Tsingy de Bemaraha. It's often referred to as 'Belo', and is not to be confused with the coastal village of Belo-sur-Mer, which lies further south. There's a phone box near Hanida Hôtel.

Hôtel du Menabe (d/tw FMg70,000/80,000) has bath rooms, but no fans. Some of the twin rooms are rather magnificent, with huge double beds. More downmarket is the **Hanida Hôtel** (r with/without electricity FMg32,000/30,000), which has rudimentary rooms, some with fans.

Mad Zebu (mains FMg20,000), on the main road about 250m down from Hôtel du Menabe, has decent meals.

Air Madagascar flies a few times weekly between Belo-sur-Tsiribihina and Morondava (FMg250,000). The Air Madagascar agent is at Mad Zebu restaurant.

The airport is about 5km out of town. There's usually at least one vehicle that meets the flights and can take you into town.

Camions-brousse (large trucks) run at least once daily between Belo-sur-Tsiribihina and Morondava (FMg25,000, four hours). Departures are usually in the morning from the ferry crossing just outside Belo. In the wet season, the road gets very muddy and the trip can take six hours; hitching a ride with a private 4WD is a better option. *Camions-brousse* also go to Bekopaka (for Parc National des Tsingy de Bemaraha) daily in the dry season, taking about five hours.

There is a ferry crossing en route to Morondava, about 1km south of Belo (Belo is on the north side of the river). The ferry, which takes vehicles, costs FMg2500 per person and takes 30 minutes to one hour going upstream (ie from Belo towards Morondava). It's much faster going downstream.

PARC NATIONAL DES TSINGY DE BEMARAHA

Parc National des Tsingy de Bemaraha is a Unesco World Heritage site and, at 66,630 hectares, is one of the largest and most spectacular protected areas in Madagascar.

The highlight is the jagged, cathedral-like limestone pinnacles, known as *tsingy*, formed over centuries by the movement of wind and water, and often towering several hundred metres into the air. Walkways and bridges allow visitors to climb on top of the smaller areas of *tsingy* (known as Petits Tsingy), while ropes and climbing equipment are needed to negotiate the larger pinnacles.

The maze-like *tsingy* (known as Grands Tsingy), once gave shelter to the mysterious Vazimba, the first inhabitants of Madagascar,

and the deep caves between them served as the venue for their ancient spiritual cults. Fragments of Vazimba pottery can still be found hidden in crevices between the rocks.

As well as the geological interest of the *tsingy*, the park also has excellent wildlife, with about 90 species of birds, eight species of reptiles, and 11 species of lemurs, including grey mouse, fork-marked, grey bamboo, sportive, brown and Decken's sifaka.

Information

Entry permits (FMg50,000 for three days) can be arranged at Angap at the park entrance on the north bank of the Manambolo River, near the ferry crossing at Bekopaka. Numerous circuits are available, costing between FMg25,000 and FMg120,000, depending on length. Guides (some of whom speak English) and porters (FMg20,000 per day) can also be arranged with Angap.

Much of the walking in the *tsingy* area of the park is pretty strenuous – gaps between the rocks are very narrow, bridges are high, and the caves under the pinnacles are cramped and dark. Anyone with a low level of fitness or vertigo might find exploring the *tsingy* difficult.

The area can only be visited between April and November; for much of the year rain makes it inaccessible. For both the Petits Tsingy and Grands Tsingy, bring good shoes, plenty of water and a torch for the numerous caves you'll be exploring. When in the park, remember that it's fady to smoke, go to the toilet outside designated areas, or point at the *tsingy* with your finger outstretched.

Tours

Given the difficulties of access, most travellers visit Tsingy de Bemaraha as part of an organised tour. Numerous travel agencies include a visit to the park in their offerings – see opposite, and the Tours sections under Morondava (p138) and Antsirabe (p84).

Tours usually last three days, starting and finishing in Belo-sur-Tsiribihina or Morondava. The Petits Tsingy, in the southern end of the park near the village of Bekopaka, is the most accessible section of the park. The much larger Grands Tsingy to the north is more difficult to reach, but more impressive.

Walks that can be undertaken from the park office include the Andadoany and Ankeligoa circuits, both to Petits Tsingy. Visits to Grands Tsingy are generally done part of the way in a car. If you don't have a car, one possibility is to walk from Bekopaka north towards Grands Tsingy, set up camp, explore the area (with a guide from Bekopaka), and then walk back to Bekopaka the next day.

Sleeping & Eating

Angap camping ground (tent pitch FMg10,000) This camp site, with showers and toilets, is near the park office. It's also possible to camp well north of here, several kilometres before reaching Grands Tsingy.

Auberge Chez Ibrahim (d FMg25,000) Near the ferry crossing, this place has basic bungalows and a restaurant.

Hôtel Relais des Tsingy (☎ 95 523 18; d with net FMg150,000-250,000) A much more upmarket option than Chez Ibrahim, with big bungalows – the more expensive of which have sitting areas. The hotel is about 2km from the ferry crossing. Meals cost FMg40,000.

There are several local hotelys in Bekopaka village and near the ferry crossing.

Getting There & Away

The park entrance, camp site and Petits Tsingy section are on the north side of the Manambolo River ferry crossing near Bekopaka, about 80km of very rough road north of Belo-sur-Tsiribihina. The Grands Tsingy section lies 20km further north. Reaching the park on your own is possible, but an organised tour is much easier.

In the dry season, there are *camions-brousse* three times a week from Morondava (FMg80,000, two days) to the Manambolo River ferry crossing via Belo-sur-Tsiribihina. Organised tours include 4WD transport to the park entrance. From the park entrance, the main way to reach the Grands Tsingy is by 4WD. It's a hot four-hour walk, so if you hike it, bring enough water. Rates for a chartered 4WD from Morondava to the park usually average about FMg700,000 per day.

MORONDAVA

pop 31,500

Morondava is a laid-back seaside town, with sandy streets and gently decaying clapboard houses, which makes a good base for organising a visit to Parc National des Tsingy de Bemaraha to the north. On the southern edge of town are tranquil mangrove swamps, which you can explore by

pirogue, observing kingfishers, egrets and other birds along the way.

Morondava's coastline is being steadily eroded by the sea. It's estimated that since 1900, several kilometres have been worn away, and the process continues. Stone breakwaters have had little effect, and several hotels built on the beach have succumbed to the waves and now lie in ruins.

Orientation

The main part of town, with the market, shops and hotels, lies stretched along Rue de L'Indépendance, which runs towards the sea roughly southeast to northwest. To the southwest is the peninsula of Nosy Kely, with numerous bungalows and beach resorts. It's bordered to the west by the sea and to the east by a mangrove swamp. To reach Nosy Kely, follow Rue de L'Indépendance to its terminus and then go left.

Information

MONEY

The BOA is just south of the main road on the eastern edge of town and the BFV-SG is at the western edge of town just off the beach road; both banks change money. Outside of business hours it's usually possible to change cash with merchants along the main street.

INTERNET ACCESS

Email and Internet access are possible at **Cyber Espace Oasis** (⊙ 8.30am-12.30pm & 2.30-7pm Mon-Sat, 9am-noon & 5-7pm Sun; per min FMg1500), next door to the Oasis Hôtel.

TELEPHONE

There are a few cardphones in town, including one at Hôtel Menabe.

TOURIST INFORMATION

The Centre de Formation Professionnelle Forestière (CFPF) office – for information on the Réserve Forestière de Kirindy – is near the Air Madagascar office, about 2km east out of town on the airport road. The **Angap** (☎ 95 524 20), for information on Andranomena and Kirindy Mite parks, is in the part of town called Andabatoara.

Beaches

The beach at Nosy Kely is fairly attractive, particularly at its southern end, although strong currents prevent swimming in many areas and views are marred by concrete pilings. Much better is the quiet beach called Betania at the southern end of the peninsula, although there is no accommodation here. To get to the beach, or for a trip through the mangroves, you can arrange transport with a local pirogue captain (about FMg1000).

Tours

The following places can organise excursions to Belo-sur-Mer, Parc National des Tsingy de Bemaraha, Tsiribihina River, Réserve Forestière de Kirindy or through the mangrove swamps; deep-sea fishing trips; and diving excursions:

Baobab Tours (☎ 95 520 12; Baobab Café) An upmarket agency specialising in deep-sea fishing and diving trips; it also organises reliable trips to Parc National des Tsingy de Bemaraha, Belo-sur-Mer and boat trips up and down the coast.

L'Oasis Hôtel (☎ 95 527 81, 032 04 931 60) The backpackers' choice – Jean 'le Rasta' speaks English and can organise a range of tours including Parc National des Tsingy de Bemaraha (about FMg1,500,000 per person for a group of three), Kirindy reserve (FMg960,000 per person for a day trip) and transfers to Belo-sur-Mer or further south down the coast.

Sleeping

There are several hotels in the centre of town, but most travellers stay at one of the complexes along the beach. Most beachfront places offer discounts in the low season. Several places closed down in the wake of the political crisis of 2002, and had yet to reopen when we visited.

TOWN

Central Hôtel (☎ 95 520 81; r with fan & bathroom FMg50,000) Located on the main road, this hotel has good-value, clean and cool rooms on the 2nd floor.

Hôtel Continental (☎ 95 521 52; d/tr with fan & bathroom FMg40,000/70,000) This is diagonally opposite the Central Hôtel. The rooms are old and dark, but clean and cool, plus ice creams are on sale in the reception.

BEACH

Almost all the beachfront places have restaurants. The following is just a selection of what's on offer.

L'Oasis Hôtel (☎ 95 527 81, 032 04 931 60; d FMg60,000; mains FMg25,000) A very friendly and lively establishment just off the beach, presided over by an affable local guy called

Jean 'le Rasta'. The bar/restaurant has live music in the evenings. The bungalows are basic, but adequate, although they can get noisy when there's a party in the bar. Bike hire and excursions can be arranged.

Trecicogne (☎ 95 520 69; trecicogne@dts.mg; r without/with bathroom FMg41,000/66,000; mains FMg15,000) A very pretty and good-value guesthouse right at the end of Nosy Kely peninsula, with a veranda overlooking the mangrove canal. The newly built wooden rooms have very clean bathrooms.

Baobab Café (☎ 95 520 12; tw FMg240,000; mains FMg45,000; 🍴 🅿 🏊) Morondava's most upmarket option has a nautical feel, with very smart and stylish rooms with fridge and TV. Twin rooms have two double beds, and four-person rooms are also available. There's a pool, snooker table and games room, and a tour agency for excursions and fishing trips.

Le Masoandro (Chez Maggie; ☎ 95 523 47; www.chez maggie.com; d FMg250,000; mains FMg40,000; 🏊 🅿) An upmarket place, with blue-and-white painted two-storey bungalows, stylishly decorated and with their own sitting area.

Morondava Beach (☎ 95 523 18; mbeach@arc.fr; d FMg90,000-120,000; set dinner FMg45,000) Big bungalows in smart grounds on a wide, windy stretch of beach. Room prices vary according to proximity to the sea. There's a restaurant on the beach.

Renala (Au Sable d'Or; ☎ 95 520 89; d/tr FMg150,000/ FMg230,000; 🍴) Smart bungalows in pale wood with tiled floors and telephones. There's an attractive two-storey restaurant with wooden verandas.

Les Philaos (☎ 95 521 02; d FMg90,000) Enormous pink-and-red two-storey bungalows, with rather tacky furnishings. Each has a sitting area downstairs. No restaurant.

Chez Zoro (r without/with bathroom FMg45,000/70,000) A well-decorated but badly organised local place on an unattractive stretch of beach behind L'Oasis Hôtel. Handy for town.

Eating & Drinking

Apart from the hotel restaurants, there are numerous small Malagasy hotelys along the main road and near the beach. Cheap eats and a good atmosphere can be had at Bar le Jamaica on the beach and Drugstore Restaurant in town.

Le Sun Beach (☎ 95 526 71; mains FMg25,000; 🕐 lunch & dinner Tue-Sun) Formerly known as Chez Cuccu, on the beach road near Les

Philaos, this place has the best reputation for French cuisine.

La Dolce Vita (Romantica; mains FMg20,000; ☺ lunch & dinner Thu-Tue) In town, La Dolce Vita has snacks and ice cream during the day, and pizza, pasta and fish dishes in the evenings.

La Capannina (☎ 95 520 69; mains FMg25,000; ☺ lunch & dinner Thu-Tue high season) On the beach road, this is an Italian place, with an attractive terrace. It's run by the Trecicogne hotel.

Magasin Zina (☺ Mon-Sat, mornings Sun) Next door to Hôtel Continental, this is the best-stocked of the shops for self-caterers.

The most popular evening drinking spots are the bar at L'Oasis Hôtel, Banana Café – a surprisingly flash nightclub on the beach road – and **My Lord** (☺ Tue-Sun), a lower-key local disco nearby. F Music Bar, next door to L'Oasis, is a clapboard bar with a fun vibe, plastic chairs, soul music and strong rum.

Getting There & Away
AIR
Air Madagascar flies several times weekly between Morondava and Antananarivo (FMg750,000), Toliara (FMg682,000) and Morombe (FMg425,000). The Air Madagascar office is on the road to the airport.

BOAT
Morondava is connected with the villages to the south by pirogues. Wooden cargo boats (without engines) depart weekly for Morombe. Facilities on most boats are very basic; bring sun protection and all the food and water you will need.

Alternatively, you can charter a pirogue between Morondava and Morombe, from where you can pick up a taxi-brousse to Ifaty. Plan on up to three days, depending on wind and weather, and expect to pay about FMg200,000 per person in a pirogue holding three people. Boat travel works best going from north to south from May to October, and south to north during the rest of the year, because of the prevailing winds. Bring food, water and sun protection, and something to keep your luggage dry. Jean 'le Rasta' at L'Oasis Hôtel can organise sailing trips down to Morombe with local boat captains.

TAXI-BROUSSE
The taxi-brousse between Morondava and Antsirabe (via Miandrivazo) takes about 15 hours and costs FMg70,000. Vehicles depart

daily, between about noon and 2pm, arriving in Antsirabe early the next morning.

Taxis-brousse also travel to Antananarivo (FMg100,000, 17 to 18 hours), departing Morondava around noon and arriving in Antananarivo around 6am the next day.

To Toliara (FMg120,000) there's *camions-brousse* three times weekly during the dry season, departing Morondava around noon and taking two days along a rough road.

Vehicles to Belo-sur-Tsiribihina depart once or twice every morning (FMg25,000, five hours).

Getting Around
Taxis between town and the airport cost FMg25,000, while shared-taxis in town cost FMg5000.

L'Oasis Hôtel rents mountain bikes for FMg50,000 per half day. Quad bikes and scooters can be hired from **Loc' Découverte** (☎ 032 04 70 619) on the beach road. A guided visit to Avenue du Baobab by quad costs FMg300,000, and scooters are FMg75,000/100,000 per half/full day.

AROUND MORONDAVA
Avenue du Baobab
One of the most photographed spots in Madagascar is the avenue of *Adansonia grandidieri* baobabs on either side of the road about 15km north of Morondava, along the road to Belo-sur-Tsiribihina. The best times to visit are at sunset and sunrise, when the colours of the trees change and the long shadows are most pronounced.

Avenue du Baobab can be reached on foot, by bicycle or taxi-brousse. The road from Morondava is sealed except for the final couple of kilometres. A taxi here from town will cost about FMg100,000 if you bargain.

Réserve Forestière de Kirindy
The Réserve Forestière de Kirindy, 60km northeast of Morondava, covers about 12,500 hectares and was established in the late 1970s with Swiss support through the CFPF as an experiment in sustainable logging and forest management. It's mostly visited by researchers, but travellers who spend a few days here could be rewarded with a glimpse of the fosa (*Cryptoprocta felix*). Madagascar's largest predator – not to be confused with the fossa – is an elusive puma-like creature. The best time to spot a fosa is in October. If you

don't get to see the fosa, you might be lucky enough to see one of Madagascar's most charming rodents, the giant jumping rat.

INFORMATION
Entry permits to the reserve cost FMg50,000 paid at the entrance. There are no official guides, but a few *pisteurs* (untrained guides who mostly speak Malagasy only) are available just to show the way to the best wildlife-viewing sites. A list of the trees you'll see en route is available at the park entrance.

Day visits from Morondava can be easily arranged, either by hiring a taxi (from FMg350,000 to FMg600,000) or through one of the tour companies on p138. As most of the lemurs in the reserve are nocturnal, it's worth staying a few hours after dark, or making an overnight visit.

WILDLIFE
In addition to the fosa, the reserve supports six species of lemurs, mainly nocturnal, including the fat-tailed lemur and the tiny mouse lemur (*Microcebus myoxinus*), believed to be the world's smallest primate. There are also 45 bird species and 32 reptile species, including the rare Madagascan flat-tailed tortoise *(Pyxis planicauda)*; the side-necked turtle *(Erymnochelys madagascariensis)*, which is Madagascar's only freshwater turtle; and numerous chameleons. Other creatures include the giant jumping rat, and several tenrec and mongoose species. Keep in mind that some animals hibernate during the winter months of June to August. For the best chance of seeing the fosa, a stay of at least three nights is needed.

SLEEPING & EATING
The reserve headquarters has a **camp site** (per site FMg25,000), **bungalows** (tw FMg50,000) and a **dormitory** (FMg40,000).

Basic meals (FMg10,000) are available at the reserve, as are soft drinks.

Before heading out to Kirindy, stop by the CFPF office in Morondava for information. Bring a good torch with you.

GETTING THERE & AWAY
Kirindy reserve lies about 60km northeast of Morondava, signposted off the road to Belo-sur-Tsiribihina. The reserve can be easily reached by taxi-brousse; ask drivers on the route between Morondava and Belo-

sur-Tsiribihina to let you off at the entrance to the road down to the reserve. From the main road, it's a 5km walk to the entrance.

Parc National Kirindy Mite & Réserve Spéciale d'Andranomena
Parc National Kirindy Mite lies 34km south of Morondava, while Réserve Spéciale d'Andranomena is around 30km to the northeast of the town. Neither park has any facilities for visitors, but camping is possible. Both areas offer excellent bird-watching – Kirindy Mite on a littoral lake near sand dunes and Andranomena on a seasonal lake close to many impressive baobabs. At the moment the parks are really only a destination for keen naturalists, but if you're interested in visiting, drop into the very helpful **Angap** (☎ 95 524 20) office in Morondava.

Sakalava Tombs & Funerary Art
The area around Morondava was once known for its numerous Sakalava royal tombs. These tombs were frequently decorated with well-executed, often erotic, funerary carvings representing life and fertility.

Because of desecration of some of the tombs by visitors in years past, many have been permanently closed, and those that are open to visitors are remote and inaccessible. If you have a specific interest, guides can be arranged through local villagers, or through hotels in Morondava.

BELO-SUR-MER
Belo-sur-Mer is an attractive seaside village and regional shipbuilding centre, and a good place to get away for a few days if you're in Morondava. There are several hotels here, including **L'Ecolodge du Menabe** (menabelo@aol.com; d FMg95,000; set dinner FMg45,000), a set of bungalows in a peaceful garden, where you can also organise diving in the area, and **Le Dauphin** (FMg75,000), which has simpler rooms.

Access to Belo-sur-Mer is by 4WD (from May to November) or boat. There are taxis-brousse between Belo-sur-Mer and Morondava, but the route is sometimes blocked. It's also possible to arrange transport with local pirogue captains. Allow plenty of time – the trip often takes more than a day – and bring all the water and food you may need. Motorised boat transfers (FMg300,000 per person, about two hours) can be arranged with tour operators in Morondava (see p138).

Northern Madagascar

CONTENTS

Northern Madagascar is one of the country's most cosmopolitan regions, with the descendants of African slaves, Indian traders, Arabic sailors and a sizeable French expat contingent mixing with the local Antakàrana.

For many visitors, Northern Madagascar's main attraction is the resort island of Nosy Be. Yet it would be a shame to miss out on the north's other attractions by sticking too closely to your sun bed. On the mainland – many areas of which are relatively unexplored – highlights include Parc National de Montagne d'Ambre and the beautiful Réserve Spéciale de l'Ankàrana, not to mention the lesser known islets and rock-climbing opportunities around Diego Suarez.

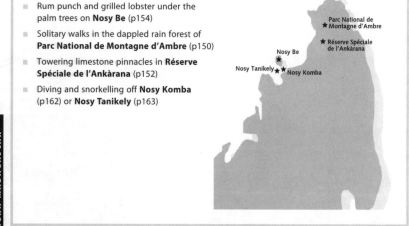

HIGHLIGHTS

- Rum punch and grilled lobster under the palm trees on **Nosy Be** (p154)

- Solitary walks in the dappled rain forest of **Parc National de Montagne d'Ambre** (p150)

- Towering limestone pinnacles in **Réserve Spéciale de l'Ankàrana** (p152)

- Diving and snorkelling off **Nosy Komba** (p162) or **Nosy Tanikely** (p163)

Parc National de
★ Montagne d'Ambre

★ Réserve Spéciale
de l'Ankàrana

Nosy Be
★

Nosy Tanikely ★ ★ Nosy Komba

■ HIGHEST POINT: 1785M   ■ PRINCIPAL TRIBE: ANTAKÀRANA

NORTHERN MADAGASCAR

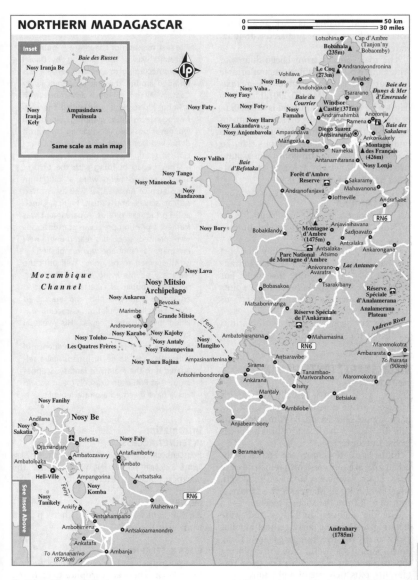

NORTHERN MADAGASCAR

0 — 50 km
0 — 30 miles

Inset

Baie des Russes
Nosy Iranja Be
Nosy Iranja Kely
Ampasindava Peninsula
Same scale as main map

Lotsohina
Bobahala (235m)
Cap d'Ambre (Tanjon'ny Bobaomby)
Vohilava
Le Coq (273m)
Andranovondronina
Andohonko
Anjiabe
Nosy Hao
Tsararano
Baie des Dunes & Mer d'Émeraude
Nosy Vaha
Nosy Fasy
Baie du Courrier
Windsor Castle (371m)
Nosy Faty
Nosy Foty
Nosy Famaho
Andramahimba
Anoronjia
Nosy Hara
Ramena
Baie des Sakalava
Nosy Lakandava
Ampasindava
Diego Suarez (Antsiranana)
Nosy Anjombavola
Ankorikakely
Mangoaka
Antsahampano
Namekia
Montagne des Français (426m)
Antanamitarana
Nosy Lonja
Nosy Valiha
Baie d'Befotaka
Forêt d'Ambre Reserve
Sakaramy
Nosy Tango
Mahavanona
Nosy Manonoka
Andranofanjava
Joffreville
Andrafiabe
Nosy Mandazona
RN6
Nosy Bory
Bobakilandy
Montagne d'Ambre (1475m)
Anjavinihavana
Sadjoavato
Antsalaka
Ankarongana
Antsalaka-Atsimo
Parc National de Montagne d'Ambre
Nosy Lava
Anivorano-Avaratra
Lac Antanavo
Bobasakoa
Tsarakibany
Réserve Spéciale d'Analamerana
Mozambique Channel
Nosy Mitsio Archipelago
Nosy Ankarea
Bevoaka
Matsaborimanga
Analamerana Plateau
Marimbe
Grande Mitsio
Ferry
Réserve Spéciale de l'Ankàrana
Androvorony
Nosy Karabo
Nosy Kajohy
Ambatoharanana
Andrevo River
Nosy Toloho
Nosy Antaly
Nosy Mangiho
Mahamasina
Maromokotra
Les Quatres Frères
Nosy Tsitampevina
RN6
Ambararata
To Iharana (90km)
Nosy Tsara Bajina
Ampasinantenina
Antsaravibe
Antsohimbondrona
Sirama
Tanambao-Marivorahona
Maromokotra
Ankàrana
Isesy
Betsiaka
Mantaly
Nosy Fanihy
Ambilobe
Andilana
Nosy Be
Anjiabeambony
Nosy Sakatia
Befetika
Nosy Faly
Beramanja
Djamandjary
Antafiambotry
Ambatozavavy
Ambato
Ambatoloaka
Ampangorina
Antsatsaka
Hell-Ville
Nosy Komba
RN6
Nosy Tanikely
Ankify
Maherivara
Andrahary (1785m)
Antsahampano
Antsakoamanondro
Ambohimena
Ankatafa
Ambanja
To Antananarivo (875km)

Getting There & Away

Air Madagascar (☎ 82 211 93; Ave Sourcouf, Diego Suarez) flies from Antananarivo to Diego Suarez daily (FMg962,000), and regularly between Sambava (FMg466,000) and Toamasina (FMg820,000), and Diego and Mahajanga (FMg577,000). Charter flights from Europe have recently begun flying into Nosy Be.

Sailing yachts regularly come into Nosy Be, and many are prepared to take passengers. Their principal destination is the Comorian island of Mayotte. For more information, see p157.

You may also be able to get a lift in a cargo boat to or from Diego Suarez. Boats go reasonably regularly from here to Mahajanga,

Sambava and Toamasina. Ask around the port for sailings, and be prepared with food, water and sun cream.

The road journey from Diego Suarez to Antananarivo is a long and uncomfortable one, particularly if you elect to do it by *taxi-brousse* (bush taxi; FMg250,000, at least two days). The worst patch of road is the 200km of the Route Nationale 6 (RN6) south of Ambanja. To Mahajanga (FMg225,000, 36 hours), expect a similarly arduous ride. To the east, the route to Ambilobe takes around two hours, followed by at least a day of pot-holes before you arrive at Iharana.

Getting Around

Air Madagascar flies from Diego Suarez to Nosy Be (FMg368,000) several times a week.

The road from Diego to Ankify (the port for boats to Nosy Be) is well-sealed and transport is easy to find along this route. For details of taxis-brousse between other points in the region, see the relevant town sections in this chapter.

Boats connect Nosy Be with various points on the mainland and surrounding islands (p157).

DIEGO SUAREZ (ANTSIRANANA)
pop 74,500

Diego, as the town is usually known (it's Malagasy name is Antsiranana), is an important port set on a small promontory jutting into one of the finest natural harbours in the Indian Ocean.

In the late 19th century the French established a naval base here, which remained until 1973. Diego saw plenty of action in WWII, when British Royal Marines arrived to wrest control of it from the Vichy French.

The old colonial buildings and wide streets give Diego a fairly genteel air, but sadly many of the buildings are falling down. Still, it's a useful base for exploring the surrounding area, with a few good restaurants, plus a couple of nightclubs.

Orientation

Diego is a sprawling place, but relatively easy to get around. Most places of interest for travellers are around Rue Colbert, on or near which most hotels, restaurants and offices are located. South of Place du 14 Octobre are taxi-brousse stations and the market.

LIBERTALIA

The first mention of the Pirate Republic of Libertalia was in a 1726 story by Daniel Defoe. According to Defoe, Libertalia was founded around the Baie des Français by Captain Misson, a French adventurer with a Robin Hood bent who sailed the seas freeing slaves and avoiding bloodshed whenever possible. He teamed up with a defrocked Dominican priest, Father Caraccioli, to set up a communist Utopia.

They began building with the help of 300 Comorians (who were a 'gift' from the Sultan of Anjouan) as well as assorted African slaves, and British, French, Dutch and Portuguese pirates. A parliament was formed, a printing press was started, crops were planted, stock was reared and a new international language was established.

All seemed to be going well until the Malagasy people living around the 'International Republic of Libertalia' descended en masse from the hills and massacred the Libertalian population. Caraccioli was killed, but Misson escaped. His eventual fate remains a mystery.

As yet, there is no physical evidence of Libertalia, and some historians have relegated it to the realms of fantasy. Sceptics argue that Robinson Crusoe's creator could easily have invented a pirate republic.

Information
INTERNET ACCESS
Housseni.com (☎ 82 225 05; Rue Lafayette; ☼ 8am-2pm & 2.30-8pm; per min FMg350) is by far the cheapest place for Internet access.

MONEY
All the banks are in the northern part of town near the port.

POST & TELEPHONE
The post office and Telecom are located on Place Foch. There are cardphones scattered around town.

TOURIST INFORMATION
Angap (☎ 82 213 20), about 2km south of town on the airport road, can provide limited information on both Parc National de Montagne d'Ambre and the Réserve Spéciale de l'Ankàrana.

DIEGO SUAREZ (ANTSIRANANA)

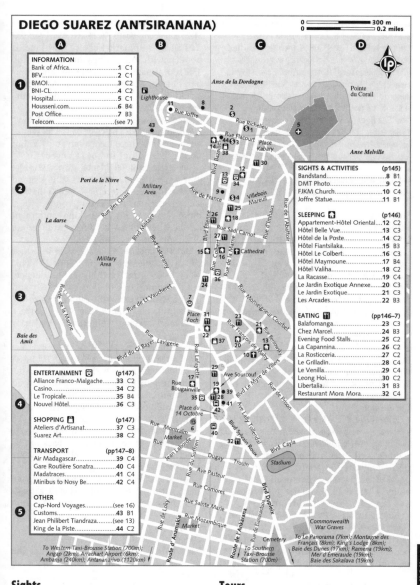

INFORMATION	
Bank of Africa	1 C1
BFV	2 C1
BMOI	3 C2
BNI-CL	4 C2
Hospital	5 C1
Housseni.com	6 B4
Post Office	7 B3
Telecom	(see 7)

SIGHTS & ACTIVITIES	(p145)
Bandstand	8 B1
DMT Photo	9 C2
FJKM Church	10 C4
Joffre Statue	11 B1

SLEEPING	(p146)
Appartement-Hôtel Oriental	12 C2
Hôtel Belle Vue	13 C3
Hôtel de la Poste	14 C2
Hôtel Fiantsilaka	15 B3
Hôtel Le Colbert	16 C3
Hôtel Maymoune	17 B4
Hôtel Valiha	18 C2
La Racasse	19 C4
Le Jardin Exotique Annexe	20 C3
Le Jardin Exotique	21 C3
Les Arcades	22 B3

EATING	(pp146–7)
Balafomanga	23 C3
Chez Marcel	24 B3
Evening Food Stalls	25 C2
La Capannina	26 C2
La Rosticceria	27 C2
Le Grilladin	28 C4
Le Venilla	29 C4
Leong Hoi	30 C2
Libertalia	31 B3
Restaurant Mora Mora	32 C4

ENTERTAINMENT	(p147)
Alliance Franco-Malgache	33 C2
Casino	34 C2
Le Tropicale	35 B4
Nouvel Hôtel	36 C3

SHOPPING	(p147)
Ateliers d'Artisanat	37 C3
Suarez Art	38 C2

TRANSPORT	(pp147–8)
Air Madagascar	39 C4
Gare Routière Sonatra	40 C4
Madatraces	41 C4
Minibus to Nosy Be	42 C4

OTHER	
Cap-Nord Voyages	(see 16)
Customs	43 B1
Jean Philibert Tiandraza	(see 13)
King de la Piste	44 C2

Sights

The **Joffre statue** (Rue Joffre) offers views over the bay and port, as does the dilapidated **bandstand** near the BFV-SG bank along the esplanade. You can buy two interesting booklets entitled *A la découverte de Diego-Suarez* from **DMT Photo** (Rue Colbert). Each has a walking tour taking in the town's historical buildings.

Tours

Tour operators that organise excursions in the region include:

Cap-Nord Voyages (☎ 82 255 06; hlcdiego.com; cap.nord.voyages@wanadoo.mg; Hôtel Colbert, Rue Colbert) Offers excursions to Montagne d'Ambre and l'Ankarana, plus car hire. It can do day trips to l'Ankàrana, followed by a drop off at Ankify for Nosy Be.

Jean Philibert Tiandraza (Bébert; ☎ 032 04 301 38; Hotel Belle Vue) A guide recommended by readers.

King de la Piste (☎ 82 225 99; www.kingdelapiste.de; Blvd Bazeilles) A German-run company that organises trips to l'Ankàrana and Montagne d'Ambre. It has its own camp sites in l'Ankàrana and two hotels on the outskirts of Diego. It also does car hire, including some no-frills budget rentals. It is a good first contact for all activities.

New Sea Roc (☎ 82 218 54; www.newsearoc.com; 26 Rue Colbert) Offering rock-climbing expeditions and equipment, New Sea Roc specialises in climbing on the Nosy Hara archipelago offshore, plus fishing, snorkelling and trekking.

Varatraz Wind Riders (☎ 82 218 54; varatraz.wr@ wanadoo.mg) Windsurf hire and trips.

Sleeping
BUDGET

Les Arcades (☎ 82 231 04; arcades@blueline.mg; Place Foch; r FMg49,000-150,000) A popular and friendly place often full of regular visitors. Rooms vary widely in comfort, price and facilities, so there's something for everyone. The best rooms are numbers 2 and 8 – if you want them, reserve in advance. There's a restaurant serving grills, burgers and Egyptian kofta, as well as a lively bar. English is spoken.

Le Jardin Exotique Annexe (☎ 82 219 33; Rue François de Mahy; d FMg95,000; **P**) A very good-value hotel with a lush garden and a tiny swimming pool. The rooms are small, neat and cheery, with quality bathrooms, fans, but no nets.

Hôtel Belle Vue (Chez Layec; ☎ 82 210 21; belle vuedie@blueline.mg; 35 Rue François de Mahy; d without/ with bathroom FMg56,000/76,000) This is another popular and often full hotel, with homely decor and a noticeboard for tours. It's a good place to get a group together for travelling. There is a fan and net in every room, and hot water in the bathrooms.

Hôtel Fiantsilaka (☎ 82 223 48; 13 Blvd Étienne; r FMg82,000-92,000; 🔀) The rooms here are fairly old and shabby, but clean, and the people are friendly. There's an upstairs restaurant with Chinese and Malagasy dishes.

MID-RANGE & TOP END

Le Jardin Exotique (☎ 82 219 33; d FMg120,000) This new upmarket place was under construction when we passed. The rooms have four-poster beds with nets, tiled floors, fans, and faintly risqué murals on the walls. There are good views over the sea, and a terrace restaurant and pool are planned.

Hôtel Le Colbert (☎ 82 232 89; www.hlcdiego.com; 51 Rue Colbert; d/tr FMg190,000/300,000; mains FMg25,000; 🔀) Diego's upmarket choice, this hotel is popular with tour groups and is often full. The rooms have a safe, telephone and mini-bar, but no mosquito nets. The Art Deco-style bistro and pavement café downstairs are stylish, but the food is average.

Hôtel Valiha (☎ 82 221 97; 41 Rue Colbert; d with bathroom FMg150,000) The cosy, well-kept white-washed rooms here have a fan and TV, but no net. Excursions can be arranged.

Appartement-Hôtel Oriental (☎ 82 239 64; Rue de la Marne; d FMg170,000-200,000; 🔀) A good choice for self-caterers – rooms have a shared kitchen and sitting room with a dining table and TV. Cooking equipment can be hired for FMg40,000, and there are discounts for longer stays.

Hôtel Maymoune (☎ 82 218 27; 7 Rue Bougainville; s/d FMg152,000/162,000; mains FMg25,000; 🔀) This place looks a bit seedy from the outside, but the rooms are good – small, pretty and bright, with a yellow-tiled floor, bathroom, TV and fridge. There's also a small terrace restaurant serving Chinese and Malagasy dishes.

Hôtel de la Poste (☎ 82 220 44; hoteldelaposte@wa nadoo.mg; Blvd Bazeilles; d FMg350,000; mains FMg35,000) A rather odd hotel with a vaguely rustic, alpine feel to the interior – lots of wood and stone cladding. The rooms have sitting areas, satellite TV and a fridge. The terrace restaurant has a view of the port.

La Racasse (☎ 82 223 64; Ave Sourcouf; d FMg150,000; 🔀) Some of the rooms out the back of this snack bar are old and shabby, and some are much better, so it pays to look at a few before deciding. The better ones have a safe, and a sitting area outside. There's a ping-pong table and TV in the restaurant.

Eating

Diego has dozens of Western-style snack bars, ice cream parlours and diners. The following is just a selection of what's on offer.

Le Venilla (☎ 82 229 25; Ave Sourcouf; mains FMg30,000-50,000; ☕ lunch & dinner Mon-Sat). The menu at this well-regarded restaurant is seasonal, but could include risotto, seafood curry or wild boar, plus a couple of regional Malagasy dishes.

Restaurant Mora Mora (☎ 032 07 788 87; Blvd Syl-vain Roux; mains FMg20,000; ☕ lunch & dinner Wed-Mon)

A cheap and friendly local restaurant with a daily menu on a blackboard. It serves an excellent green pepper sauce.

Balafomanga (☎ 82 228 94; mains FMg25,000; ☺ lunch & dinner Tue-Sun) A smart restaurant and bar with ferns, green spotlights and water features. There's a terrace outside and cosy booths at the back. The menu features seafood, dishes from Réunion, and Malagasy food.

Libertalia (☎ 032 02 208 59; Ave Lally Tollendal; mains FMg25,000; ☺ lunch & dinner Wed-Mon) This popular place has an indoor restaurant serving Malagasy and Vietnamese dishes, plus an outdoor snack bar with cheaper grills and live music on Thursday, Friday and Saturday nights.

La Rosticceria (☎ 82 236 22; Rue Colbert; mains FMg30,000; ☺ lunch & dinner Mon-Sat) A cosy, rustic and somewhat eccentric Italian restaurant, La Rosticceria serves excellent fresh pasta and a wide selection of sauces.

Chez Marcel (32 Blvd Étienne; mains FMg25,000; ☺ lunch & dinner) This lively Italian restaurant with a piano bar serves pasta and pizza. Salsa and other dance lessons are offered 3pm to 5pm Wednesday to Saturday.

Other good restaurants in town include **La Capannina** (Blvd Étienne; ☺ lunch & dinner Fri-Wed) and **Le Grilladin** (☺ lunch & dinner Tue-Sat, lunch Sun), which both have big menus featuring grills and seafood.

In the early evenings, there are good street food stands along Rue Colbert.

Leong Hoi (Rue de la Marne) is a well-stocked supermarket. Try its fresh banana tarts in the mornings – heaven.

Entertainment

Alliance Franco-Malgache (☎ 82 210 31; afdiego@ wanadoo.mg; Rue Colbert; ☺ 8.30-11.30am & 3-7.30pm Tue-Sat, 3-7.30pm Mon) The Alliance is housed in a magnificently restored Art Deco–style building, which is worth a look for its own sake. There are regular art exhibitions held here plus film screenings and concerts. The library has French books and magazines. Drop in for the latest programme of events.

On Sunday afternoon spirited football games are held in the stadium.

The town's two most popular nightclubs (much frequented by sailors from the port and male tourists, plus local lady friends) are Le Nouvel Hôtel and Le Tropicale, which are both open every night – you've

been warned. There's also a **casino** (Rue Colbert; ☺ 10am-2pm) if you fancy a game of blackjack or a go on the slot machines.

Shopping

Ateliers d'Artisanat (☎ 82 293 85; Rue Colbert) and Suarez Art, opposite Hôtel de la Poste, have local crafts for sale.

Getting There & Away

AIR

Air Madagascar (☎ 82 211 93; Ave Sourcouf) links Diego with Antananarivo (FMg962,000) daily, often via Nosy Be (FMg368,000) and Mahajanga (FMg820,000). There are also regular flights to Sambava (FMg466,000) and Antalaha (FMg639,000), as well as Maroantsetra (FMg639,000).

BOAT

There is no scheduled passenger service from Diego. However, cargo boats, which often accept passengers, travel regularly to and from coastal towns, including Mahajanga and Sambava. There are no set schedules, so you will need to inquire at the port.

TAXI-BROUSSE

Diego Suarez has three taxi-brousse stations. Most transport departs from the Southern taxi-brousse station along Route de l'Ankàrana. Vehicles heading west and north, including to Joffreville (for Parc National de Montagne d'Ambre), depart from the small western taxi-brousse station along Rte de la Pyrotechnie. Vehicles for Ambanja for Nosy Be (FMg40,000, three to five hours), Mahajanga (FMg225,000, 36 hours) and Antananarivo (FMg250,000, two days) depart from the Gare Routière Sonatra, near the Rex cinema. For Iharana, Sambava and other destinations on the northeast coast, it's quicker to get a taxi-brousse to the junction town of Ambilobe and to change into a vehicle heading east. It's possible to travel from Diego to Sambava in one long day, although taxis-brousse usually take longer. In the rainy season this route can take several days.

An alternate way of getting to Nosy Be from Diego is via a daily **minibus service** (☎ 82 210 65; Hôtel L'Orchidée, Ave Sourcouf), which costs FMg75,000, including the boat crossing to the island.

Getting Around

Diego's Arrachart airport is 6km south of the town centre. Taxis charge FMg10,000 to FMg20,000. Otherwise, you can walk out to the main road and catch a taxi-brousse into town (FMg5,000).

King de la Piste (p146) and Cap-Nord Voyages (p145) can organise 4WD rental for around FMg500,000. The driver and petrol cost extra. For motorcycle and mountain-bike rental (FMg200,000 per day), or excursions, ask at **Madatraces** (☎ 82 236 10; madatraces @malagasy.com; Ave Sourcouf).

Diego's many taxis charge FMg2500 for rides within town.

AROUND DIEGO SUAREZ
Nosy Lonja

The small island of Nosy Lonja in the middle of the Baie des Français is known in French as Pain de Sucre (Sugar Loaf) for its supposed resemblance to the much larger Sugar Loaf Mountain in Rio de Janeiro harbour in Brazil. It's off limits to foreigners and considered sacred by the Malagasy, who use it for *fijoroana* (ceremonies in which they invoke the ancestors).

Ramena

Ramena is a small village on a palm-fringed beach 18km northeast of Diego Suarez. It does not have the best beach in the Diego area, but if you have your own vehicle it's a good base for visiting Baie des Sakalava, Baie des Dunes and Mer d'Émeraude. If not, Ramena still makes a relaxing day or overnight trip from Diego.

Badamera (☎ 032 07 733 50; r FMg60,000-80,000) A few hundred metres up a hill from the beach, this popular and laid-back budget place has a shabby but stylish terrace and restaurant. The rooms and bungalows are basic and hot (no fans), but clean and with nets. Though the surrounding area is pretty scruffy, the beach isn't far away.

Villa Palm Beach (☎ 032 02 409 04; palmbeach@net courrier.com; d without/with bathroom FMg80,000/120,000) A clean and homely little guesthouse just down the hill from Badamera. Wooden-floored rooms have sea views, and there's a good selection of books and magazines to read on the beach.

Case en Falafy (☎ 032 02 674 33; www.godzilla.ch /case_en_falafy in French; r without/with bathroom FMg60,000/ 125,000; 🖳) A convivial place with a bar and a small pool. The more expensive rooms have a terrace. Tours can be arranged here.

5'Trop-Prés (☎ 032 07 740 60; r without/with bathroom FMg75,000/150,000; mains FMg22,000) A French-run place with basic but cool rooms and a terrace on the beach just up the road from Villa Palm Beach.

Restaurant L'Émeraude (☎ 032 07 725 95; set dinner FMg55,000; 🕒 lunch & dinner Wed-Mon) This rather smart restaurant on the beach has excellent food and a disco on Saturday night.

Taxis-brousse travel between Diego Suarez and Ramena (FMg5000) several times daily, though you may have to wait a while for one to leave, particularly for the trip back from Ramena. Chartering a taxi will cost about FMg100,000 return. Cycling out is no problem; see above.

Baie des Sakalava & Around

On the eastern side of the peninsula that juts into the bay east of Diego, Baie des Sakalava has a more beautiful beach than Ramena and is good for windsurfing. North of Baie des Sakalava are **Baie des Dunes** and, opposite, **Mer d'Émeraude**, where the most deserted beaches of all are to be found. You can walk from Baie des Sakalava to Baie des Dunes in about two hours, passing mangroves and interesting rock pools. To get to Mer d'Émeraude, you'll have to charter a fishing boat from Ramena or arrange a trip with one of the hotels.

Hôtel-Club de Sakalava (☎ 032 04 512 39; www .sakalava.com; d FMg150,000) arranges fishing and excursions, as well as mountain-bike, 4WD, windsurf and boat rental. To get there, head to Ankorikakely village, 13km from Diego along the main road, then walk or hitch another 5km from the signposted turn-off.

Montagne des Français

Montagne des Français is a small and attractive area of wilderness about 7km from Diego. It was named in memory of the Malagasy and French forces killed in 1942 in Allied resistance to the pro-German Vichy French forces. There are caves, the remains of a fort, abundant bird life, rock-climbing opportunities and good views across the bay. The walk towards the summit goes through interesting dry forest vegetation, and takes about two hours. To get to Montagne des Français, take a taxi-brousse along the Ramena road to King's Lodge, where you can start the walk to the top.

NORTHERN MADAGASCAR •• Joffreville **149**

King's Lodge (☎ 82 225 99; Rte de Ramena; www.king delapiste.de; d FMg200,000) is a very comfortable hotel with great views of the bay and makes a good base for climbing Montagne des Français. A botanic garden is under development, and there's detailed information available on climbing routes. The rooms include nets and fans. A set of cheaper bungalows for climbers is planned.

Le Panorama (☎ 82 225 99; Rte de Ramena; www.kingdelapiste.de; d €35; 🏊), under the same ownership as King's Lodge, is a more upmarket hotel a bit further along the same road. It has a huge swimming pool and attractive wooden bungalows on a rather dry hillside.

Windsor Castle

This 391m-high rock formation lies about 2km north of the village of Andramahimba, northwest of Diego Suarez. It served as a French fort and lookout, and was taken by the occupying British in 1942. A decaying stairway leads to the top, with good views over the **Baie du Courrier**.

Windsor Castle can only be accessed by 4WD vehicle. Follow the route west along the bay for 20km and turn north at Antsahampano. At the 32km point from Diego Suarez (which is 12km beyond Antsahampano), turn west down a track and continue for a further 5km.

Organised tours from Diego Suarez cost about FMg175,000 per person with a group of four.

THE SACRED CROCODILES OF LAC ANTANAVO

According to local tradition, Lac Antanavo lies on the site of a village that was magically flooded after its inhabitants refused to offer water to a passing sorcerer. The crocodiles that inhabit the lake are believed to be descendants of the unfortunate villagers.

Minor feeding rituals and offerings take place, usually on Saturday, with zebu meat used to attract the crocodiles to shore. It costs about FMg20,000 to watch.

Lac Antanavo – also known as Lac Sacré – is located south of Diego Suarez just off the Ambilobe to Antsiranana road. Take a taxi-brousse to Anivorano–Avaratra, on the main road about 75km south of Antsiranana, from where it's a 4km walk to the lake.

JOFFREVILLE

Established in 1902, Joffreville was once a pleasure resort for the French military, and it's easy to see why. Although the main reason to come here is to visit the adjacent Parc National de Montagne d'Ambre, this little village has a wonderfully relaxing and peaceful feel to it, with lovely views on all sides and several excellent hotels. There is an Angap office here, but it doesn't have much information – you need to go to the park headquarters.

Sleeping

Fontenay (☎ 82 236 99; cts@wanadoo.mg; r €115) This luxurious and charming hotel has very chic bungalows with stone floors, huge wood-and-marble bathrooms, CD players and four-poster beds. The restaurant in the old farmhouse, built in 1904, features a chimney designed by Gustave Eiffel, of the Tower fame. The hotel also has an orchid garden, giant tortoises and a private nature reserve with lemurs, reptiles, birds and great views over the bay of Diego. English is spoken, and excursions can be organised.

Nature Lodge (☎ 032 07 123 06; www.naturelodge -ambre.com; d €40; dinner €9) Almost as beautiful as Fontenay, and considerably cheaper, this new hotel has wooden safari-lodge style cottages with chic interiors and amazing views, and a well-decorated thatched dining room.

Auberge Sakay Tany (☎ 032 04 281 22; d/tr FMg65,000/70,000; set dinner FMg45,000) A simple, quaint guesthouse with lots of character. The three rustic, brightly painted rooms in the house share a bathroom, and there are a couple of cheaper outside rooms in the garden.

Chez Henriette (r FMg40,000; dinner FMg30,000) Another simple place with basic rooms and a little restaurant and snack bar.

The Village Store sells a few basics, but if you plan on camping in the park, you'll need to get food and other supplies in Diego. All the hotels do meals of varying standards.

Getting There & Away

Taxis-brousse run frequently from the western taxi-brousse station in Diego Suarez to Joffreville (FMg7500, two hours), 32km southwest.

You can also hire a taxi from Diego Suarez for the day from about FMg80,000 each way, including waiting time. Once in Joffreville, ask around for a driver called Armand, who will do trips up to Parc National de Montagne d'Ambre in his orange Renault 4. If you can't find him, you'll have to walk or hitch the 4km uphill to the park entrance.

PARC NATIONAL DE MONTAGNE D'AMBRE

Covering 18,200 hectares of a prominent volcanic massif, Parc National de Montagne d'Ambre is one of northern Madagascar's most visited natural attractions. All tourist development is in the accessible northern area of the park. Self-guided trails are allowed in this area, giving visitors the chance to wander blissfully alone in the magical, sun-dappled forest, perhaps stopping by one of the misty waterfalls or pausing to return the stares of a group of lemurs from high in the trees. Day visits are easily arranged from Diego, and the camp site in the forest is a lovely spot for a picnic.

Information

Angap (8am-4pm), at the park entrance a few kilometres southwest of Joffreville, can help with information, permits (FMg50,000 for three days) and guides, should you need them. The office also distributes a leaflet with a map of the self-guided trails and some information about the park.

Information about hiking in the southern reaches of the park is very sketchy; staff at the Angap offices in Diego Suarez and at the park don't know any of the routes, and no detailed maps exist.

If you want to do any serious hiking in the southern sections of the park, a guide is compulsory, and must be arranged in advance. Guide fees range from about FMg25,000 to FMg75,000 per group. The fee for night walks is FMg15,000 per group per hour. Recommended guides include Angelique and Angelin (twins!) and Laudea or Antonio, who speak English.

The park is ideal for walking during the dry season, and has about 20km of well-maintained tracks. At any time of year, come prepared for rain and leeches. During the high season, it can get very busy with package tours and groups.

Wildlife

Of the seven species of lemurs found in the park, the most notable are the crowned lemur and Sanford's lemur. Others include the rufous mouse lemur, the dwarf and northern sportive lemurs, the aye-aye and the local Montagne d'Ambre fork-marked lemur. Among other mammals, the ring-tailed mongoose is probably the most frequently observed.

Reptile and amphibian life here includes a frogs, geckos, chameleons and snakes. Some chameleons to watch for are the fairly common blue-nose chameleon (*Chamaeleo boettgeri*) and the stump-tailed chameleon.

Among the park's more than 70 species of birds are the crested wood ibis (*Lophotibis cristata*) and the malachite kingfisher (*Alcedo vintsioides*).

Hiking

Signposted walking trails in the northern part of the park take in the **Petit Lac**, a small crater lake also known as Lac de la Coupe Verte, and **Cascade Antankarana**, a beautiful waterfall flowing into a tranquil pool surrounded by fern-covered cliffs. Nearby is the path known as **Jardin Botanique**, which is a forest track lined by orchids, palms, lianas and bromeliads. Not far away, another trail leads to the small **Cascade Sacrée**, a sacred waterfall where locals often make offerings.

A longer track leads to the viewpoint over **Cascade Antomboka**, a narrow waterfall, which plunges 80m into a forest grotto. From the viewpoint there is a steep and slippery descent to the base of the cascade where you are likely to see butterflies and, with luck, crowned lemurs.

The summit of **Montagne d'Ambre** (Amber Mountain; 1475m) is reached via an approximately 11km trail heading south from the park entrance. From the camp site it's a relatively easy three- to four-hour hike, and less than an hour from the base to the summit. Just below the summit is **Lac Maudit**, where local fady prohibits swimming. Below the summit to the southeast is the larger **Grand Lac**, where you are allowed to camp.

Sleeping & Eating

The park's **Gîte d'Étape** (dm FMg40,000) and camp site are in an idyllic setting about 3km from the park entrance, at the end of an avenue of towering South American pines. The *gîte*

PARC NATIONAL DE MONTAGNE D'AMBRE

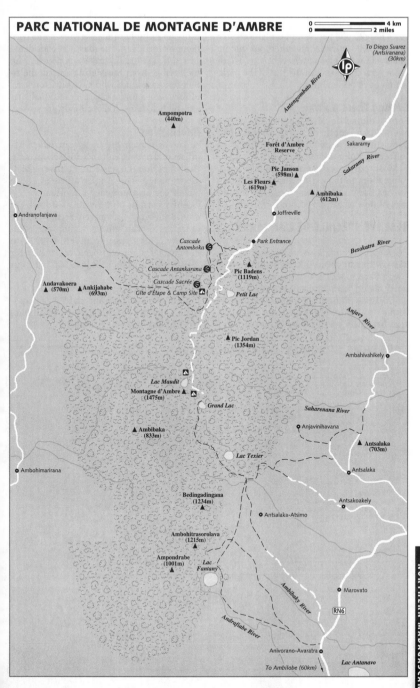

has a kitchen, and a sitting area. Camping costs FMg20,000 per person under a shelter or FMg5,000 outside, and there are picnic tables, showers, and water at the site. There are several camp sites in the rest of the park, which have no facilities.

Getting There & Away

Parc National de Montagne d'Ambre lies about 40km south of Diego Suarez. The park entrance is about 4km southwest of Joffreville along the main road.

Most tour operators in Diego Suarez arrange tours to the park, although it is easy to organise on your own. See p149 for details of how to get here from Joffreville.

RÉSERVE SPÉCIALE DE L'ANKÀRANA

At 18,225 hectares, Réserve Spéciale de l'Ankàrana encompasses the beautiful Ankàrana massif, about 100km southwest of Diego Suarez. It is a striking and undeveloped region with impressive *tsingy* (karst, or limestone pinnacles), relatively easily seen lemurs and interesting bird species, lakes and bat-filled grottoes. Running through

and under the *tsingy* are hidden forest-filled canyons and subterranean rivers, some containing crocodiles. The massif is considered sacred by the local Antakàrana people, who took refuge from the Merina among the *tsingy* and caves, and who have buried several of their kings in the caves. Traditional rites are still held here, and local fady are strong.

Information

Ankàrana is managed by Angap, which has offices at the main entrance in Mahamasina, Ambilobe and the western entrance at Matsaborimanga. The Angap office in Diego Suarez can provide general information.

Entry permits cost FMg50,000 for three days and can be arranged at the reserve entrance, as can guides, which are compulsory. Fees range from FMg40,000 to FMg80,000 per group per circuit. Fees for night walks are about FMg15,000 per hour per group.

You will need to be self-sufficient with food, water and camping supplies, including a good torch. Only very basic supplies are available in Mahamasina.

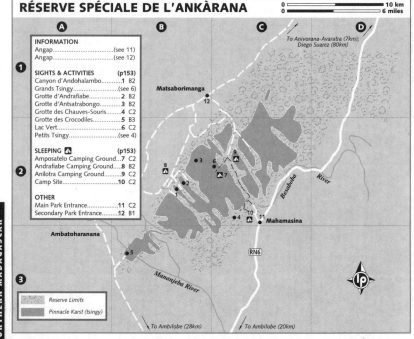

Musicians on a cargo boat, Canal des Pangalanes (p204)

Cascade Sacrée (p150), Parc National de
Montagne d'Ambre

Nocturnal frog, Réserve
Spéciale d'Analamazaotra
(p200)

Madagascar tree boa, Réserve de Nosy
Mangabe (p189)

Ylang-ylang leaves, Comoros (p160)

WAYNE WALTON

THOR VAZ DE LEON

Grande Comore coastline (p210), Comoros

Banana plantation on Anjouan (p227), Comoros

WAYNE W

As most lakes and rivers here are sacred, bathing or swimming in them is generally not permitted.

Wildlife

On the high dry *tsingy,* succulents such as *Euphorbia* and *Pachypodium* predominate, while the sheltered intervening canyons are filled with leafy cassias, figs, baobabs and other trees typical of dry deciduous forest.

Of the area's 10 species of lemurs, the most numerous are crowned, Sanford's and northern sportive lemurs. There are also woolly, rufous mouse, fat-tailed dwarf and fork-marked lemurs, Perrier's diademed sifakas and aye-ayes. Other mammals include tenrecs and ring-tailed mongooses. (Mongooses have been known to visit camping grounds at night in search of food – don't try to touch them, as they may be infected with rabies.)

Over 90 species of birds have been identified in the reserve, including the orange-and-white kingfisher, crested coua, Madagascan fish eagle, crested wood ibis and banded kestrel.

There are at least a dozen species of bats, as well as numerous chameleon and gecko species, and some (albeit rarely seen) crocodiles living in rivers in the underground caves.

Sights & Activities

It's longer and more expensive, but better for wildlife and scenery, if you go to the park's western entrance at Matsaborimanga. For this you'll need a 4WD, and the road is only passable from May to December. This is also the best entrance to use if you want to explore some of the canyons and caves on the western side of the reserve, including the 11km-long **Grotte d'Andrafiabe**.

The route to the **Grands Tsingy** and the pretty **Lac Vert** from Andriafabe camping ground passes through forest, and usually offers the chance to see lemurs, chameleons and some of Ankàrana's rich vegetation. From Andriafabe, most groups drive the 16km to Anilotra, then walk for about two hours. A second circuit from Andrafiabe camping ground (around three to four hours) takes in the Grotte d'Andrafiabe and some canyons.

Easily reached on foot from the main entrance is the impressive **Grotte des Chauves-Souris** (Cave of Bats) with superb stalactites, stalagmites and other interesting formations, and thousands of bats hanging from the walls. Nearby is a small viewpoint from where you can look over the **Petits Tsingy**.

The **Grotte des Crocodiles** (Cave of Crocodiles) is in the far southwestern corner of the reserve and is accessible by 4WD from Ambilobe. To reach the cave, turn off the road before Ambatoharanana village. You are far more likely to see lemurs and chameleons here than crocodiles.

In order to really begin to explore Ankàrana's attractions, you will need to allow at least three days, including one day each way for transport from Diego Suarez. Bring water and sun protection, as walking in the reserve can get very hot.

Tours

Organised tours to Ankàrana from Diego Suarez (p145) cost about FMg400,000 per person in a group of four for a three-day, two-night camping excursion from the Mahamasina entrance. From the Matsaborimanga entrance, the price is around FMg750,000 per person.

Sleeping & Eating

Camping grounds in the reserve include one about 3km from Mahamasina near the Petits Tsingy and Grotte des Chauves-Souris; Andrafiabe on the western edge of the reserve near Andrafiabe village; and Anilotra in the centre of the reserve near the Grands Tsingy. Anilotra is unpopular with campers, as there's no water source here, only lots of mosquitoes. Camping fees range from FMg5000 to FMg20,000 per tent per night, depending on the site. Watch out for scorpions at all of the camping grounds. You can camp outside the entrance near Mahamasina, or find local **accommodation** (about FMg25,000) in the village. **King de la Piste** (bungalows FMg50,000-100,000) has opened a new lodge just outside Mahamasina, which is a good option in the rainy season (p146).

Getting There & Away

Mahamasina village is approximately 100km southwest of Diego Suarez and about 40km north of Ambilobe (FMg5000) along the

RN6. The main reserve entrance at Maha-masina is accessible year-round, and easily reached by taxi-brousse from Diego Suarez (FMg25,000, five to seven hours). It's easy to get a taxi-brousse at the end of your trip to either Diego Suarez or Ambanja (for travelling on to Nosy Be).

To reach Matsaborimanga, turn west off the RN6 on to a rough track a few kilometres south of Anivorana–Avaratra and continue for about 35km to the reserve entrance.

AMBILOBE

Ambilobe is the nearest major town to the Réserve Spéciale de l'Ankàrana, and it is an excellent place to stock up on supplies for visiting the reserve if you are coming in from the south. It is also the junction town for transport to and from Iharana, Sambava as well as other towns on Madagascar's eastern coast.

The best accommodation option is the signposted **Hôtel de l'Ankàrana** (r FMg86,000).

A few vehicles go early every day between Ambilobe and Diego Suarez, Iharana and south to Ambanja (FMg20,000).

AMBANJA

Ambanja is a small, tree-lined town on the Sambirano River, and the junction for overland travel to/from Nosy Be. **Chez Patricia** (r without/with bathroom FMg30,000/60,000) is the best place to stay, and has a restaurant. If this is full, try **Les Bouganvilliers** (r with bathroom FMg51,000).

From Ambanja, there is daily transport to Ankify (FMg12,000), Mahajanga, Diego Suarez, and the ferry to Nosy Be. The first 200km of the RN6 south from here is particularly bad, so come prepared for a bumpy ride.

ANKIFY

The small town of Ankify is the main port for boats and ferries between the Malagasy coast and Nosy Be. There are several up-market hotels in town – try **Le Baobab** (☎ 82 293 64 in Diego; r FMg250,000), about 500m from the ferry landing.

Several taxis run daily between Ankify and Ambanja, from where it is fairly easy to find a taxi-brousse on to Diego Suarez, via Ambilobe. For details of ferries to Nosy Be, see p157.

NOSY BE & OTHER ISLANDS

pop 40,000

Nosy Be (Big Island) is Madagascar's premier beach-resort destination, with charter flights full of eager tourists clutching their baby oil and novelty sunhats, disembarking weekly at the airport. Inevitably, the island's popularity with European holidaymakers has led to a few tawdry hotel developments and busy beaches, but the good humour of the inhabitants seems untouched. With its fields of sugar cane, rum distilleries and single-gauge railway, inland Nosy Be has a faintly Caribbean atmosphere, and if you can drag yourself away from the beach there are some beautiful out-of-the-way corners to explore. If you're looking for the full bare-foot, Robinson Crusoe experience, head out to one of the smaller and less-visited islets that surround the main island.

The hotels on the island cater for all budgets, although in general they are more expensive than those of the mainland. Rates are higher at Easter, Christmas and between May and September. The climate is sunny all year round, but there's a risk of cyclones in February and March.

History

Nosy Be's first inhabitants are believed to have been 15th-century Swahili and Indian traders. Later, the island served as a magnet for refugees, merchants and settlers of all descriptions.

In 1839, the Sakalava queen Tsiomeko fled to Nosy Be and turned to the French for help in resisting her Merina enemies. In 1841, the Sakalava ceded both Nosy Be and neighbouring Nosy Komba to France.

In recent years, with increasing tourism development and local environmental pressures, deforestation has become a problem on the island, as has destruction and damage of offshore coral reefs.

Orientation

Nosy Be's capital, main port and only major town is Hell-Ville, on the island's southeastern corner. There are no good beaches but it does have banks and the Air Madagascar office.

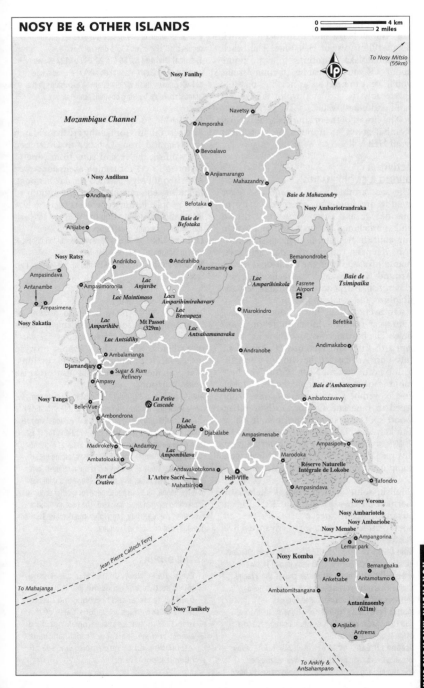

NOSY BE & OTHER ISLANDS

0 ⌷⌷⌷⌷ 4 km
0 ⌷⌷⌷⌷ 2 miles

Mozambique Channel

To Nosy Mitsio (55km)

Nosy Fanihy

Navetsy

Amporaha

Bevoalavo

Anjiamarango
Mahazandry

Baie de Mahazandry

Nosy Andilana

Andilana

Befotaka

Baie de Befotaka

Nosy Ambariotrandraka

Anjiabe

Nosy Ratsy

Andrikibo

Andrahibo

Bemanondrobe

Maromaniry

Baie de Tsimipaika

Ampasindava

Antanambe

Ampasimoronjia

Lac Anjavibe

Lac Amparihinkola

Fasrene Airport

Ampasimena

Lac Maintimaso

Lacs Amparihimirahavavy

Nosy Sakatia

Lac Amparihibe

Mt Passot (329m)

Lac Bemapaza

Marokindro

Befetika

Lac Antsahamanavaka

Andimakabo

Lac Antsidihy

Ambalamanga

Andranobe

Djamandjary

Sugar & Rum Refinery

Ampasy

Baie d'Ambatozavavy

Nosy Tanga

Belle-Vue

Antsaholana

Ambatozavavy

Ambondrona

La Petite Cascade

Lac Djabala

Djabalabe

Ampasimenabe

Ampasipohy

Madirokely

Andampy

Lac Ampombilava

Marodoka

Réserve Naturelle Intégrale de Lokobe

Ambatoloaka

Andavakotokona

Port du Cratère

L'Arbre Sacré

Hell-Ville

Ampasindava

Tafondro

Mahatsinjo

Nosy Vorona

Nosy Ambariotelo

Nosy Ambariobe

Nosy Menabe

Ampangorina

Lemur park

Nosy Komba

Mahabo

Bemangoaka

Anketsabe

Antamotamo

Jean Pierre Calloch Ferry

Ambatomitsangana

To Mahajanga

Antaninaomby (621m)

Nosy Tanikely

Anjiabe

Antrema

To Ankify & Antsahampano

The most popular beaches on Nosy Be are Ambatoloaka and Madirokely, which begin 10km west of Hell-Ville. The beach at Ambatolaka is nothing to write home about – if you're a real beach connoisseur, you'll want to head as far north as possible (preferably to Andilana) to hit the whitest sand and bluest water.

The closest of the offshore islands is Nosy Komba, about 45 minutes by motorboat from Hell-Ville.

Activities

DIVING & SNORKELLING

The seas around Nosy Be and the other islands are home to a rich diversity of marine life and offer some good diving and snorkelling. You may well see boxfish, surgeonfish, triggerfish, damselfish, clown fish, yellowfin tuna, barracuda, eagle rays, manta rays, and even the occasional whale. Around Nosy Sakatia you're likely to see clown fish, barracuda, turtles, and perhaps dolphins and whale sharks.

On average, visibility on dives is about 15m year-round – much more on good days. The best months for diving are from April to June and October to November. July and August can be windy, especially to the north around Nosy Mitsio. The best months for seeing whale sharks are October and November; and for manta rays from April to June and October to November. Good spots for snorkelling include Nosy Tanikely and Nosy Mitsio.

Prices are about €34 for a *baptême* (first dive), €32/60/282 for one/two/10 dives with equipment, and €33 for a night dive.

Courses are conducted in French or English; some staff also speak Italian or German. Prices start at about €217 for an advanced open-water course; it's best to book certification courses in advance. Dive centres include:

Blue Dive (☎ 86 616 31, 032 07 20 720; www.bluedive-madagascar.com; Madirokely & Nosy Iranja) This well-respected operator offers catamaran cruises and a range of dive excursions around the islands. It can do holiday packages and hotel bookings for all budgets.

Manta Dive Club (☎ 032 720 710; www.mantadiveclub.com; Madirokely) Offers certification courses and a range of dive excursions.

Océane's Dream (☎ 86 614 26, 032 07 127 82; www.oceanesdream.com; Ambatoloaka) Well-established operator offering catamaran-based diving cruises to Nosy Mitsio, Nosy Iranja and Nosy Radama for €497 per person, with a minimum of two people (previous certification required); it also offers CMAS dive courses.

Tropical Diving (☎ 86 616 28, 032 07 127 90; www.tropical-diving.com; Madirokely) Offers a good range of PADI courses and a variety of diving excursions to the islands; there's a booking booth in Ambatoloaka.

FISHING

The best months for fishing are from March to June, and from October to December. For sailfish, the season runs from June to October. Prices for fishing excursions start from about FMg3,000,000 per day per boat, including equipment, with a maximum of four people. Fishing operators include:

International Fisching Club (☎ 86 614 29; hotel.espadon@malagasy.com; Hôtel Espadon)

Le Grand Bleu (☎ 86 634 08; www.legrandbleunosybe.com in French; Le Grand Bleu Hotel)

Marlin Nautique (☎ 86 61315; marlin.club@simicro.mg; Le Marlin Club)

Tours

Naturally, Nosy Be is home to dozens of tour companies, some specialising in multi-day dive or snorkel cruises among the various islands, while others simply provide inter-island transport or day excursions. Many of the dive operators also organise boat excursions.

Alefa (☎ 86 615 89; www.madagascar-contacts.com/alefa in French; Madirokely beach) Alefa offers multiday excursions along the Malagasy coast in traditional wooden Sakalava sailing pirogues. Most trips sail along the coast from Nosy Be southwards, sometimes as far as Moramba (north of Mahajanga). There is onshore camping in the evenings and stops at villages along upon request. Rates are €70 per person per day all inclusive with a minimum of three people (or €210 per pirogue for smaller groups). Snorkelling equipment is included. The best months for excursions are June, July, September and October. Trips are generally not possible in February.

THE DONIA

Every June, Nosy Be holds a week-long music festival known as the Donia. Groups from Madagascar and neighbouring islands perform at venues in various parts of the island, with attendant carnival, sporting events and seminars. For French-language information, go to http://perso.wanadoo.fr/jbemizik/donia.htm.

Daniel (☎ 032 04 069 59; Hell-Ville) Glass-bottomed catamaran offering day cruises to Nosy Komba and Nosy Tanikely. Rates are FMg125,000 per person including a slap-up lunch and free rum (but excluding other drinks) and transport to and from your hotel. No reservations are necessary unless you are staying north of the Ambatoloaka/Madirokely area, in which case you will need to arrange a hotel pick-up and pay an additional fee for transfers to/from the port. Snorkelling equipment can be hired for FMg25,000. The *Daniel* departs daily at about 8.30am from the port in Hell-Ville, returning in the late afternoon. The boat can drop you off at Nosy Komba and/or Nosy Tanikely, and pick you up one or more days later for no extra cost. A minibus to the port departs Ambatoloaka at 8am daily from Location Jeunesse on the main street. Sailing time is about 45 minutes from Hell-Ville to Nosy Komba, about one hour from Nosy Komba to Nosy Tanikely, and about one hour from Nosy Tanikely back to Hell-Ville.

Island Quest (☎ 86 615 52; www.islandquest.co.za) Trips are based aboard the luxury catamaran *Bossi,* which sleeps up to eight people. This operator offers four- and five-day island cruises; diving and fishing can also be arranged. Book well in advance.

MadaVoile (Blue Planet, Escapades; ☎ 86 616 37, 86 620 80; www.madavoile.com in French; Ambatolaoaka) Three names, one reliable operator, offering a wide range of land- and sea-based tours including trips around the islands, and to Réserve Spéciale de l'Ankàrana and Parc National de Montagne d'Ambre. English and German is spoken.

Nosy Be Promenade (☎ 032 40 078 55; Ambatoloaka) A budget operator organising various day and overnight camping excursions to the outlying islands. Sample prices include FMg200,000 per person for an overnight trip to Nosy Iranja and FMg125,000 per person for a day trip to Nosy Sakatia, including lunch.

Getting There & Away
AIR
Air Madagascar (☎ 86 613 60; Rte de l'Ouest, Hell-Ville) flights links Nosy Be with Antananarivo every day (FMg962,000), often via Mahajanga (FMg681,000) or Diego (FMg368,000). Flights also go to Sambava and Dzaoudzi in Mayotte.

Air Austral (☎ 86 612 40) and **Air Mauritius** (☎ 86 612 40) both in Hell-Ville can book regular flights to Mayotte, Réunion and Mauritius.

BOAT
Two ferries (both of which take vehicles), numerous smaller and faster speedboats, and a few cargo boats connect Nosy Be with the mainland.

Cargo Boat
Cargo boats travel between Nosy Be and Mahajanga, and less frequently between Nosy Be and Diego Suarez. The trips take anywhere from 24 to 72 hours. While some boats can be relatively comfortable with passenger cabins and food provided, the smaller ones are often a nightmare. Check the blackboard outside the Auximad office at the port in Hell-Ville.

Ferry
The **Fivondronana** (☎ 032 02 358 40) leaves Nosy Be for Anstahampano port, near Ambanja, several times a week. Departure times vary according to the high tide, and the journey takes about two hours. Passenger tickets cost FMg12,500. You can buy tickets at the port or at the office on the main street.

The *Jean Pierre Calloch*, run by **MSL ferries** (☎ 86 633 13; ✆ Fri-Mon), departs Nosy Be on Monday for Mahajanga, taking about 20 hours. Ticket prices vary from FMg160,000 for a seat on deck in 3rd class to FMg350,000 for an aircraft-style seat plus meals in first class. Tickets can be bought on the ferry.

Speedboat
Various smaller speedboats depart in the morning from Nosy Be to the port of Ankify (FMg25,000, about one hour).

Yacht
Most of the private yachts passing through Nosy Be are bound for Mayotte (the passage costs about €200), with some also heading for South Africa or Mahajanga. The best place to ask is at Nandipo bar in Hell-Ville.

The yachting season in the Indian Ocean falls between August and November, before the onset of the cyclone season.

TAXI-BROUSSE
It's a long, hard ride by taxi-brousse between Diego Suarez and Ankify, the port from which boats depart from Nosy Be. On the way, taxis-brousse often stop for hours in Ambanja. Allow about a day and a half for the journey.

Getting Around
The main road on Nosy Be, between the airport and Andilana via Ambatoloaka is sealed and relatively flat. Internal roads are generally rougher and hillier.

NORTHERN MADAGASCAR

TO/FROM THE AIRPORT

Nosy Be's Fasrene airport lies about 12km from Hell-Ville on the eastern side of the island. The taxi fare from the airport to Hell-Ville is FMg20,000, or about FMg40,000 to Ambatoloaka.

CAR & MOTORCYCLE

Most tour operators and upmarket hotels can arrange car hire; expect to pay about FMg450,000 per day for a 4WD with a driver. A 4WD is not necessary unless you visit Réserve Naturelle Intégrale de Lokobe, where hiking is a better way of getting around anyway. For ordinary vehicle hire, fares are about FMg350,000 per day with a driver. **Nosy Red Cars** (☎ 86 620 35) in Ambatoloaka hire out groovy little red beach buggies (only for use on designated main roads) for €40 per day including fuel. An off-road expedition in its 4WD drive models costs €25 person per half day.

Location Jeunesse (☎ 86 614 08) in Ambatoloaka rents out Honda 250cc motorcycles (FMg175,000 per day), scooters (FMg100,000 per day) and mountain bikes (FMg50,000 per day) in mediocre condition. Be sure to check your contract and the condition of the bike very carefully before parting with any money.

TAXI & TAXI-BROUSSE

Shared-taxi fares are FMg5000 between Hell-Ville and Ambatoloaka (20 to 30 minutes), and FMg10,000 between Hell-Ville and Andilana (45 minutes). Elsewhere on the island, public transport is scarce.

Fares for charter taxis around the island are standardised, and often displayed in the reception areas of hotels; all fares are higher after 8pm. A charter between Hell-Ville and Ambatoloaka costs from FMg30,000. Chartering a taxi for the day will cost from FMg150,000 excluding fuel.

HELL-VILLE

Nosy Be's main town got its rather off-putting name from Admiral de Hell, a French governor of Réunion. At first sight the town, if not exactly hellish, does seem rather nondescript, and it's usually ignored by travellers bent on the beach. In fact, it's quite an attractive little place, with old colonial buildings crumbling into ruins among the frangipani and bougainvilleas.

Information

INTERNET ACCESS

Oasis Café (per min FMg750) offers Internet access.

MONEY

The major banks have branches in Hell-Ville for changing money and travellers cheques, plus credit card advances.

POST & TELEPHONE

The post office and Telecom office are on the corner of Boulevard de l'Indépendence and Rue Passot. There are several card-phones in town.

Sleeping

Le Restaurant d'Ambonara et ses Bungalows (☎ 86 613 67; ambonara@dts.mg; d FMg85,000-136,000) Just up from the Air Madagascar office on the way out of town, this place has comfortable bungalows with net and fan. There's a funkily decorated outdoor bar/restaurant (mains FMg25,000), with a menu that includes Swiss raclette! It's often full, so book ahead.

Hôtel Plantation (☎ 032 40 054 08; computer.serv @wanadoo.mg; Rue du Docteur Manceau; r FMg125,000-150,000; ❄) A new and charming little bar and restaurant with cheerful rooms containing fans but no nets. The restaurant serves high-class French cuisine (mains FMg40,000).

Hôtel Diana (☎ 032 40 178 76; Blvd Général de Gaulle; r without/with bathroom FMg55,000/70,000) This spick-and-span local guesthouse has good-value rooms with a fan and hot water.

Hôtel Diamant 10 (☎ 86 614 48; Rue du Fortin; r with bathroom FMg131,000; ❄) A neon-lit edifice with tiled and tacky rooms, with hot water.

Eating & Drinking

Oasis Café (☎ 86 611 57) Oasis has snacks and ice cream.

Chez Sitty (☎ 032 02 207 38; mains FMg25,000; ☿ breakfast, lunch & dinner) This place serves excellent shrimp dishes and its chocolate mousse is to die for.

Le Papillon (☎ 86 615 82; mains FMg25,000; ☿ lunch & dinner Mon-Sat) For Italian food head here.

Nandipo (☿ from 5am) This yachtsmens' hangout of choice, where many regulars get stuck into the beer by 9am, also serves food. It's a good place to find a berth on a boat headed for Mayotte or the islands near Nosy Be.

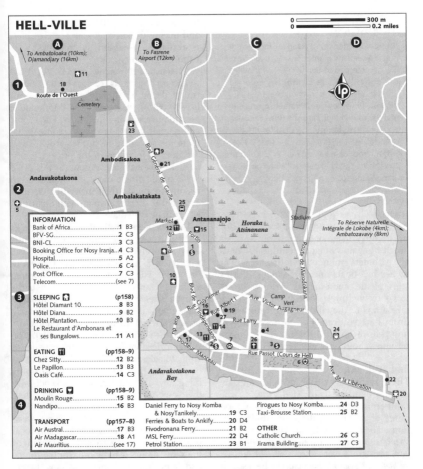

HELL-VILLE

0 — 300 m
0 — 0.2 miles

To Ambatoloaka (10km);
Djamandjary (16km)

To Fasrene
Airport (12km)

Route de l'Ouest

Cemetery

Ambodisakoa

Andavakotakona

Ambalakatakata

Market

Antananajojo

Horaka
Atsinanana

Stadium

To Réserve Naturelle
Intégrale de Lokobe (4km);
Ambatozavavy (8km)

Andavakotakona
Bay

INFORMATION	
Bank of Africa	1 B3
BFV-SG	2 C3
BNI-CL	3 C3
Booking Office for Nosy Iranja	4 C3
Hospital	5 A2
Police	6 C4
Post Office	7 C3
Telecom	(see 7)

SLEEPING	(p158)
Hôtel Diamant 10	8 B3
Hôtel Diana	9 B2
Hôtel Plantation	10 B3
Le Restaurant d'Ambonara et	
ses Bungalows	11 A1

EATING	(pp158–9)
Chez Sitty	12 B2
Le Papillon	13 B3
Oasis Café	14 C3

DRINKING	(pp158–9)
Moulin Rouge	15 B2
Nandipo	16 B3

TRANSPORT	(pp157–8)
Air Austral	17 B3
Air Madagascar	18 A1
Air Mauritius	(see 17)

Daniel Ferry to Nosy Komba	
& NosyTanikely	19 C3
Ferries & Boats to Ankify	20 D4
Fivodronana Ferry	21 B2
MSL Ferry	22 D4
Petrol Station	23 B1

Pirogues to Nosy Komba	24 D3
Taxi-Brousse Station	25 B2

OTHER	
Catholic Church	26 C3
Jirama Building	27 C3

Moulin Rouge (Le Manova) There's dancing upstairs above a restaurant and a cabaret every Tuesday night.

There are several more hard-drinking bars along the main street.

AROUND NOSY BE
Mt Passot & Crater Lakes

Mt Passot (329m), Nosy Be's loftiest point, lies about 15km north of Hell-Ville (somewhat further by road). It's a good spot for watching the sunset or admiring the view.

Some of the larger hotels arrange sunset minibus tours to the summit of Mt Passot, or you can hire a taxi to the top and walk back down (8km) to Djamandjary. You can also get here by mountain bike or motorcycle.

Réserve Naturelle Intégrale de Lokobe

The Réserve Naturelle Intégrale de Lokobe protects most of Nosy Be's remaining endemic vegetation. The reserve is home to the black lemur and several other lemur species. Other wildlife includes the boa constrictor and the giant (but harmless) Madagascan hog-nosed snakes, identified by intricate checkerboard markings.

You will need a guide to walk around in Lokobe, which can be arranged at Jungle Village (see below). There is also a fee of FMg2500 per person payable to the village chief, who will approach you with a 'ticket'. Tours with a recommended guide called Jean Robert can be arranged by most of the hotels on the island for around FMg150,000.

NORTHERN MADAGASCAR

> **YLANG-YLANG**
>
> The low, gnarled ylang-ylang (e-lang-e-lang) tree is seen in plantations all over Nosy Be. Its scented green or yellow flowers are distilled to make oil, which is exported to the West for perfume. The trees are pruned into low and rather grotesque shapes to make picking the flowers easier.
>
> The large **ylang-ylang distillery** (admissionfree; ☷ 8am-3.30pm Mon-Fri, 7.30am-2.30pm Sat) is about 3km east of Hell-Ville. You can see the ylang-ylang being distilled on Monday, Wednesday and Friday only.

Jungle Village (☎ 032 04 308 03; www.junglevillage .net; bungalows with bathroom €30; set dinner FMg60,000), in the tiny village of Ampasipohy, has six beach bungalows made from local materials, with nets and outside sitting areas. The owner has boats and can arrange fishing trips, picnics and other excursions.

To reach Jungle Village on your own, take a taxi to the village of Ambatozavavy. From here you can walk to the reserve at low tide in about 40 minutes, or go via pirogue (about FMg50,000 return).

Ambatoloaka

The tiny fishing village of Ambatoloaka, about 10km west of Hell-Ville, is the southernmost of the beaches, with a good range of accommodation and dining options. The beach itself, however, is nothing special, and the atmosphere in the village is very touristy. **Djembe disco** (admission FMg10,000; ☷ Wed-Sat & Mon) is the place to be seen in the evenings.

There is a cardphone at **L'Ylang-Ylang**; phonecards are for sale at reception. **Hôtel l'Espadon** (below) can arrange email services for its guests.

SLEEPING

Many places are often full, so it's best to reserve in advance if possible. The following is just a selection of the many hotels in Ambatoloaka.

Le Coucher du Soleil (☎ 86 616 20; coucherdu soleil@wanadoo.mg; d with bathroom FMg120,000) This Swiss-run budget hotel is about 200m above the main road on a hill and signposted. The setting is lovely, and there are good views of the sunset. It has spotless comfortable bungalows, each with a four-poster bed and mosquito net, and a terrace. Breakfast is available. It's about five minutes' walk from the beach.

Hôtel Gerard et Francine (☎ 86 614 09; geretfra@ wanadoo.mg; d without/with bathroom €35/40) A beautifully decorated family guesthouse with bright yellow walls, wooden floors and a veranda overlooking the beach. The rooms come in all shapes and sizes – some in the main house and some in the garden – and breakfast is included in the price. It's best to make advance reservations, as this place is often full. Single men are not allowed to occupy rooms on their own – they're only accepted if sharing a room with a partner, either male or female.

Les Boucaniers (☎ 032 02 675 20; www.hotel-les boucaniers.com; d €40-50) Another very beautifully decorated and friendly guesthouse, this is on a hill behind Hôtel Gerard et Francine. The rooms are very charming, with net, fan and new and stylish bathrooms. There's a rooftop restaurant/bar, a small pool, and any number of comfortable nooks in which to curl up with a book.

Caravelle (☎ 86 614 05; r with bathroom FMg150,000) A well-priced guesthouse on the way out of Ambatoloaka towards Madirokely. It's 100m or so from the beach, but the two-storey bungalows are well decorated and cool, with their own terraces and a downstairs sitting area and space for an extra bed.

La Saladerie (☎ 86 614 28; hotel.espadon@malagasy .com; r with bathroom FMg100,000) A small, local place just behind the excellent restaurant of the same name. It has clean, simple rooms and bungalows with nets and fans. Reservations can be organised through Hôtel Espadon.

Hôtel l'Espadon (☎ 86 614 28; hotel.espadon@ malagasy.com; d €71-90; ☒) Ambatoloaka's most upmarket option is comfortable but not especially charming, with a glassed-in restaurant (breakfast only), sun beds and umbrellas on the beach. The room prices vary according to view and season, but all are large, tiled and feature a TV and minibar, plus all manner of fish pictures on the walls.

EATING

Chez Angeline (mains FMg20,000) On the village street, this place has a small but good menu including zebu steak and prawns.

Chez Mama (mains FMg15,000) The staff here can whip up good rice dishes, with vegetarian options on request.

Hotel La Residence d'Ambatoloaka (mains FMg25,000) This establishment has a beachfront restaurant with good service and a few vegetarian dishes.

Karibo (pizzas FMg30,000; ☺ lunch & dinner Wed-Mon, lunch Tue) On the main road near the Hôtel L'Espadon, Karibo has passable pizzas and pasta dishes.

Safari Resto (☺ lunch & dinner Mon-Sat) Safari is a smart terrace restaurant in the middle of the village that serves salads, grilled fish and other healthy dishes.

Madirokely

Madirokely beach is just a short walk north of Ambatoloaka, with no obvious distinction between the two sections. At its northernmost end, and signposted from the beach, is the well-stocked Toko pharmacy.

SLEEPING

L'Heure Bleue (☎ 86 614 21; www.heurebleue.com; d low/high season with breakfast €55/60; ℗) Up on a hill overlooking the village, this very pretty little hotel has a terrace with great views and a small swimming pool. The fantastic bungalows, made of polished wood, have smart linen bedclothes and a front wall that slides open to reveal the view. Each has a net, fan, safe and minibar, plus a balcony with armchairs.

Le Grand Large (☎ 86 615 84; grandlarge@dts.mg; r FMg175,000-250,000; mains FMg35,000-45,000; ✗) Located right on the beach in the village, this guesthouse has smallish rooms in a variety of prices according to view and size. All have a bathroom with hot water. The unpretentious and relaxed bar/restaurant (open Tuesday to Sunday) has mostly seafood dishes with a French flavour. There are occasional barbeques on the terrace overlooking the beach.

Madiro Hôtel (☎ 032 02 273 22; www.madirohotel.com; s low/high season €60/66, d €60/72; ℗) A bigger, more upmarket hotel catering mostly to package tours from France and Italy. The rooms are large and rustic, with parquet floors, fridges and mosquito nets. Most guests are here to dive with Manta Dive Club (p156), nearby.

Le Marlin Club (☎ 86 613 15; marlin.club@simicro.mg; r per person €110; ✗) The rooms and bunga-lows are very classy, at this upmarket Italian-run hotel with brass nautical lamps and wooden floors. The bar and restaurant, however, are a bit tacky. There's a snack bar on the beach, and facilities for watersports, diving and fishing excursions.

EATING

Tsimanin Kafé (☎ 032 04 016 00; mains FMg45,000) A 'gastronomic' French restaurant in an attractive wooden building on the beach. Expect lobster profiteroles, prawns in oyster sauce and so on, plus a few lighter lunch dishes. Unfortunately there is not much for veggies, but there's an extensive wine list.

Mama Lily (mains FMg10,000) At the other end of the scale, this friendly *hotely* in the middle of the village does cheap and tasty Malagasy meals.

Ambondrona & Belle Vue

Ambondrona beach is on a small bay north of Madirokely. To get here by road, follow the road north to the sugar cane railway then turn left at the first drivable track and follow it down towards the water. Just north of Ambondrona is a beach known as Belle Vue. From here northwards, the beaches and villages are much quieter and more attractive than at Ambatoloaka and Madirokely.

Domaine de Manga Be (☎ 86 616 30; urslinder@wanadoo.mg; r from FMg150,000) A very stylish and original self-catering complex aimed predominantly at families. The bungalows, studio apartments and rooms come in all shapes and sizes, but all are beautifully decorated, with kitchens or kitchenettes, nets and fans. A bistro and a supermarket are planned. If you pay a supplement you can hire an apartment complete with a cook to prepare your meals.

Tsara Loky (☎ 86 610 22; d FMg40,000-180,000; mains FMg27,000) This local place right on the beach has a good restaurant (order in advance) and a variety of rooms and bungalows – the best have bathrooms and hammocks outside, the cheapest are basic rooms in the main house.

Le Jolie Coin (☎ 032 40 055 72; fax 86 612 57; d with breakfast FMg150,000) A local place with slightly grubby rooms on a rather swampy bit of beach. Some rooms have an upstairs floor, and one has a kitchenette.

Nosy Be Hôtel (☎ 86 614 06; www.nosybehotel.com; d €70-92; 🏊 P) Catering predominantly to package tours, this hotel is very luxurious and tastefully decorated, with friendly staff. It's right on the beach, set in a lush garden.

Djamandjary

Djamandjary (dza-*man*-dzar) is Nosy Be's second-largest community. It's home to a working **rum refinery** (admission FMg20,000; 🕙 Mon-Fri).

Just east of town is a **sugar mill**, with two decaying but functional 1903 steam locomotives. These are still occasionally used during the cutting season (May to August) to transport cane along part of Nosy Be's mostly abandoned 37km of railway line.

Orangea (☎ 86 610 67; www.orangea-nosybe.com in French; d FMg325,000; P) Sweeping lawns lead down to the brightly coloured restaurant and pool deck at this cheerful and well-organised small hotel. The whitewashed rooms contain cushions made from African fabrics, fans, and hot water in the bathrooms. An excellent choice for accommodation or a lunch stop (reserve in advance).

Vanila Hôtel (☎ 86 615 23; vanilahotel@simicro.mg; d low season with breakfast €67-79, high season €91-105; 🏊 P) An upmarket beach hotel that caters more to couples and families than tour groups. It has a warm atmosphere, charming orange rooms, two bars and a restaurant, and bikes can be hired (FMg75,000 per day). Sailing, diving and excursions can be arranged here.

Ampasimoronjia

Ampasimoronjia is the next village up from Djamandjary. There are several hotels between here and Andilana, to the north.

Le Grand Bleu (☎ 86 634 08; www.legrandbleu nosybe.com; d with breakfast FMg300,000; P 🍴) On a hill overlooking the sea (lots of stairs), the bungalows here are very pretty, with blue-and-white walls and wooden floors. Each has a four-poster bed with a mosquito net, and a minibar. There's a lagoon pool and a Jacuzzi, a TV lounge and a terrace restaurant with a wood-fired pizza oven. Deep-sea fishing and quad-bike tours can be arranged.

Corail Noir (☎ 86 634 47; www.corailnoirhotel.com; s/d €40/80; 🏊 P) A big new resort hotel that's under the same management as Nosy Be hotel and Madiro-Hôtel. It has all the luxury trimmings, but not much character yet, and the beach in front of it is pretty average. The rooms have a safe, minibar, telephone and TV.

Chanty Beach (☎ 86 614 73; http://travel.to/Chanty-Beach; r low/high season per person €37.50/45) A charming, but perhaps rather staid, German-run guesthouse in a neat garden right on the beach. Some of the clean bungalows have their own kitchenette, and there's a small restaurant/bar.

Le Relais (☎ 86 615 10; r without/with bathroom FMg70,000/100,000) This is a no-frills, but friendly backpackers-style place, about five minutes' walk from the beach. There's a funky bar with a ping-pong table, and meals can be arranged. It also has bikes and boats for hire.

Andilana

Andilana is the most beautiful of the accessible beaches on Nosy Be, with a crescent of perfect white sand and turquoise water. A big package hotel is under construction in the next bay, but hopefully the residents will remain within the hotel limits and not spill over onto Andilana beach.

Belvedere Hotel (☎ 86 614 25; r FMg150,000-250,000; 🏊) is a very peaceful and pretty hotel perched on a bluff overlooking the beach. The rooms are huge, with mosquito nets and bright red '80s-style bathrooms. There's a restaurant and bar here, too.

Chez Loulou (set menu FMg100,000; 🕙 lunch & dinner), on the beach, has the same owner as Belvedere. On Sunday it organises a delicious buffet lunch (all-you-can-eat FMg100,000) on the beach, with live Malagasy music. Arrive early if you want any food, as it's very popular with expats.

OFFSHORE ISLANDS
Nosy Komba

The small volcanic island of Nosy Komba lies midway between Nosy Be and the mainland. Being the nearest offshore island to Nosy Be, it's very popular for day trips from the main island, usually combined with Nosy Tanikely. Prices for these are about FMg125,000 including lunch. Alternatively, you can hire a local pirogue from Hell-Ville for FMg10,000.

Boats land at Ampangorina, where there is an interesting craft market and some semi-tame black lemurs. There's a fabulous beach at Anjiabe, on the southwest coast.

Hôtel Les Floralies (☎ 032 04 944 21; d with bathroom FMg100,000) is the most developed of the two hotels on the island. It has simple bungalows on a magnificent beach, with a shady wooden deck and convivial bar/restaurant (mains FMg25,000). Snorkels and fins can be hired. **Hôtel Madio** (Ampangorina; r without/with bathroom FMg30,000/75,000) is a simple, local place. Chez Yolande, nearby, has seafood dishes with local sauces, and can hire out boats.

Nosy Tanikely

Nosy Tanikely is 10km west of Nosy Komba. It is an officially protected marine reserve and one of the better remaining snorkelling and diving sites in the area, with coral, numerous fish and the occasional sea turtle. Snorkelling equipment can be hired near the picnic area for FMg25,000.

Camping is possible, but you'll need to bring everything with you. If you're having lunch on the beach, make sure your operator takes all its rubbish away when you leave.

Most organised day tours combine Nosy Tanikely with Nosy Komba, using the beach on Nosy Tanikely for a lunch-time picnic.

It's also possible to visit by pirogue from Nosy Komba; you can arrange this with the hotels there or with locals. The trip takes about two hours each way, so bring a hat and sunscreen.

Nosy Sakatia

Nosy Sakatia, just off the west coast of Nosy Be, is quiet and tiny (3 sq km). It offers the opportunity to wander along forest tracks, see baobabs, fruit bats or chameleons, and to do some diving.

Sakatia Passions (☎ 86 614 62; www.sakatia-passions.com in French; s/d full board €95/130) has bungalows in a coconut plantation and a seafood buffet every Sunday. Sailing, fishing and diving can be arranged.

To get to Sakatia Passions, you need to go to Chanty Beach hotel in Ampasimoronjia, and radio across for a boat transfer. Day trips to the island are offered by some of the tour companies listed on p156.

Nosy Mitsio

Nosy Mitsio is a small and beautiful archipelago about 55km northeast of Nosy Be. The archipelago's main attraction lies in its excellent dive sites. There is a beach camp site on the southwestern side of Grande Mitsio.

On Nosy Tsara Bajina is the very upmarket **Hôtel Tsara Bajina** (☎ 86 612 49; tsarabanjina@magic.fr; full board per person €144). Boat transfers from Nosy Be cost €64.

Tropical Diving (☎ 032 07 127 90; www.tropical-diving.com) and **Le Marlin Club** (☎ 86 613 15; marlin.club@simicro.mg), both in Madirokely on Nosy Be, organise multiday camping/diving trips to Nosy Mitsio.

The trip between Nosy Be and Nosy Mitsio takes about four to six hours. Most of the dive and tour operators on p156 can arrange transfers to the islands.

Nosy Iranja

Nosy Iranja, southwest of Nosy Be, actually consists of two islands, the larger and inhabited Nosy Iranja Be (about 200 hectares), and the smaller Nosy Iranja Kely (13 hectares). The islands are connected by a 1.5km-long sand bar, negotiable on foot at low tide. Sea turtles regularly lay their eggs on the beaches.

The hyper-luxurious **Hôtel Nosy Iranja** (☎ 86 616 90; www.iranja.com in French; s/d per person €170/85; ✷ P), on Nosy Iranja Kely, has chic hexagonal bungalows with decks, hammocks and easy chairs. Inside is a fourposter bed, a CD player and a wood-and-stone bathroom complete with hairdryer. Naturally, an array of water sports, diving, fishing and boat excursions can be arranged. Helicopter transfers and a gym are also at your disposal. There's a three-night minimum stay at the hotel, which needs to be booked in advance at the hotel's office in Hell-Ville.

Should your budget not quite stretch to all this, the only other option is to arrange a homestay with the villagers on Nosy Iranja Be.

The trip from Nosy Be to Nosy Iranja takes about two hours in a speedboat; longer in slower vessels. The tour and dive companies on p156 offer trips to the island from about FMg275,000 per person.

Eastern Madagascar

Sometimes called the Vanilla Coast, the Cyclone Coast and the Pirate Coast, the long east coast of Madagascar has enough lush rain forests, glorious white beaches and long waterways to keep visitors exploring it for months. The region stretches from southern Farafangana, up past the old colonial resort of Toamasina, to the island of Sainte Marie and as far as the Masoala Peninsula in the extreme northeast.

Despite its many exciting natural features, the region's poor infrastructure (caused in part by the cyclones of its nickname) makes getting about an adventure in itself. In the course of a trip around eastern Madagascar, you could find yourself chugging along canals on a flat-bottomed barge, racing along switchback roads, climbing aboard a ponderous cargo boat, or hiking through thick forest with a line of porters.

Conversely, the well-surfaced road between Antananarivo and Toamasina is one of the most travelled by visitors to Madagascar, who flock to see (and hear) the indri, Madagascar's biggest lemur, in Parc National d'Andasibe-Mantadia. Further north, another increasingly popular holiday destination is Île Sainte Marie, an offshore island whose palm-fringed beaches are beginning to overshadow those of the better-known Nosy Be as a paradise for sun-worshippers.

Climatically, eastern Madagascar is the wettest part of the country, particularly between December and March, and is also the area that suffers most from severe cyclones. The last major damage was done in 2000, when cyclones Eline, Gloria and Hudah flattened whole towns and made thousands homeless.

HIGHLIGHTS

- Watching whales off the shores of **Île Sainte Marie** (p176)
- Trekking in the remote forests of the **Masoala Peninsula** (p192)
- Searching for aye-ayes in the trees along **Réserve de Nosy Mangabe's** (p189) golden beach
- Boating past reed huts and coffee factories on the **Canal des Pangalanes** (p204)
- Listening for eerie wail of the indri, Madagascar's largest lemur, at **Parc National d'Andasibe-Mantadia** (p199)

Nosy Mangabe ★ ★ Masoala Peninsula

★ Île Sainte Marie

Parc National d'Andasibe-Mantadia ★

Canal des Pangalanes ★

| ■ HIGHEST POINT: 1785M | ■ PRINCIPAL TRIBES: BETSIMISARAKA, TSIMIHETY, ANTAIMORO |

EASTERN MADAGASCAR

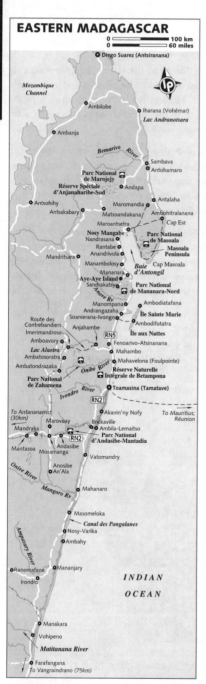

EASTERN MADAGASCAR

0 _____ 100 km
0 _____ 60 miles

Getting There & Away
AIR
Air Madagascar has flights from Antananarivo to Toamasina (FMg638,000, one hour) daily; and several times a week from Antananarivo to Manakara (FMg750,000), Farafangana (FMg820,000), Île Sainte Marie (FMg750,000, 1½ hours) and Mananjary (FMg682,000). You can also fly from Diego Suarez, Sambava or Antalaha to Maroantsetra, Mananara and Toamasina twice a week.

Air Austral and Air Mauritius fly from Toamasina to Réunion, continuing on to Mauritius.

BOAT
Toamasina is linked to Mauritius and Réunion by passenger boat which departs approximately every two weeks. For more information, see p172.

Cargo boats from Diego Suarez occasionally round the Masoala Peninsula as far as Maroantsetra, but they are few and far between and facilities are minimal.

LAND
The Route Nationale 2 (RN2) from Antananarivo to Toamasina is well-served by *taxis-brousse* (bush taxis) and buses. It's not a ride for the carsick – the road twists and turns endlessly, and drivers don't slow down for the corners.

From the south, travel by road is only possible with plenty of time and patience, and even then you'll only get as far as Mananara, 225km south of Toamasina. Travel by road from the north is only possible as far as Antalaha. After that, put on your walking boots, flag down a passing cargo boat, or quickest of all, buy an air ticket.

Getting Around
AIR
Air Madagascar makes small plane hops up and down the northeast coast from Toamasina or Antananarivo, stopping at Maroantsetra (FMg577,000 from Toamasina) and Mananara (FMg470,000). Several weekly flights connect Île Sainte Marie to Toamasina (FMg368,000). Ambatondrazaka is likewise connected several times a week by small plane to both Antananarivo and Toamasina.

BOAT

From rusty-bottomed canal barges to over-loaded cargo vessels, boats figure highly on the transport map of the east.

The French-built Canal des Pangalanes, which runs from Farafangana to Toamasina, is silted up and impassable in places but definitely the main thoroughfare of the region. Regular cargo vessels and motorboats ply the most visited northern waters between Ambila-Lemaitso and Toamasina. For more details, see p204.

Boats replace taxis-brousse as the main form of public transport for the coastal towns north of Soanierana-Ivongo. Few of the boats have any passenger facilities, however, and none have fixed schedules – it's simply a matter of hanging around the ports and waiting for something going your way to arrive. Several ferries a day, some equipped with such luxuries as seats and lifejackets, do the run across from the mainland to Île Sainte Marie. See p179 for details.

BUS & TAXI-BROUSSE

From the towns on the RN2, you'll be able to find onward transport to places like Andasibe and Ambatondrazaka, although once off the RN2 the roads are generally poor.

North of Toamasina, taxis-brousse continue daily as far as Soanierana-Ivongo, from where you catch the boat to Île Sainte Marie. Taxis-brousse are usually prevented from travelling further north due to collapsed bridges and enormous potholes. Likewise, no taxis-brousse go south from Toamasina, but further down the coast the towns of Mananjary, Manakara and Farafangana are linked by regular, if rickety, vehicles.

TRAIN

The once-famous passenger train service between Antananarivo and Toamasina is presently suspended. There are, however, high hopes that it will be back on track (!) sometime in 2004, after an injection of South African investment. Check at the station in Antananarivo for the latest news.

The only other trains in the region are the cargo engines that run up and down the single-gauge railway linking some of the villages on the Canal des Pangalanes. These are supposedly forbidden from taking passengers, but if you're lucky you should be able to talk your way on board.

TOAMASINA (TAMATAVE)

pop 174,000

Toamasina (often still known by its French name Tamatave) was developed as a resort during colonial times. Photographs from a hundred years ago show French holiday-makers posing in long bathing costumes in front of wooden beach huts. These days, the town is a popular holiday destination among the more affluent Malagasy. Every Sunday, come rain or shine, the town's fashionable youth gather on the seafront to promenade, flirt and ride around in high-wheeled *pousse-pousse* (rickshaws).

Despite its reputation as a pleasure resort, first impressions of the town are not edifying, especially if you arrive during one of the frequent downpours. Once-grand colonial buildings, now covered in greeny-black mould, line the streets. Many of the palm trees that adorn the town's wide boulevards and avenues have lost their tops, and the potholes in the road are so deep you can step into them up to your knees.

But despite this atmosphere of decay, Toamasina is a vibrant and important town, a centre of commerce for the east and one of the country's major ports. It's also a convenient spot to break the journey between Antananarivo and Île Sainte Marie, or to organise a trip down the Canal des Pangalanes.

HISTORY

The origin of the Malagasy name Toamasina is disputed. One theory states that it was derived from the Portuguese name São Tomás (St Thomas), while another attributes it to King Radama I's first visit to the seaside in 1817; it is said that the king knelt to taste the water and said (surely stating the obvious), 'Toa masina' ('It is salty').

During the political strife in 2002, the Toamasina region was one of centres of support for former president Didier Ratsiraka, whose family originated in the area. Militant factions blockaded the RN2, cutting the main fuel supply lines to Antananarivo. The blockades were removed by force, but not before a thriving black market trade in petrol had sprung up.

TOAMASINA (TAMATAVE)

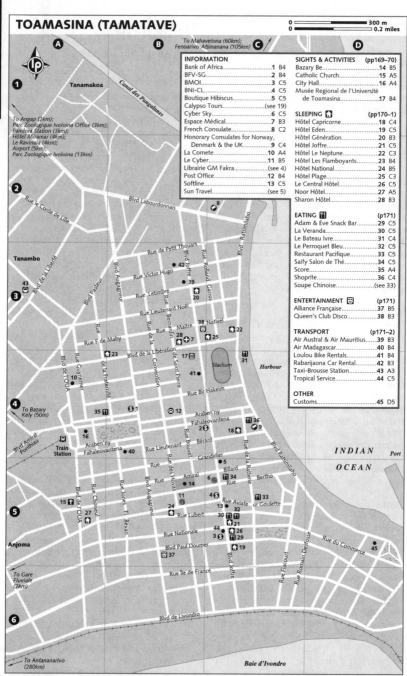

0 — 300 m
0 — 0.2 miles

To Mahavelona (60km);
Fenoarivo-Atsinanana (105km)

Tanamakoa

Canal des Pangalanes

To Angap (2km);
Parc Zoologique Ivoloina Office (3km);
Pandora Station (3km);
Hôtel Miramar (4km);
Le Ravinala (4km);
Airport (5km);
Parc Zoologique Ivoloina (13km)

INFORMATION
Bank of Africa...........................1 B4
BFV-SG.....................................2 B4
BMOI..3 C5
BNI-CL......................................4 C5
Boutique Hibiscus.....................5 C5
Calypso Tours...................(see 19)
Cyber Sky.................................6 C5
Espace Médical.........................7 B3
French Consulate.......................8 C2
Honorary Consulates for Norway,
  Denmark & the UK.................9 C4
La Comete...............................10 A4
Le Cyber.................................11 B5
Librairie GM Fakra................(see 4)
Post Office..............................12 B4
Softline..................................13 C5
Sun Travel.........................(see 5)

SIGHTS & ACTIVITIES (pp169–70)
Bazary Be...............................14 B5
Catholic Church......................15 A5
City Hall.................................16 A4
Musée Regional de l'Université
  de Toamasina.......................17 B4

SLEEPING (pp170–1)
Hôtel Capricorne.....................18 C4
Hôtel Eden.............................19 C5
Hôtel Génération.....................20 B3
Hôtel Joffre............................21 C5
Hôtel Le Neptune....................22 C3
Hôtel Les Flamboyants............23 B4
Hôtel National.........................24 C5
Hôtel Plage............................25 C3
Le Central Hôtel......................26 C5
Noor Hôtel.............................27 A5
Sharon Hôtel..........................28 B3

EATING (p171)
Adam & Eve Snack Bar............29 C5
La Veranda.............................30 C5
Le Bateau Ivre........................31 C4
Le Perroquet Bleu...................32 C5
Restaurant Pacifique...............33 C5
Saify Salon de Thé..................34 C5
Score.....................................35 A4
Shoprite.................................36 C4
Soupe Chinoise..................(see 33)

ENTERTAINMENT (p171)
Alliance Française....................37 B5
Queen's Club Disco.................38 B3

TRANSPORT (p171–2)
Air Austral & Air Mauritius.......39 B3
Air Madagascar......................40 B4
Loulou Bike Rentals.................41 B4
Rabarijaona Car Rental.............42 B3
Taxi-Brousse Station...............43 A3
Tropical Service......................44 C5

OTHER
Customs.................................45 D5

Rue le Conte de Lille

Blvd Labourdonnais

Tanambo

Rue de la Liberté

Blvd Pasteur

Blvd Augagneur

Rue de Petit Thouars

Rue Victor Hugo

Rue Joffre

Rue Roland Garros

Rue Letimbre

Rue Lieutenant Noël

Rue Benardin

Rue Maitre

Rue Nativel

Rue F de Mahy

Blvd de la Libération

Blvd Guyverner

Blvd de l'OUA

Blvd de la Fraternité

de la Convention

de Saint Pierre

Stadium

Harbour

Rue Bir Hakeim

To Bazary
Kely (50m)

Blvd Amiral
Ponthiau

Train
Station

Araben'ny
Fahaleovantena

Araben'ny
Fahaleovantena

Rue Lieutenant
Bérard

Rue Bouret

Grandidier

Rue de la Batterie

Blvd Ratsimilaho

*INDIAN
OCEAN*

Port

Rue des Hovas

Rue Amiral
Billard

Rue
Bertho

Rue Choiseul

Rue Jones

El Bevan

Blvd Augagneur

Rue Aviate
ur Goulette

Rue Lubert

Rue Nationale

Blvd Paul Doumer

Blvd Joffre

Rue Flacourt

Rue Romain Desfosse

Rue du Commerce

Blvd de l'OUA

Rue Île de France

Anjoma

To Gare
Fluviale
(2km)

Blvd de Livondro

To Antananarivo
(280km)

Baie d'Ivondro

ORIENTATION

Major streets running roughly north–south include Blvd Joffre (the main commercial street, with many of the town's shops and hotels) and Blvd Ratsimilaho, along the waterfront. Araben'ny Fahaleovantena (aka Ave Poincaré) is the main east–west thoroughfare, joining the waterfront with the train station.

INFORMATION
Bookshops

Librairie GM Fakra (Rue Joffre; 🕙 Tue-Sun, afternoon Mon), near BNI-CL, has a few English newspapers and magazines, plus maps of the region and postcards.

Internet Access

For email try **Cyber Sky** (Blvd Joffre; per min FMg150; 🕙 8am-9pm Mon-Sat) or **Le Cyber** (☎ 53 307 84; Rue Aviateur Goulette; per min FMg150; 🕙 7.30am-7.30pm).

Medical Services

Espace Médical (☎ 032 07 088 23, 53 315 66; Blvd de la Libération; 🕙 24hr), near Sharon Hôtel, is clean and well equipped.

Money

The **Bank of Africa** (BOA; main branch; Blvd Augagneur) is a few blocks east of the train station. **BNI-CL** (Blvd Joffre) and **BMOI** (Blvd Joffre) both have ATMs that will accept Visa cards. There's also a **BFV-SG** (Cnr Blvd Joffre & Araben'ny Fahaleovantena). **Hôtel Le Neptune** (☎ 53 324 26; Blvd Ratsimilaho) is sometimes willing to change travellers cheques outside of normal banking hours.

Post & Telephone

The main post office can be found on Araben'ny Fahaleovantena. There are several cardphones around town.

Tourist Information

Angap (☎ 53 327 07; Rte d'Ivoloina) is a few kilometres out of town on the road to the airport. It offers general information about national parks in the region. **Parc Zoologique d'Ivoloina** (Rte d'Ivoloina; p172) has an office a bit further on from Angap offering information about visits to the park.

TOURS

The following companies can assist with car hire, excursions down the Canal des Pangalanes, air packages to Île Sainte Marie and trips to Parc Zoologique Ivoloina, Mahambo and the beach resorts north along the coast.

Boutique Hibiscus (☎ 53 321 77; fax 53 334 03; Blvd Joffre) Booking agency for Hotel des Pangalanes. A half-day trip on the Canal des Pangalanes costs FMg750,000 per boat.

Calypso Tours (☎ 53 312 90; calypsotour@netcourrier .com; Blvd Joffre) A budget tour company attached to Hôtel Eden.

La Comete (☎ 53 339 53, 032 40 022 42; Blvd de l'OUA) Speedboat transfers to hotels on Canal des Pangalanes. From FMg1,500,000 per boat (takes 10 people).

Rabarijaona Car Rental (LCR; ☎ 53 301 52; grace .tours@dts.mg; Rue Victor Hugo) Cars from are FMg400,000 per day, drivers are FMg30,000 extra.

Softline (☎ 53 329 75; softline@dts.mg; 20 Blvd Joffre) Luxury cruises on the Canal des Pangalanes. A day trip with picnic lunch cost FMg300,000 per person.

Sun Travel (☎ 53 333 82; suntravel@wanadoo.mg; 30 Blvd Joffre) Day trips to Parc Zoologique Ivoloina cost FMg200,000. A day on the Canal des Pangalanes including picnic lunch cost FMg380,000 per person.

SIGHTS & ACTIVITIES
Musée Regional de l'Université de Toamasina

University Museum (admission by donation; 🕙 9am-4pm Mon-Sat) consists mostly of posters in French outlining the general history of Africa, plus a few dusty exhibits of farming tools, local geological forms, and fishing implements. It's worth half an hour of your time on a rainy afternoon.

Markets

Toamasina's colourful **Bazary Be** (Big Market) sells fruit, vegetables, spices, handicrafts and beautiful bouquets of flowers if you feel the need to brighten up your hotel room. The **Bazary Kely** (Little Market) sells fish and produce. It occupies the ruins of a commercial complex on Blvd de la Fidelité, west of the train station.

Swimming

Hôtel Miramar (☎ 53 332 15; off Rte de l'Aéroport; 🕙 Mon-Sun) has a clean 50m pool near the sea. It costs FMg15,000 for nonguests. You can also use the slightly grubby-looking pool at the **Hôtel Le Neptune** (☎ 53 322 26; Blvd Ratsimilaho) on the seafront, which charges FMg10,000 for nonguests. A better bet is the 25m pool at the **Le Bateau Ivre** (☎ 53 302 94; Blvd Ratsimilaho), in the centre of town, which has free swimming if you eat in the restaurant (see opposite) or charges FMg10,000 if you don't.

SLEEPING

As befits its status as a holiday town, Toamasina is fairly well provided with hotels, albeit mostly faded and overpriced. There are lots of mosquitoes in Toamasina, so opt for a hotel with nets, or bring your own.

Budget

Hôtel Les Flamboyants (☎ 53 323 50; Blvd de la Libération; r without/with air-con FMg85,000/98,000; 🔣) A very good-value choice – airy rooms have a balcony, mosquito net, phone and bathroom. There's a TV downstairs in the excellent restaurant.

Le Ravinala (☎ 53 308 83; fgbaril@wanadoo.mg; Rte de l'Aéroport; r without/with toilet FMg76,000/86,000; mains FMg25,000) Funky polished bamboo furniture makes this friendly beach guesthouse a very attractive-looking option. There's an attached restaurant open Wednesday to Monday.

Hôtel Eden (☎ 53 312 90; calypsotour@netcourrier .com; Blvd Joffre; r without/with toilet FMg50,000/60,000) The rooms at this new backpackers' hotel have a fan but no mosquito nets. It's a handy place to organise tours on the Canal des Pangalanes.

Hôtel Capricorne (☎ 53 331 66; Rue Lieutenant Bérard; r with bathroom FMg64,000) Not a bad budget option – the Capricorne is fairly basic, but clean and quiet. The biggish rooms have a telephone, but no mosquito nets. There's a bar on site.

Hôtel National (Hôtel Étoile Rouge; ☎ 53 322 90; Rue Lubert; d with bathroom FMg67,500, d with air-con FMg125,000; 🔣) About the same standard as Hôtel Capricorne, the small, noisy but clean rooms have a fan but no mosquito nets.

Hôtel Plage (☎ 53 320 90; hotel_plage@simicro.mg; Blvd de la Libération; d with bathroom FMg65,000, with hot water FMg80,000) Once you pass the rather postmodern coloured sculptures in the lobby, the big rooms at this rather scruffy hotel are just about adequate. There are (ageing) fans, but no nets. Go for the more expensive rooms – the cheaper ones are next to the disco.

Mid-Range

Hôtel Génération (☎ 53 321 05; fax 53 328 34; Blvd Joffre; s/d with bathroom FMg87,750/147,000; 🔣) The Génération has cheerful pink rooms with colourful bedspreads, TV, balcony and even a fridge. The English-speaking staff are helpful and friendly, and the restaurant is one of the best in town. Slightly cheaper rooms without air-con are also available.

Le Central Hôtel (☎ 53 340 86; fax 53 341 19; Blvd Joffre; d/tw with bathroom FMg135,000/158,000; 🔣) The Central has smart rooms with balconies, elegant four-poster beds and mosquito nets, plus phone and TV. Its restaurant, Le Veranda, is around the corner.

Hôtel Joffre (☎ 53 323 90; fax 53 332 94; Blvd Joffre; sodefi@dts.mg; r with bathroom & fan/air-con FMg110,000/ 135,000; 🔣) With its marble floors, wooden reception desk and pavement café, the Joffre exudes faded colonial charm. Once inside, however, the rooms are merely functional rather than luxurious. All have mosquito nets, a TV and phone, and some have a balcony. The hotel is used by organised tours and in the high season is often full, so it's best to book in advance.

Hôtel Miramar (☎ 53 332 15; fax 53 330 13; off Rte de l'Aéroport; d with fan/air-con FMg170,000/200,000; 🔣 🔣) A slightly faded but upmarket establishment on the beach about 4km north of town. Each of the good-quality bungalows, some with TV, have a little sitting area outside, but none have mosquito nets. There's a 50m swimming pool and a quiet garden. Be careful when walking on the beach, as there have been reports of muggings in the area.

Noor Hôtel (☎ 53 338 45; Blvd de l'OUA; r without/ with air-con FMg110,000/125,000; 🔣) Smallish, but the spick-and-span rooms have mosquito nets and tiled floors. There's a bright and cheerful breakfast room and bar.

Top End

Neither of Toamasina's top-end hotels is particularly special, offering little in the way of character, and only slightly more comfort than the mid-range options.

Sharon Hôtel (☎ 53 304 20; fax 53 331 29; Blvd de la Libération; d with TV & phone €60, ste with Jacuzzi €105; 🔣 🅿) A sparklingly modern and clean hotel, furnished in fake walnut with red nylon carpets and gilt trimmings. Rooms have a safe and fridge; bathrooms have an apricot-coloured basin, full bathtub and free condoms – everything the out-of-town businessman could desire. There's a pool, a sauna and a gym on site, and a pizzeria in the courtyard. Visa cards accepted.

Hôtel Le Neptune (☎ 53 322 26; fax 53 324 26; Blvd Ratsimilaho; d/tr €65/75; ⚡ Ⓟ 🏊) With a good location overlooking the sea, the Neptune has a greenish swimming pool and a sundeck with plastic chairs, a casino, slot machines and a disco (open Monday to Saturday). The fairly plush rooms have marble bathrooms, old-fashioned balconies, a TV and minibar, and fluffy towels, but no mosquito nets.

EATING

Le Veranda (☎ 53 334 35; off Blvd Joffre; set dinner FMg40,000; 🕑 lunch & dinner Mon-Sat) This upmarket peach-coloured restaurant technically belongs to Hotel Central, but it enjoys great popularity in its own right with French expatriates. The set three-course dinner changes daily, and the big menu features a range of Malagasy, European and Chinese dishes.

Le Bateau Ivre (La Piscine; ☎ 53 302 94; Blvd Ratsimilaho; mains FMg40,000; 🕑 lunch & dinner; 🏊) Toamasina's latest leisure spot combines a rather expensive seafood restaurant with a 25m swimming pool (open from 9am) and live music in the evenings. It's a great place for kids, but the pool gets packed at weekends. Swimming is free if you eat here, FMg10,000 if you don't.

Le Perroquet Bleu (☎ 032 40 270 55; Rue Lubert; mains FMg25,000; 🕑 breakfast, lunch & dinner) A very cosy, warm and welcoming little restaurant. The open kitchen dishes out real Italian pizza alongside local rice dishes, while the blue parrot of the name squawks cheerfully on his perch.

Hôtel Génération (Blvd Joffre; set dinner FMg40,000) Of the hotel restaurants, this is one of the best, with excellent service and a good range of Chinese, European and Malagasy dishes.

Sharon Hôtel (Blvd de la Libération; mains from FMg30,000) The restaurant at the Sharon is a good one for vegetarians, with its decent selection of Indian vegetarian dishes alongside upmarket staples such as lobster thermidor.

Hôtel Les Flamboyants (Blvd de la Libération; mains FMg25,000-35,000) Has a good selection of locally prepared seafood in an attractive terrace restaurant.

Hôtel Joffre (Blvd Joffre) The elegant dining room here has good French food and suitably deferential service.

Restaurant Pacifique (Rue de la Batterie; mains FMg10,000-15,000; 🕑 lunch & dinner Tue-Sun) If you feel like Chinese food, try Pacifique which has a café called Soupe Chinoise next door.

Adam & Eve Snack Bar (☎ 53 334 56; Blvd Joffre; lunches FMg10,000; 🕑 breakfast, lunch & dinner Tue-Sun) For snacks and drinks, head to Adam & Eve Snack Bar, which has an outdoor bar and dishes up Malagasy dishes as well as juice, ice cream and crêpes.

Saify Salon de Thé (☎ 53 331 81; Blvd Joffre; snacks FMg5000; 🕑 breakfast & lunch) As an alternative to Adam & Eve try this place up the road, which has nondescript patisserie and slow service, but fresh juice and good ice cream.

If you're craving European luxuries, try Shoprite or Score supermarkets.

ENTERTAINMENT

Alliance Française (☎ 53 334 94; aftamatave@dts.mg; Blvd Paul Doumer) Has French film screenings a few times a week.

Popular nightspots include **Queen's Club Disco** (off Blvd Joffre; 🕑 nightly from 9pm), the expensive nightclub and casino at **Hôtel Le Neptune** (🕑 Mon-Sat; see Sleeping above) and **Pandora Station** (Rte de l'Aéroport; 🕑 Thu-Sun) which also has a snack bar.

GETTING THERE & AWAY
Air

Air Madagascar (☎ 53 323 56; Araben'ny Fahaleovantena) flies daily between Toamasina and Antananarivo (FMg639,000), sometimes via Île Sainte Marie (FMg368,000). There's weekly flights which connect Toamasina with Sambava (FMg682,000), Mananara (FMg466,000), Maroantsetra (FMg577,000), Ambatondrazaka (FMg306,000), Antalaha (FMg682,000), and Antsiranana (FMg820,000). Be warned that during the vanilla season (June to October), the planes that fly up and down the northeast coast can be full.

Weekly flights on **Air Austral & Air Mauritius** (shared office ☎ 53 312 43; 81 Blvd Joffre) link Toamasina with Port Louis (Mauritius) and St-Denis (Réunion).

Boat

Boat travel is generally slow and uncomfortable, but is often the only option when roads on the northeast coast are impassable because of weather, which is most of the time. Cargo boats leave from Toamasina for Île Sainte Marie, Mananara, Antalaha, Antsiranana and Taolagnaro, although you generally have to wait to find one that accepts passengers (you will need to bring all your own food and water). Standards vary widely; cabins are sometimes available, but on most boats you can expect to be bedding down on deck. Fares and schedules vary wildly. You will need to ask around in the port area, and be prepared to wait at least several days.

The MS *Mauritius Trochetia* leaves Toamasina for Réunion and Mauritius approximately every two weeks. Return fares to Réunion are €365/235 for a 1st/2nd-class cabin. To Mauritius and back, fares are €497/342. For tickets, go to **Tropical Service** (☎ 53 336 79/89; 23 Blvd Joffre), near the Hotel Joffre.

Taxi-Brousse

The taxi-brousse station at the northwestern edge of town serves Antananarivo as well as points north as far as Soanierana-Ivongo (FMg30,000, four hours) and south as far as Mahanaro. Along the route between Toamasina and Antananarivo there are minibuses and coaches throughout the day (FMg40,000, seven hours). It is best to leave early to ensure that you reach your destination during daylight.

There are taxis-brousse departing throughout the day to Moramanga (FMg30,000, four hours).

Train

There was no regular train service to/from Toamasina at the time of research. Plans are afoot to reinstate train services, so inquire at the Toamasina or Antananarivo stations for an update.

GETTING AROUND

Taxis between town and the airport (5km north of town) cost FMg25,000. Taxi rides within town cost FMg5000.

With its wide, flat avenues, Toamasina is ideal for cycling. For bike rental try **Loulou Bike Rentals** (Blvd Joffre; full-/half-day rental FMg15,000/30,000; 🕒 7.30am-6pm), opposite the stadium.

Rabarijaona Car Rental (LCR; ☎ 53 301 52; grace.tours@dts.mg; Rue Victor Hugo) has cars from FMg400,000 per day. Drivers are FMg30,000 extra. You can also hire cars through **Sun Travel** (☎ 53 333 82; suntravel@wanadoo.mg; 30 Blvd Joffre) or ask at **Le Perroquet Bleu** (☎ 032 40 270 55; Rue Lubert) restaurant about private car-hire deals.

Pousse-pousses charge from FMg2000 per trip within the centre of town.

NORTH OF TOAMASINA

PARC ZOOLOGIQUE IVOLOINA

The **Parc Zoologique Ivoloina** (admission FMg20,000; 🕒 9am-5pm) is a conservation-friendly and very well-run zoo and botanical garden just north of Toamasina. The Madagascar Wildlife Trust, supported by zoos and conservation organisations around the world, has set up an education centre, captive breeding programmes for endangered species and a halfway house for animals being reintroduced into the wild. The zoo's beautiful grounds contain more than 100 lemurs from a dozen different species, including the aye-aye, as well as radiated tortoises, tree boas and tomato frogs. There are both caged and wild lemurs; feeding is not permitted.

The botanical garden contains more than 75 species of native and exotic plants, and there is a model farm on site designed to demonstrate sustainable agricultural methods. It is possible to hire a pirogue (traditional canoe) around the lake, or to picnic on the shores. There is a kiosk on the grounds with a small selection of drinks and snacks.

All explanations are in Malagasy or French, but you can buy some notes on the zoo in English (FMg5000).

For detailed information on Ivoloina, and on how your local zoo can support conservation efforts in Madagascar, stop by the office of the **Madagascar Fauna Group** (☎ 53 308 42; mfgmad@dts.mg; Rte de l'Aéroport), 4km north of central Toamasina.

Ivoloina's **camp site** (tent sites FMg10,000), in a pretty spot next to the lake, has toilets, showers and sheltered picnic tables.

Parc Zoologique Ivoloina is 13km north of Toamasina. A charter taxi from town costs around FMg25,000 per hour. Taxis-brousse from Toamasina to Ivoloina village (FMg5000) leave every hour or two. From Ivoloina village it is a scenic 4km walk to the park entrance. Organised tour companies in Toamasina charge about FMg200,000 per vehicle (maximum three people).

AMBATONDRAZAKA
pop 35,000

Ambatondrazaka (am-baton-draz-*aka*) is the major town near **Lac Alaotra**, Madagascar's largest body of water. The lake supports 74 species of water birds, and the shores are home to the endangered Alaotran gentle lemur. For more information about the lake and the battle to save it, see the boxed text below. One of the few places where the road meets the lake is at Andreba, on the east of the lake (accessible by taxi-brousse from Ambatondrazaka), where there is a lemur reserve. Ask for the *responsable* of the reserve, who will organise a canoe and a guide. It is best to visit the reserve in the early morning.

Hôtel Voahirana (☎ 54 812 08; r FMg50,000) near the market has clean rooms and a reasonable restaurant and can help organise treks in the region. **Hôtel Max** (☎ 54 813 86; d without/with bathroom FMg30,000/90,000), near the train station is more comfortable – more expensive rooms have TV.

Air Madagascar connects Ambatondrazaka with Toamasina (FMg306,000) and Antananarivo (FMg368,000) a few times a week.

To get to Ambatondrazaka from Toamasina, go to Moramanga (FMg30,000, 5½ hours) from where a taxi-brousse leaves most days for Ambatondrazaka (FMg25,000, four to six hours). The road is good until you reach Moramanga, and is rough from there to Ambatondrazaka. Direct taxis for Ambatondrazaka also depart several times weekly from Antananarivo's eastern taxi-brousse station (FMg30,000).

From Ambatondrazaka, there is usually at least one vehicle daily to Imerimandroso (FMg10,000, one to two hours).

ROUTE DES CONTREBANDIERS

The Route des Contrebandiers (Smugglers' Path) is a muddy and slippery five- to six-day trek connecting Imerimandroso (50km north of Ambatondrazaka on the eastern edge of Lac Alaotra) with the village of Anjahambe, about 35km to the west of Mahambo. Historically, the Route des Contrebandiers was used by smugglers bringing goods from Réunion and Mauritius into the Merina highlands.

Today, few travellers attempt the trek, primarily because access is difficult and the going is very hard. If you do attempt the trail, you'll need camping equipment, including a waterproof groundsheet, although some villages along the way have small hotels. You'll need to be self-sufficient

---

LAC ALAOTRA

The area around Lac Alaotra is a centre of biodiversity, with three species found nowhere else on earth – the Alaotran gentle lemur, the Madagascar pochard and the Alaotran little grebe. Sadly, Lac Alaotra exemplifies the environmental damage that affects many parts of Madagascar, with the latter two species probably extinct.

Population growth, hunting, burning and clearance of marshes, escalating fishing pressure, the pollution from pesticides, and invasion by introduced plants and fish species have all contributed to the degradation. As the area's original forest cover was lost, striking erosion gullies (seen if you fly from Antananarivo to Ambatondrazaka) have leaked their sterile sediment onto the surrounding rice fields.

The good news is that steps are being taken to restore the ecological balance. The Durrell Wildlife Conservation Trust has led a five-year project to raise awareness of the value of the marshes, to raise pride in the Alaotran gentle lemur and to gain commitment to wise use of the wetlands. The government has added Alaotra to the international Ramsar convention list of important wetlands, promising to maintain its biodiversity.

Fishermen have agreed to limited mesh sizes and a closed season. Villagers protect marsh areas, plant new marshes, and have decreased marsh burning and clearance. Fish catches are increasing and lemur populations are recovering. There is now hope that the tide of environmental degradation can be turned at Alaotra.

Joanna Durbin, Durrell Wildlife Conservation Trust

EASTERN MADAGASCAR

THE MYSTERY OF THE STOLEN BONES

In the last few years, nearly 1000 ancestral tombs in the Ambatondrazaka region have been broken into by thieves intent on stealing human bones. Although the thieves themselves have often been caught and sentenced, the reason behind the crimes remains mysterious. The unknown traffickers, who have so far evaded capture, offer as much as US$4000 for a kilogram of bones.

The thefts of the bones, which are regarded as sacred, have caused widespread distress among families of the region, and wild rumours abound as to what they could be wanted for, with suggested culprits ranging from foreign mafiosos to desperate AIDS victims convinced the bones could cure them. No convincing theory has yet been raised, however, and the thefts continue.

---

with food. Water is available, but you will need a good filter. Seek out a guide from Hôtel Voahirana in Ambatondrazaka.

MAHAVELONA (FOULPOINTE)

Mahavelona, more commonly known as Foulpointe (fool-point), is a small, nondescript coastal town near some white-sand beaches. There are sharks offshore; swimming anywhere away from the hotels area, which is protected by a reef, is risky. The best beaches and the more expensive hotels are to the south of town.

Ruins of the 19th-century Merina **Fort Hova** are about 500m north of Mahavelona. Its walls, which are 6m high and 4m thick in places, are made from coral, sand and eggs, similar to the material used in the walls of Ambohimanga near Antananarivo (p76).

Sleeping & Eating

Au Gentil Pêcheur (☎ 57 220 16; d/f FMg76,000/ 121,000) At the southern end of town, about 300m from the main road, these simple bungalows have tiled floors, which are very close to a rather swampy looking beach. The restaurant (dishes from FMg19,000) has seafood from FMg25,000 and cheaper dishes.

Hôtel Génération Annexe (☎ 57 220 22; d/tr FMg92,000/110,000; dishes around FMg25,000) Nearby Au Gentil Pêcheur and under the same management as Hôtel Génération in Toamasina, this place is a step up. The thatched bungalows are set in a peaceful garden, and have a bathroom with hot water. The cheery terraced restaurant is only 20m from the beach.

Le Grand Bleu (☎ 57 220 06/7; tw/f with bathroom FMg150,000/300,000; set dinner FMg60,000; 🕮) About 800m east of the road and signposted, Le Grand Bleu is better still, with cute little wickerwork bungalows that are very well-maintained and contain big, modern bathrooms. Pirogue trips on the sea cost FMg30,000. Bookings can be made through the Hôtel Joffre in Toamasina.

Manda Beach Hôtel (☎ 57 220 00; mandabeach@ dts.mg; d/tr with fan & net FMg183,000/263,000; 🕮) Upmarket and about 100m south of Le Grand Bleu, the smart beachside bungalows here have polished wooden walls, sundecks and ethnic-printed bedcovers. The hotel's stretch of beach is the best you'll find in town, and it has a swimming pool and tennis courts in the grounds. Transfers here from Toamasina cost FMg200,000 for two people.

At the northern end of the village, **Le Lagon** (☎ 57 220 28; d FMg60,000) and **Vakoa** (☎ 57 220 18; d FMg80,000) both have scruffy but clean bungalows, and bars and restaurants over a little pond near the beach. Le Lagon is apparently building a swimming pool. The beach here is distinctly uninviting, brown and rocky, but it's not far to walk to a better bit of sand further south.

Getting There & Away

Mahavelona lies 58km north of Toamasina. Minibuses depart from the Toamasina taxi-brousse station daily, generally in the mornings (FMg10,000, 1½ hours). Hotel vehicles going from Mahavelona to Toamasina will give you a lift for the equivalent of the taxi-brousse fare.

Several vehicles daily pass Mahavelona while heading south to Toamasina from Soanierana-Ivongo. The time they pass Mahavelona depends on what time the ferry from Île Sainte Marie arrives at Soanierana-Ivongo. If you need to catch a taxi-brousse to Soanierana-Ivongo, stand by the side of the road before 9am.

MAHAMBO

Mahambo is a coastal village with a safe swimming beach and luxuriant vegetation that comes right down to the shore in some places.

In a meadow about 50m from the beach, **Ylang-Ylang** (☎ 57 300 08/9; camping/d/tw FMg25,000/ 50,000/75,000) has pretty little bungalows, each with easy chairs outside. Meals can be arranged in the garden restaurant.

The beach in front of **La Pirogue** (☎ 57 301 71; bungalow low/high season FMg100,000/175,000; set dinners FMg25,000-50,000) is a bit rocky, but the rooms themselves are well-maintained, with hot water, and there's a seafood restaurant, too.

Motel Récif (☎ 57 300 50; d FMg80,000), on the beach, is quite a long walk from town. It has good French food, although the rooms, with grubby linen and cold water, aren't up to much.

Mahambo is 30km north of Mahavelona and about 90km from Toamasina. If you plan on heading to one of the beach hotels, ask the taxi driver to drop you at the intersection, then walk about 2km down a sandy track heading east. For information on travel along the coast north of Toamasina, see opposite.

FENOARIVO-ATSINANANA

The bustling spice-growing town of Fenoarivo-Atsinanana (usually referred to as just Fenoarivo – which means 'Thousand Warriors' – or Fénérive-Est) was the first capital of the Betsimisaraka. It was here in the early 1700s that the founder, Ratsimilaho, united the tribe and proclaimed himself king. Ratsimilaho's tomb is on a tiny island just offshore. About 3km south of Fenoarivo is Vohimasina – the ruins of an old **pirate fort** with triangular water wells. You can also visit a nearby **clove factory**.

The town has a post office, a lively market, a cardphone and a BOA bank.

Sleeping & Eating

Le Girofle d'Or (☎ 57 300 43; d/tr FMg53,000/73,000; mains FMg15,000) In the centre of town near the École Protestante and not far from the market, this place has basic rooms sharing a clean bathroom, and a restaurant serving Malagasy food.

Le Girofle Beach (☎ 57 300 42; r without/with bathroom FMg53,000/63,000) The beach annexe,

overlooks the beach about 1.5km east of town, but the bungalows are fairly grotty.

Hôtel Paradisa Kely (☎ 57 300 06; r FMg60,000) Next door to the Girofle Beach, it's about the same standard.

Hôtel Belle Rose (☎ 57 300 38; d/tr with bathroom FMg80,000/140,000) About 500m from the centre on the road leading to the hospital, this is a bit more comfortable than the other options.

Getting There & Away

Fenoarivo is about 15km north of Mahambo, and is serviced by taxis-brousse on the Toamasina to Soanierana-Ivongo route.

PARC NATIONAL DE ZAHAMENA

West of Fenoarivo-Atsinanana is the 41,402-hectare **Parc National de Zahamena** (admission FMg50,000). Still in the development stage, Zahamena protects important areas of rain forest and about a dozen species of lemur.

The park is managed by Angap with support from Conservation International; for information, contact the **park office** (☎ 57 300 33) in town. There are some basic camping grounds in the park. You will need to be self-sufficient with food, water and equipment. You can also reach Zahamena from Ambatondrazaka.

SOANIERANA-IVONGO

Soanierana-Ivongo is a small town notable primarily as a port for boats to and from Île Sainte Marie. If the pronunciation of the name defeats you, you can get away with referring to it as 'Sierra-Ivongo'.

There are no good accommodation options, so it's best to try to time your travels to avoid having to stay overnight. If you do stay, the best place is **Hôtel Les Escales** (bungalows FMg25,000), next to the boat jetty. Les Escales is also the place to come for boat and taxi-brousse information and tickets, although the touts will be sure to find you as soon as you step out of your vehicle. There is a restaurant here – order well in advance as meals can take hours to cook.

Taxis-brousse head to Soanierana-Ivongo from Toamasina (FMg25,000, three to four hours), departing from around 6am every morning. However, they are not necessarily coordinated with the ferry departure from Soanierana-Ivongo (which varies according

LAC ALAOTRA & PARC NATIONAL DE ZAHAMENA

to the tides); try to get on the first vehicle heading north.

Taxis-brousse heading south to Toamasina wait for the launches and ferry from Île Sainte Marie. (For information on boat connections to and from the island, refer to p179.)

The road from Soanierana-Ivongo north to Mananara is dignified with the name Route Nationale 5 (RN5). However, it is actually no more than a collection of deep potholes joined together with dust or mud, depending on the season. There are six major river crossings en route, served by ferries and/or fragile bridges. Assuming there are any taxis-brousse running, and that nothing else goes wrong (a big assumption), you can make it in about two days (taxis-brousse stop when darkness falls and continue the next day).

There have been several instances of taxis-brousse overturning along this route or falling through weak bridges. In all of Madagascar's rough journeys, this particular one stands out – so it's only to be attempted by the seriously masochistic or truly desperate. Should this describe you, you can expect to be quoted about FMg150,000 for the taxi-brousse journey. Private vehicles attempting the route will charge about the same for a lift.

The only other way to get up the coast from Soanierana-Ivongo is to take a boat across to Île Sainte Marie, then look for another boat for the onward journey.

ÎLE SAINTE MARIE

The slender 57km-long island of Île Sainte Marie (its Malagasy name, Nosy Boraha, is rarely used) lies 8km off the coast. Once the haunt of pirates, the island has seen a big influx of tourists in recent years, and hotels have proliferated – it is now jokingly called '*Île des Vazahas*' ('island of foreigners') by locals. Despite this, Île Sainte Marie still retains considerable charm – particularly in the small villages that dot the lush agricultural interior – and the beaches are world-class.

If you're not the type to lie immobile for days working on your tan, Île Sainte Marie's rugged interior is a particularly good place for hiking, cycling or motorcycling. Naturally, watersports are on offer everywhere, and between July and September the waters around the island play host to migrating humpback whales (p191).

Rain can be expected year-round on Île Sainte Marie, although the weather is usually least wet from late August to late November. Between December and March, the island is subject to violent cyclones.

Because it sees so many visitors, prices for food are slightly higher on Île Sainte Marie than on the mainland.

HISTORY

The Malagasy name of the island, Nosy Boraha, is presumed to mean 'Island of Ibrahim' or 'Island of Abraham', a name

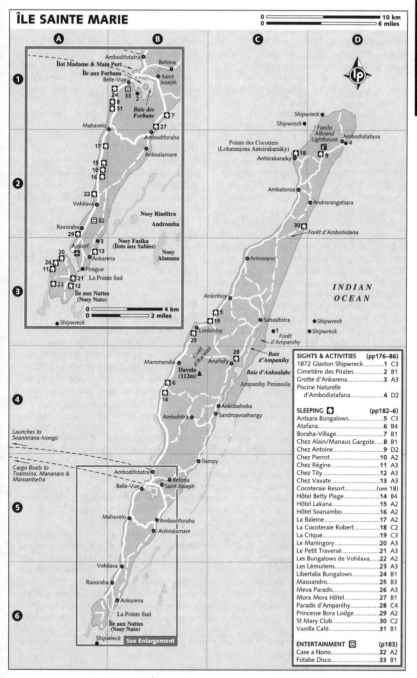

ÎLE SAINTE MARIE

perhaps bestowed by early Arabic or Jewish settlers. The commonly used French name, Île Sainte Marie, is derived from Santa Maria, the name originally given to it by early-16th-century Portuguese sailors.

French settlers attempted to found a colony on Île Sainte Marie in the 1640s, but were thwarted by strong tropical fevers, which killed most of the pioneers. From then on the island became the hideout of a motley international band of English, Portuguese, French and American pirates. Presumably the swashbucklers had stronger constitutions than the law-abiding settlers – or the rich pickings from silk-laden ships passing en route to India made the profits worth the risk.

At this point, a Frenchman named Jean-Onésime Filet (known as 'La Bigorne') was shipwrecked on a beach of Sainte Marie while fleeing an affair with the wife of a fellow officer in Réunion. One of the local women who found him and restored him to health was none other than Princess Bety of Betsimisaraka, daughter of King Ratsimilaho (himself the son of an English pirate). Bety and La Bigorne were married, and in July 1750, after the death of her father, Bety ceded the island to France.

In 1752, the widow of Ratsimilaho organised a revolt, massacring French settlers, exiling Bety to Mauritius and returning control of the island to the Betsimisaraka. In 1818, the French returned, eventually turning the island into a penal colony. In recognition of Princess Bety's magnanimous gift to France, the independence agreement of 1960 allowed the inhabitants of Île Sainte Marie to choose between French and Malagasy nationality. Although the majority chose Malagasy, many retain French names.

INFORMATION

The only place to get money (cash, Visa advances and travellers cheques) is at the **BFV-SG** (7.30-11.30am & 2-4pm Mon-Fri), next to the small boat harbour in Ambodifotatra.

The post office is in the upper part of Ambodifotatra, just south of the main part of town. There's a telephone office in the main street.

Internet access is available at the **La Baleine** (per min FMg1000), just south of Ambodifotatra.

ACTIVITIES
Diving & Snorkelling

Île Sainte Marie may not have all the coral it once did, but it still offers some decent diving. The good months are from July to January; the best time is from October to December. Dive centres are often closed from February to May.

THE PIRATE KINGDOM

By the early 18th century, Île Sainte Marie had become the headquarters of the world's pirates. At one stage, the pirate population of Madagascar numbered close to 1000. English and French naval policing had slowed profits in the once-lucrative Caribbean to a trickle, so Madagascar, and Île Sainte Marie in particular, was an ideal base from which to ambush traders sailing around the Cape of Good Hope between Europe and the Far East.

One of history's most infamous pirates, Captain Kidd, arrived on the island after a long siege on the high seas. The wreck of his ship, the *Adventure,* was discovered by divers in 2000 at the entrance to Baie des Forbans, but much of Kidd's treasure has never been found...

The pirates frequently married local women, and their offspring came to be known as Zana-Malata (Children of Mulattos). Of these, it was Ratsimilaho, the son of a Malagasy princess, Antavaratra Rahena, and an English pirate, Thomas White, who would have the greatest impact on Madagascar. Ratsimilaho was leader of the Zana-Malata and, thanks to a number of military successes, became founder and chief of the unified Betsimisaraka.

John Avery, a British pirate, established himself in about 1695 at Baie d'Antongil near present-day Maroantsetra. One of his raids was on the ship of a Mogul maharajah on his way to Mecca. Among the booty was the daughter of an oriental sovereign, whom Avery took as his bride. After making treaties with neighbouring pirate leaders, he proclaimed himself ruler of Antongil. It isn't known what eventually became of Avery, but some historians believe he returned to England to live out his days incognito.

Some popular diving sites are found around the two shipwrecks in the far north and along the eastern coast, offshore from Sahasifotra. The dive centres and some hotels also rent out snorkelling gear. The main dive centres, all with offices in Ambodifotatra, are:

Il Balenottero (☎ 57 400 36; www.ilbalenottero.com) Single/double dives FMg200,000/360,000. Whale-watching FMg200,000 per half day. PADI Open Water course FMg1,800,000. Multiday yacht cruises and fishing trips can also be arranged.

Le Lemurien Palmé (☎ 032 04 607 34; www.lemurien -palme.com) Dives from FMg200,000, try dives FMg250,000. Also offers whale-watching and motorcycle hire.

Mahery-Be Dive Centre (☎ 57 401 48; somasub@ ifrance.com) Offers dives and courses at the same prices as both the others, plus boat hire for FMg1,500,000 per day.

Fishing

Il Balenottero, Chez Clevice, Le Maningory and some of the upper-end hotels organise big game fishing expeditions. Prices start from €133 per half day. Fishing is best between late September and March/April.

Whale-Watching

Every year from July to September, several hundred whales swim through the waters off Île Sainte Marie, with many staying in Baie d'Antongil to the north to give birth or to look for mates. During this time, the dive centres, hotels and tour companies on Île Sainte Marie organise whale-watching excursions around the island. Prices average about FMg200,000 per person.

Be sure the boat is seaworthy before handing over your money, and don't go out in bad weather. For those who read French and want more detailed information on the whales, look for the *Petit guide pratique à l'usage des observateurs des baleines à bosse à Madagascar* (about FMg25,000), which is on sale at some of the top-end hotels. For more details about whales, see p191.

TOURS

Most of the mid-range and top-end hotels organise tours around the island by 4WD, pirogue or boat, including day excursions to Île aux Nattes, Pointe des Cocotiers at the north of the island, and Baie d'Ampanihy. Prices vary according to where you start your tour.

WARNING

Many areas of the coast north and south of Ambodifotatra are home to sea urchins. Check locally before going swimming and always wear something on your feet.

Chez Clevice (☎ 032 02 33 148; Ambodifotatra) can organise excursions including whale-watching (FMg200,000 per half day for a group of five), and boat trips to the beach at La Crique (FMg200,000 per person). You can also arrange boat transfers or day trips from here to the mainland towns of Manompana and Ampanihy (to both towns it's FMg300,000 per person).

GETTING THERE & AWAY
Air

Air Madagascar flies daily between Île Sainte Marie and Antananarivo (FMg750,000), frequently via Toamasina (FMg368,000). Flights to Mananara (FMg209,000), Maroantsetra (FMg368,000), as well as destinations further north, go via Toamasina. Flights are often full; in the vanilla season (June to October) book as far in advance as possible, and reconfirm all bookings.

The office of **Air Madagascar** (☎ 57 400 46; Ambodifotatra) is down a side road past the telephone office.

Boat

Since the sinking of the ferry *Samsonette* in 2000, the only way of reaching Île Sainte Marie by boat is on one of a number of small launches that make the trip from Soanierana-Ivongo (FMg35,000 one way). Sailings are often cancelled in bad weather or rough seas; if in doubt about conditions, it's best to wait until the weather is better before attempting the crossing and to carefully choose one of the more seaworthy boats. The most seaworthy of these is the *Rozina* (which does the trip in about two hours). It departs from Île Sainte Marie at about 7.30am and from Soanierana-Ivongo around 11am. On the *Rozina*, try to get a seat at the front where it's drier.

All the launches have offices by the ports in Ambodifotatra and Soanierana-Ivongo. Before sailing, all passengers are required to go to the police station in Soanierana-

Ivongo to register. For all crossings, bring plastic or something waterproof to protect you and your luggage.

Many travellers usually fly one way between Antananarivo and Île Sainte Marie and then travel the other way overland, stopping off at a few places along the way. You can travel by road and ferry or launch between Toamasina and Île Sainte Marie via Soanierana-Ivongo in one day if you get an early start.

Cargo boats also sail between Île Sainte Marie and Mananara, Maroantsetra and Toamasina. There are no set schedules; inquire at the port on Îlot Madame. Departures from Île Sainte Marie are often in the evening or at night. For more information, see the Getting There & Away sections of individual town chapters.

GETTING AROUND

Most roads on Île Sainte Marie are in bad condition, particularly the road running north from Ambodifotatra towards Pointe des Cocotiers.

To/From the Airport

The airport is located at the southern tip of the island, 13km south of Ambodifotatra. Hotel transfer prices range from FMg10,000 to FMg150,000 one way, depending on distance and hotel.

Taxis-brousse usually charge FMg10,000 between the airport and Ambodifotatra. A private taxi costs FMg35,000.

Car & Motorcycle

A few places rent out cars with a driver for expeditions around the island. Try Hôtel Soanambo in the south of the island, or Boraha-Village hotel. Rates are around FMg500,000 for a 4WD.

Hiring a motorcycle is a good way of getting around the island and seeing off the beaten track parts of Île Sainte Marie. Many of the roads are heavily potholed, so you'll need to be a fairly confident rider to negotiate them safely.

Il Balenottero (☎ 57 400 36; www.ilbalenottero .com), next to the harbour in Ambodifotatra, rents motorcycles for FMg250,000 per day, as does Le Lemurien Palmé (☎ 032 04 607 34; www.lemurien-palme.com). Many hotels also have motorcycles for hire, and a 'chauffeur' can often be arranged.

Bicycle

Île Sainte Marie is ideal for mountain bikes, although some of the roads at the northern end of the island (particularly the road north of Lonkintsy) are too rutted and rough to be enjoyable – particularly in the rainy season, when they can become very slippery.

Le Lemurien Palmé (☎ 032 04 607 34; www .lemurien-palme.com) and many hotels also rent bicycles. Places to try include Libertalia Bungalows south of Ambodifotatra, and La Cocoterie Robert in the far north. The going rate is FMg15,000/30,000 per half/full day.

Boat

The agencies listed under the Diving & Snorkelling (p179) and Tours (p179) sections, as well as the upper-end hotels, can help arrange boat rental. Prices average about FMg1,500,000 per day for a boat for up to four people.

Inexpensive pirogue trips along the coast, or to Île aux Forbans or Île aux Nattes can be arranged with locals.

Taxi-Brousse

There are a few taxis-brousse on Île Sainte Marie. Most run along the route between the airport and Ambodifotatra; a few travel north along the road from Ambodifotatra as far as La Crique. Elsewhere on the island, they are few and far between.

Sample fares include Ambodifotatra to Libertalia (FMg5000); Ambodifotatra to the other hotels south of Ambodifotatra (FMg10,000); and from Ambodifotatra to Lonkintsy village (FMg15,000).

AMBODIFOTATRA

Ambodifotatra (am-bodi-*foot*-atr) is Île Sainte Marie's only town. It really just consists of one long, dusty main street extending from the harbour. Ambodifotatra is very much a one-horse town, but it's got several decent restaurants.

Sights

Sites of interest in the town itself include Madagascar's oldest **Catholic church**, which dates from 1857 and was a gift to the island from Empress Eugénie of France, and a granite **fort** (1753), which is now closed to the public.

Just south of the fort is the **tomb of Sylvain Roux**, France's first commercial attaché on the east coast of Madagascar. At the northern end of town is the **tomb of François Albrand**, a French military commander of the island who died in 1826 at 31. If you read French, try to decipher the rather melancholy epitaph.

A **market** is held daily in the town centre.

CIMETIÈRE DES PIRATES

This appropriately eerie and overgrown pirate cemetery is located beside Baie des Forbans about a 20-minute walk southeast of the causeway.

Access to the private cemetery is via an isolated foot track, which crosses several tidal creeks, slippery stones and logs. The cemetery can only be reached on foot at low tide, but it may be possible to get here by pirogue – ask at the Boraha-Village hotel for details.

ÎLE AUX FORBANS

This small island, located opposite the cemetery in Baie des Forbans, is the site of the ruins of an ancient **gateway**. Its significance is unknown, but it is thought to have been a pirate landmark or lookout post.

ÎLOT MADAME

This tiny island at the entrance to Baie des Forbans is connected by two causeways to Ambodifotatra to the north and Belle-Vue, in the south. The island served as the fortified administration centre of the French East India Company until it was taken over by local government offices. It has a deep harbour for larger cargo boats and yachts.

Sleeping & Eating

Unless you are on a tight budget or are waiting for a boat out of the harbour, there is little of interest in staying in Ambodifotatra, where there is no beach.

La Bigorne (☎ 57 401 23, 55 400 67; Arabe Angleterre; d with bathroom FMg80,000; mains FMg25,000) The best choice in town. Very well-maintained polished dark-wood bungalows behind a good French restaurant have fans, but no nets. There's a dining terrace on the wooden veranda in the garden.

Les Palmiers (☎ 57 402 34; d with bathroom FMg60,000; breakfast FMg15,000) A little compound with smart, good-value bungalows

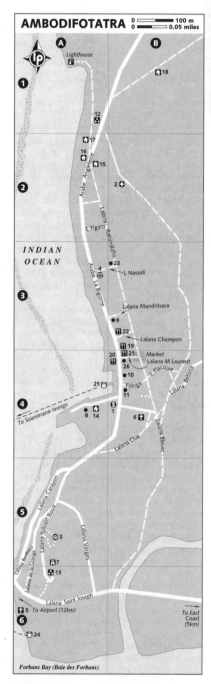

AMBODIFOTATRA

with a fan and net, up a path from the centre of town. There's cold water only in the bathrooms.

La Polina (Au Bon Coin; ☎ 57 402 30; Arabe Angleterre; r with bathroom FMg100,000; mains FMg25,000) A big, new and rather tacky place overlooking the sea. Each bungalow has its own four-poster bed with mosquito net, but the rooms are quite small. There's a disco on Wednesday and Sunday nights, and a workshop next door, so it could get pretty noisy.

Le Drakkar (☎ 57 400 22; d without/with bathroom FMg40,000/60,000) A colonial-looking old house that has a rather Caribbean air to it. It's a bit scruffy, but charming, with rum, soul music, kids and dogs everywhere. The bungalows behind the house are quite simple, but perfectly clean and adequate. The restaurant (mains FMg18,000) serves cheap seafood. An interesting option if you're on a budget.

Hôtel-Restaurant Zinnia (☎ 57 400 09; r without/with hot water FMg55,000/60,000; mains FMg25,000) The bungalows behind the main house here are rather basic, but have their own bathrooms. The rooms upstairs above the restaurant are big and well decorated, sharing a bathroom with hot water. There's a noisy generator next door, which might keep you awake at night; try ear plugs.

On the main street of Ambodifotatra, La Bigorne, Restaurant Le Relais and Vanille et Orchidée all offer a variety of fish and seafood dishes with a French flavour.

Choco Pain, near the harbour, sells pastries, cheese and a few other imported items.

For cheap eats, try the food stalls that appear in the market area around 6pm daily.

Chan Kan, in the centre of town, and the supermarket near Hôtel Zinnia are the best stocked places for groceries, although supplies at both are fairly limited.

SOUTH OF AMBODIFOTATRA
Ankarena

At the southeastern tip of Île Sainte Marie is a fine stretch of peaceful reef-protected beach and a deep **cave** in the base of the cliffs, which is home to hundreds of bats. The cave has given rise to several pirate legends, most of which concern hidden treasure. To reach Ankarena, walk across the small hill to the east of the airport.

Sleeping & Eating

Most of the island's hotels are along the strip between Ambodifotatra and the airport. The beach is narrower here, but still white and beautiful, and staying close to the town and airport will save you spending time and money on transfers to remoter parts of the island. Another advantage is that the hotels are close enough together for ease of evening dining.

The smaller and better-value bungalow complexes in the south and around the island have limited space and are frequently booked out during the high season (mid-December to mid-January, April to May, and July to October), as well as on weekends and Malagasy holidays, so it's worth making reservations at these times. Reduced rates are usually available in the low season.

BUDGET

Chez Alain (postal address BP 515, Île Sainte Marie; camping/d FMg10,000/30,000) This budget camp site also has reed bungalows with no electricity. About 3.5km south of Ambodifotatra. Malagasy meals can be arranged.

La Baleine (☎ 57 401 34; lantoualbert@wandadoo .mg; bungalows without/with bathroom FMg35,000/70,000, with hot water FMg80,000) A bit more comfortable than Chez Alain, but still fairly simple – although the bungalows here have nets.

Meals in the restaurant (meals FMg35,000) and Internet access (FMg100 per minute) is available.

Vanilla Café (☎ 032 07 09 050; d with bathroom FMg70,000) A small place near Chez Alain/ Manaos Gargote, which has basic bungalows with shower and shared toilet. There's a good beach here.

Chez Vavate (☎ 57 401 15; r FMg65,000) A slightly eccentric setup at the top of a hill overlooking the airport. Neat little bungalows have good views over the sea, and there's a beach at the bottom of a steep path. Snorkelling is possible nearby.

MID-RANGE & TOP END

Libertalia Bungalows (☎ 57 403 03; libertalia@dts.mg; d with bathroom FMg98,000; mains FMg25,000) About 2.5km south of Ambodifotatra, this is one of the classiest mid-range choices on the island. The setting and beach are lovely, there's snorkelling off a private jetty and the bright blue-and-white bungalows have fans and mosquito nets. It's a small place on a small beach, but it's friendly and very well maintained. Excursions and rental bikes can be arranged.

Chez Pierrot (☎ 57 401 43; r with bathroom low/high season FMg100,000/125,000; set dinner FMg38,000) Spick-and-span bungalows with bright bedcovers are arranged in a neat garden with cropped lawns next to the sea. Each bungalow has its own deckchairs, and hammocks are strung here and there in the shade. Good value.

Les Bungalows de Vohilava (☎ 57 402 50; vohilava@malagasy.com; r with bathroom FMg120,000) The rooms here are absolutely enormous, with a similarly huge attached sitting room and terraces with hammock. It's a low-key and very relaxed place, with a bar, a good beach, and some pet tortoises. You can hire bikes, motorcycles and kayaks here. The restaurant (meals around FMg20,000) does snacks and evening meals.

Hôtel Lakana (☎ 57 401 32; lakana@dts.mg; r low/high season FMg150,000/190,000, with bathroom FMg180,000/230,000; mains FMg35,000) This is a well-regarded but perhaps slightly overpriced hotel with a set of bungalows on stilts over the sea (each has its own bathroom back on land) and smarter rooms (with inside bathrooms) clustered together in the garden. There's a shop, restaurant and bar on site. Various excursions can be arranged, along with bike, car or motorcycle hire.

Hôtel Soanambo (☎ 57 401 37; hsm@dts.mg; s/d low season €27/32, high season €32/42; dinner €12; 🍴 P 🛏) One of Sainte Marie's most upmarket complexes, with rows of whitewashed bungalows strung along a narrow beach. The cheaper bungalows, although very well-decorated, are small for the price. Bigger, plusher bungalows with TV and telephone, and 'condos' with a sitting area are also available. There's a pool and sundeck, a pontoon for swimming at low tide, tennis courts and car/motorcycle/mountain-bike hire. It's very comfortable, but a bit 'resorty', and often full with package tours.

Princesse Bora Lodge (☎ 57 040 03; www.princesse -bora.com; d half board per person low/high season FMg360,000/425,000) The most luxurious of the lot. The huge round bungalows have a fan, net, safe, suspended wooden bed, enamel bathroom, terrace and balcony. You even get a little footbath outside for washing the sand off your feet! Some two-storey family bungalows are also available. The beach has comfortable sun beds and an outdoor shower, but there's no pool. The restaurant (sandwiches FMg15,000) is quite expensive, naturally. The hotel organises conservation-friendly whale-watching trips in conjunction with an organisation called **Megaptera** (www.multimania.com/megaptera). There is also a wide range of watersports, diving and excursions on offer.

Entertainment

The main nightlife spots are Fotabe Disco, about 1.5km south of Ambodifotatra, and Case a Nono near the airport.

NORTH OF AMBODIFOTATRA

The west coast north of Ambodifotatra also has some good beaches. The hotels here are further apart and a little bit harder to access. North of La Crique, the road is abysmal, so you're better off going by boat. **Piscine Naturelle d'Ambodiatafana**, the natural swimming holes at the northeastern tip of the island, are a series of hollow basins in the coastal rocks, which are filled by the high tide. To reach them, walk 8km northeast along the main track from Ambatoroa on the west coast. Access with a motorcycle or mountain bike is possible, although it's tough going.

Southwest of Ambodiatafana and along the same access track is the **Fanilo Albrand lighthouse**. From the ridge, it's possible to sometimes see as far as Maroantsetra and the Baie d'Antongil.

Sleeping

Accommodations in this section are listed from south to north in each price range.

BUDGET

Atafana (☎ 032 04 637 81; r without/with hot water FMg80,000/120,000; meals FMg35,000) A very friendly and welcoming family-run place. The bamboo bungalows are fairly simple for the price, with four-poster beds with mosquito nets and spacious bathrooms. The more expensive rooms have a little sitting area as well. This is a great spot to watch the sunset, and swimming is possible even at low tide. Family bungalows for five people are also available. The food is better value than the rooms.

Antsara Bungalows (☎ 57 401 59; r FMg25,000-95,000; dinner FMg45,000) On the other side of the road from a rather swampy looking beach, this charming old wooden building on stilts has bungalows up the hill behind it, plus a few down by the water. Room facilities vary widely, from barely functional huts to rooms with bathrooms and hot water.

Chez Antoine (r without/with bathroom FMg25,000/60,000; dinner FMg20,000) This well-established and fun local place in the far north offers good value if you don't mind being miles off the beaten track and not being on the beach. Antoine can also cook a slap-up lunch for those on their way to Piscine Naturelle d'Ambodiatafana. Very peaceful.

MID-RANGE & TOP END

Hôtel Betty Plage (☎ 57 400 66; lemurienpalme aol.com; d/f with bathroom FMg90,000/130,000; set dinner FMg45,000) This good-value hotel is the base for the Lemurien Palmé dive operation. The bungalows are smart and spacious, with mosquito nets, and the beach is narrow, but sandy. It's a very comfortable place to base yourself if you're planning lots of diving.

Masoandro (☎ 57 040 05; masoandro@simicro.mg; r half board per person €53) Masoandro, near Lonkintsy, is definitely the most chic of Sainte Marie's hotels – the interiors of the main building and bungalows are decorated in a stunning ethnic style that brings in many elements of traditional Malagasy design. The beautifully simple bedrooms have polished wood floors, cream cotton bedcovers

and murals on the walls. Steps run down to a sandy bay beach from the hotel.

La Crique (☎ 57 401 60; d without/with bathroom FMg95,000/117,000) La Crique's rooms have mosquito nets and verandas with deckchairs from which you can look out to sea over a tidy rose garden. The shared bathrooms only have cold-water showers. There's a terraced restaurant (dinner is FMg55,000). Airport transfers cost FMg47,000 per person, or you can get here by taxi-brousse (FMg15,000 from Ambodifotatra); ask to be dropped at the top of the rutted track that leads down to the hotel.

La Cocoterie Robert (☎ 57 401 70; s/d FMg130,000/150,000; set dinner FMg60,000) This long-established hotel has wooden bungalows with big, clean bathrooms in a gorgeous spot among the palm trees. The beach here is one of the best on the island. The downside is that it's rather difficult to get to – you have to call the hotel for a boat transfer from La Crique (FMg95,000 per person), or the airport (FMg135,000 per person). There are some bikes for hire.

Cocoteraie Resort (☎ 57 401 73; soanamb.tan@simicro.mg; s low/high season €34/47, d low/high season €44/68; dinner €12) Next door to La Cocoterie Robert, this is a much more upmarket place on the same fantastic beach. The bungalows are painted a rather gaudy yellow and green, but are very well constructed and decorated. The hotel is managed by the same people as Soanambo in the south, and has the same rather resorty feel to it. Excursions and watersports are all on offer. Airport transfers (€25 per person) combine boat and car.

ÎLE AUX NATTES

Also known as Nosy Nato, Île aux Nattes is off the southern tip of Île Sainte Marie. It's got just about everything you could want from a tropical island – curving white beaches, turquoise sea, a lush green interior and a good range of cheap and chilled-out guesthouses, plus one upmarket hotel. Access is via pirogue (FMg5000 one way), leaving from the beach just southwest of the airport runway. You can swim or walk across the narrow channel at low tide; the water is about chest height. If you're heading around to the southern tip of the island, a pirogue transfer shouldn't cost more than FMg25,000.

The island itself can be explored on foot in less than three hours – but why hurry? Better to stay a night – or several nights – and adjust to the feeling of sand between the toes.

Sleeping

The places below don't have telephone numbers and many of them are located on nameless streets; asking around is your best bet.

Chez Tity (r FMg60,000; dinner FMg40,000) This is a friendly local place popular with backpackers with a bit more character than the rest. Some of the simple huts have their own deck on stilts over the sea. The beach is quite narrow here. Snorkelling equipment and pirogues can be hired.

Les Lémuriens (r without/with bathroom FMg50,000/75,000) This set of very simple A-frame bungalows, with mosquito nets, are among lush vegetation at the southern tip of the island. Wildlife is much in evidence – you can expect lemurs in the dining room and crabs scuttling across the bedroom floor at night. The restaurant is quite popular with French expats.

Chez Régine (r FMg60,000) Some readers have highly recommended this simple, inexpensive guesthouse in a peaceful spot on the west coast of the island. The food is very good, but order several hours in advance.

Le Maningory (☎ 032 709 005; www.madagascar.com/maningory; s/tw/d with bathroom FMg200,000/235,000/240,000; set dinner FMg60,000) The most upmarket option on Nosy Nato sits on a lovely beach in the northwest of the island. The smart bamboo-and-wood bungalows, set slightly back from the beach, have verandas, draped mosquito nets and hot water, while the deck bar/restaurant with easy chairs and *foosball* (table football). It's rustic, tasteful and incredibly relaxing. Excursions, fishing and diving can be arranged. Rates include breakfast and transfers. If you get a pirogue here from the airport beach, the hotel will pay the boatman.

Meva Paradis (☎ 032 022 07 80; r FMg125,000; bungalow with bathroom FMg175,000) This rather overpriced and empty hotel sits in manicured gardens on the west coast. The beach is excellent, though, and the bungalows in particular are very comfortable. No hot water.

Le Petit Traversé (☎ 57 402 54; r FMg100,000) A simple and overpriced option, but it's got a good beach and is right opposite the airport, so you can get off the plane and be up to your neck in turquoise sea very soon afterwards. No hot water.

NORTHEAST COAST

The wildest and least visited part of the island, the northeast coast can be reached via the cross-island road just outside Ambodifotatra. It's a good hike or bike across, but makes for a bumpy car ride. The sand on the east coast beaches is *not* firm enough for motorcycles and the bush is too thick to ride in. The road to the southern hotels is surfaced, so access is easy.

The **Ampanihy Peninsula** offers relative isolation and a beautiful stretch of sand. It is separated from the mainland by the narrow Baie d'Ampanihy. The easiest access to the peninsula is by pirogue from the village of Anafiafy, followed by a five-minute walk across the peninsula's narrowest point to the beach.

Mora Mora Hôtel (☎ 57 401 14; moramora@malagasy.com; r without/with bathroom FMg150,000/200,000) This slightly overpriced hotel has a glass-walled restaurant on stilts with a sea view and lots of books – a good place to while away some time if you're here when it's raining. Two of the rooms are on a pontoon over the ocean, and share a bathroom. There's almost no beach here at all, so you swim off the jetty. The hotel is about 5km southeast of Ambodifotatra; there are two access roads (both signposted).

Boraha-Village (☎ 57 400 71; www.boraha.com; s/d half board per person €70/45) An excellent and very well-run upmarket hotel, with fantastic food and personal service. The very smart bungalows have big sliding doors, safes, verandas and bright, tasteful décor. There's a huge range of imaginative 4WD and boat excursions on offer, plus fishing, a cookery school and massages. The hotel also runs a tour of the Canal des Pangalanes, concentrating on the behind-the-scenes life of the villages. Guides speak English.

Paradis d'Ampanihy (fax 57 402 78, addressed to Hélène; r without/with bathroom FMg30,000/50,000; dinner FMg35,000) The place to stay if you want to spend time on the Ampanihy Peninsula, this little local hotel in Anafiafy plans to open an annex on the peninsula itself. The

EASTERN MADAGASCAR

restaurant's speciality is dishes with coconut sauce. There are guides for visiting the nearby forest.

St Mary Club (☎ 57 040 08; stmaryclub@netclub.mg; s/d with bathroom FMg230,000/350,000; 🛏 🅿) A new and empty Italian-run luxury hotel right up on the northeast tip of the island. If any guests arrive to give it some atmosphere, this could be an excellent option. There's a swimming pool, a huge lounge/dining room, and huge, smart bungalows with safe and air-con.

THE VANILLA COAST

Once north of Soanierana-Ivongo, you're into the remote northeast corner of Madagascar, centre of the vanilla industry.

The recent vanilla boom has led to a new prosperity in the northeast, with many peasant farmers abandoning other crops such as coffee to grow more vanilla. More money, however, has not led to more development, and the infrastructure in the northeast remains very limited, with no roads to speak of and not much in the way of telephone services. People in this area are much more interested in vanilla than tourism, so guides, porters and competent hotel staff are hard to find in some places.

PARC NATIONAL DE MANANARA-NORD

The very remote Parc National de Mananara-Nord (23,000 hectares) encompasses some of the last remaining lowland rain forest in Madagascar. An additional 1000 hectares of offshore islets and their surrounding reefs are protected as a marine national park. The largest of these islets is Nosy Atafana, southeast of Mananara town.

Mananara-Nord is the only known habitat of the hairy-eared dwarf lemur, but lemurs are not the main attraction in the park, and are not always seen by visitors. The park also protects indris, diademed sifakas, brown lemurs, ruffed lemurs and aye-ayes, as well as a variety of geckos (including the endemic uroplatus and day geckos), and dugong, whales and offshore reef life. The area's primary appeal – apart from its forest – is the opportunity to get to know a remote area of Madagascar and

experience rural Malagasy life. The park is still in an early stage of development, so the staff ask that travellers give them advanced warning of their visit via the Angap offices in Antananarivo, Maroantsetra or Mananara. Turning up in the park unannounced is not encouraged, as guides and facilities still need to be arranged in advance.

Information

Entry permits for Mananara-Nord (including Nosy Atafana) cost FMg50,000 for three days. Guide fees range from FMg25,000/ 50,000 per half/full day to FMg150,000 for four days. Porter fees are the same. Guides in the park are still inexperienced and not employed full-time, so to get a good one, and make sure he's available, you'll need to contact the Angap offices in Antananarivo, Maroantsetra or Mananara in advance. The best English-speaking guide is Luther.

VANILLA

The vanilla plant was introduced to Madagascar from Mexico by French plantation owners, who named it *vanille* (*lavanila* in Malagasy), from the Spanish *vanilla* or 'little pod'. It is a type of climbing orchid, *Vanila planifolia*, which attaches itself to trees. The vanilla seeds grow inside a long pod hanging from the plant and each pod contains thousands of seeds, which are collected and cured in factories. Dark-brown or black pods are the most desirable because of their stronger aroma.

Madagascar is one of the world's largest producers of vanilla, which – together with other spices such as cloves and pepper, and essences such as ylang-ylang – traditionally has accounted for about one-third of the country's exports. It grows most abundantly in the northeastern parts of the country, particularly on the northeast coast where the hot and wet climate is ideally suited for its cultivation.

Cyclone Hudah, which destroyed more than 20% of Madagascar's vanilla crop in 2000, caused a shortage of supply, a huge escalation in price – in 2003, a kilo of vanilla was changing hands for as much as FMg2,000,000 – and a subsequent increase in vanilla-related crime, including thefts and even murders.

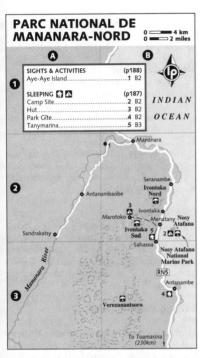

PARC NATIONAL DE MANANARA-NORD

0 —— 4 km
0 —— 2 miles

SIGHTS & ACTIVITIES	(p188)
Aye-Aye Island.................................1	B2

SLEEPING	(p187)
Camp Site..2	B2
Hut...3	B2
Park Gîte...4	B2
Tanymarina......................................5	B3

INDIAN

OCEAN

Mananara

Seranambe
Ivontaka
Nord

Antanambaobe

Marotoko   Ivontaka
Menatany   Nosy
Atafana
Ivontaka
Sandrakatsy   Sud

Sahasoa

Nosy Atafana
National
Marine Park

RN5

Antanambe

Verezanantsoro

To Toamasina
(230km)

The only topographical maps of the area are those put out by FTM (p250). These are not available in Mananara, so you will need to purchase it in advance in Antananarivo. A rudimentary map of the park is available from Angap in Mananara.

Hiking

Two circuits are available in Parc National de Mananara-Nord, although others are in the pipeline for the future. The circuits both start at Sarasota, about 2.5km south of Mananara. From here you head north along the sparsely travelled coastal road, then west towards the forest of Vintana Sud (four hours). After spending the night at the village of Partook, on the edge of the forest, continue southeast the next day to return to Sahasoa.

The second circuit available in the park is a trip by boat to Nosy Atafana. You can of course combine the circuits by doing the walk and then the boat trip afterwards, or vice versa. For any trip in the park, you'll need to be self-sufficient with food and water. A limited amount of camping

equipment is for hire in the park office at Sahasoa.

Hiking in the park is fairly hard going, so you'll need to be fit to attempt a trek here.

Sleeping & Eating

In Antanambe, **Tanymarina** (Chez Grondin; r from FMg75,000) has rooms and chalets. There is a restaurant here, plus a boat for visits to Nosy Atafana.

There are **gîtes** (r or camping FMg10,000) run by the park in Sahasoa and Antanambe. Both have rooms, a camp site, shower and toilets.

In Marotoko village, at the edge of the forest of Ivontaka Sud, there is a hut where you can stay overnight and some rivers nearby for washing. On Nosy Atafana there is a camp site with a water supply; bungalows are planned.

Getting There & Away

The park's remoteness makes it very hard to get to. For visits to Nosy Atafana, you can hire a boat from Mananara or Antanambe. Boat transfers to Nosy Atafana take about 2½ to three hours (one way) from Mananara, and about 30 minutes from Sahasoa. However, boats (FMg1,000,000) are expensive. The park is planning to buy a boat of their own, which will bring the cost down considerably. If you go to Nosy Atafana from Mananara, you'll need to call into Sahasoa on the way to pick up your guide (this must be arranged in advance with the park office in Mananara).

For visits to Ivontaka Sud, you'll need to get to Sahasoa – five hours in a 4WD, six hours by bike, or a long day on foot.

NOSY ATAFANA NATIONAL MARINE PARK

Nosy Atafana, offshore to the southeast of Mananara town, consists of three islands and the surrounding coral reef. As well as good **snorkelling**, it offers the chance to observe a unique **coastal forest** not found on the mainland.

Nosy Atafana is easily visited on a day trip from Mananara. It's possible to walk between the three islands at low tide.

MANANARA

pop 33,000

Mananara is a small and very out-of-the way town set in an attractive clove- and vanilla-producing area at the southern entrance to Baie d'Antongil. The coast south of Mananara is particularly striking, with small, isolated fishing villages and little else – certainly not any serviceable roads. Mananara has seen big social changes of late, as the price of vanilla has boomed. As a result, large shiny 4WD cars bump up and down the potholed streets. Auctions are hosted at the Saturday evening parties in the town hall, in which newly-rich vanilla barons prove their status by paying ludicrous prices for random objects such as roast chickens.

Mananara is also the starting point for visiting Parc National de Mananara-Nord, the Marine National Park of Nosy Atafana and tiny Aye-Aye Island. For a bit of snorkelling, walk along the long peninsula behind the airport, which has some white sand beaches and coral about 100m offshore. Watch out for sea urchins here.

There is electricity in Mananara, but no telephone service.

Aye-Aye Island

This small, privately owned island in the Mananara River offers the opportunity to observe aye-ayes in their natural environment. Access to the island costs FMg30,000 per person, including car and pirogue transport. It's not an untouched wilderness, but a charming spot nonetheless, and is presided over by the friendly caretaker, Narcisse, his wife, children and dozens of chickens. You can visit the island for a couple of hours after dark, but there's also a small **gîte** (FMg20,000) on the island if you want to stay overnight. Bring a torch and mosquito repellent.

You're almost guaranteed to see an aye-aye here – they have adapted to living in the palm trees, boring holes in coconuts with their very sharp teeth and then spooning out the flesh with their skeletal middle finger. You'll also have the chance to spot brown lemurs, tiny *Microcebus* (mouse lemurs), fat-tailed dwarf lemurs, grey bamboo lemurs and over 40 species of birds. There are no guides, but researchers are occasionally in residence and will show you around.

The best way to reach the island is by boat, arranged through Chez Roger in Mananara (see following). Alternatively, you can walk for about 4.5km along the

paved road that leads west along the river from Mananara towards Sandrakatsy, and then cross over to the island via pirogue.

Sleeping & Eating

Chez Roger (r FMg60,000) In the centre of town, this is the best place, especially if you want to visit Aye-Aye Island. The big and comfortable bungalows have bathrooms (bucket showers), and the restaurant (from FMg15,000) does slap-up meals.

Hôtel Aye-Aye (r FMg65,000; 🏊) Near the airport this hotel is also a good spot, with a small pool, bungalows among the palm trees, and a great selection of rums.

Entertainment

Mananara is, surprisingly, a bit of a party town. Every Friday, Saturday and Sunday night there is a disco and *bal* (party) either at the Hôtel de Ville in the middle of town or at Snack Bar restaurant, around the corner from Chez Roger.

Getting There & Around
AIR

Most visitors to Mananara arrive by air. Several Air Madagascar flights per week connect Mananara with Toamasina (FMg466,000), Maroantsetra (FMg250,000) and Antananarivo (FMg681,000). You can also fly from Mananara to Sambava or Antalaha on the north coast, via Maroantsetra.

Be warned – during the vanilla season from June to October, the small planes that fly between Mananara, Toamasina and Maroantsetra are usually full weeks in advance, so book well ahead to make sure you don't get stuck. Ramanaraibe Export, about 300m west of town over a bridge, is the agent for Air Madagascar in Mananara.

BOAT

Cargo boats sail relatively frequently between Mananara, Île Sainte Marie, Maroantsetra and Toamasina. There are usually several departures, depending on the weather, although there are no set schedules. This journey is only really safe between September and March – at other times the sea is much too rough to make the journey.

Inquire at the small port in Mananara – boats often come in and leave again fairly quickly, so you'll have to return often on the chance of finding a ship in port. Fares between Mananara and Île Sainte Marie or Maroantsetra average about FMg50,000; the trip takes at least eight hours, often sailing through the night. Decent boats to look for include *Estilina, Geralda II* and *Tsiriry*. Occasional cargo boats go as far as Sambava, Antalaha or even Diego Suarez in the north. There are no facilities of any kind on the boats – bring sun protection (an umbrella is handy for shade), food and water.

TAXI-BROUSSE
Mananara lies 127km north of Soanierana-Ivongo. There are occasional taxis-brousse between Mananara and Toamasina in the dry season, but the road is abysmal and getting worse.

From Mananara north to Maroantsetra, the road is also in bad condition, and entails several river crossings; there are occasional taxis-brousse during the dry season. Inquire about taxis-brousse departures in the market or at Chez Roger.

MANANARA TO MAROANTSETRA
If you have the time and energy, Mananara to Maroantsetra (114km) is a beautiful walk or mountain-bike ride along the very rough coastal road, which sees almost no vehicle traffic.

Manambolosy, 20km north of Mananara, is the first major town and has a basic **hotel** (r FMg25,000). **Tanjora**, also with a **hotel** (r FMg25,000), is 15km north, followed in a further 15km by the village of **Anandrivola**, which has a sandy lagoon and bungalows at the **Jolex Hotel** (r FMg40,000); meals and motorcycle lifts can be arranged.

About 17km further on is **Rantabe**, from which you can take a pirogue trip 15km upriver through forest. South of town is a beach and some offshore coral. **Bungalows** (r FMg25,000) are available.

Just north of Rantabe you will need to cross the Rantabe River in a pirogue. Transport to Maroantsetra is sometimes waiting on the other side. If not, continue on foot for 12km to **Nandrasana**, from where there are usually at least three vehicles daily to Maroantsetra (FMg20,000).

Water is sometimes available in Nandrasana, Rantabe and Manambolosy, and you can get fresh fish in all the villages, but you'll need to bring most supplies with you.

If you're coming south from Maroantsetra, you can hire guides (FMg200,000) and porters (FMg150,000) for the trip – see p190 for details.

RÉSERVE DE NOSY MANGABE
The thickly forested island nature reserve of Nosy Mangabe (520 hectares) is located in Baie d'Antongil about 5km offshore from Maroantsetra. With its dark-green forested hills rising dramatically out of the surrounding sea, and a wonderful yellow sickle of beach, the island has a magical, otherworldly feel rather like a location from *Jurassic Park*. It rains a lot on Nosy Mangabe, however, so you could well end up seeing all this through a wall of water.

The main attraction of Nosy Mangabe is its flourishing population of aye-ayes, which were introduced in 1967 to protect them from extinction. Nosy Mangabe's aye-ayes are fairly elusive these days, and a sighting is by no means guaranteed. Besides the aye-ayes, the island is home to mouse lemurs, white-fronted brown lemurs and black-and-white ruffed lemurs, all of which are fairly easily spotted if you stay overnight.

Walking through the forest in the dark, your torch will pick out a host of reptiles and amphibians – Nosy Mangabe is home to the leaf-tailed gecko *(Uroplatus fimbriatus)*, one of nature's most accomplished camouflage artists; several species of chameleons; many frogs; and several snake species, including the harmless *Pseudoxyrohopus heterurus*, which is believed to be endemic to Nosy Mangabe, and the Madagascar tree boa.

There are several walking trails on the island and a small waterfall. At one end is a beach called Plage des Hollandais, with rocks bearing the scratched names of some 17th-century Dutch sailors. From July to September, you can see whales offshore.

Information
An entry permit for the Réserve de Nosy Mangabe (which is not included in the permit for nearby Parc National de Masoala) costs FMg50,000 for three days. Guides (compulsory) are FMg50,000 per group per day. Night walks cost FMg45,000 for groups of up to four, plus FMg20,000 for the guide's evening meal. Some guides (ask

for Angeline or Suzette) will cook in the evenings for an extra fee.

Permits can be obtained at the Parc National de Masoala office in Maroantsetra, or on the island itself.

Sleeping & Eating
There is a very well-equipped **camping ground** (tent sites FMg15,000) at the Angap station on the western edge of the island. It has picnic tables, shelters, a kitchen and toilets, and a waterfall nearby provides the showers. You'll need to bring camping and cooking equipment, food, water or purifying tablets, and cooking fuel. Camping equipment can be rented through 3M Loisirs in Maroantsetra (below), and sometimes through the guides at the reserve.

Getting There & Away
Boat transfers to Nosy Mangabe can be arranged with the guides based at the Parc National de Masoala office in Maroantsetra, or with 3M Loisirs (below). Rates for a return day trip are about FMg350,000 per boat with a minimum of three people. The trip takes 30 to 45 minutes and may occasionally be cancelled or postponed if the weather is bad, so it's best not to schedule a flight too close to your planned return from the island.

MAROANTSETRA
Maroantsetra (maro-ant-*setr*), set on Baie d'Antongil near the mouth of the Antainambalana River, is a remote and isolated place full of languid charm, surrounded by beautiful riverine scenery. It's well worth spending a day or two exploring the area on foot, quad or mountain bike. On the way you'll pass vanilla plantations, wave-pounded beaches, and the occasional chameleon on the side of the road – plus, of course, dozens of waving children.

From July to September there's a good chance of seeing breeding and birthing **humpback whales**.

Maroantsetra's climate is one of the wettest in Madagascar, with close to 3500mm of rain annually. May to September are the wettest months, although rain can fall at any time of year. The nearest good beach to Maroantsetra is **Navana**, which has a backdrop of virgin rain forest. It's a 30-minute boat ride from town.

Information
BOA has a branch here for changing cash and travellers cheques.

Contact **Angap** (7.30am-noon & 2.30-6pm), two blocks down from the market, behind Maroantsetra's two large radio towers, to organise treks across the Masoala Peninsula, visits to Nosy Mangabe or trips to Parc National de Mananara-Nord. The Parc National Mascala office is also located here.

Activities
KAYAKING
Sea kayaking is an excellent way to explore the shores around Maroantsetra and the Masoala Peninsula, and there are numerous excellent routes. **Kayak Masoala** (www.kayakafrica.com/madagascar.asp) have set up several kayaking camp sites on the peninsula and run trips there from Maroantsetra. Inquire at Le Coco Beach (opposite) for information.

QUAD, MOTOR OR MOUNTAIN BIKING
A great way to get out and explore the area around Maroantsetra is by mountain bike. If that sounds too energetic, rent a quad or motorcycle, both of which are just about the only motor vehicles that can make it far along the very rough RN2. All bikes can be hired in town (see below).

CANOEING
The tour companies listed below can organise trips by pirogue up the various rivers outside Maroantsetra. Some include a visit to a vanilla plantation and treatment plant. Maroa Tours also organises overnight camping trips by motorised pirogue to the Makira rain forest, newly added to the Parc National de Masoala. These can be a good alternative to Nosy Mangabe if the sea is too rough.

Tours
There's a lot to do in Maroantsetra, and several well-organised ways of doing it. English-speaking guides are easy to find.

3M Loisirs (write to Boite Postale 83, 512 Maroantsetra) Near the small bridge leading to Coco Beach Hotel, 3M Loisirs has a selection of good-quality sporting and camping equipment for hire, including snorkelling gear (FMg25,000 per day), tents (FMg25,000 per day), quad bikes (FMg350,000 per day), 4WD

THE WHALES OF BAIE D'ANTONGIL

Every year between July and September, Baie d'Antongil, just south of Maroantsetra, is the site of the migration of hundreds of humpback whales *(Megaptera novaeangliae)*. The whales make their way from the Antarctic northward to the warmer waters around Baie d'Antongil, where they spend the winter months breeding and birthing before the long journey back to Antarctica. En route the whales swim past Fort Dauphin and Île Sainte Marie, where they are often sighted offshore.

Humpbacks can measure up to 15m in length and weigh as much as 35,000kg. Despite their size, they are exceptionally agile, and capable of acrobatic moves such as breaching (launching themselves completely out of the water with their flippers). Humpbacks are also renowned for their singing, which is presumed to be related to mating patterns. Humpback songs can last up to an hour, and are considered to be the most complex of all whale songs.

To maximise your chances of observing the whales and their acrobatics, try to go out on a day when the water is calm – although conditions on the bay vary widely, so the water may be calm in one area and rough in another.

The Wildlife Conservation Society (WCS; in Maroantsetra) and the American Museum of Natural History (AMNH, based in New York City) have a long-term research and conservation programme for humpback whales and other marine mammals, with a field base on Nosy Mangabe. The WCS-AMNH project has drafted a set of guidelines aimed at ensuring the well-being and safety of both whales and whale-watchers. These have since been adopted as national law in Madagascar, and local boat operators have been trained to operate within the guidelines, ensuring that disturbance to the whales by whale-watchers will be minimal.

To ensure that you go out with experienced and trained guides and boat operators, organise your trip through the office of Parc National de Masoala in Maroantsetra. Expect to pay from about FMg350,000 for a half-day trip.

For details of the whale-watching project, have a look at the website of the **American Museum of Natural History** (http://research.amnh.org/biodiversity/center/programs/whales.html).

vehicles (FMg500,000 per day), motorcycles (FMg400,000 per day) and canoes (FMg200,000). It also arranges river excursions (FMg200,000 per half day), and boat trips to Nosy Mangabe (FMg300,000 return) or the Masoala Peninsula.

Maroa Tours (☎ 57 720 06; c/o Le Coco Beach) Rakoto, an English-speaking Angap guide and 'fixer', does excursions by pirogue to villages upriver from Maroantsetra (FMg125,000 per person for groups of two or more), along with visits to Nosy Mangabe and the Masoala Peninsula. The tours include visits to a vanilla and cinnamon farm and village weaving workshops. The best time to see vanilla is between October and June. Rakoto can also organised guided treks to Mananara.

Relais du Masoala (see following) Maroantsetra's most upmarket hotel organises overnight excursions in the surrounding area, including the Masoala Peninsula (FMg800,000 per person) and to Nosy Mangabe (FMg280,000 per person for groups of at least two).

Sleeping

Relais du Masoala (☎ 57 721 43/42, in Antananarivo ☎ 22 219 74; relais@simicro.mg; cortezmd@bow.dts.mg; r FMg300,000; P) This is a very tranquil and well-decorated upmarket hotel about 2.5km east of town overlooking a small canal, with the bay and the mountains in the distance. The luxurious bungalows scattered through the leafy grounds have two double beds, huge bathrooms, decks, fans and mosquito nets. A variety of excursions can be arranged from here.

Le Coco Beach (☎ 57 702 06; camping FMg15,000, r without/with toilet FMg75,000/100,000) This friendly mid-range hotel has comfortable, well-maintained bungalows and a good restaurant set amid coconut palms. Those of you who are arachnophobes should watch out for spiders' webs and their large occupants strung between the trees at night! Le Coco Beach is a good place to meet other travellers and get a group together for trips further afield. Cross over the small bridge and turn right, about 800m from the centre of town.

Hôtel Antongil (☎ 17 via post office; r FMg50,000; dinner FMg12,500) There are big, breezy upstairs rooms with fans and mosquito nets around a wide wooden veranda at this two-storey building in the centre of town. Rooms share toilets. The small restaurant serves Malagasy meals.

Le Maroa (in Toamasina ☎ 032 04 225 20; d/tr with bathroom FMg60,000/75,000) Near the Parc National de Masoala office, Le Maroa has a good restaurant (lots of varieties of *soupe chinoise*) and decent bungalows with fans and mosquito nets.

Hôtel du Centre (☎ 48 via post office; r without/with bathroom FMg30,000/40,000; meals FMg20,000) A basic place with rooms in wooden sheds. Meals can be arranged in the evenings.

Eating

Places for a good meal include Les Grillades, near Le Coco Beach, Bar Blanc Vert nearby, and the restaurant at **Le Maroa** (in Toamasina ☎ 032 04 225 20; mains FMg15,000).

The restaurant at **Le Coco Beach** (☎ 57 702 06; mains FMg20,000) is good value. Try Rakoto's punch coco here – it's legendary. Meals at **Relais du Masoala** (☎ 57 721 43/42, in Antananarivo ☎ 22 219 74; relais@simicro.mg; cortezmd@bow.dts.mg; dinner FMg50,000) are more refined, and there are some delectable desserts. Rive Gauche, in a pretty spot near the harbour, is open in the early evening for ice creams and snacks.

If you're stocking up for a camping trip, Maroantsetra is good for self-caterers. It has great bread, which is available at the market, along with a modest selection of fruits and vegetables.

Getting There & Away
AIR
Air Madagascar flights connect Maroantsetra several times a week with Antananarivo (FMg681,000), Toamasina (FMg577,000), Sambava (FMg306,000), Mananara (FMg250,000) and Antalaha (FMg250,000). The Air Madagascar office (at Ramanaraibe Export) is a few kilometres from town on the road to the airport. Flights to/from Maroantsetra are often full, especially between June and November – be sure to reconfirm your ticket. Weather may affect plane schedules, particularly during the rainiest months (July to September).

BOAT
During most of the year, the only alternative to flying is to get a cargo boat to or from Maroantsetra. Boat travel is not a safe option between July and September, when the seas are rough.

There are unscheduled but regular sailings between Maroantsetra and Île Sainte Marie (from FMg150,000, 10 hours), Toamasina (about FMg150,000, two days), Antalaha (FMg150,000, 12 to 15 hours) and Mananara (FMg50,000, nine hours). Enquire at the port in Maroantsetra, and then be prepared for inevitable delays. The boats that take passengers are sometimes extremely overloaded, and some do capsize, so if the boat looks too full, don't get on. Good boats to look out for to Mananara are *Estilina*, *Geralda II* and *Tsiriry*. To Île Sainte Marie or Toamasina, look out for *Savannah*, *Red Rose* or *Rosita*.

Mroa Tours, 3M Loisirs and Relais du Masoata (p191) can arrange speedboat transfers to various points on the Masoala Peninsula.

TAXI-BROUSSE
Maroantsetra lies 112km north of Mananara at the end of a 'road', which is more of a rutted cart track with several river crossings en route. Occasional taxis-brousse connect the two towns during the dry season from October to December, but this is not a method of transport to be relied upon. To the north of Maroantsetra, there are no roads, and hence no taxis-brousse.

Getting Around
The airport is about 7km southwest of town. Maroantsetra has a few taxis, which all charge FMg15,000 for a trip out to the airport.

Alternatively, it's possible to get a lift in the Air Madagascar vehicle (FMg5,000); ask at the Air Madagascar office when you reconfirm your ticket.

MASOALA PENINSULA & PARC NATIONAL DE MASOALA
The Masoala (mash-wala) Peninsula is the site of a 210,000-hectare national park containing one of the best rain forests in the country. It also encompasses three protected marine areas: Tampolo Marine Park on the peninsula's southwestern coast;

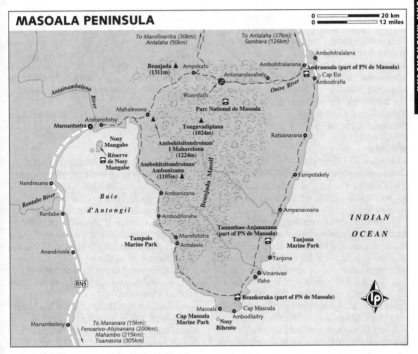

MASOALA PENINSULA

0   20 km
0   12 miles

To Marofinaritra (30km);
Antalaha (50km)

To Antalaha (37km);
Sambava (126km)

Ambohitralalana

Beanjada ▲   Ampokafo
(1311m)

Ambohitralanana   Andranoala (part of PN de Masoala)
Cap Est

Antananandavehely

Ambodirafia

Onive River

Antainambalana River

Mahalevona

Waterfalls

Parc National de Masoala

Andranofotsy

Tongavadipiana
(1024m)

Maroantsetra

Ratsianarana

Nosy
Mangabe

Ambohitsitondroinan'
I Mahavelona
(1224m)

Réserve
de Nosy
Mangabe

Ambohitsitondroinan'
Ambanizana
(1105m) ▲

Beanjada Massif

Fampotakely

Nandrasana

Baie
d'Antongil

Ambanizana

Rantabe River

Ampanavoana

Rantabe

Ambodiforaha

Tanambao-Anjanazana
(part of PN de Masoala)

INDIAN

Tampolo
Marine Park

Marofototra
Antalavia

Tanjona
Marine Park

OCEAN

Anandrivola

Tanjona

Vinanivao
Ifaho

RN5

Beankoraka (part of PN de Masoala)

Masoala   Cap Masoala

Manambolosy

To Mananara (15km);
Fenoarivo-Atsinanana (200km);
Mahambo (215km);
Toamasina (305km)

Cap Masoala
Marine Park

Ambodilaitry

Nosy
Bihento

Cap Masoala Marine Park at the tip of the peninsula; and Tanjona Marine Park on the southeastern coast. Most of the park is spread across the central part of the peninsula, extending southwest to the coast by Tampolo Marine Park. There are several small discrete parcels *(parcs détachés)* elsewhere on the peninsula, including Andranoala, near Cap Est, Tanambao-Anjanazana, contiguous with Tanjona Marine Park, and Beankoraka, near the tip of the peninsula.

Masoala Peninsula is one of Madagascar's premier **trekking** areas. It also offers excellent opportunities for **sea kayaking**, **snorkelling** and **swimming**. At the peninsula's southernmost tip is the beautiful **Cap Masoala**, which can be reached on foot or by bicycle from Cap Est. Masoala Peninsula is exceptionally wet. The months between October and December are somewhat drier and are the best months for trekking, although you should be prepared for rain at any time of the year. June and July are the rainiest months, therefore river levels are highest at this time.

Information

Parc National de Masoala is administered by Angap in collaboration with the Wildlife Conservation Society (WCS). Park headquarters are at the Angap office in Maroantsetra. There is also a Parc National de Masoala and Angap representative based in Antalaha.

The best place to arrange permits, guides and treks across the peninsula is at the Angap office in Maroantsetra. The guides here are well organised, and many speak English. Treks can also be arranged in Antalaha or in Ambodirafia, near Cap Est, although the staff and guides there don't speak English.

Permits cost FMg50,000 for three days. Guide fees start at FMg50,000/45,000 per day/night for visits to the park. For trekking circuits (194), guide/porter fees are FMg350,000/175,000 for the Maroantsetra to Antalaha circuit; and FMg50,000/40,000 per day for a tour of the peninsula and FMg600,000/275,000 for Maroantsetra to Cap Est. Food, including for the guides and porters, is not included in these rates and is supposed to be paid by you, although there may be some room for negotiation on this. One reason for the comparatively high fees is that they include the days that the guides and porters need to walk back to Maroantsetra after depositing you in Antalaha or Cap Est (food for this return portion is the responsibility of the guides and porters themselves.) Guides are also required for visiting the marine parks.

Wildlife

The Masoala Peninsula is famous for its dramatic vegetation, which includes primary forest, rain forest and coastal forest as well as a variety of palm and orchid species.

Ten lemur species are found on Masoala, including the red-ruffed and eastern fork-marked lemurs. The helmeted vanga shrike is most often seen here. There are also several tenrec and mongoose species, 14 bat species, 60 reptile species and about 85 bird species, including the rare serpent eagle and Madagascan red owl (both found on the peninsula's west coast).

The marine national parks protect mangrove ecosystems, coral reefs, dolphins and turtles. For details about whales in Baie d'Antongil, see p191.

Hiking

The main hiking routes are the Maroantsetra to Antalaha direct trip (three to five days); the Maroantsetra to Cap Est route (five to eight days); and a tour of the whole peninsula, which involves starting at Antalaha, travelling to Cap Est by car or bike, trekking to Cap Masoala, then taking a boat to Maroantsetra via Nosy Mangabe. Several shorter routes taking in smaller sections of the peninsula are possible, particularly if you're based at the ecobungalows on the peninsula's west coast.

Of the three main routes, Maroantsetra to Antalaha, which passes through rice paddies and gentler terrain, is the easiest but also dullest, although all the treks are fairly demanding and involve numerous slippery, muddy stretches. If you want to see forest, the best option is the trek from Maroantsetra to Cap Est.

There are river and stream crossings along both routes – primarily small, low streams on the Maroantsetra to Antalaha

trek, and some deeper, faster-moving rivers between Maroantsetra and Cap Est (which means you may be wading up to waist or chest height, depending on the time of year, often over slippery rocks). Inquire at the Parc National de Masoala office (p190) about trail conditions when you arrive.

You need an official guide for all treks on the peninsula (p193).

Sleeping & Eating

Ecolodge Chez Arol (http://arollodge.free.fr; Ambodiforaha; camping per person FMg15,000, s/d/tr FMg50,000/75,000/90,000; dinner FMg50,000) Travellers rave about the good French food at Chez Arol and its wonderful position between the beach and the forest. Numerous trekking and snorkelling trips can be arranged from here. It has a booking office in Maroantsetra, 200m east of the bank.

Chez Giuseppe (d FMg30,000; dinner FMg30,000) A set of bungalows on the beach nearby Chez Arol, at Tampolo.

Ambanizana on the west coast has **bungalows** (r FMg30,000) run by Le Coco Beach in Maroantsetra. You can also camp at the Angap base here.

Kayak Masoala (mea@dts.mg; camp sites per person FMg50,000, 9-night all-inclusive trip per person €994) Several wilderness camp sites with bow tents and dining shelters at Cap Masoala are run by Kayak Masoala. The company organises trips here by motorboat, followed by guided sea-kayak tours of the offshore islands. Snorkelling, diving, bird-watching and fishing are also possible. For details, ask at Le Coco Beach (p191) in Maroantsetra.

On the Maroantsetra to Cap Est trek, most nights are spent in villages, where it is customary to pay between FMg5000 and FMg10,000 per person per night to the village chief. However, you should still carry a tent, as some villages are too small to be able to offer accommodation.

There are designated **camping grounds** (camp sites FMg15,000) all the way round the peninsula, including at Marofototra, Cap Masoala, Ambodilaitry, Ifaho and Cap Est. These have wells and shelters for tents, but you'll need to bring in all other equipment.

Bottled water and basic supplies are usually available in bigger villages such as Mahavelona, Ampokafo and Antanandavahely, but you will need to be self-sufficient with most food. There are water sources en route – bring a good purifier.

CAP EST

Remote and beautiful Cap Est is Madagascar's easternmost point. Ambodirafia, southeast of Ambohitralanana on the coast, has an Angap station and is the starting point for treks down the east coast of the peninsula. The walk from here to Cap Masoala takes about four days. The numerous rivers en route must be crossed by pirogue; allow at least three days for cycling one way.

Résidence du Cap (☎ 032 04 539 05; r with bathroom FMg75,000; set dinners FMg40,000) is Cap Est's main hotel. It has been destroyed by cyclones and rebuilt twice in four years. Assuming it's still standing by the time you get there, it has five bungalows, electricity from a generator, and a restaurant. It's located about 4km southeast of Ambohitralanana and makes a good base for trekking.

Hôtel du Voyageur (Ambodirafia; r FMg15,000) has simple but picturesque bungalow accommodation with bucket showers. It also has Malagasy meals. Further towards Cap Masoala at Vinanivao is **Chez Marie** (r FMg15,000), a similarly simple place.

Cap Est is linked to Antalaha by two taxis-brousse daily (FMg25,000, four hours) in the dry season. You can also get there by mountain bike (four to six hours), which can be rented in Antalaha.

To travel to and from Cap Est or Cap Masoala by sea, ask in Antalaha's small harbour about cargo boats heading around the peninsula. Once in Cap Masoala it's possible to take a boat on to Maroantsetra, although this should be arranged in advance if possible or you could be in for a long wait. It's also possible, but hard walking, to continue up the western side of the peninsula by foot to Maroantsetra (four to six days).

ANTALAHA

pop 30,000

Antalaha, a prosperous coastal town, suffered significant damage during Cyclone Hudah in April 2000 and Cyclone Hiary in 2002. Numerous buildings, including the airport, were partially destroyed and

vanilla production was dealt a severe blow, but little sign of the damage now remains in the town centre.

Apart from being a relaxing place to stop if you are travelling up or down the east coast, Antalaha makes a good starting point for visiting Cap Est, about 50km to the south.

Information

The Angap and Parc National de Masoala representative (for arranging permits and guides) is in town next door to the Chamber of Commerce.

Antalaha is well known in Madagascar's expat circles for its excellent dentist – inquire at the Kam-Hyo pharmacy opposite Hôtel Florida if you need his services. There are also banks in Antalaha for changing money, and a good **Internet café** (per 15 min FMg5000) – look for the orange sign next to Pharmacy Kam-Hyo.

Tours

Hôtel Océan Momo (☎ 032 02 340 69) can help organise excursions in the area, as can Le Corail restaurant (p196) and **Henri Fraise Fils Travel Service** (☎ 88 810 33; at the port). Le Corail also rents mountain bikes.

Sleeping & Eating

Hôtel Océan Momo (☎ 032 02 340 69; www.ocean -momo.com in French; d with bathroom FMg200,000; mains FMg35,000) This comfortable hotel on the beach about 100m south of the port is Antalaha's most luxurious option. The imposing white bungalows, in rows next to the beach, have tiled floors, dark wood furniture and four-poster beds with mosquito nets. The restaurant is equally impressive – large and tastefully decorated, with a range of seafood on the menu.

Chambres Liane (☎ 032 04 763 60; r with bathroom FMg60,000) Small but well-kept rooms with mosquito nets but no fans, and friendly staff.

Hôtel Florida (☎ 032 07 161 90; r with bathroom FMg75,000, with hot water FMg90,000; ⚒) On the main road opposite the white pharmacy, this is a step up. Some more expensive rooms with air-con are also available.

Hôtel Nany (☎ 032 40 051 89; at the port; r with bathroom FMg75,000) Basic whitewashed rooms around a cheery courtyard full of palm trees. Cold water only in the showers.

Le Corail (☎ 032 04 539 05; ☺ lunch & dinner Tue-Sun) Le Corail has good French food, great desserts, and rents out mountain bikes. It's also the booking office for Residence du Cap hotel, and the owner can give advice on trekking on the peninsula.

Fleur de Lotus (☺ dinner) Near Hôtel du Centre, this is one of Antalaha's better dining options; it has a good Chinese menu selection.

For inexpensive food and home-made ice cream, try Salon de Thé Joice, near the police station just south of the market.

Getting There & Around

AIR

Air Madagascar (☎ 88 813 22) has flights linking Antalaha several times weekly with Sambava (FMg250,000), Maroantsetra (FMg250,000) and Antananarivo (FMg820,000).

The airport is 12km north of town. Taxis between town and the airport charge a ridiculous FMg20,000 per person, so you might want to catch a taxi-brousse from the main road by the airport turn-off for FMg7000.

BOAT

Cargo boats sail regularly between Antalaha and Maroantsetra (about FMg150,000), sometimes also stopping near Cap Est. There are no set schedules; inquire at the port about sailings. There are also cargo boats to other areas along the east coast, including Toamasina, Sambava and Iharana.

TAXI-BROUSSE

Heading north, there are usually several taxis-brousse each day between Antalaha and Sambava (FMg20,000, three hours). Departures are from the taxi-brousse stand about 2km north of town.

Heading south, two taxis-brousse daily go to Cap Est (FMg25,000, four hours) in the dry season. Taxis-brousse towards Cap Est depart from the taxi-brousse station on the way to the airport from town. If you're taking a mountain bike to Cap Est, the taxis-brousse can tie it on top.

SAMBAVA

pop 28,000

Sambava is a sprawling beach town set between the sea and the soaring Marojejy massif on Madagascar's rugged northeastern coast about halfway between Maroant-setra and Antsiranana. The town is nothing special in itself, but makes a good base for exploring the surrounding area, which produces coffee and cloves as well as vanilla. If you want to swim off Sambava's beaches (which are long and sandy, but hot and blustery) inquire locally about sharks and currents.

All major banks have branches in Sambava for changing money – you may find yourself using them more often than expected, as everything in Sambava is fairly expensive compared to other towns in the region.

Best (☎ 88 922 48; best.sambava@wanadoo.mg; Rte Principale; per min FMg1000), 100m from Paradise Hotel, has Internet access.

Tours

Sambava Voyages (☎ 88 921 10) in the centre of town can organise excursions in the surrounding area. These include visits to a vanilla factory or nearby coffee plantations (about FMg100,000 per person); transport to Andapa or Antalaha (FMg350,000 per day for the vehicle); and day trips along the river in a pirogue, returning on foot through the villages (FMg260,000 per person, including lunch).

Sleeping & Eating

Hôtel Orchidea Beach II (☎ 88 923 24; Plage des Cocotiers; r with bathroom FMg116,000; mains FMg30,000) A rustic, welcoming establishment that has more charm than any other in town. Just across the road from the beach, it has small but well-maintained rooms with fans but no mosquito nets. The friendly restaurant serves a good selection of seafood. Cold water only in the bathrooms.

Hôtel Las Palmas (☎ 88 920 87, in Antananarivo ☎ 22 593 96; fax 88 921 73; Plage des Cocotiers; r without/with air-con FMg150,000/180,000; ☺) Nominally Sambava's most upmarket hotel, this place has a good position on the beach, but is decent rather than luxurious. The rather small rooms, with pink plastic bathrooms, have fans or air-con, but no nets. There's a terrace restaurant (mains FMg25,000 to 35,000) and some beach umbrellas. The hotel runs excursions to the palm and vanilla plantations outside town (FMg60,000 per person).

Hôtel Paradise (☎ 88 922 97; Rte Principale; d/tr FMg130,000/160,000; mains FMg20,000) This place is highly kitsch but comfortable, with a huge, flashy Chinese-run edifice, a good restaurant and obliging staff. Rooms are vast and cool, but noisy, with fans but no mosquito nets, and painted *trompe l'oeil* bedheads.

Sava Hôtel (☎ 88 922 92; Rte Principale; r without/with bathroom FMg75,000/85,000) A fairly uninspiring place with big, shabby rooms and a cheap restaurant (steaks FMg20,000, prawns FMg15,000).

Hotel Carrefour (☎ 88 920 60; r without/with air-con FMg130,000/250,000; 🔀) A once grand, now faded hotel, down by the beach at the north end of town. If you arrive here after 8pm you won't be able to check in.

Getting There & Around
Air Madagascar (☎ 88 920 37; Rte Principale) flies from Sambava several times weekly to Antananarivo (FMg962,000), sometimes via Maroantsetra (FMg306,000) and Toamasina (FMg368,000). There are also several flights weekly to Diego Suarez (FMg466,000).

The airport is situated about 2km south of town. Taxis to the airport from town cost FMg2500, or you could walk.

Taxis to Antalaha (FMg20,000; three hours) and Andapa (FMg20,000, 2½ hours) depart from the hectic taxi-brousse station in the market at the southern end of town. Transport to Iharana (FMg20,000, 2½ hours) and on to Diego Suarez (FMg100,000; about 17 hours) departs from the northern taxi-brousse station.

ANDAPA
Andapa lies in an attractive agricultural valley in one of Madagascar's most important rice-growing areas. Nothing in particular happens in Andapa, but the beauty of the surrounding countryside, the cool climate and the friendly, untouristy atmosphere make it a great place to kick back and just take in a slice of Malagasy life. From town there are a couple of easy and scenic **hikes**, one which passes through rolling rice fields to a set of impressive rapids about 3km northeast of town. You can also walk 2km south to a waterfall, surrounded by vanilla plantations and fishponds.

There is a very helpful **WWF/Angap office** (wwfandapa@wwf.mg; BP 28, 205 Andapa) in Andapa, from which to arrange treks to the nearby Parc National de Marojejy and Réserve Spéciale d'Anjanaharibe-Sud. If you want to visit either of these areas from Andapa, you'll need at least three days.

Hôtel Vahasoa (r with bathroom from FMg50,000) is a very friendly and homely hotel with a restaurant serving fantastic food. A slap-up, multicourse Chinese dinner, often including lobster, costs FMg50,000. The charming owners, Mr and Mrs Tam Hyok, can help with advice on hikes in the surrounding area or visits to the National Park. Taxis-brousse will drop off or pick you outside the door on request.

Hôtel Beanana (r with fan & bathroom FMg92,000) is the only other place in town – it's on the way into the village, but it doesn't have a restaurant.

There are also several hotely in town serving very simple Malagasy-style meals.

Andapa lies 109km southwest of Sambava along a winding, sealed road which passes through spectacular scenery. Taxis-brousse go daily between the two towns for about FMg20,000 (2½ hours). If you start early, it's quite possible to get to Andapa as a day trip from Sambava.

PARC NATIONAL DE MAROJEJY & RÉSERVE SPÉCIALE D'ANJANAHARIBE-SUD
The rugged and precipitous Marojejy (Marojezy) massif rises north of the road between Andapa and Sambava. It is part of a 60,050-hectare national park that protects a remote wilderness area noted for its vegetation, including over 2000 types of plants, and the spectacular views from the upper reaches of the forest. The park is also home to 11 species of lemurs, including the aye-aye, the silky sifaka *(Propitecus candidus)* and the helmeted vanga shrike, endemic to the region. There are over 100 bird species, about 70% of which are endemic to Madagascar, as well as numerous species of frog and chameleon.

The Réserve Spéciale d'Anjanaharibe-Sud (18,250 hectares), to the southwest of Parc National Marojejy, gained attention in 1997 when the Takhtajania perrieri – a small tree in the Winteraceae family, which is believed to have existed on earth about 120 million years ago – was rediscovered here.

At the park's lower elevations the landscape is dominated by thick rain forest, while above about 800m, the rain forest is replaced by highland forest. At the highest elevations, rising up to the peak of Mt Marojejy at 2133m, the primary vegetation cover consists of heath, mosses and lichens.

It can get very cold at the higher altitudes. Trails in the park and up to the summit are very hard and steep, so this destination is for fit trekkers only.

Both Marojejy and Anjanaharibe-Sud are administered by the World Wide Fund for Nature (WWF). Local communities on the borders of the park manage portions of the forest in partnership with WWF.

The turn off to Marojejy is near Manantenina village, 40km from Andapa on the Sambava road (near the 66km post). Once in the park, there are three camp sites, each at different altitudes. The first two camp sites have huts with beds, but the third and highest is a camping ground only. The Réserve Spéciale d'Anjanaharibe-Sud features most of the same vegetation as the park, but walking here is easier. The best times to visit the parks are from April to May and September to December.

For information, and guides and permits (FMg50,000), contact **WWF** (wwfandapa@wwf.mg; BP 28, 205 Andapa) in Andapa or the WWF welcome office in Manantenina. **Sambava Voyages** (☎ 88 921 10; Sambava) can also arrange visits to the park.

IHARANA (VOHÉMAR)

Iharana (commonly known as Vohémar) lies 153km north of Sambava along a mostly sealed road. It is the last stop north on the east coast before the (rough) road heads inland to Ambilobe and Diego Suarez. Like Sambava and Antalaha, Iharana is a vanilla-producing centre.

One of the main sites of interest for visitors is **Lac Andranotsara**, 7km south of Iharana. It is also known as Lac Vert (Green Lake) because of its coloration by algae. Nearby is a good beach. According to legend, there was once a village at Andranotsara, which one night sank into the earth under the weight of an irritable seven-headed monster who curled up there to sleep. This incident was followed by seven days of rain, which flooded the indentation. The crocodiles that inhabit the resulting lake are thought to be reincarnations of the villagers, and various *fady* (taboos) are in effect. It's possible to walk from Iharana to Lac Andranotsara, though you'll need to ask directions locally.

The main hotel in Iharana is the **Sol y Mar** (☎ 88 630 42; vohemarina@vohemarina.com; r

FMg60,000-190,000), with decent bungalows, some more expensive rooms, and a good restaurant.

Hôtel-Restaurant La Cigogne (☎ 88 630 65) is known for its food. **La Floride** (meals FMg15,000), not far from the Sambirano pharmacy, has good meals, although you'll need to order in advance. There are also some simple rooms here.

Another place to try is **Hotely Kanto** (meals FMg10,000), which has good Malagasy dishes.

Air Madagascar has a few flights weekly connecting Iharana with Diego Suarez (FMg368,000), Nosy Be (FMg368,000) and Antalaha (FMg368,000).

Taxis-brousse travel daily between Iharana and Sambava (FMg20,000, four to five hours). There is usually one vehicle daily between Iharana and Daraina (four hours, 60km), northwest of Iharana en route to Ambilobe, where there's a basic hotely. At least several vehicles weekly continue on to Diego Suarez during the dry season, via Ambilobe. The stretch between Iharana and Ambilobe is very rough, and can take anywhere from 12 to 20 hours. The journey from Ambilobe on to Diego Suarez is only about two hours.

SOUTH OF TOAMASINA

MORAMANGA
pop 24,000

The market town of Moramanga lies along the Antananarivo–Toamasina road, 30km west of Andasibe and 115km east of Antananarivo. It's a necessary stop for travellers heading to or from Parc National d'Andasibe-Mantadia on public transport.

BOA has a branch in town for changing money.

The **Musée de la Gendarmerie** (Police Museum; Camp Tristany; admission FMg10,000; ☺ 8am-noon & 2.30-5.30pm Mon-Fri, 9-11am & 2-5pm Sat & Sun), about 1km southwest of the market, exhibits cannons, police uniforms, a vintage taxi-brousse and, strangely, an enormous bunch of dried marijuana.

Grand Hôtel (☎ 56 823 81; r with bathroom FMg56,000; mains FMg10,000), on the main road opposite the taxi-brousse station, has big, dark rooms with private showers but shared toilets. Try to get a room at the back – they're quieter. The restaurant serves Malagasy food.

Hôtel Emeraude (☎ 56 821 57; d/tw with bathroom FMg92,000/97,000), just a few doors west of Grand Hôtel, and also on the main road, has slightly overpriced rooms with toilets and hot water. There is a *salon de thé* downstairs.

Down the track to the side of the Grand Hôtel, where the taxis-brousse to Brickaville stop, are two clean and basic local hotels, Hôtel Nadia and Hôtel Sarah.

Restaurant Coq d'Or (☎ 55 820 45; ☽ lunch & dinner Mon-Sat, lunch Sun; mains FMg15,000), just off the main road opposite Grand Hôtel, serves *soupe chinoise,* fried chicken and other Malagasy meals.

La Flore Orientale (☎ 56 820 20; ☽ lunch & dinner; mains FMg25,000) is a Chinese restaurant with an extensive menu, east of Grand Hôtel.

Taxis-brousse leave regularly to Moramanga from Antananarivo's eastern taxibrousse station (FMg10,000, three hours). There are direct taxi-brousse connections from Moramanga to Andasibe (FMg5000) every few hours.

To get to Toamasina (FMg30,000, 5½ hours), you will need to wait on the main road (near the Tiko shop) until a vehicle coming from Antananarivo arrives with space.

PARC NATIONAL D'ANDASIBE-MANTADIA

This 12,810-hectare park encompasses two distinct areas: the smaller **Réserve Spéciale d'Analamazaotra** (often referred to as Périnet, its French colonial-era name) in the south by Andasibe; and the much larger **Parc National d'Andasibe-Mantadia** to the north. The park, which consists of beautiful primary forest studded with lakes, is the home of the rare indri, Madagascar's largest lemur. The wonderous indri has been described as looking like 'a four-year-old child in a panda suit' and is famous for its eerie wailing cry, which sounds like something between a fire siren and the song of an operatic tenor – it's an amazing experience to behold. Indris can be heard calling almost daily in Réserve Spéciale d'Analamazaotra, mainly early in the morning and at dusk.

The Réserve d'Analamazaotra – which is where most visitors come to – tends to fill up during July and September, Madagascar's tourist high season. The best times to visit are from September to January, and

in May. During the winter months of June to October, the park can get very cold, so bring enough warm clothing with you. If the weather has been wet (which it often is), watch out for leeches.

Information

Entry permits (three days FMg50,000) are valid for visiting both d'Analamazaotra and Mantadia, and can be purchased at the Angap office at the main park entrance. Guides can also be arranged here; don't hire guides who approach you in Andasibe or Moramanga, as only official guides (who will be allocated to you at the park entrance) can work in the park. All of the guides speak French and some also speak English, German, Spanish, Italian or Japanese – but check before setting out, as some are prone to exaggeration about their linguistic skills. Guide fees range from FMg20,000 per four-person group for a two-hour tour to FMg60,000 for the six-hour Circuit Aventure. Night walks (FMg40,000) are only allowed on the perimeter of the park.

Wildlife

In d'Analamazaotra, there are about 60 family groups of two or five indris; their cry, which can be heard up to 3km away, is used to define a particular group's territory. Indris are active on and off throughout the day, beginning about an hour after daybreak, which is usually the best time to see them. Despite the incredible cacophony

---

THE LEGEND OF THE BABAKOTO

The indri is known in Malagasy as 'babakoto', meaning 'Father of Koto'. The word indri actually means 'look up there', and was mistaken for the animal's name by a European explorer being shown the babakoto by locals!

Tradition relates that the babakoto got its name when a young boy named Koto climbed a tree in the forest in search of honey. Koto disturbed a bee's nest and, stung all over, released his grip on the branches. He was saved from falling to the ground by the indri, which caught him in its arms, and thus earned its name. To this day, it's *fady* (taboo) for villagers to kill or eat indris.

of sound that comes out of the forest, each individual only calls for about four or five minutes per day. Indris eat complex carbohydrates, and therefore need to spend much of their day in a sedentary manner digesting their food. They spend most of their time high in the forest canopy, feeding, sleeping and sunning themselves. Despite their slothful appearance, their powerful hind legs make them capable of 10m horizontal leaps from tree to tree – perfectly balanced despite their lack of a tail, which is a short stump.

The indris are very much the stars of the show, but other species you may see include woolly lemurs, grey bamboo lemurs, red-fronted lemurs, black-and-white ruffed lemurs and diademed sifakas. Eleven species of tenrec, the immense and colourful Parson's chameleon and seven other chameleon species are also found here. Over 100 bird species have been identified in the park, together with 20 species of amphibian.

Réserve Spéciale d'Analamazaotra

The entrance to d'Analamazaotra is 2km along a sealed road from Andasibe. Because the reserve is small, most of it can be covered in short walks. The best time for seeing (and hearing) indris is early in the morning, from 7am to 11am.

Before you begin exploring, it is worth visiting the museum at the park reception, which has a display on indris and information about the park.

Analamazaotra has two small lakes, **Lac Vert** (Green Lake) and **Lac Rouge** (Red Lake). Behind the Angap office is the **Parc aux Orchidées**, which is at its most attractive in October (but is almost completely dried up by late summer).

There are three organised walking trails. The easiest and most popular trail is the **Circuit Indri 1** (about two hours), which includes the main lakes and the territory of a single family of indris. The slightly longer **Circuit Indri 2** (two to four hours) visits the lakes and encompasses the patches of two separate families of indris. The **Circuit Aventure** (up to six hours) does all of the above plus more strenuous walking. Night walks take place along the road on the perimeter of the reserve. You will probably be able to see tenrecs, and mouse and dwarf lemurs

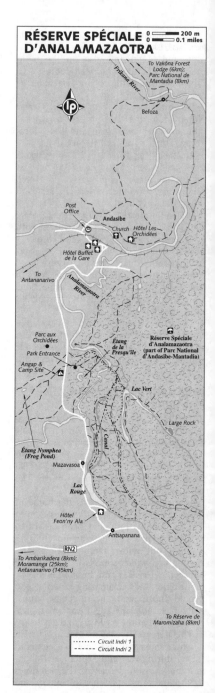

RÉSERVE SPÉCIALE D'ANALAMAZAOTRA 0 — 200 m / 0 — 0.1 miles

Irikama River
To Vakôna Forest Lodge (6km); Parc National de Mantadia (8km)
Befoza
Post Office
Andasibe
Church Hôtel Les Orchidées
Hôtel Buffet de la Gare
To Antananarivo
Analamazaotra River
Parc aux Orchidées
Park Entrance
Angap & Camp Site
Étang de la Presqu'île
Réserve Spéciale d'Analamazaotra (part of Parc National d'Andasibe-Mantadia)
Lac Vert
Large Rock
Étang Nymphea (Frog Pond)
Canal
Mazavasoa
Lac Rouge
Hôtel Feon'ny Ala
Antsapanana
RN2
To Ambarikadera (8km); Moramanga (25km); Antananarivo (145km)
To Réserve de Maromizaha (8km)
········· Circuit Indri 1
- - - - - Circuit Indri 2

on this walk – bring along a strong torch (flashlight), and discourage your guide if they try to take an illegal walk into the forest itself.

Parc National de Mantadia

The Parc National de Mantadia (10,000 hectares), about 17km north of d'Analamazaotra, was created primarily to protect the indris. It also hosts two species of lemur not found in Analamazaotra: the diademed sifaka and the black-and-white ruffed lemur. The park – which is a quiet, beautiful area with numerous waterfalls – is undeveloped and seldom visited compared with its popular neighbour to the south.

Established (easy) circuits include Circuit Rianasoa (guides FMg20,000, one hour); Circuit Chute Sacrée (guides FMg20,000, about 1½ hours); and Circuit Tsakoka (guides FMg40,000, about three hours). Guides, information and permits can all be obtained at the main park entrance near Andasibe. To visit Mantadia, you'll need your own transport, and camping equipment if you're planning to stay the night.

Most travellers stay in or near the very charming village of Andasibe (see below). The closest hotel to Mantadia is Vakôna Forest Lodge. You can **camp** (tent sites FMg25,000) behind the Angap office at the main park entrance. You'll need to get a permit first, and can arrange to leave your gear at the office while visiting the park.

The **camping ground** (tent sites free) just outside Parc National de Mantadia has no facilities.

For details about how to travel to and from the park entrance, see p202. To get to Mantadia from the park entrance, you will need to arrange your own vehicle or bicycle, or to arrange transport with park staff. Vehicles can sometimes be hired through the Angap guides or at Hôtel Feon'ny Ala (FMg150,000 to FMg400,000 in Andasibe).

RÉSERVE DE MAROMIZAHA

This 10,000-hectare reserve about 8km southeast of Parc National d'Andasibe-Mantadia, offers good camping, numerous walking tracks, stands of rain forest and panoramic views. The area is also home to 11 lemur species, although you probably won't see many. They include diademed sifakas and black-and-white ruffed lemurs, both of which are also found at Mantadia. Visits here can be organised with the guides at Parc National d'Andasibe-Mantadia. The reserve is accessible from the park gate via an easy trail. No permit is necessary.

ANDASIBE

Andasibe (an-da-see-*bay*) is a former logging village that makes a convenient base for visiting both the Réserve Spéciale d'Analamazaotra and Parc National de Mantadia. It's also a very charming little place in its own right, bisected by a railway line that's currently defunct but due to re-open in 2004.

Sleeping & Eating

Hôtel Feon'ny Ala (☎ 55 857 71; r FMg60,000, d/tw with bathroom FMg114,000/132,000; set dinners FMg45,000) This very well run mid-range lodge has a glorious setting right on the edge of the forest, close enough to hear the indris call (the hotel's name means 'Song of the Forest'). The bungalows are rather close together but very comfortable, with hot showers. The restaurant does good evening meals and picnic lunches. It's about 400m from the T-junction leading to Andasibe from the main Antananarivo–Toamasina road, and about 1.5km south of the entrance to Parc National d'Andasibe-Mantadia.

Vakôna Forest Lodge (☎ 22 213 94; www.hotel-vakona.com; d with bathroom low/high season FMg280,000/330,000; mains FMg40,000; **P**) Andasibe's most upmarket hotel is one of the best-regarded in Madagascar. It's set in a 'forest' of eucalyptus trees about 9km uphill from the village. The terracotta-coloured bungalows, scattered through gardens filled with palms and bougainvilleas, have wood floors, whitewashed walls, big bathrooms, a mini-bar, safe and terraces. The main building is a beautiful glass-walled restaurant with a sun deck and a log fire, set in the middle of a lake. In the hotel's grounds are a zoo and crocodile farm (residents/non residents FMg10,000/25,000), a lemur sanctuary and an equestrian centre (FMg45,000 per hour). To get here you will need to have your own vehicle, arrange a pick-up through the hotel (one way FMg60,000), walk, or try to hitch a lift.

Hôtel Buffet de la Gare (☎ 56 832 08; s/d bungalow with bathroom FMg168,000/210,000; set dinners FMg50,000) This Andasibe institution, which is housed in a declining but still impressive 1938 building on the station platform, has played host over the years to wildlife luminaries such as Sir David Attenborough and Gerald Durrell. These days it makes up in retro character what it lacks in facilities. However, the bungalows 500m up the road are positively luxurious, with stone hearths and log fires. Some simple rooms are also available in the main building for FMg50,000.

Hôtel Les Orchidées (r FMg50,000) Housed in a wooden building in the centre of the village (signposted), this guesthouse has basic rooms with shared facilities. Malagasy meals are available at the restaurant a few doors down.

Getting There & Away

From Antananarivo, the best way to reach Andasibe is to take a taxi-brousse to Moramanga, and from there get a regular taxi-brousse to Andasibe, which will drop you at your hotel. Otherwise, you can take any taxi-brousse along the Antananarivo–Toamasina road to the T-junction, from where you'll need to walk or hitch the 3km to Andasibe (but only 400m to Hôtel Feon'ny Ala). From Toamasina, there are direct taxis-brousse most days to and from Moramanga.

Returning to Antananarivo or Toamasina from Andasibe, go first to Moramanga, and get a vehicle from there. Vehicles passing Hôtel Feon'ny Ala on the way out of the village can be very full, so you might be better off walking into Andasibe first.

Charter taxis in Antananarivo charge from FMg300,000 for a return day trip to Parc National d' Andasibe-Mantadia. Allow at least three hours each way, and keep in mind that to arrive early enough to have a chance of hearing the indris, you'll have to leave by 6am.

MANANJARY
pop 24,500

Mananjary (manan-dzar) is an agreeable, relaxed backwater sliced into two parts by the Canal des Pangalanes. It is also a local centre for production of vanilla, coffee and pepper.

Every seven years, the small Antambohoaka tribe holds mass circumcision ceremonies in Mananjary, known as *sambatra* (the actual operations are now performed in the hospital). Similar ceremonies are also held in surrounding villages.

North of Mananjary at Ambohitsara is the locally revered **White Elephant** sculpture. This relic is attributed to the Zeïdistes, descendants of the prophet Mohammed who first landed at Iharana on Madagascar's northeast coast and then moved south. Despite the name, it bears little resemblance to an elephant.

On the ocean side of the canal, **Hôtel Sorafa** (☎ 72 942 50; fax 72 943 23; r with bathroom FMg80,000), formerly called the Solimotel, has decent rooms on the seafront and a restaurant. Mountain bikes can sometimes be hired here.

The most comfortable place in town is **Hôtel Jardin de la Mer** (☎ 72 942 24; d with bathroom FMg98,000), near the water, about 1km from the centre of town with well-kept bungalows and a good restaurant. The hotel organises trips on the canal and in the surrounding area.

Air Madagascar flights link Mananjary once or twice weekly with Antananarivo (FMg681,000), Manakara (FMg306,000), Farafangana (FMg425,000) and Fort Dauphin (FMg682,000).

Daily taxis-brousse connect Mananjary with Fianarantsoa (FMg50,000, six hours) and Manakara (FMg40,000, four hours). For Manakara, you may need to get off at the junction village of Irondro and wait for a connection.

There is no direct road access from Mananjary to Toamasina.

MANAKARA
pop 31,500

Manakara is a quiet Malagasy town with-wide unpaved streets and an end of the world feel. It is known primarily as the terminus of the train line from Fianarantsoa. Manakara has some long, pine-fringed beaches, although sharks and strong currents mean that swimming is not possible here.

Manakara is divided into two parts. In the centre, known as Tanambao, are the train and taxi-brousse stations, the market and some hotels. Over the lagoon-like estuary of the Manakara River is the old seaside district of Manakara-Be, where you'll find several banks, a post office, a few hotels and the beach.

For bicycle, car or boat trips in Manakara's surrounding area, as well as excursions along the Canal des Pangalanes, contact **Sylvain** (☎ 72 216 68), an English-speaking guide.

Sleeping & Eating

Les Flamboyants (☎ 72 216 77; lionelmanakara@dts .mg; d with shared bathroom FMg43,000; 🖳) This is an exceptionally good-value guesthouse in the centre of town, with a shady 1st-floor terrace and French poetry on the bedroom walls. There's also lots of local information available. This is the first guesthouse the *pousse-pousses* from the station will take you to.

Magneva Hôtel (☎ 72 714 73; d with bathroom FMg70,000) If you don't mind being about 2km out of town, this is a very comfortable and peaceful option. The big, tiled rooms and bungalows set amid tranquil gardens have hot water, and a car is available for going in and out of town. Ring for a pickup, as it's too far to go in a *pousse-pousse*.

Leong Hôtel (☎ 72 216 88; r with bathroom, TV & balcony FMg60,000/100,000/135,000) Rooms all have fans, mosquito nets and hot water at this spick-and-span Chinese-run place on the road down to the beach. There's a snack bar on site.

Hôtel Parthenay Club (☎ 72 216 63; Manakara-Be; bungalow without/with bathroom FMg60,000/75,000; mains FMg17,000; 🍴) A slightly decaying but still charming hotel in gardens down by the beach, with a rather forbidding-looking concrete swimming pool and a tennis court (plus racquets). The restaurant food has a good reputation.

Hôtel Morabe (r FMg50,000) and **Le Délice** (r FMg50,000) are two good, simple local hotels near the market. The food at Le Délice is excellent.

La Guinguette (☎ 72 213 92; mains FMg20,000; 🕙 lunch & dinner Wed-Mon) Down by the beach in Manakara-Be, La Guinguette has a good selection of seafood and French dishes. Chez Elysa, diagonally opposite Les Flamboyants, serves drinks and snacks, and has a lively atmosphere and there's occasional live music.

Getting There & Away

AIR

Air Madagascar flights link Manakara a few times a week with Antananarivo (FMg750,000), sometimes via Farafangana (FMg250,000) and Mananjary (FMg306,000). There is one flight weekly to Fort Dauphin (FMg682,000). The Air Madagascar office is in the Hôtel Sidi complex, opposite Les Flamboyants.

TAXI-BROUSSE

At least one taxi-brousse daily connects Manakara and Ranomafana (FMg50,000, six hours) continuing to Fianarantsoa (nine hours). These wait until at least 4pm before setting off, so you'll arrive at your destination in the middle of the night. There is usually one direct vehicle daily to Mananjary (FMg40,000, four hours) and Farafangana (FMg20,000, three hours).

The taxi-brousse station is located 2km north of town.

TRAIN

Most travellers prefer to travel at least one way by train from Fianarantsoa; see p94 for details.

Getting Around

There are no taxis in Manakara so the only way of getting around is in one of the hundreds of *pousse-pousses*. The *pousse-pousse* men here are particularly rapacious in soliciting fares; to avoid them, hire a bike from a man called 'Boy' near the market (half/full day FMg15,000/30,000).

FARAFANGANA

pop 22,000

Farafangana is at the southern extreme of the Canal des Pangalanes, and is 109km by road south of Manakara. It is a quiet town with nothing special to do, but has a friendly, relaxed ambience.

Hôtel Les Cocotiers (☎ 73 911 87; ranarson@dts.mg; r FMg75,000) and its annexe **Le Coco Beach** (☎ 73 911 88) provide the best lodgings in town.

There is generally a daily taxi-brousse travelling between Farafangana and Manakara (FMg20,000, three hours). There is no public transport along the 315km road to Fort Dauphin, so you'll have to fly. Air Madagascar has weekly flights for around FMg649,000.

CANAL DES PANGALANES

The Canal des Pangalanes is a collection of natural rivers and artificial lakes that stretches approximately 600km along the east coast from Toamasina to Farafangana, although it's only navigable from just north of Mananjary. More than its rather dull scenery, the canal's charm comes from the procession of boats of all shapes and sizes on its waters, and the small villages on the banks. Here you can stop to see eels drying in the sun, visit local coffee factories, or talk with fishermen mending their wooden pirogues under the trees.

The best times to tour the Canal des Pangalanes are from March to May and September to December.

Tours

Most organised tours cruise from Toamasina to one of the nearby lakes, stay overnight at a lakeside hotel – where you may be able to do some water sports or hiking – and then return to Toamasina. Few organised tours travel along the canal for any great distance. In addition to the operators listed on p169, the following companies do trips along the canal:

Boogie Pilgrim (☎ 22 530 70; www.boogie-pilgrim.net) This Antananarivo-based tour operator organises trips to and from its hotel, Bush House, on Lac Ampitabe.

Boraha-Village (☎ 57 400 71; www.boraha.com) This hotel on Île Sainte Marie organises very high-quality trips on the canal, with the emphasis on local life, agriculture and fishing. Guides speak English.

L'Aziza (☎ 032 07 008 66; l.aziza@netcourrier.com) No-frills, budget trips on flat-bottomed canal boats from any point on the Pangalanes to any other cost FMg200,000 per person per day, including lunch. It also does hotel bookings. Reduced rates for groups.

Getting There & Away

You can travel along the canal in either direction by boat, by taxi-brousse along a parallel inland road or by cargo train. For all travel on the canal, allow plenty of time, and be prepared to spend time on boats without any amenities at all – not even seats!

To find a boat heading down the canal from Toamasina, ask around at the *gare fluviale* about 2.5km from the centre of town.

NORTHERN CANAL DES PANGALANES

To Mahavelona (60km)

Toamasina (Tamatave)
Gare Fluviale

Ivondro River

Canal des Pangalanes

Lac Andovolaline

Lac Nosive　Ankarefo

RN2

Lac Sarobakina

Lac Takanivona　Tampina

Ankanin'ny Nofy

Ambinaninony　Andrano-Koditra

Le Reserve d'Akanin'ny Nofy

Rongaronga River

Lac Ampitabe

Lac Irangy

Ampanotoamaizina

Lac Rasoamasay

Lac Rasobe

INDIAN OCEAN

Manombato

To Antananarivo (260km)

Lac Anjaraborona

Brickaville

Ambila-Lemaitso

To Vatomandry (60km); Mananjary (275km)

There are no fixed sailing schedules, so you may have to wait a while. To continue down the canal each day, you will need to keep asking about onward public boats or pirogues, which can be chartered. Allow three to four days between Toamasina and Ambila-Lemaitso, travelling by pirogue and staying in villages en route. If you take public boats all the way, reckon on about FMg100,000 per person, not including accommodation, for the whole trip.

If you are coming from Antananarivo, the usual places to start a tour of the canal are Manombato, a tiny village on the shores of Lac Rasobe, or Ambila-Lemaitso, where there are several hotels (below).

Watch out for the green barge called *Imitso*, which runs from Toamasina to Vatomandry, carrying merchandise and a few passengers (the fare is FMg7500 from Ankanin'ny Nofy to Toamasina).

LAC AMPITABE & ANKANIN'NY NOFY

One of Lake Ampitabe's chief attractions is **Le Reserve d'Akanin'ny Nofy** (☎ 030 55 851 30; admission FMg40,000; ☉ dawn-night), a private wildlife park with several species of lemur, including Coquerel's sifaka and some very tame black-and-white ruffed lemurs. There's also a good selection of reptiles on another island just offshore, and some comfortable bungalows (FMg150,000) for overnight stays. Meals can be arranged and cost FMg50,000.

Bush House (☎ 22 530 70; www.boogie-pilgrim.net; s/d per person FMg257,000/197,000, s/d bungalow per person FMg310,000/234,000), just across from the reserve, has charming staff, a great atmosphere and simple but rustically attractive rooms. Rates include full board. Walks, boats or canoe trips can be arranged to visit local village projects supported by the hotel, as well the lemur reserve and the sea beach on the other side of the lake. All the guests eat together in the evenings, and the food is superb. Speedboat transfers from Toamasina/Manombato cost FMg675,000/1,575,000 per boat of up to six people. Near Bush House is l'Île aux Nepenthes, an islet containing hundreds of carnivorous pitcher plants.

Just around the lake from Bush House is **Hôtel Pangalanes** (☎ 53 321 77; r FMg180,000; set dinners FMg55,000), which has somewhat squashed bungalows, with two small rooms in each sharing a bathroom and small sitting area. There are also some rooms on stilts over the

lake, which share bathrooms back on land, and are the same price as the bungalows.

LAC RASOAMASAY

The main place to stay here is **Ony Hôtel** (☎ 030 55 850 88; r FMg100,000; set dinners FMg50,000), on the northern side of the lake. Camping is also possible.

LAC RASOBE & MANOMBATO

On the southwestern edge of Lac Rasobe and about 1km south of the village of Manombato lies a beautiful white-sand beach with a number of (expensive) hotels spread along it. This is the starting point for many tours of the northern canal area. Manombato village is connected with the main road by a sandy 7km track (4WD only). The turn off from the RN2 is about 11km north of Brickaville. There's no public transport from Brickaville, so you'll have to charter a car in Brickaville or hitch or walk from the turn off.

The best hotels here are **Chez Luigi** (☎ 56 720 20; d/tr FMg150,000/200,000; set dinner FMg65,000), which has large and luxurious bungalows and does waterskiing, transfers and canoe trips, and **Les Acacias** (☎ 56 720 35; socyin@ simicro.mg; d without/with hot water FMg120,000/150,000; set dinners FMg55,000), which offers boat hire to Ankanin'ny Nofy for FMg600,000 per boat of up to six people. **Hotel Rasoa Beach** (☎ 56 720 18; d FMg140,000) has good-value six-person rooms for FMg190,000, but is otherwise overpriced.

The cheapest option is the basic **Hibiscus** (r FMg50,000; mains FMg20,000), which has shared bucket showers and is slightly away from the beach.

AMBILA-LEMAITSO

This sleepy seaside village, regularly flattened by cyclones, is a good place to start a tour of Canal des Pangalanes. There's a long, white beach, but ask about sharks and currents before swimming. Canoes (FMg30,000 per day) can be hired from **Kayak Nari** in the centre of town.

Just after the ferry crossing as you come from Brickaville is the friendly **Le Nirvana** (r with bathroom FMg70,000; mains FMg20,000), a very atmospheric but decaying set of bungalows on a narrow strip of land between the canal and the sea. There's a peaceful wooden jetty overlooking the canal. This is a good place to find out about transport up and down the canal, and can help with bookings for *Aziza* (p204).

In the village itself, **Hôtel Relais Malaky** (☎ 56 720 22; d/tr FMg65,000/75,000) has a faded, colonial air and sea views, with a decent restaurant downstairs. A bit further outside the village is **Hotel Ambila Beach** (☎ 030 23 847 85; camping FMg10,000, tr with bathroom FMg75,000), which has a terrace overlooking the river. **Le Tropicana** (r FMg40,000) is the cheapest option, with basic bungalows on a small beach on the river.

To get to Ambila-Lemaitso from Brickaville, you'll have to charter a private car in town to follow the sandy road from the northern edge of town east for about 18km to a small ferry crossing over the canal. From the ferry crossing, it's another 4km north along a sandy track to Ambila-Lemaitso. At Ambila-Lemaitso you can inquire about boats heading up or down the canal.

BRICKAVILLE

Brickaville, reached by taxi-brousse from Moramanga (FMg25,000, three hours) or Toamasina (FMg20,000, 5½ hours), is an old sugar-cane growing town on the RN2 between Antananarivo and Toamasina. Near the train station, **Hôtel Mevasoa** (r FMg35,000) has simple but clean accommodation with a bucket shower. There is a small hotely serving good meals. Other places to try include the similar Hôtel-Restaurant Le Florida and Hôtel Des Amis.

Comoros

THOR VAZ DE LEON

Comoros

COMOROS

Early seafaring Arabs called the Comoros Djazair al Qamar, meaning 'Islands of the Moon', which gave rise to the modern name Comores in French and Comoros in English. It's not hard to see the inspiration for the name – the moon hangs brilliantly behind the palm trees, silvering the ageing stone of crumbling Swahili palaces and reflecting off white-sand beaches. The crescent moon also appears on the country's flag as a symbol of the Muslim faith, brought here in the 9th century and still the dominant force on the islands.

The Comoros are seldom visited by travellers, but for those who do make it, the four islands offer everything from active volcanoes to virgin rain forests and giant bats to fossil fish. Superimposed on all this are the charm of the Comorian people and the mysterious appeal of the Swahili culture, which originated in a heady mix of Arab traders, Persian sultans, African slaves and Portuguese pirates.

The Comoros are divided into two political parts – the independent Union des Comores and French-controlled island of Mayotte. The independent Union des Comores consists of three islands – Grande Comore (also known as Ngazidja), Anjouan (or Ndzuani) and Mohéli (Mwali or Moili). The fourth island in the group, Mayotte (or Maore), is a *collectivité territoriale* (overseas territory) of France. The Comoros' political situation is as volcanic as the islands' geography, with more than 20 coups d'état having taken place since independence in 1975. A new Comorian president rarely has time to order his dark suit or military frogging for the official portrait when armed men are once again knocking on his door...

COMOROS

HIGHLIGHTS

- Wandering the labyrinthine stone streets of Moroni's and Mutsamudu's old **Arab quarters** (p217 and p231)
- Swimming in the sea and camping on the beaches of **Parc Marin de Mohéli** (p226)
- Hiking among plantations in **Anjouan's** (p229) cool, misty highlands
- Swimming with sea turtles off the coast of Mayotte in **Sazilé** (p236)

★ Moroni

Mutsamudu
★
★ Anjouan

★
Parc Marin
de Mohéli

Sazilé ★

■ HIGHEST POINT: 2360M | ■ LANGUAGES: SHIMASHIWA (SWAHILI), FRENCH, ARABIC

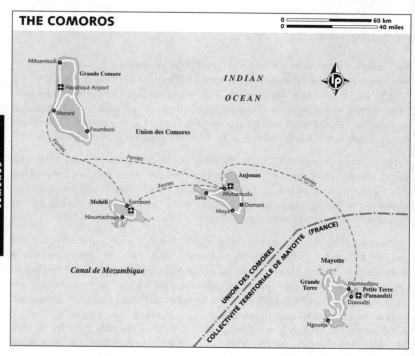

GRANDE COMORE

pop 363,000

The largest (60km by 20km) of the independent Comoros islands, Grande Comore (known as Ngazidja by the Comorians) is also the most economically developed and wields the most political power. Away from the handsome main town, Moroni, the island is dominated by the 2360m Mt Karthala, the largest active volcano in the world, which last erupted in the 1970s, burying a nearby village.

The island is fringed by solidified lava and sandy beaches of various hues, from brilliant white to dark volcanic grey. What little agricultural land is available lies in the south where there are banana, breadfruit, cassava, vanilla, ylang-ylang and coconut plantations. Most of the island's population and activity is concentrated on the west coast. The sparsely populated and dramatically beautiful east coast remains quiet and traditional, with only a few tiny thatched-hut villages.

History

For information on the precolonial history of the Comoros, see the History chapter on p28.

SULTAN SAÏD ALI & THE FRENCH

In 1881 the ambitious sultan Saïd Ali formed a coalition with the French to oust the previous incumbent and take over as the *tibe* (grand sultan) of Grande Comore. This provided the French with a foot in the door, and after just a few years the island was in the hands of French planters. In 1908 Grande Comore was formally annexed by France, eager for a strategic base in the area as a counterweight to the British hold on nearby Zanzibar. The French maintained their grip on the islands for nearly a century.

AHMED ABDALLAH ABDEREMANE

In a referendum held in 1974, the population of Grande Comore, along with that of Anjouan and Mohéli, voted for independence. The population of Mayotte elected to stay under French rule. Less than a year

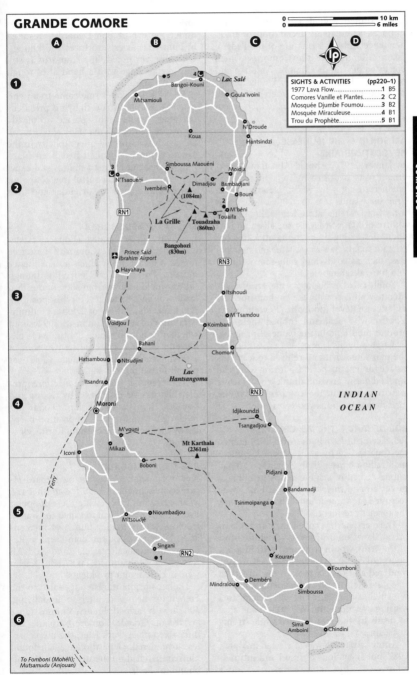

GRANDE COMORE

0 — 10 km
0 — 6 miles

SIGHTS & ACTIVITIES	(pp220–1)
1977 Lava Flow	**1** B5
Comores Vanille et Plantes	**2** C2
Mosquée Djumbe Foumou	**3** B2
Mosquée Miraculeuse	**4** B1
Trou du Prophète	**5** B1

COMOROS

Lac Salé
Bangoi-Kouni
Mitsamiouli
Goula'ivoini
N'Droude
Koua
Hantsindzi
Simboussa Maouéni
Moidja
N'Tsaouéni
Dimadjou
Bambadjani
Ivembéni
Bouni
(1084m)
M'béni
Touaifa
La Grille
Touadzaha
(860m)
Bangohozi
(830m)
RN1
RN3
Prince Saïd
Ibrahim Airport
Hayahaya
Itsihoudi
M'Tsamdou
Voidjou
Koimbani
Bahani
Chomoni
Hatsambou
Ntsudjini
Itsandra
Lac
Hantsangoma
RN3
INDIAN
OCEAN
Moroni
Idjikoundzi
Tsangadjou
M'vouni
Mt Karthala
(2361m)
Iconi
Mikazi
Boboni
Pidjani
Bandamadji
Tsinmoipanga
Nioumbadjou
Mitsoudjé
Singani
RN2
Kourani
Foumboni
1
Mindralou
Dembéni
Simboussa
Sima
Amboini
Chindini

Ferry

To Fomboni (Mohéli);
Mutsamudu (Anjouan)

later, Ahmed Abdallah Abderemane announced a unilateral declaration of independence and the formation of the Federal Islamic Republic of the Comoros, which consisted of Grande Comore, Anjouan and Mohéli. In December 1975, France recognised the new government, then stood back and waited for the fireworks, which began almost immediately.

ALI SOILIH & THE JEUNESSE RÉVOLUTIONNAIRE

In January 1976, Ahmed Abdallah Abderemane was overthrown in a mercenary-engineered coup by Soilih. Determined to drag the islands into the 20th century and away from colonial attitudes, Soilih imposed a form of Maoist-Marxist socialism and set about destroying the past and attacking behaviour that he saw as wasteful and destructive, such as costly and elaborate wedding and funeral ceremonies.

Soilih ruled using a private army of illiterate youths bearing the euphemistic title of Jeunesse Révolutionnaire (Revolutionary Youth), who beat and robbed their way around the island in the name of progress. Frustrated by his lack of success, Soilih lost the plot somewhat and refused to leave his palace for lengthy periods, during which he smoked marijuana and drank whisky while watching films in the company of young girls drawn from his youth brigade.

BOB DENARD & THE MERCENARIES

Relief came in 1978 in the form of 29 French mercenaries led by a moustached Frenchman calling himself 'Bob Denard', who had a long record of staging coups in dubious places around the world. Denard had been recruited by Ahmed Abdallah Abderemane, the former president.

The mercenaries arrived on Grande Comore at dawn on 13 May 1978 whilst most of the army was in Anjouan. Within a few hours Soilih's reign was over. The army surrendered and people took to the streets to celebrate. Reinstated as president, Abdallah returned to the island two weeks later to a rousing welcome and Ali Soilih was shot to death by the mercenaries while 'trying to escape'.

Ahmed Abdallah was re-elected in March 1987, but allegations of fraud and intimidation tactics by the government – and a

'presidential guard' led by mercenaries under the eye of Bob Denard – resulted in numerous arrests, tortures and killings. One observer noted: 'the Comoros is still run like a village with a handful of tough men in charge'.

In 1989 Abdallah's rule came to an end when he was shot to death by his presidential guard while in his palace, ironically known as Beit el Salama (House of Peace). Denard was suspected of complicity in the assassination – Abdallah had been planning to disband his mercenaries and expel him – and he seized control in a coup, but was quickly forced to surrender and then deported.

SAÏD MOHAMED DJOHAR

In 1990 Saïd Mohamed Djohar was declared winner of the Comoros' first free presidential elections since independence in 1975. For a while it looked as though things would improve, but soon opposition leaders began to jockey for his position. After the dissolution of Djohar's administration and a referendum in 1992 about whether or not he should continue to rule, a group of soldiers backed by two sons of assassinated president Abdallah took over the airport and radio station.

The eventual presidential elections predictably suffered disruption by rioting and boycotts from the opposition. Djohar was re-elected, with the main opposition party, led by Mohammed Taki Abdul Karim, close behind.

BOB DENARD (AGAIN)

Not to be deterred, the ageing Denard returned in September 1995 for another try. With the aim of displacing the unpopular President Djohar, Denard sailed to Grande Comore with a motley bunch of mercenaries. Djohar was captured and sent to Réunion for 'medical reasons', and Saïd Ali Kemal and Mohammed Taki Abdul Karim were declared joint presidents.

Djohar's prime minister appealed to the French for help and, after some dallying, 600 heavily armed French commandoes arrived on Grande Comore by plane and inflatable raft. A week later, the mercenaries surrendered. Denard once again found himself marched up the steps of an aircraft bound for Paris.

MOHAMED TAKI ABDUL KARIM

In elections held in December 1996, Mohammed Taki Abdul Karim was elected as president. At this point, after 20 years of simmering resentment, the situation between the islands of the Comoros finally erupted. Mohéli and Anjouan declared themselves autonomous republics and rejected any attempt at compromise by the central government in Grande Comore.

President Taki resorted to a military landing on Anjouan, which ended in humiliation when the government's forces were driven back to their boats by the furious Anjouan militia. By late 1998 Grande Comore seemed to be plunged into complete anarchy. Things came to a head, again, when President Taki died suddenly of a 'heart attack' in November 1998. In a climate of utter confusion, an interim government was appointed.

COLONEL AZZALI & THE NEW UNION

On 30 April 1999, another military coup, this time staged by Colonel Assoumani Azzali, ousted the interim government. He promised that the islands would return to civilian rule, with a new constitution and a new name – L'Union des Comores – by 2002. Elections were held in April 2002 both for the presidency of the Union and the administrations of the reunited, but more autonomous, islands of Grande Comore, Mohéli and Anjouan. Azzali declared himself the winner of the Union elections, despite complaints of vote rigging from the opposition. Each of the three islands – Anjouan, Grande Comore and Mohéli – elected their own president.

These presidents are now squabbling like the sultans of old, forming factions against each other and within their own administrations. The situation, with four presidents and only three islands, has led to political and administrative confusion, with businessmen protesting that they don't know which government to pay their taxes to!

Orientation

Grande Comore's Prince Saíd Ibrahim Airport lies about 19km north of Moroni, the capital, in the village of Hayahaya. Boats arriving in Grande Comore come into the port in central Moroni. Moroni is the only place on the island with any real infrastructure, but tarmac roads in reasonably good condition run around the perimeter of the island, with those in the north being in the best condition.

After a short time travelling around Grande Comore, you will notice one annoying factor: there are no signposts anywhere. To know where you are and where you are going, you will have to guess, follow a detailed map or keep asking people.

Information

Only the larger villages on Grande Comore have telephone and postal services. Fax and email facilities are only available to the public in Moroni, although the more up-market hotels (at this point only the Royal Itsandra outside Moroni; – see p220) are sometimes able to organise fax services for their guests. The Banque pour l'Industrie et le Commerce in Moroni (see p217) can change cash and travellers cheques.

Grande Comore, like the other islands in the group, is overwhelmingly (although tolerantly) Muslim. Visitors are asked to dress modestly when away from the beach, meaning no shorts or low-cut tops for women, and no bare-chested men. Topless swimming or sunbathing are unacceptable. During the holy month of Ramadan, the population of the Comoros fasts from dawn to dusk. During this time, many restaurants are closed, and shops and other businesses open earlier and close earlier, especially on Fridays. Travellers should respect the sensibilities of the population and refrain from eating, drinking or smoking in public during daylight hours.

There are no money-changing facilities at the airport, so make sure you have enough euros (or, at a pinch, US dollars) to pay for a taxi to your hotel and to last until you get to a bank.

El Maarouf Hospital (Map p216; ☎ 73 26 04; Rte Magoudjou, Moroni) has recently been revamped with a large injection of overseas aid, and is now just about acceptable for minor medical problems. In other emergencies call the **police station** (Map p216; ☎ 74 46 63; Ave des Ministères, Moroni).

Activities

The range of activities on Grande Comore may well increase dramatically if the planned renovation of the luxurious Le

COMOROS

Galawa Beach Hotel in Mitsamiouli goes ahead. For the moment, however, no-one is offering watersports beyond the dive company listed below.

DIVING
Grande Comore is the only island of the independent Comoros that has a proper dive centre. **Itsandra Plongée** (☎ 73 29 76; pou mka@ifrance.com; 1 dive CF15,000, 5 dives CF71,300, NAUI Open Water course CF112,000), based on the beach in the village of Itsandra, is French-run and by all accounts fairly reputable. It's not always open, however, so you'd be best to ring or email them in advance – ask for Karin.

HIKING
Grande Comore has some very rewarding hikes, including to Mt Karthala and La Grille.

Mt Karthala
Although it's possible to climb Mt Karthala in a very long day, it's a much better idea to carry camping equipment and spend a day or two exploring the summit. The trek should only be attempted during the dry season (between April and November). The most popular routes begin at M'vouni or further up at Boboni – however, the road between M'vouni and Boboni is almost impassable by normal vehicles, so you will have to take a 4WD or trek there. It takes at least seven hours to climb from M'vouni to the summit and about five hours to the summit from Boboni.

Although the summit and the crater are frequently clear, the slopes are normally blanketed in thick mist for much of the day. The best and most sheltered camp site is within the crater itself. The general consensus is that you'll need a local guide to show you the way up. Be sure to carry all the food and water you'll need for the trip, and don't underestimate the amount of water you'll require. Unless you are really fit, you may want to take a porter, which should cost less than half of what you end up paying for the guide.

Contact one of the tour operators listed on p217, or **Comores Travel Services** (☎ 77 00 55; comotour@yahoo.fr; Mbéni; tent hire CF5000, 2-day expedition per person CF74,000), who specialise in taking walkers up the volcano and can hire out camping equipment. When arranging a trip, always be sure to sort out any particulars, such as who will provide and carry food, water and equipment.

La Grille
If you don't have time to do Mt Karthala, La Grille, the northern massif of Grande Comore, also offers a couple of hiking options. From the villages of Ivémbeni and Simboussa Maoueni in the heights above the west coast village of N'Tsaouéni, walking tracks lead up and over the massif to the east coast. Ask one of the companies (see above) to help arrange guides and plan routes.

Getting There & Around
AIR
Grande Comore is currently served by the following international airlines:

Air Austral (Map p216; ☎ 73 31 44; www.air-austral .com in French; Rue Magoudjou, Quartier Oasis, Moroni) Flies several times a week between Moroni, Mayotte, Mauritius and Réunion. Connections in Mayotte for flights to Madagascar.

Air Madagascar (Map p216; ☎ 73 55 40; www.air madagascar.mg; Quartier Oasis, Moroni) Used to fly between Moroni and Mahajanga on the west coast of Madagascar, with connections to Antananarivo. At the time of research this service was suspended, but it may well be worth checking to see if it's resumed.

Air Seychelles (☎ 73 31 44; www.airseychelles.net; Rue Magoudjou, Quartier Oasis, Moroni) Flies weekly between Moroni and Malé, with connections to Paris.

Air Tanzania (Map p216; ☎ 73 54 26; www.airtan zania.com; Quartier Oasis, Moroni) Flies weekly from Moroni to Dar es Salaam and Zanzibar.

Sudan Airways (☎ 73 23 10; www.sudanair.com) Flies weekly between Paris and Moroni, via Khartoum.

Yemenia (☎ 73 14 00/3; www.yemenairways.net) Flies weekly between Sana'a and Moroni, with connections to Paris.

As well as the international flights listed above, Grande Comore is served by two internal airlines, which fly their small planes almost daily to the islands of Anjouan and Mohéli, with Comores Aviation also providing services to Mayotte.

Comores Aviation (Map p216; ☎ 73 34 00; comores .avi@snpt.km; Rte Corniche, Moroni) and **Comores Air Service** (Map p216; ☎ 73 33 66; cas@snpt.com; Blvd El Marrouf, Moroni) provide a reasonably efficient and easy way to fly between the islands. Fares range from CF20,000, for a hop from

Moroni to Mohéli, to CF58,000 to go from Moroni to Mayotte. Comores Air Service does a circular ticket taking in all three islands for CF68,000. Both airlines can also fly you to Zanzibar (CF130,000 one way) or Dar es Salaam in Tanzania (CF140,000 one way). Comores Air Service also goes to Nairobi and Mombasa in Kenya (both CF140,000 one way).

BOAT

Boats regularly ply between Grande Comore and the other islands in the archipelago, with Anjouan probably being the easiest destination to get to. If you've got a bit longer to wait you could find a boat to go further afield without too much difficulty – the usual destinations are Zanzibar, Mombasa in Kenya, or Mahajanga in Madagascar. To find a boat, head for the port in Moroni where various makeshift offices along the seafront display the latest comings and goings on blackboards outside.

Boats vary widely in quality and safety, so try to see the vessel before you buy your ticket. One of the best is *Alliance des Iles* to Anjouan (CF1100, five hours). To get to Mayotte, fares are fixed and expensive at around €85. Mohéli boats are smaller and less frequent as the port is often ignored by bigger ships (CF6500, four to six hours).

CAR

Hiring a car on Grande Comore can only be arranged in Moroni. Prices are reasonably standard – CF15,000 for a day, plus petrol. Most cars can be hired with a driver for the same price, which is a good idea since roads are steep and winding and signposts non-existent. See p217 for details on car hire.

TAXI-BROUSSE

Long-distance routes are served by *taxis-brousse* (bush taxis), which mostly take the form of minibuses, although there are a few *bâchés* (converted pick ups) too. Because the east coast is so sparsely populated, very few taxis-brousse travel between M'beni and Chomoni, and between Pidjani and Chomoni, so circling the entire island by public transport is very difficult (but not impossible). Like everything else on the island, public transport seems to slow down between 11.30am and 3pm, and after dark (or by 4pm during Ramadan) it virtually stops.

MORONI

Moroni had its beginnings as the seat of an ancient sultanate, which carried on trade within the region, primarily with Zanzibar. In Comorian, the name means 'in the heart of the fire', certainly in reference to its proximity to Mt Karthala. Moroni is a beautiful and friendly town, and a great introduction to the Comoros if you've just arrived. Wandering the narrow streets of the old Arab quarter, you'll find ladies in their colourful wraps chatting to each other on their doorsteps, and grave groups of white-robed men whiling away the hours between prayers with games of dominoes played on smooth stone benches.

At sunset Moroni harbour must be one of the most beautiful sights in the Indian Ocean. The fading orange light is reflected by the coral-walled Ancienne Mosquée du Vendredi (old Friday mosque, p217), the whitewashed buildings of the seafront and the dozens of wooden boats moored between volcanic rock jetties. At dusk there are often hundreds of men and boys swimming here, with the giant silhouettes of fruit bats flapping overhead.

Orientation

From the airport at Hayahaya, the quickest and easiest way into Moroni is by hopping into a shared-taxi with some other passengers, which will cost you CF1000 (or about €2). If you arrive in the port, you can simply walk or hail a shared-taxi to take you to your chosen hotel.

From the north a couple of main roads lead to the appropriately named Ave des Ministères, where there are some government offices, including the tourist office. The confusing medina (old Arab quarter), with its maze of narrow lanes, is found between the harbour and the bazaar. The Ave de Republic Populaire de China, which passes the port and stadium, is thus named because it ends at the huge, incongruous and Chinese-built Peoples' Palace.

Information
BOOKSHOPS

Nouveautes (☎ 73 00 43; Rte Magoudjou) sells current local newspapers, older French magazines and newspapers, a full range of maps for each island in the Comoros, and a handy Comorian–French dictionary.

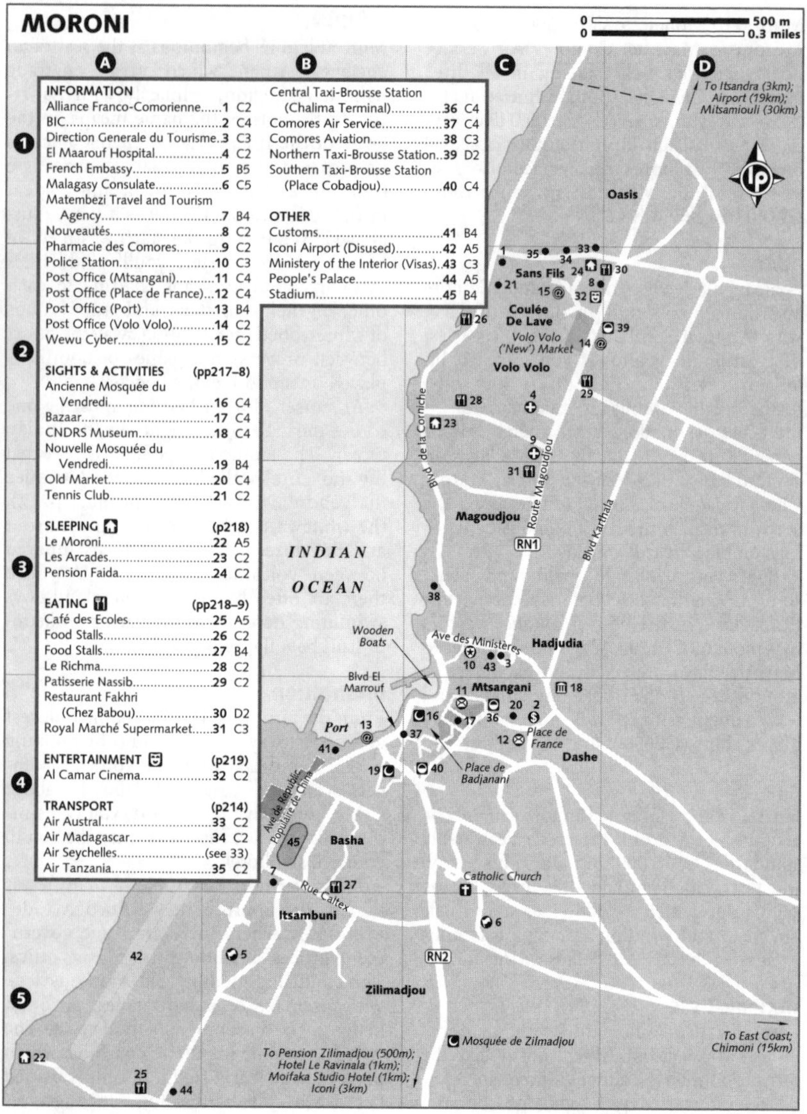
MORONI
0 500 m
0 0.3 miles
A
B
C
D
1
2
3
4
5
INFORMATION
Alliance Franco-Comorienne......1 C2
BIC......2 C4
Direction Generale du Tourisme..3 C3
El Maarouf Hospital......4 C2
French Embassy......5 B5
Malagasy Consulate......6 C5
Matembezi Travel and Tourism Agency......7 B4
Nouveautés......8 C2
Pharmacie des Comores......9 C2
Police Station......10 C3
Post Office (Mtsangani)......11 C4
Post Office (Place de France)...12 C4
Post Office (Port)......13 B4
Post Office (Volo Volo)......14 C2
Wewu Cyber......15 C2
SIGHTS & ACTIVITIES (pp217–8)
Ancienne Mosquée du Vendredi......16 C4
Bazaar......17 C4
CNDRS Museum......18 C4
Nouvelle Mosquée du Vendredi......19 B4
Old Market......20 C4
Tennis Club......21 C2
SLEEPING (p218)
Le Moroni......22 A5
Les Arcades......23 C2
Pension Faida......24 C2
EATING (pp218–9)
Café des Ecoles......25 A5
Food Stalls......26 C2
Food Stalls......27 B4
Le Richma......28 C2
Patisserie Nassib......29 C2
Restaurant Fakhri (Chez Babou)......30 D2
Royal Marché Supermarket......31 C3
ENTERTAINMENT (p219)
Al Camar Cinema......32 C2
TRANSPORT (p214)
Air Austral......33 C2
Air Madagascar......34 C2
Air Seychelles......(see 33)
Air Tanzania......35 C2
Central Taxi-Brousse Station (Chalima Terminal)......36 C4
Comores Air Service......37 C4
Comores Aviation......38 C3
Northern Taxi-Brousse Station..39 D2
Southern Taxi-Brousse Station (Place Cobadjou)......40 C4
OTHER
Customs......41 B4
Iconi Airport (Disused)......42 A5
Ministery of the Interior (Visas)..43 C3
People's Palace......44 A5
Stadium......45 B4
To Itsandra (3km); Airport (19km); Mitsamiouli (30km)
Oasis
Sans Fils
Coulée De Lave
Volo Volo ('New') Market
Volo Volo
Blvd de la Corniche
Route Magoudjou
Blvd Karthala
Magoudjou
RN1
INDIAN OCEAN
Wooden Boats
Ave des Ministères
Hadjudia
Mtsangani
Blvd El Marrouf
Port
Place de France
Dashe
Place de Badjanani
Ave de Republic Populaire de Chine
Basha
Catholic Church
Rue Caltex
Itsambuni
RN2
Zilimadjou
Mosquée de Zilmadjou
To East Coast; Chimoni (15km)
To Pension Zilimadjou (500m); Hotel Le Ravinala (1km); Moifaka Studio Hotel (1km); Iconi (3km)

CULTURAL CENTRES

Alliance Franco-Comorienne (☎ 73 10 87; afc@snpt.km; Blvd de la Corniche; ⏲ 7.30am-10pm Mon-Sat) organises French courses, sports classes and even cabaret and karaoke! There's a library with French books, magazines and videos, Internet access, regular exhibitions and a hall for concerts. Films – all dubbed into French – cost CF200 and are shown weekly. Some activities are only open to members. The **cafeteria** (snacks CF1000; ⏲ 7.30am-10pm Mon-Sat) also serves alcohol.

INTERNET ACCESS

Internet and fax services are available at the post offices at Volo Volo, to the north of town, and at the port. Surfing costs CF25 a minute. Internet access is also possible at Le Moroni hotel (see p218) and the Alliance Franco-Comorienne (opposite). **Wewu Cyber** (☎ 73 15 30; wewucyber@snpt.km; per hr CF1500), also in Volo Volo behind the new market, claims to be open 24 hours a day.

MEDICAL SERVICES

See p213 for details of emergency medical services in Moroni. For minor problems, try **Pharmacie des Comores** (☎ 73 22 73; Rte Magoudjou; ☘ 8am-1pm & 4-7pm Sat-Thu, 8-11.30am & 4-7pm Fri).

MONEY

The only place to change cash or travellers cheques is the **Banque pour l'Industrie et le Commerce** (BIC; ☎ 73 12 04; Pl de France; ☘ 7.15am-2pm Mon-Thu, 7.15-11am Fri, closes 1hr earlier during Ramadan). They can also do advances on Visa cards for a hefty commission.

POST & TELEPHONE

All four **post offices** (☎ 7.30am-2.30pm Mon-Thu, 7.30-11am Fri, 7.30am-noon Sat) have phone boxes; buy a card from one of the eager salesmen outside, then give it back afterwards – you only pay for the units you use.

TOURIST INFORMATION

There's no official tourist office in Moroni offering information, but you can get a helpful list of hotels and pensions from the government-run **Direction Generale du Tourisme** (☎ 74 42 43; dg.tourisme@snpt.km; Ave des Ministères; ☘ 7.30am-2.30pm Mon-Thu, 7.30-11.30am Fri, 7.30am-noon Sat).

TRAVEL AGENCIES

For excursions within Grande Comore, try these two agencies:

Le Moroni (☎ 73 52 42/64/74; lemoroni@bow.snpt.km; Ave Ali Soilih) This upmarket hotel organises day trips taking in all the island's major attractions. A boat trip to the beaches at the north of the island costs €25 per person, a full-day island tour costs €45, while a two-day expedition up Mt Karthala is €150. All prices are based on a group of four.

Matembezi Travel and Tourism Agency (☎ 73 04 00; agence.matembezi@snpt.km; Rue Caltex) This very professional and friendly tour operator can organise hikes, picnics and other day and half-day trips for around €20. It also organises hikes up Mt Karthala, and rents cars with or without driver from €30 per day, excluding fuel.

Sights

ARAB QUARTER (OLD TOWN)

The area around the port and the Ancienne Mosquée de Vendredi (old Friday mosque) is a convoluted medina with narrow streets lined with buildings dating back to Swahili times. It's reminiscent of a miniature version of Zanzibar's Stone Town and almost as intriguing. Here you can spend at least an hour wandering aimlessly, chatting with locals or joining in a game of dominoes or *bao* (an ancient African game played using a board carved with 32 holes). Watch for the elaborately carved Swahili doors found on many houses.

THE TWO FRIDAY MOSQUES

The most imposing structure along the waterfront is the off-white, **Ancienne Mosquée du Vendredi** a two-storey building with elegant colonnades and a square minaret. The original structure dates back to 1427, though the minaret was added early this century.

These days Friday worship has moved to the magnificent **Nouvelle Mosquée du Vendredi** (new Friday mosque) next to the port. In between prayers, the steps outside the mosques serve as a meeting place for the town's menfolk, many dressed in the traditional *kanzu* (long white robe) and *kofia* (skull cap). To see the interior of any of the mosques, you have to be male, appropriately dressed (in long trousers) and go through the ritual washing of the feet before entering.

THE BAZAAR & OLD MARKET

Moroni's bazaar and old covered market, which sprawl down the road past the BIC bank, are a hectic mess of noise, smell and colour. Women in gaily coloured *chiromani* (cloth wraps), their faces plastered in yellow sandalwood paste, huddle over piles of fruit, vegetables and fish, waving off clouds of flies and trying to avoid being crushed by the throngs of pedestrians and vehicles jostling through the bottleneck. In among it all are wide boys (hawkers) flogging plastic sunglasses, Muslim zealots haranguing the crowds, and toddlers playing in the dust. The men in the bazaar generally don't mind being photographed or filmed, although it's polite to ask first. The women will either screech refusals and wave you away, or demand outrageous sums of money for their pictures.

COMOROS

MUSEUMS

The interesting **Centre Nationale de Documentation et de Recherche Scientifique (CNDRS) Museum** (Musée des Comores; ☎ 73 20 64; Blvd Karthala; admission CF750; ⊙ 8am-1pm Mon-Thu, 8-11am Fri, 8am-noon Sat) has a display about the eruption of Mt Karthala; some Shiraz tombs from Mohéli; clothes, music and *galawas* (wooden sailing canoes) from all four islands; and the showpiece – a pickled coelacanth fish caught off Anjouan in 1985 (see the boxed text on p229). There is also a library, although all but one or two books are in French.

Activities

If you fancy a game of tennis when you're in Moroni, call into the **Tennis Club** (☎ 73 34 84; Blvd de la Corniche). The club building also houses a gym, which you can book through the club.

Sleeping

Moroni has more options than anywhere else in the independent Comoros, although all will seem way overpriced if you've just arrived from Madagascar. Some places quote in euros, others in Comorian francs, but in practice you can pay with either currency anywhere.

HOTELS

Le Moroni (☎ 73 52 42; lemoroni@bow.snpt.km; Ave Ali Soilih; s/d with breakfast €57/76; ⊠ ▯ ☲) Moroni's only international-standard hotel is the place to be if you really need a business centre, a swimming pool, an excursion desk, a bar, a restaurant and even giant chess! The rooms are new-looking and comfortable, though small, with minibar, satellite TV and phone. Recommended are the pizzas in the restaurant, which also does the usual steaks and seafood, from CF3000. There are a couple of decent vegetarian options too.

Moifaka Studio Hotel (☎ 73 15 56; hmoifaka@ snpt.km; s/d CF12,750/15,000, with balcony & minibar CF15,750/18,000; ⊠) Moifaka is an excellent option if you can do without all the extras provided by Le Moroni. Rooms are modern, clean and tiled, with TV and good en suite bathrooms. The only disadvantage is that it's hard to find, as it's far out of town in the suburbs towards Iconi. Take a taxi.

Les Arcades (☎ 73 19 42; Blvd de la Corniche; r €25, breakfast €4; ⊠ ☲) Lukewarm reports from travellers about this big pink edifice

suggest the staff are rather offhand, but it's modern and clean. Rooms have nets, telephones and TV. A swimming pool is under construction.

PENSIONS

Hotel Le Ravinala (☎ 73 51 90; d with fan/air-con CF12,000/15,000; ⊠) A very welcoming and friendly establishment, although difficult to find and far from town. Screened rooms have TV and telephones, but shared bathrooms. Bigger rooms with bathroom (full-size bath) and nets are also available. There's a comfortable sitting room and a restaurant (red-bean curry CF2500).

Pension Faida (☎ 73 22 11; Quartier Oasis; s/d CF7500/10,000) The budget traveller's choice – a couple of rooms in a family home, with rudimentary shared bathroom, although one of the rooms has its own. It's noisy, rickety (the handles fall off the doors) and lacking in polish, but friendly and homely. Monsieur will hire himself and his car out for excursions for CF15,000 per day plus petrol.

Pension Zilimadjou (☎ 73 16 96; d without/with bathroom CF10,000/13,000) Lost in the southern suburbs, this is another hard-to-find place, but it's good value, with simple and clean rooms with nets, a little garden and terrace, and good bathrooms.

Eating & Drinking

Eating and drinking options are severely limited in Moroni, especially if you're here during Ramadan. Cheapest eats in town are the little food stalls and hole-in-the-wall restaurants along Rue Caltex and Blvd de la Corniche, although hygiene standards are low. Café des Écoles, on the road towards Le Moroni, has been recommended, although it was closed when we visited. If you're self-catering in Moroni, try the **Royal Marché Supermarket** (Route Magoudjou).

Restaurant Fakhri (Chez Babou; ☎ 73 21 29; Quartier Oasis; curries CF3500; ⊙ lunch & dinner Tue-Sun) Run by a family of voluble Indians, this is definitely the liveliest restaurant in town – featuring a huge terrace lit up with fairy lights and a pavement ice cream bar. The menu includes kebabs (cooked on an open barbecue), huge curry dishes (one portion is enough for two people), samosas and sandwiches, plus lots of fresh juice. There are vegetarian options, although not all the dishes on the menu are always available. The ice cream is to die for, and half the town turns up to get it in the evenings.

Le Richma (☎ 73 27 68; Rue Ambassadeur; seafood CF3000; ☿ lunch & dinner Wed-Mon) Quite an up-market place, with a cosy bar that's popular with expats. Portions are quite small, so order some extra rice. Try the *pilao* (similar to an African paella).

Patisserie Nassib (Rte Magoudjou; brioche CF300; ☿ 6am-11pm) The best patisserie in town turns into a little café at night, serving burgers, kebabs and rice dishes, which can all be washed down with fresh fruit juice and yogurt. There's also football on TV.

Entertainment

Entertainment in Moroni comes more in the form of gasbagging with the ever-friendly locals than anything remotely organised, but there are regular films and concerts shown at the Alliance Franco-Comorienne (see p216).

The **Al Camar Cinema** (☎ 73 01 00; Rte Magoudjou) is no longer a cinema, but instead stages occasional concerts.

Getting There & Around

There are three taxi-brousse stations in Moroni. The northern taxi-brousse station, near the new market in Volo Volo, serves the north and east. Vehicles here go to Itsandra (CF300, 20 minutes), the airport at Hayahaya (CF500, 30 minutes), Mitsamiouli (CF700, one hour), and as far as M'beni on the northeast coast. For destinations in central Grande Comore, mainly Chomoni (CF500, 40 minutes), taxis-brousse leave from the Chalima terminal, which is lost in the labyrinthe old town – ask a local to lead the way.

To southern destinations such as Foumboni (CF700, 1½ hours), taxis-brousse leave from the southern taxi-brousse station at Place Cobadjou, near the new Friday mosque.

Once in town, getting around is as easy as walking or flagging down one of the hundreds of shared-taxis, which will pick you up and deposit you anywhere in town for CF300, or a bit more for further destinations. You can easily take a shared-taxi from town to the airport (CF1000), Itsandra (CF500) or Iconi (CF500).

AROUND GRANDE COMORE
Itsandra

With its startling white-sand beach and excellent choice of hotels, the village of Itsandra is conveniently located about 4km north of Moroni, and is a very good place to base yourself for a stay in Grande Comore. It was here that Bob Denard's mercenary forces arrived in 1978, resulting in the fall of Ali Soilih (see p212).

Motel Vanille (☎ 73 28 08; RN1; s/d CF10,000/13,500) is a very good-value place and ideal if you don't mind being out of Moroni. Rooms have a sitting area, satellite TV, kitchen with fridge, bedroom with fan and mosquito net, and private bathroom. There's a supermarket underneath the hotel, and the owners will arrange for a cleaner if you're staying longer than a few days. You can also order a few Comorian specialities to be cooked for you. Car hire is available.

Another excellent place to stay is **Pension Amal** (☎ 73 35 17; pensionamal@yahoo.fr; RN1; r CF10,000; ☐). It has a few rooms in a pretty garden, and is quiet and peaceful. The rooms are spacious and very cool, with fan and private bathroom. There's no restaurant, but meals can be provided to order and it does breakfast (CF1500).

The only 'proper' restaurant in Itsandra is the unimaginatively named **Restaurant Itsandra** (☎ 73 29 76) inside the dive club on the beach (see p214). It serves up the usual fare – grilled fish, chicken, chips and rice – for about CF3000. But Itsandra is near enough to Moroni for you to take a shared-taxi into town to eat in the evenings.

Hatsambou

On the coast 3km north of Itsandra is the village of Hatsambou, visible from RN1 about 20m lower than the road. The Comoros is the world's second-largest producer of vanilla (after Madagascar) and here, on the inland side of the main road, is a small **shed** where green vanilla is graded and sorted. The workers can explain the vanilla producing and sorting processes (in French).

You can arrange **fishing trips** in local galawas for about CF15,000 per day (plus petrol) for up to four people in a motorised galawa, or about CF5000 for half a day in a simple two-person, human-powered galawa. If the sea is rough, however, this won't be possible.

COMOROS

Since the demise of Le Galawa Beach Hotel at the northern tip of the island, the **Royal Itsandra Hotel** (☎ 73 35 17; itsandrahot@snpt .km; RN1; s/d €46/66; ⚡) is now the only up-market beach hotel in Grande Comore. It's not especially charming or Comorian, but it's entirely acceptable and has a lovely private beach and a good restaurant (fish soup CF3000). Rooms are spacious, light and have sea views as well as a telephone, TV and full-size bathtub. There's a casino and piano bar to provide the nightlife and every so often the hotel does a seafood buffet outside among the palm trees. Transfers from the airport can be arranged for CF5000 per car.

N'Tsaouéni

The sleepy village of N'Tsaouéni is also believed to be the final resting place of Caliph Mohammed Athoumani Kouba, a cousin of the Prophet Mohammed, and one of the founders of Islam in the Comoros. The location of his tomb is the subject of some dispute but the best case can be made for the recently renovated **tomb** beside the old and crumbling Friday mosque. The building housing the tomb has a magnificently carved door, and the tomb itself is inside a larger cement structure, draped in colourful cloths. To see the tomb, ask the guardian, who lives in the house opposite the door, to let you in.

The rose-coloured, 14th-century **Mosquée Djumbe Foumou** is also worth a look. Ask to be allowed inside – the interior is painted a lovely yellow ochre, with pink paint and relief work around the mihrab (the niche indicating the direction of Mecca).

Mitsamiouli

Right on the northern tip of the island, Mitsamiouli is the second-largest town on Grande Comore, with a long, sandy beach that serves as a popular venue for football games. However, like Itsandra, the beaches are a bit public for sunbathing or relaxing, and there isn't a lot of shade. Because Mitsamiouli was home for years to a luxury South African hotel, many of the locals here speak some English.

The only place to stay in Mitsamiouli since the demise of the five-star Le Galawa Beach Hotel (which may well have reopened under a new name by the time you read this) is the fairly decent **Le Maloudja**

(☎ 78 81 56; r with breakfast CF15,000, bigger bungalows €46; ⚡). It's in a lovely spot, with a magnificent beach and a small pocket of forest that's good for watching birds or even lemurs. It's very no-frills at the moment, but due for total renovation if Le Galawa is reopened, and may even become part of a single, larger hotel. If you have a tent, or aren't too bothered about home comforts, this is a great beach to hang out on.

Almost opposite the road leading to Le Maloudja, **Mi-Amuse** (☎ 78 81 92; grills CF3000; ☾ lunch & dinner, disco Fri & Sat) is a good restaurant, bar and disco. There's also a small ylang-ylang plantation and distillery behind the main building, plus a magnificent baobab tree on the other side of the road.

Café Philosophique (Rue du Ralima; local dishes CF1000; ☾ lunch & dinner) is an excellent place in the centre of the village, which serves local food and organises cultural tourism excursions, often focused on Comorian music and dance.

Trou du Prophete

The French name of this small bay, 2km east of Le Maloudja hotel, translates rather inelegantly as 'hole of the prophet' – its much prettier local name is Zindoni. Legend has it that the Prophet Mohammed once made landfall in the harbour, but it almost certainly once served as a haven for 17th-century pirates. It's now a popular leisure spot bordered by a few French holiday villas (including the former home of Bob Denard). It's signposted off the main road, but doesn't have much of a beach.

Bangoi-Kouni & Lac Salé

In the small village of Bangoi-Kouni, about 3km further on, is the so-called **Mosquée Miraculeuse** (Miracle Mosque). No-one in the village knows anything of its origins and it's reputed to have constructed itself in a single night.

Another legend connected with the village is that of the nearby **Lac Salé**. A sorcerer supposedly arrived at a neighbouring village and asked for a drink of water. Refused by miserly villagers, he retaliated by sending a magic flood to drown them all, and thus created the lake. Even today villagers in Bangoi-Kouni are said to offer a coconut to thirsty travellers to prevent the same fate befalling them.

The vibrant blue saltwater lake sits in a deep crater between the shore and RN3, about a kilometre or so east of Bangoi-Kouni. It's easily visible from the main road, and you can walk around the crater rim, with great views of the coast. Legend has it that stones thrown from here are mysteriously deflected and always fall short of the water.

M'beni

M'beni is home to Grande Comore's only official ecotourism attraction – an essential oils distillery and experimental farm known as **Comores Vanille et Plantes** (☎ 77 02 34; www.comores-online.com/cvp/ecomusee.htm in French; admission free). There's a shop selling spices, essential oils, jam, honey and local crafts; a distillery and vanilla treatment plant; an interesting collection of local plants and herbs; and even a pen full of ostriches! Most of this is designed to find new ways of improving agricultural production by breeding strains of plants and trees resistant to disease, but it's also a well-thought-out tourism project, and a green and pleasant place to visit. There's a small snack bar, too.

Chomoni

About halfway down the east coast, Chomoni is probably the best beach along this part of the island because of its position beside a sheltered bay, and fascinating mixture of black lava and white sandy beach. You can stay at the very basic **Restaurant-Bungalows Djoka** (☎ 77 61 70; r CF5000), which has basic palm-thatch bungalows with nets right on the beach. There are no bathrooms of any kind, although the staff will bring you a bucket of fresh water on request. The restaurant can cook curries, fish dishes and rice for about CF2500, and provide (warm) soft drinks.

Foumboni & Bandamadji

The town of Foumboni on the south-eastern corner of Grande Comore is the island's third-largest community. Whiter and brighter than Moroni, Iconi or Itsandra, little-touristed Foumboni has a more exotic feel than the west-coast towns, and local people appear truly stunned at the sight of visitors.

Along RN3, 12km north of Foumboni, lies the village of **Bandamadji**, where several

ancient tombs have been discovered. It is believed that they date back to the early 16th century and contain the remains of early Portuguese navigators and traders who followed in the wake of Vasco da Gama. You can get there by taking a taxi-brousse from Foumboni.

Chindini

More open and airy than the villages further north, Chindini has an idyllic beach immediately west of town, with plenty of spots to pitch a tent. From the beach there's a view across to this unusual looking village, which sits on a very exposed, nearly treeless expanse of coastline. There's also a shipwreck rusting on the rocks. When the weather is clear, you can see the neighbouring island of Mohéli across the channel. If you're hankering to get over there, speak with local galawa owners, who occasionally make the 50km trip across (CF7500, two hours). Beware of doing this trip in bad weather, though.

Singani

The village of Singani, on the way from Moroni to Foumboni, likes to think of itself as the Pompeii of the Indian Ocean, and with pretty good reason. During the eruption of Mt Karthala in April 1977, locals spoke of the 'sky turning red like sunset'. The lava flow swept through the village, destroying everything in its path – only the school was spared.

Two weeks before the eruption occurred, a madman had taken to running through the village streets, warning people of an impending eruption. No-one listened, but three days prior to the eruption the earth began to quake and the man's warnings were taken more seriously. After the initial eruption, the village was evacuated before the lava reached the inhabited area and no-one was threatened except the man himself, who elected to remain in the school. Strangely enough, the stream of lava parted and spared the building. There he remained for several days until rescuers managed to dig through the lava. By that time, he'd lost whatever grip he'd ever had on reality. The only people in Singani who benefited from the volcano were the local football team – the ash was levelled into a large playing field.

COMOROS

Iconi

Iconi is the oldest settlement on Grande Comore and was the original capital, the seat of the Sultan of Bambao. It suffered badly at the hands of Malagasy pirates from the 16th to the early 19th centuries. In 1805 a particularly determined wave of pirates sent many of the inhabitants of Iconi fleeing the town. When the invaders killed their leader, the women of Iconi threw themselves off the cliffs into the sea rather than face capture.

In March 1978, a second tragedy took place in Iconi when Ali Soilih's youth gangs massacred unarmed citizens protesting his policies forbidding Comorian tradition and religious fervour. There's a plaque commemorating them on the wall of the sultan's palace in the centre of the village.

The most imposing buildings in Iconi are the 16th-century **Palais de Kaviridjeo** (the former home of the sultan), and the still-shiny **Nouvelle Mosquée du Vendredi** (new Friday mosque). Also have a look also at several residences dating back to the times of the sultans, including a single wall of **La Fortaleza**, a palace attributed to early Portuguese sailors.

MOHÉLI

pop 31,000

Mohéli (also called Mwali or Moili) is the smallest, wildest, least populated and least developed island of the Union. The island's south coast, coral reefs and dramatically craggy offshore islets are protected by the Comoros' only national park, the Parc Marin de Mohéli, which protects dolphins, whales and sea turtles. Bird-watchers will also find plenty to interest them at Lac Dziani Boundouni on the western edge of the island, and there's even a good chance of spotting the rare mongoose lemur in the remaining stands of rain forest.

In spite of its backwater feel (or because of it), Mohéli is, for many travellers, the most interesting and inviting of all the islands. An excellent ecotourism project funded by the European Union (EU) means that simple bungalow accommodation is easy to find in attractive spots all over the island.

History

In 1830 the Malagasy prince Ramanetaka arrived on Mohéli (up to this time the island was dependent on Anjouan) and staged a coup which left him in power as sultan. He was succeeded by his young daughter, Djoumbé Saoudy, who took the name of Fatima I.

The French hoped to gain a foot in Mohéli's door by sending a governess, Madame Droit, to see to the young sultaness's education, but this was to no avail. Love, however, succeeded where education failed. Fatima began an affair with the Frenchman Joseph François Lambert, a trader, adventurer and ship owner from Mauritius who had been made a duke by the queen of Madagascar. Lambert was able to gain control of great tracts of land on Mohéli and set up plantations with his British partner, William Sunley. In 1867, after the affair had begun to wane, Fatima abdicated the throne and fled the Comoros with a French gendarme, opening the way for the island to become a French protectorate.

Throughout colonialism and the independence that followed, Mohéli, by virtue of its small size and low economic value, was forced into a back seat position in the affairs of the Comoros. In the 1990s after years of 'humiliation' by France and the independent Moroni-based government, Mohéli's leaders declared its independence from the other islands. Reconciliation with the Moroni government was only achieved in April 2000, when Mohamed Saïd Fazul was elected leader of Mohéli under a new constitution that kept the three islands as one nation, but provided each with greater autonomy.

Orientation

Mohéli's small size makes it easy to explore if you've got your own car, although not all the roads are tarmac. Taxis-brousse don't circumnavigate the island, as they can't do the stretch between Mirénéni and Miringoni. The Parc Marin encompasses the whole south coast, from Itsamia to N'Drondroni, and the islands off Nioumachoua.

Information

Mohéli is the smallest and least developed of the Comoros, and few of the villages outside Fomboni have a piped water supply or electricity networks. Medical facil-

MOHÉLI

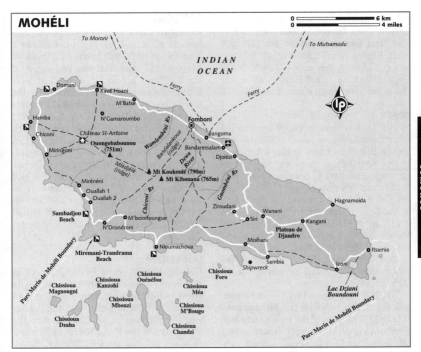

ities are severely limited and if you develop any serious health problems, you'll need to fly out to the French-run Mayotte. There are telephone, email and postal services in Fomboni, but not much in the way of communications elsewhere on the island.

Hiking
CROSS-ISLAND TREKS

Mohéli is so small it's easy to traverse the island in one long day, or you could camp midway. A particularly fine walk begins along the Dewa River east of Fomboni, then climbs steeply up to the interior of the island and eventually descends to the south coast a couple of kilometres east of Nioumachoua.

Another route, across the western end of the island, begins at Miringoni, then climbs steeply through rain forest and agricultural land to the ruined mountain hut Château St-Antoine on the top of the Mlédjélé ridge. From here it's about a 1½-hour walk to Kavé Hoani on the north coast. The same trek can be started at Hamba, a beach just north of Miringoni.

WESTERN MOHÉLI

Just northwest of Nioumachoa, beyond the inhabited area of town, a track begins that follows the southwestern coast and occasionally ventures up into the hills before eventually reaching Miringoni. It's a beautiful coastline and a worthwhile hike, especially if you have camping equipment and make a two-day trip out of it. For a shorter hike, simply walk from Ouallah 1 (the last point on the taxi-brousse route) to Miringoni along the unsurfaced road, which should take about an hour.

Since tracks on both these hikes can get very confusing and often change with the seasons, you'll need a guide to show you the way. The best place to find one is at the eco-tourism project bungalow at Miringoni.

Getting There & Around
AIR

The **Mohéli airport** (Map p223) is in the village of Bandaressalam, about 4km east of the capital Fomboni, on the north coast. Taxis-brousse run sporadically along the road past it into town, or you can try to hitch.

Mohéli is served by both the Comoros' internal airlines, **Comores Aviation** (Map p225; ☎ 72 03 86) and **Comores Air Service** (Map p225; ☎ 72 01 55). Flights travel almost daily to Mayotte (CF38,000), Anjouan (CF20,000) and Grande Comore (CF20,000). Both airline offices are in the main street of Fomboni.

BOAT
Mohéli isn't as well served by boats as the other three Comoros islands; its small size means that it is often ignored by cargo boats. Nonetheless, there are some boats arriving and departing reasonably regularly to the neighbouring islands – try *Alliance des Iles* to Grande Comore (CF6500, four to six hours). The cargo boat **Frégate des Iles** (Map p225) also sometimes stops in Mohéli on its way between Mayotte and Moroni (€75, nine hours). For more up-to-date information about this ask in the office called Chic Safari halfway down the main street.

To find out about boat movements, look for bits of paper on the **'message trees'** (Map p225) in front of the police station in Fomboni's main street. Boat departures are also announced on local radio. Boats usually come in to the port at Bangoma, 1½km east of the town centre.

There's also a chance of finding a *pirogue* (dugout canoe) owner in Kavé Hoani to take you across to Chindini on Grande Comore (CF7500, two hours).

CAR
All five hire cars on Mohéli cost the same – CF15,000 per day without petrol – there's a petrol station on the main street. You can get a car with driver at Akmal Resto (see p226). Make sure you agree on the total price before taking the car to avoid misunderstandings.

TAXI-BROUSSE
Taxis-brousse go from Fomboni to points all over the island including Miringoni (CF500, 1½ hours), Ouallah 1 and 2 (CF600, 2½ hours), Itsamia (CF300, one hour) and Nioumachoua (CF600, two hours). Most places only see one or two taxis-brousse a day, so it's hard to do a day trip to any of them, but there are simple bungalows in each of the above villages if you need to stay the night.

FOMBONI
Unsurprisingly for such a small place, Fomboni is quiet and sleepy in the extreme. There's no old Arab town like those in Moroni and Mutsamudu, and most of the buildings are low-rise and low-tech. Once you've walked up and down the main street (which has no name) a couple of times, cast an eye over the market and visited the jetty, you've pretty much experienced all that the town has to offer. Mohélians are a bit quieter and less outgoing than their counterparts on Grande Comore and Anjouan, but they are still unfailingly friendly and courteous, so as long as you aren't looking for action-packed entertainment, Fomboni is a good place to just wander about, taking in everyday Comorian life.

Orientation
Getting lost is not a likely prospect in Fomboni – there's really only one main street, which arrives from the airport in the east, meanders along past the market and the government buildings next to the shore, passes the Hotel Relais de Singani, then sets off west towards Domoni. Taxis-brousse generally come to a halt just outside the market, or at the junction just past the Comores Aviation office. Standing on the appropriate side of the main street and waving at any that pass will get you where you need to go.

Information
EMERGENCY
In an emergency, call Mohéli's **police station** (☎ 72 01 27) or **hospital** (☎ 72 80 38), both on the main street.

INTERNET ACCESS
Email and Internet access is provided by the excellent **Centre de Ressources** (☎ 72 04 60; 10 min CF450; ☷ 8.30am-noon & 3-5.30pm), which also has a well-stocked library, with French magazines, novels and local newspapers.

MONEY
Because the island is so small, there's no full-time bank on Mohéli, just a part-time branch of the Banque de l'Industrie et le Commerce (BIC), which opens every second Tuesday morning, when the 'bank' arrives by plane in a canvas bag!

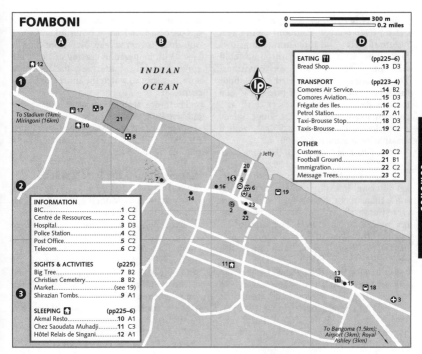

FOMBONI

INDIAN
OCEAN

To Stadium (1km);
Miringoni (16km)

Jetty

INFORMATION
BIC.................................1 C2
Centre de Ressources.............2 C2
Hospital..........................3 D3
Police Station....................4 C2
Post Office.......................5 C2
Telecom...........................6 C2

SIGHTS & ACTIVITIES (p225)
Big Tree..........................7 B2
Christian Cemetery................8 B2
Market.......................(see 19)
Shirazian Tombs...................9 A1

SLEEPING (pp225–6)
Akmal Resto......................10 A1
Chez Saoudata Muhadji............11 C3
Hôtel Relais de Singani..........12 A1

EATING (pp225–6)
Bread Shop.......................13 D3

TRANSPORT (pp223–4)
Comores Air Service..............14 B2
Comores Aviation.................15 D3
Frégate des Iles.................16 C2
Petrol Station...................17 A1
Taxi-Brousse Stop................18 D3
Taxis-Brousse....................19 C2

OTHER
Customs..........................20 C2
Football Ground..................21 B1
Immigration......................22 C2
Message Trees....................23 C2

To Bangoma (1.5km);
Airport (3km); Royal
Ashley (3km)

COMOROS

POST & TELEPHONE
The post office and Telecom are opposite each other on the road leading to the jetty. At the time of research a new post office was under construction, which will apparently be situated near the hospital at the eastern end of town.

Sights & Activities
There's not a lot in the way of official sights in Fomboni. You can take a look at the very overgrown gravestones of Joseph François Lambert (see p222) and his business partner, William Sunley, in the **Christian cemetery** next to the football ground; on the other side of the pitch are some even more overgrown **Shirazian tombs**.

You can wander around the small **market** down by the shore, and marvel at the size of some of the fish being dismembered – to see them arriving off the fishing boats you'll need to be at the area around the market at about 4pm. As far as recreational activities are concerned, the options are limited to a game of *bao* or Scrabble with some of the leisurely gentlemen who gather

under the **big tree** near the Christian cemetery. You can also watch, or perhaps join in, a game of **football** (soccer) on the sports ground or at the stadium on the western edge of town.

Sleeping & Eating
There's no longer any problem finding accommodation or food in Fomboni – there are now four entirely acceptable places to stay, three with restaurants. If you're self-catering, choices are limited to tinned sardines, cheese spread and vegetables from the market. Try the **bread shop** (9am), next door to the Comores Aviation office, for fresh loaves.

Chez Saoudata Muhadji (Pension Farsifa; 72 05 21; s/d CF5000/10,000, with breakfast CF6000/12,000) This very friendly little B&B is run by the delightful Madame Muhadji and her son Farook. The double rooms, with fans and nets, are spotless, as is the shared bathroom. The only disadvantage is that there are no twin rooms. The building is unmarked, so you'll have to ask the way – everybody knows it.

Akmal Resto (☎ 72 00 50; crm@snpt.km; s/d with breakfast CF10,000/16,000) Fomboni's only real restaurant has good little straw bungalows next door, with private bathrooms (cold water only), nets, fans and even televisions! The manager is very knowledgeable about the island and has cars for hire (CF15,000 for the day, including driver). Fish and chicken dishes, served with huge salads and followed by fruit, are CF3000, while a massive lobster costs CF4000.

Hotel Relais de Singani (☎ 72 05 45; s/d with breakfast CF13,500/18,000; restaurant dishes from CF2500) This claims to be Fomboni's most upmarket hotel, but in reality it doesn't offer much more than any of the others. The rooms are clean but small, with private bathrooms (no hot water), fans and nets. The atmosphere is a bit run-down and the staff a bit too laidback. They have a restaurant, where you need to order well in advance. There's also a minibus for hire at CF25,000 per day.

Royal Ashley (☎ 72 08 45; Bandaressalam; r with bathroom CF6000) The cheapest and most basic of Fomboni's hotels, the Royal Ashley is situated right opposite the airport. It's shabby but cheerful, with a good restaurant serving main dishes from CF1500.

Getting There & Around

For more information about getting to and from Fomboni, see p223.

AROUND MOHÉLI

With sandy beaches, primary rain forests, tranquil lakes and best of all, the fascinating offshore islets of the *parc marin* (marine national park), Mohéli is a fantastic place to explore on foot or in a car. There are ecotourism projects in the villages of Itsamia, Nioumachoua, and at Ouallah 1 and 2.

Itsamia

Itsamia is a fairly substantial village with a sweep of sandy, if slightly grubby beach. **Sea turtles** visit the beach at night during high tide to lay their eggs. Visitors can observe the turtles with the help of a local guide, and then learn more about life of this endangered animal in the education centre, known as La Maison des Tortues (Turtle House). Guides cost CF1500 per person, and you'll need a good torch, although you mustn't shine it directly on to the turtles until they have started to lay. Guides are

also available to take visitors bird-watching at **Lac Dziani Boundouni**, a beautiful and tranquil three-cornered lake, 3km from the village. With its peaceful grazing cattle, white egrets and blue butterflies, the lake is a stunning spot to watch the sunset, or have a picnic.

There are simple **bungalows** (r with private bathroom CF5000) on the beach at Itsamia, and a small restaurant area. Meals can be arranged for about CF1500. You can camp here for a one-off fee of CF1000.

Nioumachoua & the Parc Marin de Mohéli

Nioumachoua is Mohéli's second-biggest community, and is home to the only proper hotel outside Fomboni. The village is hot, dusty and low-rise, but all this is compensated for by the magnificent view – the five islets of the *parc marin* rise steeply out of the turquoise sea just offshore, some of the them ringed by tempting yellow-sand beaches. The beach in the village itself is similarly wide and golden, but fairly dirty.

The Nioumachoua ecotourism association (known to the locals simply as L'Association) has a boat for hire which takes visitors out to the islands for snorkelling, picnics or overnight stays. The cost is a steep CF12,000 per boat, or CF15,000 if it comes back the next day to pick you up (guests at Mohéli Bungalows pay CF10,000). A guide to show you the snorkelling sites and explain the ecology of the park will cost CF2000. Bargaining is not possible, nor can you find an alternative boat, as prices are fixed by L'Association.

There are no facilities on the islands, which means you will have to bring everything with you, including water and food (and then take all your rubbish with you when you leave).

Mohéli Bungalows (☎ 72 60 38; fax 72 60 37; r with breakfast per person CF21,000, half board per person CF27,500) in a lovely position on a semi-private beach, has a garden and breezy terrace. The fairly decent bungalows have nets and fans, plus private bathrooms (no hot water). Excursions can be arranged to Itsamia and other villages, and a boat (CF10,000) and snorkelling equipment is available for trips to the *parc marin*. A three-course dinner of fish or various other seafood in the restaurant costs CF6500, and a picnic lunch is CF2200. It's overpriced and often full, especially during Mayotte's school holidays, but it's the only option on the island if you want to stay in a proper beach hotel.

L'Association also maintains a row of three little **rooms** (s/d CF6000/7500), which have nets and bathrooms, but are lacking electricity. They're easy to find, right under the baobab trees next to L'Association headquarters. Next door is the **Restaurant Baobab** (main dishes CF1500), a cute-looking straw hut with local cloths on the tables. They serve fish dishes, manioc, bananas and so on. Order well in advance.

Ouallah 2

The next village after Nioumachoa is confusingly known as Ouallah (or Wela) 2. It's a tiny little place elevated a few hundred metres above sea level, with the stunning beach of **Sambadjou** just downhill from the village. Nearby is the **Cascade de Mirémani**, a waterfall which cascades prettily on to the beach. The **bungalows** (s/d CF3000/4000) are in a beautiful spot on the beach and have a water source, but only the most rudimentary of bathrooms (although there are plans to improve them) and no electricity. Meals can be cooked to order. There's also a boat for hire.

Ouallah 1

Ouallah 1 is the last village accessible by taxi-brousse from Nioumachoua, and is home to the grandly titled Maison des Livingstones, a ecotourism centre named after the giant Livingstone's fruit bat. There is a set of well-built **bungalows** (s/d with breakfast CF3000/4000) with nets and a separate sanitation block. Meals can be cooked to order from about CF1500.

There's also a guide (CF2500 per person or CF4000 per couple) available to walk with visitors through the forest to the roosting place of the bats. It's a steep and slippery walk, three hours there and back, and the bats, when you reach them, are a bit far away to see clearly. But it's still worth doing for the experience of walking in the forest and the chance to learn more about the island's flora – the guide will explain the various plants used in local medicines.

Miringoni

Isolated somewhat by its lack of a decent access road from Ouallah 2, Miringoni is set among thick vegetation on the west coast of Mohéli. A steep 4km walk along the track inland from Miringoni will bring you to a forest hut known as Château St-Antoine high on the ridge. From this 690m point, there's a fine view down to the coast over one of the Comoros' greatest expanses of primary forest. The walk takes three to four hours there and back from Miringoni. You can stay in the village's only **bungalow** (CF3000), which has lovely views of the coast. You can also find an ecoguide here to take you into the forest. Meals can be arranged.

ANJOUAN

pop 252,000

Anjouan, known as 'pearl of the Comoros' by its inhabitants, is the most scenic of the islands, with a varied and beautiful landscape. The island is thickly covered with clove trees, banana plants, ylang-ylang plantations and endless notched palm trees. Through this mosaic of green moves the rural population: the ladies swaying under their loads of firewood or stacks of cassava; the men, machetes in hand, setting off in the cool of the morning to cut new palm thatch for their roofs. Up in the highlands, the air is blissfully cool and mists often descend, the trees of the rain forest dripping moisture on to the giant, swooping bats that live in them.

The Anjouanais are fiercely proud of their identity, and declared independence from the rest of the Comoros in 1996. It has been reluctantly coaxed back into the Union, but relations remain uneasy with the other islands, and many Anjouanais working on Grande Comore or Mayotte have returned home in the face of violent persecution.

History

During the latter part of the 19th century, Sultan Abdallah III of Anjouan ran into problems with his long-term supporters, the British, over his continued holding of slaves. When he agreed to halt the practice, Anjouan's landowners revolted – they depended on slaves to farm their plantations. In April 1886 the ageing sultan travelled to France, which had a more relaxed approach to the issue of slavery, and signed the treaty making the island a French protectorate. In 1912, the island joined the other three Comoros in becoming a full colony of France.

The destinies of the three islands remained on a parallel course throughout the series of coups d'état that characterised politics in the Comoros over the next 12 years. But in March 1996 the volcanic tensions created by years of federalism and centralism finally erupted.

In 1997 the Anjouan government, led by the self-elected president Ibrahim, declared full independence from the Federal government in Grande Comore. Almost immedi-

ately guerrilla war broke out between the supporters of President Ibrahim and those who wanted Anjouan to remain part of the Federation.

Anjouan rejected any attempt to bring the island back into the Federal Republic until 2001, when a new 'military committee' led by Major Mohamed Bacar seized power on Anjouan with the aim of rejoining the Comoros. Bacar survived two coup attempts in quick succession, and held on to power long enough to become president of Anjouan in the elections held in April 2002.

At press time, Bacar was still president, and continues to wrangle with the President of the Union, Assoumali Azzali, for power over the island.

THE COELACANTH – A FISH CAUGHT IN TIME

Three days before Christmas 1938, Marjorie Latimer, a young museum curator in East London, South Africa, discovered a strange, pale-blue fish on a trawler in the port. It was 1.5m long, with white spots, hard scales and fleshy protuberances that resembled limbs. She contacted Dr JLB Smith, a university professor and amateur fish expert, for help in identifying it.

When Smith first saw the fish, he said, 'the sight hit me like a white-hot blast'. He recognised it as a coelacanth, a fish only known from fossil records and thought to have become extinct over 60 million years ago. The coelacanth was a hot contender as one of the species that crawled out of the sea to found life on earth – and thus to be one of the earliest ancestors of man. To find it still in existence was the marine equivalent of stumbling upon a living dinosaur. Smith christened the fish *Latimeria Chalumnae* in honour of its finder, and devoted the next 14 years of his life to finding another one. Posters were printed offering fishermen from Mozambique to Mombasa £100 for the capture of a specimen, and Smith and his wife trawled the East African coast for months on end to no avail.

Four days before Christmas 1952, a fisherman named Ahamadi Abdallah set off in his *galawa* (Comorian dugout canoe) from Domoni, on the southeast coast of Anjouan. He hooked a bizarre-looking fish with hard scales and limb-like fins, and was just about to start cleaning and gutting his catch when the local teacher happened by and remembered something about a crazy *mzungu* (white person) offering a reward for a fish like that...

On Christmas Eve, Smith received a cable from Eric Hunt, an English sea captain in the Comoros. 'Have coelacanth', it said. Smith was a man possessed. He had to get to the fish before it rotted. In desperation, he contacted the Prime Minister of South Africa, DF Malan, and convinced him to lend a South African Air Force plane for the scientific rescue mission. After a frantic race against time Smith arrived in the Comoros, and flew the fish straight back to South Africa and posterity. Abdallah got his reward, and Smith, and the Comoros, became famous overnight.

Since then, obsessed scientists have been visiting the Comoros regularly to look for the coelacanth. No-one, however, has succeeded in establishing how many exist, and none have yet been taken alive. The species is now protected under international law, and celebrated as part of the Comoros' national heritage. To see a coelacanth, visit the Centre Nationale de Documentation et de Recherche Scientifique museum in Moroni, Grande Comore (see p218). For more information on the coelacanth, visit the website www.dinofish.com.

Orientation

Anjouan's airport lies just outside the village of Ouani, about 6km north of the capital, Mutsamudu. Boats arriving in Anjouan come into the port in central Mutsamudu. Anjouan is shaped like an elongated triangle, with three main roads connecting the major towns on the island – Bambao, Domoni and Mutsamudu.

Information

The larger towns of Anjouan have telephone and postal services, but only very limited fax and email facilities are available in Mutsamudu. The BIC bank in Mutsamudu (see p231) can change cash and travellers cheques.

There are no money-changing facilities at the airport, so make sure you have enough euros (or US dollars) to pay for a taxi to your hotel, and to last until you get to the bank.

Medical facilities in Anjouan are extremely limited, so you will need to fly to Mayotte should you require any serious treatment.

Hiking

Anjouan is in many ways the best of the Comoros islands for hiking, as its wooded highlands have the coolest climate. Try to walk from the coast into the hills rather than the other way round, so that you've reached enough altitude to stay cool by the time the sun is at its height.

THE CRATER LAKES

On the slopes of Mt Ntingui are two crater lakes, Lac Dzialaoutsounga (697m) and Lac Dzialandzé (910m). Together, they make a nice day trek from the village of Bambao on the east coast, or from the village of Koni-Ngani to the west. To do the walk, trek or find a taxi-brousse to Dindi, about 7km west of Bambao. From Dindi, the track climbs, passing Lac Dzialaoutsounga on the left, and after 2km arrives at the Col de Pomoni. The track to the right climbs for 1km through a semi-wooded area to Lac Dzialandzé. From here you can walk around the lake, with great views of the crater and surrounding farmland, to Koni-Ngani, where you can pick up a taxi-brousse back to Bambao, and then on to Domoni or Mutsamudu.

MT NTINGUI

It's a hard and steep climb from Lac Dzialandzé up to the normally cloud-covered summit of 1595m Mt Ntingui, the highest point on Anjouan. On a rare clear day, it affords a view over all four islands of the archipelago. At this point, you can either descend to Mutsamudu or return to the Col de Pomoni, and descend through the village of Lingoni to Pomoni on the west coast. Alternatively, you can climb up to Mt Ntingui from Mutsamudu – follow the road from Mutsamudu to the village of Hombo, then ask your way from there.

JIMILIME & THE NORTHEAST

The far northeast of Anjouan, accessible only on foot or by boat, offers another option for exploring off the beaten path. One easy day walk begins at Col de Patsi (700m), which is about 11km above Ouani. The trekking route begins by ascending 1090m-high Mt Djadjana, then following the ridge down through inhabited areas to the traditional village of Jimilime. You can also walk from Ouani directly over the ridge and down to Jimilime and Hayoho on the opposite coast.

Getting There & Around

AIR

Anjouan is served by both the Comoros' domestic airlines, **Comores Aviation** (Map p231; ☎ 71 04 82; nts.mutsa@snpt.km; Mutsamudu) and **Comores Air Service** (☎ 71 12 32; Ouani). Flights go from Anjouan to Mayotte (CF43,000), Moroni (CF31,000) and Mohéli (CF20,000) almost every day, but for flights to destinations further afield, you'll have to connect in Mayotte or Moroni.

BOAT

The port in Mutsamudu is well served by the region's sea traffic. To find a boat to your chosen destination, check the chalked-up ship movements on the blackboards propped up at intervals along the seafront. Alternatively, just ask around in the town square or contact **Agence Tourisme Verte** (RECA Mroni; Map p231; danielmoitane@yahoo.fr; town square; ✆ 8am-1pm & 4-9pm). Look out for the *Alliance des Iles*, which goes to Mohéli (CF6500), or the *Ile d'Anjouan*, which is the newest boat to Mahajanga (two days) in Madagascar. Tickets cost €45 to Mayotte and CF11,000 to Moroni. Boats to destinations further afield, such as Zanzibar (CF75,000, two days), come along once a week or so.

CAR

If you're driving around Anjouan in September, try to avoid the carpets of cloves spread out to dry on the roads! Agence Tourisme Verte (see above) rents cars for about CF16,500 per day, including driver and fuel. A guide (some of whom speak English) costs another CF10,000 per day. The Hôtel Al Amal (see p232) also rents cars, although their prices are way higher.

TAXI-BROUSSE

Taxis-brousse are infrequent and slow down after around 3pm. In Mutsamudu, taxis-brousse leave from the town square in front of the post office. There are regular services between Mutsamudu and Domoni (CF500), Bimbini (CF450), Ouani (CF100) and Moya (CF150) from early morning until mid-afternoon. Distances are short, but the steep and winding roads mean the journey is slow going.

MUTSAMUDU

First impressions of Mutsamudu are not edifying. The place is unbelievably filthy – piles of rubbish fill every crevice, litter the streets and choke the shoreline and the river that runs through the town square. Cattle live on it, munching away on the refuse and defying veterinary science by looking surprisingly healthy.

Before too long, however, you'll be as used to the rubbish as the locals clearly are, and start to enjoy the attractions of the town. There are plenty – the views from the ruined citadel; the narrow, spice-scented streets of the large and well-preserved medina (founded in 1492); and the friendly, laid-back atmosphere of the seafront and

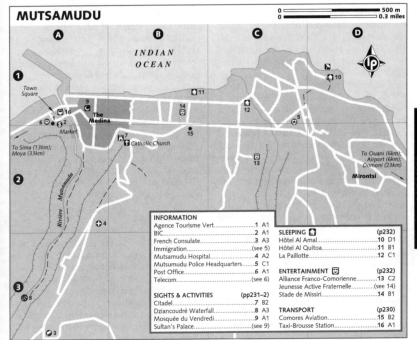

MUTSAMUDU

INDIAN
OCEAN

Town
Square

The
Medina

Market

Catholic Church

To Sima (13km);
Moya (33km)

Rivière Mutsamudu

To Ouani (6km);
Airport (6km);
Domoni (23km)

Mirontsi

COMOROS

INFORMATION
Agence Tourisme Vert......................**1** A1
BIC..**2** A1
French Consulate..............................**3** A3
Immigration....................................(see 5)
Mutsamudu Hospital........................**4** A2
Mutsamudu Police Headquarters......**5** C1
Post Office......................................**6** A1
Telecom..(see 6)

SIGHTS & ACTIVITIES   (pp231–2)
Citadel...**7** B2
Dziancoudré Waterfall......................**8** A3
Mosquée du Vendredi.......................**9** A1
Sultan's Palace...............................(see 9)

SLEEPING   (p232)
Hôtel Al Amal.................................**10** D1
Hôtel Al Quitoa...............................**11** B1
La Paillotte.....................................**12** C1

ENTERTAINMENT   (p232)
Alliance Franco-Comorienne............**13** C2
Jeunesse Active Fraternelle..........(see 14)
Stade de Missiri..............................**14** B1

TRANSPORT   (p230)
Comores Aviation.............................**15** B2
Taxi-Brousse Station........................**16** A1

the town square, where you can chat with the old men in their immaculate white robes, fingering prayer beads as they gather outside the mosques.

Orientation
Most of Mutsamudu stretches along two parallel (unnamed) main streets, from the port area to the Hôtel Al Amal about 750m away. Between the two streets is a fascinating maze of lanes and shops in the medina, known as the Arab quarter. Next to the port is the town square, where you will find the main offices, the bank, taxis-brousse and most of the town's unemployed menfolk.

Information
EMERGENCY
In an emergency, call **Centre Médical Urbain de Mutsamudu** (☎ 71 13 07) or **Mutsamudu Police Headquarters** (☎ 71 02 00).

INTERNET ACCESS
The Hôtel Al Quitoa (see p232) has access to email for guests, although the connection doesn't always work.

MONEY
The only bank on the island is the **Banque pour l'Industrie et le Commerce** (BIC; ☎ 71 01 71; town square; 8.30am-3.30pm Mon-Fri). There's no problem changing travellers cheques here and the procedure is quite efficient.

POST & TELEPHONE
The main post office is on the town square, and has a cardphone outside for calls.

TRAVEL AGENCIES
There's no official tourist office or tour company in Anjouan. For car hire, excursions and information about boats, contact the helpful Monsieur Daniel at **Agence Tourisme Verte** (RECA Mroni; danielmoitane@yahoo.fr; town square; 8am-1pm & 4-9pm). He can also arrange homestays with local families, and provide guides for hiking (CF20,000 per day). The office is right next door to the BIC bank.

Sights
Overlooking Mutsamudu, up a steep stairway from the road above the medina, is the ruined, cannon-laden **citadel**, constructed

with British money in 1860 to defend the town against Malagasy pirates. The citadel was damaged in a 1950 cyclone, but still affords great views across the town and the new harbour, which was financed by Arab interests.

Wandering through the narrow stone streets of the medina is the best form of sightseeing in Mutsamudu. You can stop to admire the **mosquée de vendredi** (Friday mosque), the half-ruined **Sultan's Palace** and the occasional **covered bridges** that link one side of the street to the other. These were constructed centuries ago to allow high-born Swahili women to visit friends and neighbours without having to show themselves immodestly in the streets. Likewise, the smooth **stone benches** (barazas in Comorian) set into the doorways of the richer houses allowed the master of the household to receive male visitors outside without compromising the propriety of his womenfolk.

There is also an easy walk from Mutsamudu up the river gorge to the pretty **Dziancoundré Waterfall**. The only decent **beach** within walking distance of town is run by the Hôtel Al Amal. Nonguests can use it for a small fee.

Sleeping & Eating

Eating and sleeping options are few and far between in Mutsamudu, and all are relatively expensive, although there are a couple of food stalls in the town square, which sell fresh bread and the occasional beef kebab most evenings.

Hôtel Al Quitoa (Hôtel de la Plage; ☎ 71 07 00; henribondar@yahoo.fr; r without/with bathroom CF5000/7500; 🖳) The rooms at this friendly and helpful guesthouse are fairly basic, but they do have mosquito nets and fans, and the restaurant features a comfy TV corner and serves beer. The staff are very knowledgeable about the island and can help plan hikes and excursions into the hills. The food (dishes about CF3500) is plentiful and good – mainly local seafood curries and grills.

La Paillotte (☎ 71 05 24; s/d CF7500/12,000) The rooms behind this very good restaurant are rather hot, but in good condition. They feature fans, nets, and private bathrooms (no hot water) – in some you even get an electric alarm clock. The choice of dishes in the restaurant is fairly limited – omelettes, fish,

chicken and apparently even lobster – but tasty. Prices start at about CF2500.

Hôtel Al Amal (☎ 71 10 17; sat@snpt.km; s/d CF19,500/24,500; 🖳 🗶 P) Anjouan's only 'proper' hotel is a rather unlovely concrete edifice about half a kilometre from the centre of town. It has a small yellow-sand beach (sometimes covered in oil), a swimming pool (sometimes full of rubble), and fairly modern rooms with telephones and televisions. The restaurant, with a smart bar (it even serves cocktails), has a very grand menu featuring dishes such as magret de canard (duck fillet) and tuna carpaccio (CF3500 to CF5500), but it doesn't always manage to live up to its promise.

Entertainment

There's even less in the way of formal entertainment in Mutsamudu than there is on Grande Comore. You could try asking the **Alliance Franco-Comorienne** (afc@snpt.km) about music or theatre performances. Football and basketball matches are sometimes held in the Stade de Missiri in the centre of town. Table tennis tournaments and concerts are held in the Jeunesse Active Fraternelle (JAF) building next door.

Getting There & Around

For more information about getting to and from Mutsamudu, see p230.

AROUND ANJOUAN

The interior of Anjouan, although heavily populated and farmed, is very beautiful and excellent for hiking and exploring. There are lots of opportunities for interesting walks; if you're feeling energetic, take camping gear and turn any combination of the three main routes (west of Bambao, north of Pomoni and south of Mutsamudu) into a cross-island trek. The roads are steep and dizzily winding – you'll need a steady nerve and a heavy hand with the horn if you're driving yourself. Once off the main roads, the paths are generally seasonal and very confusing – you'll either need to take a local guide with you or keep asking the way. Luckily the inhabitants of Anjouan are extremely friendly and happy to help, often walking several kilometres out of their way to put strangers on the right track.

For more details about hiking around Anjouan, see p229.

Domoni

Domoni, halfway down the east coast, was the original capital of the island and now has the second-largest population. The local embroidery here is especially masterful and Domoni is also the source of some of the Comoros' finest woodcarving. The town is guarded by an ancient fortified wall and a ruined tower, built to protect the town from Malagasy pirates.

The old town is even more winding and maze-like than the medina in Mutsamudu, with carved Swahili doors and stone reliefwork lintels on the bigger houses and palaces. Look out for the ladies painting each other's faces with sandalwood paste on the many staircases, and the little straw rooms constructed on the roofs of the stone houses to catch the sea breeze.

A more recent addition in Domoni is the **mausoleum** of president Ahmed Abdallah Abderemane, assassinated in 1989 by his presidential guard. With its brilliant white walls and four high minarets, it's now the most imposing structure in town, if not the entire country.

Motel Loulou (☎ 71 92 35; r CF15,000; ✖) is a few minutes' walk up from town towards the police station and the road to Ajaho. You can also ask taxis-brousse to drop you there. The rooms are brand new and gleaming, with tiled floors, mosquito nets and private bathrooms. Breakfast or meals can be served on order – dishes are around CF3000.

Moya

This scruffy little village overlooks a beautiful white beach – easily the best on Anjouan, and arguably the best in the Comoros. The beach is protected by a reef and offers excellent swimming and rock scrambling, as well as passable snorkelling when the seas are calm.

You'll be joined in the water by dozens of naked boys, who like to roll in the sand while wet and then offer their ghost-like faces for photographs. Be extra careful about leaving your possessions on the beach. Don't buy seashells from the local kids – the practice is illegal and environmentally harmful. Start early if you want to take a day trip on the taxi-brousse from Mutsamudu – the trip here can take up to two hours. Better to stay overnight in the local hotel, enjoy a seafood feast and watch the spectacular sunset.

The only place to stay is the **Moya Plage Hotel** (r with breakfast CF5000), set above the beach in a shady spot with great views. The tiny rooms, which have communal bathrooms (someone in the family can often boil some water for you) and mosquito nets, are hot and basic, but the management is very friendly, the drinks are cold and the food is fantastic.

Meals in the restaurant cost CF4000, or CF5000 for the house speciality – enormous lobsters in vanilla or coconut sauce. You'll need to order at least two hours in advance.

Sima & the West

Twenty kilometres west of Mutsamudu, Sima is one of the oldest settlements in the Comoros and certainly the oldest on Anjouan. Its mosque, **Mosquée Ziyarani**, was constructed in the 15th century over the top of a mosque built in the 11th century. From Sima, the circular island route splits; the main road heads south towards Marahare and Moya, and another continues 5km west through Kavani, with the landscape becoming wilder on the way to the sheltered fishing village of **Bimbini**.

An hour's canoe ride from Bimbini lies **Île de la Selle**, which has good opportunities for bird-watching and interesting mangrove forests, but no real beach. Ask in the village if you'd like to go there.

MAYOTTE

pop 194,000

The biggest difference between Mayotte and the other Comorian islands is that politically, Mayotte is a *collectivité territoriale* (overseas territory) of France and its people are French citizens. Despite large infusions of money aimed at bringing the island's economy and infrastructure into parity with the *Metropole* (as mainland France is known), Mayotte remains economically poor, with a clear gulf between the local population and the French expatriates.

Under French administration, Mayotte has for the most part enjoyed relative peace and stability. The Mahorais, as the people of Mayotte are called, are uncharitably known as 'the spoilt children of the Republic' by the other Comorians; and to the casual visitor at least both the Mahorais and Mayotte's French

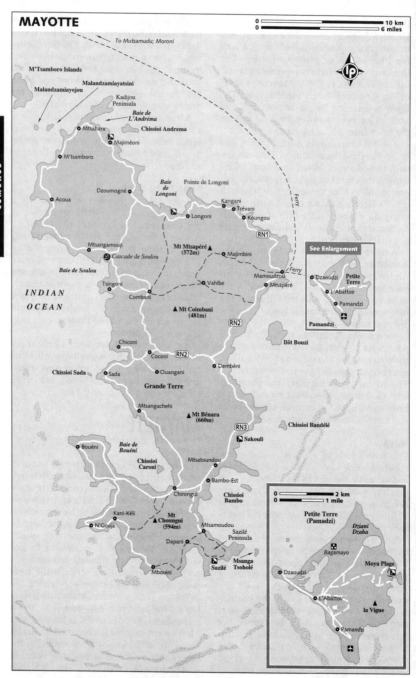

MAYOTTE

0 — 10 km
0 — 6 miles

To Mutsamudu; Moroni

M'Tsamboro Islands

Malandzamiayatsini
Malandzamiayojou

Kadijou
Peninsula

*Baie de
L'Andréma*

Mtsahara

Majiméoni

Chissioi Andrema

M'tsamboro

Dzoumogné

*Baie
de
Longoni*

Pointe de Longoni

Acoua

Kangani
Trévani
Koungou

Longoni

RN1

Mtsangamouji

Cascade de Soulou

Mt Mtsapéré
(572m)

Majimbini

Baie de Soulou

Tsingoni

Combani

Vahibe

Mamoudzou

Mtsapéré

INDIAN
OCEAN

Mt Coimbani
(481m)

RN2

See Enlargement

Dzaoudzi

Petite
Terre

L'Abattoir

Pamandzi

Pamandzi

Chiconi

Coconi

RN2

Ilôt Bouzi

Chissioi Sada

Sada

Ouangani

Dembéni

Grande Terre

Mtsangachehi

Mt Bénara
(660m)

RN3

Chissioi Bandélé

Sakouli

Bouéni

*Baie de
Bouéni*

Chissioi
Caroni

Mtsatoundou

Bambo-Est

Chissioi
Bambo

Chirongui

0 — 2 km
0 — 1 mile

Petite Terre
(Pamadzi)

*Dziani
Dzaha*

Kani-Kéli

Mt
Choungui
(594m)

Mtsamoudou

Sazilé
Peninsula

N'Gouja

Dapani

Sazilé

Msanga
Tsoholé

Bagamayo

Moya Plage

Dzaoudzi

Mbouini

L'Abattoir

la Vigue

Pamandzi

Ferry

expats are considerably less friendly than the inhabitants of the other three islands. Tensions come from the presence on the island of illegal Comorian workers and economic migrants from Anjouan and Mohéli.

If you are a budget traveller, be aware that Mayotte is a *very* expensive place. Thanks to a population of well-paid French bureaucrats, prices for meals and private transport are the same, or more, than in France, and bargaining is all but impossible. Underwater enthusiasts will love Mayotte for its fantastic diving, sailing and snorkelling opportunities; other travellers might be inclined to give it a miss.

History

During the mid-19th-century 'scramble for Africa', Sultan Adriansouli, who had gained quite a few enemies during his rise to power, formed an accord ceding the island to the French in exchange for protection from his rivals. The official transfer of Mayotte took place in May 1843 and the island was transformed from a sultanate into a haven for French planters and slaveholders, then a full colony of France.

A majority of Mahorais voted against independence in a referendum held in 1974, and when Ahmed Abdallah Abderemane unilaterally announced the independence of all four islands, Mayotte's leaders cabled France asking for their intervention. French Foreign Legionnaires and a couple of warships were sent to patrol the territory, and the Comoros' transition to independence went ahead without Mayotte. Another referendum was held in 1976, during the height of Ali Soilih's chaotic reign in the independent Comoros, and this time a whopping 99% of the population voted to stay with France. The UN regularly calls on France to hand Mayotte back to the Union des Comores, but faced with a population staunchly opposed to a break with France the French seem disinclined to do so. Plans are in fact afoot to change the island's status from a *collectivité territoriale* to a full *départment d'outre mer* (overseas department) like Réunion, which would bring even closer administrative links with France.

Orientation

The 'island' of Mayotte actually consists of three main islands: Grande Terre (356 sq km), the central island which contains the largest town, Mamoudzou, and adjacent industrial zone; Petite Terre (Pamandzi; 18 sq km), where the airport is located; and the rock of Dzaoudzi, linked to Petite Terre by a causeway. The latter two islands are just a short ferry ride from Mamoudzou, which has the bank and main shopping area.

Information

The various shops, offices and businesses that you'll need while in Mayotte are divided between Mamoudzou, Petite Terre and various villages around the island.

There are no English publications for sale on Mayotte. The most popular daily newspaper is *Mayotte Hebdo*, on sale at kiosks for €1.50.

In an emergency, telephone Mayotte's **police** (☎ 17), **fire service** (☎ 18) or **hospital** (☎ 61 1515).

The companies that organise excursions within Mayotte are very much geared towards large groups and quite expensive. Try **Maoré Aventure** (☎ 62 30 87; siri-za-maore@wandadoo.fr; Ouangani), which can organise whale- and sea turtle–watching expeditions.

Be aware that you *cannot* change Comorian or Malagasy francs anywhere on Mayotte. There are no money-changing facilities at the airport, so make sure you arrive with enough euros to get yourself into town.

Activities

DIVING & SNORKELLING

Dive specialists report that Mayotte is one of the most biologically diverse sites in the world, with more than 600 species of fish inhabiting the great coral reef that encircles the island. The island is also on the migration routes of various species of sailfish and marlin. Not surprisingly the island has a number of dive companies. Prices start at about €35 for one dive, €180 for five dives, or €240 for a level one CMAS course. The following is just a selection of the companies operating:

Aqua Diva (☎ 61 81 59; aquadivadive@wanadoo.fr; Kaweni)

Lagon Maoré (☎ 60 14 19; jardinmaore@wanadoor.fr; N'goudja) Attached to Le Jardin Maoré hotel on the south coast. Also does boat excursions, whale-watching and big game fishing.

Le Lambis (☎ 60 06 31; lambis.plongee-mayotte@wana doo.fr; Blvd des Crabes, Dzaoudzi)

SAILING & BOAT TRIPS

With the biggest lagoon in the world, Mayotte is home to a plethora of sailing companies. For a fuller list, consult the Comité du Tourisme du Mayotte (see p238). Half-day excursions in the lagoon generally cost around €35; a full day on the water is €45.

Mayotte Découverte (☎ 61 19 09, 69 17 24; Mamoudzou) Does trips in an extraordinary craft called *Le Visiobul*, which has an enormous Perspex bubble underneath it!

Mayotte Voile (☎ 69 02 59; Plage de Sakouli) Based on the brown-sand beach at Sakouli. Offers sailing and windsurfing lessons, boat excursions and canoeing.

Sea Blue Safari (Map p237; ☎ 61 07 63; sea.blue.safari@caramail.com; Rue du Commerce, Mamoudzou) Specialises in dolphin- and whale-watching.

HIKING

Although not as scenic as the other islands of the Comoros, there are still a few good walks to be done in Mayotte. For excellent and detailed maps indicating the best walking routes in Mayotte, pick up a copy of the excellent booklet *Mayotte à Pied*, available at bookshops in Mamoudzou.

Sazilé Peninsula

From the village of Mtsamoudou at the southeastern corner of the island, there's an 8km circuit track which takes in the little visited beach of Sazilé, where you'll find sea turtles offshore and the colourful dunes of Magikavo. Just offshore is the lovely exposed sand bar known as Îlot du Sable Blanc. This is a popular destination for day trips but be warned that the beach is very exposed, with no shade.

The route can be easily walked in a couple of hours, excluding stops, but access to Mtsamoudou can be a problem so allow all day for the trip. To get there from Mamoudzou, look for a taxi-brousse going directly to Mtsamoudou. If you're unsuccessful, take one going to Chirongui via Mtsamoudou and get off at Bambo-Est. From there, it's a 5km walk (or you could hitch) to Mtsamoudou and the start of the circuit. The way to the beach is marked by paint on stones. Boats to the islet will be easiest to find at weekends.

Mt Mtsapéré

A good day circuit from Mamoudzou will take you to the summit of Mt Mtsapéré (572m), the highest point in northern Mayotte. Begin by heading west out of Mamoudzou along Rue de la Convalescence and climb to the tiny village of Majimbini, 4km from Mamoudzou. Keep going until you arrive at the summit, just a little more than 1km from the village.

Once you've admired the predictably vegetated peak, either return the way you came, or bear left and follow the ridge route, which descends through the village of Vahibe and meets the coast about 3km south of Mamoudzou.

Getting There & Around

AIR

Mayotte is served by the following international airlines:

African Express Airways (☎ 61 64 20; abrahair@wanadoo.fr; Kaweni) Flights to Nairobi.

Air Austral (Map p237; ☎ 60 90 90; mayotte@air-austral.com; Place du Marché) Flights to Nosy Be and Mahajanga in Madagascar, Réunion and Mauritius. Also has an office opposite the ferry terminal in Dzaoudzi.

Air France (Map p237; ☎ 61 10 52; issoufali.mayotte@wanadoo.fr; Place du Marché) Flights to France via Réunion.

Air Madagascar (Map p237; ☎ 60 10 52; tsc@snpt.km; Dzaoudzi) Weekly flights to Mahajanga, and sometimes Nosy Be, in Madagascar.

Air Mozambique (LAM; Map p237; ☎ 61 61 85; royal.travel@wanadoo.fr; 70 Rue de L'Agriculture) Flights to Pemba and Maputo in Mozambique.

Air Seychelles (Map p237; ☎ 62 31 00; ario-mayotte@wanadoo.fr; Place Mariage, Mamoudzou) Flies weekly between Malé and Mayotte.

Comores Aviation (Map p237; ☎ 61 62 00; comores.aviation-MAY@wanadoo.fr; Rue du Commerce) The only one of the Comoros' two internal airlines to serve Mayotte. Tickets cost €116 to Moroni, €86 to Anjouan and €101 to Mohéli.

BOAT

Getting to and from Mayotte by boat is fairly difficult and very expensive, as the Mahorais authorities fix prices and no bargaining is not possible. A ticket to Anjouan will cost €45, or to Moroni €85. *Nousra* is the best boat on this route. The best bet is simply to ask around the port area in Dzaoudzi.

CAR & MOTORCYCLE

The cheapest car-hire deals are to be had at **MultiAuto** (☎ 69 22 99; location-multi-autos@wanadoo.fr; Kaweni; ☉ Mon-Sat), which sometimes goes as low as €19 per day with unlimited kilometres. For scooters, try **Jéjé** (☎ 69 39 92; 27 Rue du Commerce) in Mamoudzou, which hires Vespa mopeds with helmet and lock for €20 per day. No-one on the island hires out mountain bikes.

TAXI-BROUSSE
Taxis-brousse are one of the only reasonably priced things on Mayotte – the fare is €2.50 to points north of Mamoudzou, such as M'Tsamboro (40 minutes), or €4 if you go as far south as N'goudja (about an hour). There are three taxi-brousse stations in Mamoudzou – the one next to the port is for vehicles south, the one on Place du Marché has departures for the centre of the island, and the one a bit further down Avenue Adrian-Souli is for destinations heading north.

MAMOUDZOU
Most of Mayotte's shops, restaurants and businesses are concentrated in Mamoudzou, and the neighbouring industrial zone of Kaweni. Here European-style paint warehouses and tyre emporiums are mixed with the same rotting vegetables, open drains and piles of rubbish you'd see in any Third World port. All in all it's a sprawl, lacking any of the charm or architectural interest of the towns of the independent Comoros.

Information
BOOKSHOPS
The best bookshop in the Comoros is **La Maison des Livres** (☎ 61 14 97; marielaure.maison.des .livres@wanadoo.fr; Place Mariage, Mamoudzou), which has maps, guides to Mayotte and the surrounding countries, novels and magazines, all in French.

INTERNET ACCESS
PC Services (☎ 60 29 08; m.pcservices@wanadoo.fr; RN1 Kaweni), about a kilometre from Mamoudzou's centre in the suburb of Kaweni, is a personal computer shop with seven machines, but they're closed at weekends. **Cyber Club** (☎ 62 62 1; 24 Route de Vahibé, Passamainty; 10 min €1; ☯ 9am-10pm Mon-Sat) is also just outside Mamoudzou and they serve snacks.

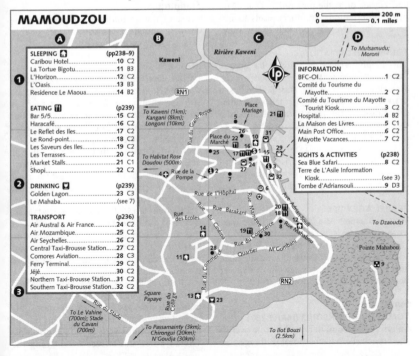

MAMOUDZOU

0 ————— 200 m
0 ————— 0.1 miles

SLEEPING	(pp238–9)
Caribou Hotel	10 C2
La Tortue Bigotu	11 B3
L'Horizon	12 C2
L'Oasis	13 B3
Residence Le Maoua	14 B2

EATING	(p239)
Bar 5/5	15 C2
Haracafé	16 C2
Le Reflet des Iles	17 C2
Le Rond-point	18 C2
Les Saveurs des Iles	19 C2
Les Terrasses	20 C2
Market Stalls	21 C1
Shopi	22 C2

DRINKING	(p239)
Golden Lagon	23 C3
Le Mahaba	(see 7)

TRANSPORT	(p236)
Air Austral & Air France	24 C2
Air Mozambique	25 C2
Air Seychelles	26 C2
Central Taxi-Brousse Station	27 C2
Comores Aviation	28 C3
Ferry Terminal	29 C2
Jéjé	30 C2
Northern Taxi-Brousse Station	31 C2
Southern Taxi-Brousse Station	32 C2

INFORMATION	
BFC-OI	1 C2
Comité du Tourisme du Mayotte	2 C2
Comité du Tourisme du Mayotte Tourist Kiosk	3 C2
Hospital	4 B2
La Maison des Livres	5 C1
Main Post Office	6 C2
Mayotte Vacances	7 C2

SIGHTS & ACTIVITIES	(p238)
Sea Blue Safari	8 C2
Terre de L'Asile Information Kiosk	(see 3)
Tombe d'Adriansouli	9 D3

Rivière Kaweni

Kaweni

To Mutsamudu; Moroni

RN1

Place Mariage

Place du Marché

To Kaweni (1km); Kangani (8km); Longoni (10km)

To Habitat Rose Doudou (500m)

Rue de la Pompe

Rue de l'Hôpital

Rue Barakani

Rue des Ecoles

Rue du Chemin

Rue du Commerce

Quartier M'Gombani

Square Papaye

Rue du Stade

Rue du Collège

To Le Vahine (700m); Stade du Cavani (700m)

To Passamainty (3km); Chirongui (20km); N'Goudja (30km)

To Ilot Bouzi (2.5km)

RN2

To Dzaoudzi

Pointe Mahabou

To Ilot Bouzi

COMOROS

MEDIA

Ask at the Comité du Tourisme (see below) for *Le Cart-é-plan de Mayotte*, which has very detailed maps, or *Le Guide*, published monthly, which has lists of duty doctors and pharmacies.

MONEY

Only one bank, **Banque Française Commerciale Ocean Indien** (BFC-OI; ☎ 61 10 91; Rue Mariazé; ☒ 7.30am-noon & 1.30-3.30pm), will change foreign currency or travellers cheques and do advances on Visa and MasterCard. It also has ATMs, which should theoretically give you money on a Visa card. This is the main branch and is located directly opposite the ferry terminal. The bank gets horribly crowded, so get there about 30 minutes before opening to avoid the queues.

POST & TELEPHONE

The **main post office** (☎ 61 11 03; ☒ 7am-5pm Mon-Fri, 7-11am Sat) is on Rue de l'Hôpital. To make telephone calls, you'll need to buy a *telecarte* (phonecard) for one of the public telephones. Cards are on sale at most shops and kiosks, or at the post office. Dial ☎ 00 before international numbers. Calls to Europe or the USA cost about €0.25 a minute.

TOURIST INFORMATION

The helpful **Comité du Tourisme du Mayotte** (☎ 61 09 09; ctm@mayotte.tourisme.com; Rue de la Pompe, Mamoudzou; ☒ 7.30am-4.30pm Mon-Fri) also has a branch at the airport and smaller information kiosk by the ferry terminal, which is open on Saturdays. They are the best place to come for lists of the *chambres d'hôte* (B&B-style accommodation) around the island, although their information isn't always up-to-date. They can also provide information on diving and sailing companies.

TRAVEL AGENCIES

Mayotte Vacances (Map p237; ☎ 61 25 50; mayotte-vacances@wanadoo.fr; Place du Marché, Mamoudzou) organises boat trips and picnics on various islets in the lagoon, tours of Grande Terre and car hire. Prices average about €55 per person per day, or €25 for a half day.

Sights

TOMBE D'ADRIANSOULI (MAP P237)

Sultan Adriansouli handed Mayotte over to the French. Perhaps he is not well regarded these days, because his tomb lies in ruins. However, the expansive public gardens surrounding the tomb are a pretty enough area of large shaded trees and grass, with views of the bay.

ÎLOT BOUZI (MAP P234)

Îlot Bouzi, a large island in the Mayotte lagoon, is a fauna-conservation area for Mayotte's own species of lemur, *Lemur fulvus mayottensis*. Three hundred and fifty *makis*, as the lemurs are commonly known, roam the island, some of which are used to people and can be handled and stroked. The *makis* are endangered in Mayotte because of poaching, culling by farmers (who blame them for raids on plantations) and encroaching urbanisation. The lemurs can be visited by contacting **Terre de L'Asile** (Map p237; ☎ 61 03 30), the conservation organisation that maintains the island. They have an information point in the kiosk, just opposite the ferry terminal in Mamoudzou. A visit, including the 5km boat transfers, costs €15 per person.

Sleeping

Most of the accommodation in Mamoudzou is aimed at visiting businesspeople and is therefore expensive.

BUDGET

Habitat Rose Doudou (☎ 61 04 48; rose.doudou@wanadoo.fr; 16 Route de Majimbini; s/d/studio €25/35/45) A quiet, family-run *chambre d'hôtes* with a good choice of rooms and prices, and the opportunity to self-cater – there's a well-equipped kitchen for guests to use. You can also rent studios with bathroom, kitchen and one bedroom. The disadvantage is that it's quite far out of town – follow the road past the hospital, then look for the signpost at the crossroads.

L'Horizon (☎ 65 95 98; 9 Rue Mahabou; r with breakfast €40; ☒) Another homely *chambre d'hôtes* that has big, modern rooms with private bathroom. It's convenient, friendly and has good views over the lagoon – therefore it's often full.

L'Oasis (☎ 61 12 23; oasis.mayotte@wanadoo.fr; 97 Rue du Commerce; s/d €26/34; ☒) This is a restaurant which has fairly scruffy rooms attached with shared bathrooms, plus one or two bigger rooms with private bathrooms. There's a bar and terrace overlooking the lagoon, but none of it has much class. The daily three-course menu cost €8 and is quite good value.

Residence Le Maoua (☎ 61 00 53; residence.le.maoua@wanadoo.fr; Rue Marindrini; s/d with bathroom €23/38) Smallish rooms with fans and nets, not too far from town. High on mosquitos, low on charm, but just about acceptable, and under renovation so it may improve.

MID-RANGE

Caribou Hotel (☎ 61 14 18; hotelcaribou.mayotte@wanadoo.fr; Place du Marché; s/d €73/82; 🌐 P) Mamoudzou's most upmarket hotel, with a restaurant and snack bar, business services and a rather plasticky feel. The rooms, however, are comfortable and have satellite TV and telephones. The snack bar (sandwiches €4) is a popular meeting place for the town's French population.

La Tortue Bigotu (☎ 61 11 32; la.tortue.bigotu.hotel@wanadoo.fr; s/d €65/69; 🌐 P 🏊) Another upmarket place a bit further out of town. The fairly smart but small rooms have televisions and big bathrooms. There's a small pool, a terrace, barbeque area, bar and a fishtank. The restaurant does seafood, grills and pizzas for about €14.

Eating & Drinking

There is a fairly good selection of restaurants in Mamoudzou, most of which double as bars. There's not much in the way of cheap eats – the market stalls down by the port serve fried bananas and the occasional omelette for around €2, but get there early before the flies have done too much damage. You can also find evening food stalls around the stadium in the suburb of Cavani.

RESTAURANTS

Le Vahine (☎ 61 14 49; 12 Rue du Stade; fish curries €5; 🕐 lunch & dinner Mon-Sat, dinner Sun) Excellent, friendly service, big portions and reasonable prices mean this cheerful place is often packed, although the menu is very limited. If you can't get a table, have a wander in the area, which has several cheap restaurants and cafés.

Le Rond-point (☎ 61 04 61; 2 Rue du Commerce; mains €15-25; 🕐 lunch & dinner Mon-Sat) A good wine list and a cocktail menu complement the French gastronomy and the lagoon view in this fairly classy establishment.

Les Terrasses (☎ 61 06 12; 1 Bis Rue du Commerce; seafood €12-16; 🕐 lunch & dinner Tue-Sat, dinner Sun) Another classy French restaurant, specialising in seafood. As the name suggests, there's a big terrace with a seaview.

Le Reflet des Iles (☎ 61 10 30; Place du Marché; pizzas €8; 🕐 lunch & dinner Mon-Sat) An insalubrious location, right by the noisy roundabout in the centre of town, but the bar and restaurant are nicely decorated and relaxing.

CAFÉS & SANDWICH BARS

Les Saveurs des Iles (☎ 61 29 76; 10, Rue du Commerce; rice dishes €7; 🕐 lunch Mon-Sat) One of the few places in Mamoudzou that serves local curries, chicken and coconut rice. It's on the 1st floor, away from the exhaust fumes.

Bar 5/5 (Place de la Jetée; curries €4) Another cheap and local place with daily specials chalked up on a blackboard. It's a good place to sit while waiting for le barge (ferry), although the service was terrible when we visited.

Haracafé (Place du Marché; crepes €3) A little coffee bar next door to Le Reflet des Iles. Does herbal teas, fresh juice and delicious crepes.

SELF-CATERING

Shopi supermarket (Place du Marché) Provides all those Western treats you may have been dreaming about, but at prices to match. You can pick up cheaper vegetables and fish at the market.

NIGHTCLUBS

Mamoudzou boasts two fairly average discos, the down-to-earth **Golden Lagon** (Rue du Commerce; admission €10) and **Le Mahaba** (Place du Marché; admission €15), where smart dress is required.

Getting There & Around

A regular ferry known as le barge takes cars, bikes, trucks and foot passengers between Mamoudzou and Dzaoudzi, with a journey time of about 10 minutes. Foot passengers cost only €0.76 per person, but cars are €15. You only pay on the Mamoudzou side. The ferry departs every 30 minutes between 6am and 10.30pm, then every hour until 12.30pm. There are ferries until 2.30am on Saturdays.

Within Mamoudzou, shared-taxis cost a standard €0.70 for rides around town.

GRANDE TERRE

Most of the route that encircles Mayotte is paved, but the uneven coastline, especially in the north, makes for lots of twisting and bending and is rather slow going, so don't try to cover too much ground in a day.

Sights & Activities

As you travel around Mayotte, watch out for the interesting and colourful **bangas**, small bachelor houses constructed by young men and painted with humourous sayings and philosophies such as 'la vie celibataire est la vie superbe' (the bachelor life is a superb life). Often, several friends will share the same banga, each encouraging the other to complete his education before marrying and starting a family. Off the far northwestern tip is a group of islands collectively known as **M'Tsamboro**. They are very difficult to reach by public transport, but offer superb swimming and snorkelling. The travel agencies listed on p236 organise day trips by boat around the islands for about €55 per person. Alternatively contact **Restaurant le Choizil** (☎ 62 52 36; Hamjago), which has a boat and organises day trips with lunch.

On the chocolate-coloured west-coast beach of Soulou is the **Cascade de Soulou**, an unusual 8m-high waterfall that plunges directly into the sea (or onto the beach at low tide). Be careful if driving down the rough track that leads to the waterfall, 2km south

of Mtsangamouji – hire cars are regularly trashed on this route.

Sea turtles often come and lay their eggs on the beaches of the peninsula of **Sazilé** in the extreme southeast of Mayotte, and the sand island opposite. To get here, it's a 4km walk from the trailhead on the road between the villages of Mtsamoudou and Dapani. If you're there in the daytime, you'll need to don a snorkel and fins to see the turtles, which are a bit wilder and shyer than their counterparts in N'goudja (see opposite).

Sleeping & Eating

There are a few scattered B&Bs and homestays in the villages around Mayotte; but these can be very hard to find. The best thing to do is get an up-to-date list of what's available from the Comité du Tourisme in Mamoudzou (see p238) before setting out, and ring ahead to get proper directions. There are no camp sites on the island, but in some places you may be allowed to pitch a tent. Likewise there are one or two little restaurants around the island, but you're mostly confined to the hotel restaurants listed below.

Hôtel Le Sakouli (☎ 60 63 63; sakouli.hotel@wanadoo.fr; Plage de Sakouli; s/d €120/175; ⊠ P ⊠) The most upmarket beach hotel on the island, with a fantastic horizon swimming pool, a Jacuzzi and a panoramic terrace. The rooms are big and tiled, with a TV, full-sized bathtub and balcony. If you come for lunch in

---

RESPONSIBLE TURTLE WATCHING

■ When in the water, keep your distance and avoid disturbing resting, sleeping or actively feeding turtles.

■ Approach turtles slowly and calmly, and move away if the turtle shows signs of distress.

■ Never try to feed, catch or ride turtles.

■ Don't shine torches on the female turtles on the beach until they have actually started laying their eggs.

■ Never shine torches or point camera flashes directly into turtles' eyes – photograph from behind.

■ Leave turtle eggs and hatchlings (baby turtles) undisturbed.

■ Do not interfere with the hatchlings' crawl to the sea as this could jeopardise their survival.

■ Never photograph hatchlings – they are very sensitive to light.

■ Limit your viewing to 30 minutes at a time.

■ Never buy products made from turtle shells, or foodstuffs made from turtle parts – these are illegal.

the restaurant (€15) you are allowed to use the pool. Prices go up at Christmas and New Year and during school holidays.

Le Jardin Maoré (☎ 60 14 19; jardin.maore@wanadoo.fr; Plage de N'goudja; s/d low season €82/124, high season €96/152; 🏊) More rustic than Le Sakouli, but on a much better beach and with the added draw of virtually guaranteed sea-turtle viewing. During the day you can snorkel with the habituated turtles that live just off the beach, and during the night watch them come up on to the shore to lay their eggs. The food and service in the restaurant (buffet lunch €15) are generally average, but Le Jardin's bungalows are very well decorated, with raffia walls, draped mosquito nets and platform beds. There's also a fully equipped dive and watersports centre on site (see p235). The restaurant gets very busy with French expatriates at weekends.

Baie des Tortues (☎ 62 62 53; la-baie-des-tortues@wanadoo.fr; Bouéni; s/d with breakfast €55/77) A rather elegant restaurant (lunch €11), just outside the village of Bouéni on the southeast coast. There's a decent beach (you can see sea turtles here as well) and some well-maintained bungalows with fans, nets, televisions and balconies.

Villa Maora (☎ 67 74 40; anita-gerome@wanadoo.fr; Kangani; r with bathroom €38; 🏊) This friendly B&B is a very good option if you have your own car – it's signposted off the main road into the village of Kangani. The rooms have nets and televisions, and there's also a little terrace for breakfast.

Getting There & Around
For more information about getting to and from Grande Terre, see p236.

PETITE TERRE
The island of Petite Terre, with two villages named Pamandzi and L'Abattoir, is connected to the rock of Dzaoudzi (a sort of poor man's version of the Rock of Gibraltar) by a causeway. Until the arrival of the foreign legion in 1962, it served as the capital of Mayotte, and still functions as its military centre. Two small islands comprise Petite Terre, which, being considerably quieter and cleaner than Mamoudzou, has become the affluent high-rent district of Mayotte. It's here that most of the European community live.

Pamandzi has a pretty, tranquil beach known as **Moya Plage**, and a volcanic crater called **Dziani Dzaha**, but there's very little of interest on Dzaoudzi beyond a few handsome colonial buildings and a single hotel.

Near the coast on the western side of Pamandzi there is the archaeological site of **Bagamoyo**. Researchers working at the site have uncovered pottery, tombs and glass beads indicating a 10th-century Shirazian settlement.

Information
BFC-OI Petite Terre (☎ 60 26 45; Rue Commerce, L'Abattoir; 🕐 7.30am-noon & 1.30-3.30pm) changes foreign currency and travellers cheques. It also does advances on Visa and MasterCard and has an ATM. Go early to avoid the queues.

Sleeping
Le Rocher (☎ 60 10 10; lerocher@wanadoo.fr; Boulevard des Crabes, Dzaoudzi; s/d €54/62; 🏊 Ⓟ) This is Petite Terre's most upmarket place, so you can expect lots of gilt, fake Grecian statues and potted palms. The rooms are a bit worn but still comfortable. Some have balconies and views of the lagoon, while others come with full-sized bathtubs. There's a pricey restaurant onsite and a disco called **Ningha** (🕐 Mon-Sat), which charges €15 entry for men, but women enter free of charge – go in drag.

L'Albatros (☎ 60 31 43; 137 Route Nationale, Pamandzi; r with breakfast €30) Right next to the airport, this is a cheery yellow-painted *chambre d'hôtes*, with a bar often full of garrulous middle-aged Frenchmen. Rooms are good value, with fans and nets, but uncomfortable beds. The food in the restaurant (daily menu €9.50) is OK. A satellite TV and a comfy sofa make this a good place to while away time waiting for flights at the airport.

Villa Raha (☎ 62 03 64; 13 Rue Smiam, Pamandzi; s/d €25/42, with bathroom €27/68) Despite scruffy rooms and vague management, this is an acceptable place in a quiet area. Some of the rooms share a little sitting area. Dinner (€10) can be arranged.

Lagon Sud (☎ 60.06 20; lagon_sud_leroux@yahoo.fr; Blvd des Crabes, L'Abattoir; s/d €26/42) Slightly rundown, but with lovely views, this hotel is on the main road between Dzaoudzi and Pamandzi, in front of a mud beach.

Eating & Drinking

Auberge de L'île (☎ 60 14 57; Route de Moya, L'Abattoir; nightly menu €18) A typical French restaurant, serving frogs' legs, *terrine de crabe* (crab) and other delights.

Le Faré (☎ 60 13 31; Blvd des Crabes, L'Abattoir; daily dish €10-13; ✆ dinner Tue, lunch & dinner Wed-Sun) A bar with a limited selection of food, situated next to Lagon Sud on the causeway. There's a little beach and a pool table; it gets very full at weekends.

Le Triskell (☎ 60 12 26; Rue du Four à Chaux; mains €10; ✆ lunch & dinner) A decent little bar/bistro, with a pool table and a TV. Attracts a loyal following of expats.

Entertainment

CMAC (☎ 61 11 36; Dzaoudzi; admission €2) Just up the road from Le Rocher hotel, this cultural association shows French films several nights a week. The reception desk at Le Rocher has a program, or check the posters around Mamoudzou.

Getting There & Around

The redoubtable *barge* brings passengers over to Petite Terre from Mamoudzou (see p239 for full details). Once you're there, you can whiz anywhere on the island in shared-taxis, which cost between €0.70 and €1.10, depending on where you're going.

Directory

CONTENTS

ACCOMMODATION

In most Malagasy and Comorian towns, it's usually possible to find a decent, relatively clean room (with bathroom) from about €13 a night. In this guide, 'budget' refers to places that charge under €8.50 a night; 'mid-range' refers to places that charge €8.50 to €17; and 'top end' refers to all establishments that charge more than €17 per night.

In tourist areas such as Nosy Be and Île Sainte Marie, prices are a lot higher during the high season between June and August and around Christmas, New Year and Easter. Unless otherwise noted, prices quoted in this book are high-season prices. It's better, but not essential, to make advance reservations during high season.

PRACTICALITIES

- In Madagascar, check out the French-language newspapers *Midi Madagasikara*, *Madagascar Tribune* and *L'Express de Madagascar*. In the Comoros, pick up the government-run *Al Watwan*, also in French.

- Madagascar TV stations include Marc Ravalomanana's MBS, as well as the semiprivate MA-TV, RTA, OTV and RTT. In the Comoros, MTV (not the American music channel!) shows local music and some films dubbed into French.

- Voltage in those places in Madagascar and the Comoros that have electricity is 220V. Outlets take European-style two-pin round plugs.

- Madagascar and the Comoros both use the metric system.

Single rooms are rare; so you'll usually have to pay for a double. Many hotels in Madagascar and the Comoros simply have one kind of room (usually with one double and one single bed) and charge the same regardless of occupancy. A standard *chambre double* (double room) has *chambres familiale* (one double bed), but many also have an extra *lit supplémentaire* (single bed). A *chambre twin*, with two single beds, is often more expensive than a double. Lots of places have *chambres familiales* (family rooms) for four or more people.

Camping & Gîtes D'Étape

Camping is possible in most areas of Madagascar and the Comoros. Camp-site facilities vary, from hot showers, toilets and well-equipped cooking areas, to nothing more than a cleared area of bush. Some national parks also have basic hostels known as *gîtes d'étape*, as well as one or two tents for hire, but these are not always very high quality.

Homestays

In rural areas you can sometimes arrange informal homestays by politely asking around a village for a place to sleep in return for payment. Pay a fair fee (about FMg25,000 per room is appropriate) and if possible provide your own food – your hosts may barely have enough to feed themselves.

Hotels & Bungalows

Hotels in Madagascar and the Comoros are also known as *pensions*, *chambres d'hôte*, *residences* or *auberges*. Pensions and *chambres d'hôte* are the simplest. Note that the word *hotely* in Madagascar refers not to a hotel, but to a simple restaurant, although often these have basic rooms as well.

Cheaper rooms (which often take the form of separate bungalows) have their own shower or basin and you share a toilet (WC). Other, more expensive rooms have bathrooms including toilet. Cheapest of all are rooms with a shared toilet and bathroom, known as *salle de bain commune*.

Hot water and a decent blanket or two are worthwhile luxuries in the *hauts plateaux* (highlands) region of central Madagascar. Conversely, air-conditioning or a fan can make sleeping easier in hotter areas. It's best to bring your own mosquito net, plus something to hang it with. A pair of earplugs also comes in handy.

ACTIVITIES
Cycling & Motorcycling

Madagascar is a good country for mountain biking. Cheap Chinese-made bicycles can be hired in many places. For any long-distance trip you will need to bring your bike from home. For more information on cycling, see p261.

In some parts of Madagascar, motorcycles or quad bikes are available for exploring off the beaten track. If you're looking to do some serious motorcycling, contact **Trajectoire** (☎ 94 433 00; www.trajectoire.it), a company based in Toliara in the south. For additional information, check the website of **Madagascar on Bike** (www.madagascar-on-bike.com).

Diving & Snorkelling

Madagascar and the Comoros are the ideal places to lower yourself over the side of a boat and into another world. The areas around Ifaty (p110), Île Sainte Marie (p178), Nosy Be (p156) and Mayotte (p235) are some of the best. There are companies in every dive spot competing to offer internationally recognised diving courses and trips for qualified divers.

RESPONSIBLE DIVING

Please consider the following tips when diving and help preserve the ecology and beauty of the reefs.

- Never use anchors on the reef and take care not to ground boats on coral.

- Avoid touching or standing on living marine organisms or dragging equipment across the reef. If you must hold on to the reef, only touch exposed rock or dead coral.

- Practise and maintain proper buoyancy control. Major damage can be done by divers descending too fast and colliding with the reef.

- Spend as little time as possible within caves, as your air bubbles may be caught on the roof leaving organisms high and dry.

- Don't collect or buy corals or shells or loot shipwrecks.

- Take home all your rubbish and any litter you may find, too.

- Do not feed the fish.

Most dive operators insist on checking your general ability, health and qualifications before you can enrol in a diving course. If you are not sure if diving is for you, many places offer a *baptême*, which is also known as a 'try dive'. Some dive instructors speak English, Italian and German as well as French. Many dive centres in Madagascar are closed between February and May, when diving conditions are least favourable.

Hiking & Trekking

A pair of sturdy shoes and a willingness to walk is more or less essential to any trip to Madagascar. In a single week you could easily find yourself marching in single file along a rocky, boiling ridge with acres of yellow grass on all sides, then a few days later slithering downhill through stands of giant bamboo with rainwater trickling down your neck.

The most popular hiking areas in the country include Parc National d'Andringitra (p97), Parc National de l'Isalo (p108), the Réserve Spéciale de l'Ankàrana (p152) and

RESPONSIBLE HIKING

To help preserve the ecology and beauty of Madagascar and the Comoros, consider the following tips when hiking:

Rubbish

- Carry out all your rubbish; never bury it (digging disturbs soil and ground cover, encourage erosion and the rubbish may be dug up by animals). Make an effort to carry out rubbish left by others, too.
- Minimise waste by taking minimal packaging and no more food than you will need. Use reusable containers.

Human Waste Disposal

- Where there is no toilet, bury your waste. Dig a small hole 15cm (6in) deep and at least 100m (320ft) from any watercourse. Cover the waste with soil and a rock.
- Remember that in some areas of Madagascar, going to the toilet outside certain designated areas is *fady* (taboo). Ask your guide or local people for advice on this.

Washing

- Don't use detergents or toothpaste in or near watercourses, even if they are biodegradable.
- For personal washing, use biodegradable soap and a water container at least 50m (160ft) away from the watercourse. Disperse the waste water widely to allow the soil to filter it fully.
- Wash cooking utensils 50m (160ft) from watercourses with a scourer or sand instead of detergent.

Erosion

- Hillsides and slopes are prone to erosion. Stick to existing tracks and avoid short cuts.
- If a well-used track passes through a mud patch, walk through the mud so as not to increase the size of the patch.
- Avoid removing the plant life that keeps topsoils in place.

Fires & Low-Impact Cooking

- Don't depend on open fires for cooking. The cutting of wood for fires causes rapid deforestation. Cook on a light-weight kerosene, alcohol or Shellite (white gas) stove and avoid those powered by disposable butane-gas canisters.
- If you light a fire, use an existing fireplace. Don't surround fires with rocks. Use only dead, fallen wood. Discourage your guide from collecting too much firewood.
- Ensure that you fully extinguish a fire after use. Spread the embers and flood them with water.

Wildlife Conservation

- Don't buy items, such as tortoiseshell, made from endangered species.
- Discourage the presence of wildlife by not leaving food scraps behind. Place gear out of reach.
- Don't feed the wildlife as animals can become dependent on handouts, leading to unbalanced populations and disease. Make it clear to park authorities that you disapprove of baiting.

Environmental Organisations

- For more information about conservation in Madagascar, contact the **Durrell Wildlife Conservation Trust** (in UK ☎ 01534 860 000; www.durrellwildlife.org) or **Conservation International** (www.conservation.org).

the Masoala Peninsula (p194). Hiking highlights in the Comoros islands include the picturesque hills of Anjouan (p229), the rain forests of Mohéli (p223) and the ascent of Grande Comore's Mt Karthala (p214), an active volcano.

It's not all hard going, but a reasonable level of fitness is required for most areas. In many places, such as Parc National de Ranomafana (p90) or the Masoala Peninsula (p194), trekking involves some mud, stream crossings, leeches and slogging through rice paddies – particularly during the rainy season. In the more dry areas of the south and west, such as Parc National de l'Isalo (p108), the main challenge is likely to be the heat.

For most hikes you will need sturdy shoes, a water bottle, first-aid kit and waterproofs. For longer treks, you'll need to be self-sufficient with water, food and camping equipment, and in almost all cases you'll need a guide. Porters are also available in many places. For routes off the beaten track, bring along a topographical map and a compass or GPS device.

Rock Climbing

The area around Diego Suarez, such as Montagne des Français (p148), in northern Madagascar, and the region west of Parc National d'Andringitra, such as the Tsaranoro Massif (p98) are best for rock climbing.

For more information on rock-climbing trips in the north, contact **New Sea Roc** (www.newsearoc.com) and for details of opportunities in the Andringitra region, contact **Camp Catta** (www.campcatta.com).

Sailing & Kayaking

Madagascar and the Comoros offer miles of coastline to explore and a variety of vessels to sail in, from tiny wooden pirogues to luxury catamarans. See Nosy Be (p156) and Mayotte (p236) for listings of sailing operators.

The waters around the Masoala Peninsula in northeastern Madagascar are ideal for sea kayaking. **Kayak Masoala** (www.kayakafrica.com/mada gascar.asp), a company based in Maroantsetra, runs boat-supported sea kayak trips to beautiful Cap Masoala on the peninsula's southern tip. For more information, see p190.

Surfing & Windsurfing

Surfing and windsurfing are growing sports in Madagascar, especially around Toliara and Fort Dauphin (p117). Bring all your own equipment as it can be hard to hire. The best season for windsurfing is August to February, whereas surfing is possible from March to September.

BUSINESS HOURS

Offices, post offices and banks are normally open from 8am to noon and 2pm to 3.30pm or 4pm weekdays. Most shops are also open until 5.30pm or 6pm on weekdays and 8am to noon on Saturday. In hotter areas opening hours may be different – from about 7am to 11.30am and about 3pm to 6pm on weekdays.

In the Comoros, government offices and banks close around noon on Friday for prayers and don't reopen in the afternoon. During the holy month of Ramadan restaurants are closed and many businesses, shops and government offices open around 7am and close at lunchtime for the rest of the day. The dates of Ramadan change every year – to find them, check out www.holidays.net/ramadan/dates.htm.

Most restaurants are open from noon to 2pm for lunch, and in the evenings from about 6.30pm to 8pm.

CHILDREN

With few formal children's attractions or childcare facilities, Madagascar and the Comoros are both reasonably hard places to travel with young children, so junior travellers are a fairly rare sight. Some national parks and zoos (eg the Croq Farm in Antananarivo and the Andasibe-Mantadia, l'Isalo and Ranomafana National Parks) have visitors centres with exhibitions geared towards helping children understand issues of biodiversity and conservation.

Disposable nappies are available in Antananarivo's supermarkets, but are hard to find elsewhere. Many hotels provide *chambres familiales* or double rooms with an extra single bed geared for use by parents and children. Some of the more upmarket hotels provide a *menu enfant* (children's menu) and high chairs in their restaurants.

For more information, check out Lonely Planet's *Travel with Children* by Cathy Lanigan and Maureen Wheeler.

CLIMATE

Madagascar experiences a variety of climatic conditions. Most rainfall occurs on the east coast and in the far north, while areas southwest of the highlands remain dry for much of the year.

Average maximum temperatures vary from about 30°C in coastal areas (although the mercury has climbed as high as 44°C on occasion) to around 25°C on the *hauts plateaux*. In Antananarivo and other highland areas, temperatures during the winter months can drop to 10°C and even lower during the night. Temperatures at the country's highest elevations may be as low as -10°C during June and July. Along the western coast, temperatures are high year-round.

The Comoros have a tropical climate, with a wet season from the months of October to April. The heaviest rainfall occurs between December and April and amounts can reach as high as 390mm (15in) in a month.

Temperatures are extremely hot even during the wet season, rarely dropping below 19°C at any time of year. The central, higher parts of the islands (especially Anjouan) remain significantly cooler than the coasts.

For more information on the best time to travel in Madagascar and the Comoros, see p9.

CUSTOMS

It's forbidden to take the following out of Madagascar: live plants (including vanilla); mounted insects, tortoiseshell; fragments of *Aepyornis* (elephant bird) eggshell; precious stones (in export quantities only); jewellery; antique coins; fossils; funerary art and antiquities. The export of coral and seashells is forbidden in the Comoros islands and Mayotte.

Officially, you aren't allowed to take more than FMg25,000 out of Madagascar. For more detailed information, check the website of **Malagasy customs** (www.madagascar-contacts.com/douanes in French).

DANGERS & ANNOYANCES

Travelling around Madagascar and the Comoros is not inherently dangerous, and there is no reason for you to be overly concerned about your personal safety. However, as when travelling anywhere in the world, some common-sense precautions are always warranted.

Beaches & Forests

Some areas along the Malagasy and Comorian coastlines are subject to danger from sharks and strong currents. Make sure to seek local advice before heading into the water. To avoid stepping on sea urchins, wear shoes when walking on the beach or swimming.

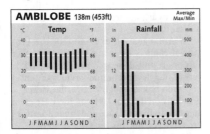

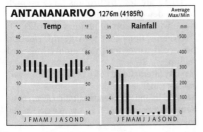

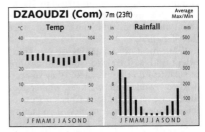

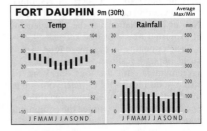

In rain forests, watch for leeches in muddy areas or during the rainy season. Wear your socks over your trousers, apply insect repellent, and carry salt to remove any that do get in. Mosquitos are also ubiquitous – wear insect repellent, especially at dawn and dusk.

Crimes

As a Western traveller you will stand out as someone who is wealthy, which increases your vulnerability. Petty theft is the main risk – don't keep valuables in a pack or external money belt, and watch your pockets in crowded areas. Leave expensive jewellery and watches at home. To avoid trouble with the police, carry your passport with you at all times (a photocopy is not sufficient).

Road Accidents

A combination of packed, unroadworthy vehicles, reckless drivers and poor-quality roads makes *taxi-brousse* (bush taxi) travel in Madagascar, and to a lesser extent the Comoros, fairly hazardous. To minimise the risks, try to avoid night travel if possible.

Annoyance on taxi-brousse comes in the form of inadequate legroom and deafening music blasting from tinny speakers. Consider an inflatable cushion and a pair of earplugs.

Touts & Guides

Be wary of organising trips with someone you meet at the airport on arrival in Madagascar. It's always best to wait and get a recommendation from your hotel or other travellers first.

While most official guides are very competent and well trained, some guides are reluctant to do the full circuit they've been paid for, while others ask for higher fees than those set by the park. Check prices before parting with your money. If you aren't satisfied with your guide for any reason, report the matter to the Association Nationale pour la Gestion des Aires Protégées (Angap; National Association for the Management of Protected Areas) or park office.

When booking an organised tour, clarify at the outset (ideally in writing) what your agreement is with the tour operator. It's also a good idea to try to meet your guide in advance to gauge their language abilities. For camping trips, try to see the equipment you will be using.

POLITICAL INSTABILITY

Both Madagascar and the Comoros have been subject to bouts of political instability in the past few years. While the situation in both countries is now calm, it's important to check the latest information before travelling. Check travel advisories issued by the foreign department of your home government. These can be found on the following websites:

Australia (☎ 1300 139 281; www.dfat.gov.au /travel)

Canada (☎ 1800 267 6788; www.voyage.gc.ca)

New Zealand (☎ 64 4439 8000; www.mft.govt .nz/travel)

United Kingdom (☎ 0870 606 0290; www.fco .gov.uk)

United States (☎ 202 647 4000; http://travel .state.gov)

DISABLED TRAVELLERS

Madagascar and the Comoros have few, if any, facilities for the disabled. This, combined with a weak infrastructure in many areas, may make travel here difficult.

Public transport is very crowded and unable to accommodate a wheelchair unless it is folded up. Travelling by rental car is the best option.

The Réserve Privée de Berenty (p122), near Fort Dauphin, and Parc National de l'Isalo (p107) are the most accessible of Madagascar's nature reserves for those with a disability.

In Antananarivo and most of the provincial capitals there are hotels with either lifts or ground-floor accommodation. While most bungalow accommodation – the most common type of lodging in Madagascar – is generally on the ground floor, there are often steps up to the entrance and inner doorways are often too narrow for a wheelchair.

There are few bathrooms large enough to manoeuvre a wheelchair in, and almost none with any sort of handles or holds.

Organisations that provide information on world travel for the mobility impaired include:

Mobility International USA (☎ 541 343 1284; www .miusa.org; USA)

National Information Communication Awareness Network (Nican; ☎ 02 6285 3713; www.nican.com.au; Australia)

Royal Association for Disability & Rehabilitation
(☎ 020 7250 3222; www.radar.org.uk; UK)
Society for the Advancement of Travel for the Handicapped (SATH; ☎ 212 447 7284; www.sath.org; USA)

EMBASSIES & CONSULATES
Madagascan Embassies & Consulates
Australia (☎ 02 92 99 2290; tonyknox@ozemail.com.au; 6th level, 100 Clarence St, Sydney NSW 2000)
Canada (☎ 613 744 7995; ambmgnet@inexpress.net; 649 Blair Rd, Ottawa, K1J 7M4, Ontario)
Comoros (☎ 73 18 69; consmad@snpt.km; BP 349, Moroni)
France (☎ 01 45 04 62 11; ambamadparis@tiscali.fr; 4 Ave Raphael, Paris 75016)
Germany (☎ 02 28 95 35 90; ambamad@aol.com; Rolandstrasse 53-170, Bonn-Bad Godesberg)
Italy (☎ 3 6 30 77 97; ambamad-rm@flashnet-it.netclub.mg; Viaricardo Zandonai 84, 400 194 Roma)
Japan (☎ 03 3446 72 52; 2-3-23 Moko Azabu, Minako-Ku, Tokyo)
Kenya (☎ 02 218 393; mbnbo@africaonline.co.kc; BP 41723, Hilton Hotel, 1st fl, Nairobi)
Mauritius (☎ 0686 50 15; Rue Guiot Pasceau, Floreal)
Netherlands (☎ 10 4255212; 97 Heemraadssingel, 3022 CB Rotterdam)
Seychelles (☎ 03 40 30; BP 68 Plaisance, Mahe)
South Africa (☎ 011 442 33 22; PO Box 786098, Sandton 2146)
United Kingdom (☎ 020 8746 0133; 16 Lanark Mans, Pennard Rd, London, W12 8DT)
United States (☎ 202 265 5522; malagasy@embassy.org; 2374 Massachusetts Ave, NW, Washington, DC 20008)

Comorian Embassies & Consulates
For Mayotte, see your nearest French embassy.
France (☎ 01 40 67 90 54; 20 Rue Marbeau, Paris)
Germany (☎ 02 2345 4444)
Kenya (☎ 02 22 29 64)
South Africa (☎ 012 343 9483)
United Kingdom (☎ 020 7460 1162; 16 Lanark Mansions, Pennard Rd, London, W12 8DT)
United States (☎ 212 223 27 11; 420 East 50 St, New York, NY 10022)

Embassies & Consulates in Madagascar
Norway, Denmark and the UK have honorary consulates near the port in Toamasina.
    The following embassies and consulates are mostly in Antananarivo.
Canada (Map pp64-5; ☎ 22 425 59; c.canada@dts.mg; Lot II 169 Villa 3H Ivandry)
Comoros Antananarivo (Map pp64-5; ☎ 032 02 404 506; Rue Doktor Villette, Isoraka); Mahajanga (⊙ 8am-1pm

Mon-Sat) A block behind the Air Austral office, this embassy can issue Comorian visas.
France (Map pp64-5; ☎ 22 214 88; 3 Rue Jean Jaurès, Ambatomena) Near the Shanghai Hotel.
Germany (☎ 22 238 02; 101 Rue Pasteur Rabeony, Ambodiroatra)
Italy (Map pp60-1; ☎ 22 284 43; 22 Rue Pasteur Rabary, Ankadivato) East of the centre.
Japan (☎ 22 261 02; Rte Fort Duchesne Ampasanimalo)
Mauritius (☎ 22 321 57; Rte Circulaire Anjahana) South of the centre.
Netherlands (☎ 22 224 22; 88 Lotissement Bonnet Ivandry) North of the centre.
Seychelles (Map pp64-5; ☎ 22 632 02; 18 Rue Jean Jaurès, Ambatomena) Near the Shanghai Hotel.
South Africa (☎ 22 423 03; Rte d'Ambohimanga, Ambohitrarahaba)
United Kingdom (Map pp60-1; ☎ 22 273 70; Lot III, 164 Ter Alarobia Amboniloha)
United States (Map pp64-5; ☎ 22 209 56, 22 212 57; 14 Lalana Rainitovo, Haute-Ville) East of the UCB bank.

Embassies & Consulates in the Comoros
France (☎ 73 0615; Avenue de Republic Populaire de China, Moroni, Grande Comore)
Madagascar (☎ 7318 69; consmad@snpt.km; Moroni, Grande Comore)

FESTIVALS & EVENTS
Madagascar
Alahamady Be (March) The low-key Malagasy New Year.
Santabary (April/May) The first rice harvest.
Fisemana (June) A ritual purification ceremony of the Antakàrana people.
Famadihana (June to September) Literally the 'turning of the bones', these reburial ceremonies are held especially during August and September.
Sambatra (June to December) Circumcision festivals held by most tribes between June and September, and in November and December in the southwest.

The Comoros
Comorian festivals are based around the Muslim calendar, which changes from year to year. For more information on holidays, see p250.

FOOD
Budget restaurants as listed in this guide are usually food stalls or small Malagasy *hotelys*; they are open only until about 8pm, and serve mainly rice dishes or snacks for under €2. Mid-range restaurants serve plain French food, including staples such as *steack frites* (steak and chips), costing about €4 for

a main course. Top-end restaurants serve French haute cuisine, which might include lobster profiteroles or goose-liver paté for around €7 per main course.

For more information, see p36.

GAY & LESBIAN TRAVELLERS

Homosexual practices are illegal in Madagascar and the Comoros for persons under 21 years of age. Homosexuality is not openly practised, and there are no organisations catering to gay and lesbian travellers. Overt displays of affection – whether among couples of the same or opposite sex – are culturally inappropriate.

HOLIDAYS

In the Comoros, and to a lesser extent in Madagascar, accommodation and flights are often harder to find during French school holidays, when many expats from Mayotte and Réunion travel in the region. To find out when these holidays are, look up the website www.ac-reunion.fr/academie/calendri.htm, which is in French.

Government offices and private companies close on the following public holidays; banks are generally also closed the afternoon before a public holiday.

Madagascar

New Year's Day 1 January
Insurrection Day 29 March – celebrates the rebellion against the French in 1947.
Easter Monday March/April
Labour Day 1 May
Anniversary Day 8 May
Organisation of African Unity Day 25 May
Ascension Thursday May/June – occurs 40 days after Easter.
Pentecost Monday May/June – occurs 51 days after Easter.
National Day 26 June – Independence Day.
Assumption 15 August
All Saints' Day 1 November
Christmas Day 25 December
Republic Day 30 December

The Comoros

The main holidays for Muslim Comorians are Islamic and based on the lunar calendar, so the dates change each year. The biggest celebration is Id-ul-Fitr, which marks the end of the fast of Ramadan. The other major Islamic holiday is Id-el-Kabir, also known as Id-el-Haj, which marks the beginning of the pilgrimage to Mecca.

These four dates are designated as specific public holidays:
New Years Day 1 January
Labour Day 1 May
Organisation of African Unity 25 May – Celebration Day.
Independence Day 5 July

In addition to those celebrated above, Mayotte also observes Bastille Day (14 July) and Christmas Day (25 December).

INSURANCE

A travel-insurance policy to cover theft, loss and medical problems is essential. Some policies specifically exclude dangerous activities, which can include scuba diving, motorcycling or even trekking.

You may prefer a policy that pays doctors or hospitals directly rather than you having to pay on the spot and claim later.

Check that the policy covers an emergency flight home. This is an important consideration for Madagascar, given the cost of air tickets to most destinations.

For more advice about health-insurance policies, see p267.

INTERNET ACCESS

Many Internet providers in Madagascar and the Comoros (including some post offices) run fast and reliable services. The cheapest services, mostly available in provincial capitals, cost about €0.02 per minute, while in more remote places the cost might be as high as €0.10 per minute.

For details of useful websites for travellers to Madagascar, see p12.

LEGAL MATTERS

The use and possession of marijuana and other recreational drugs is illegal in Madagascar and the Comoros. If you are arrested, ask to see a representative of your country. Madagascar is strict in enforcing immigration laws, so don't overstay your visa. The legal age of consent for heterosexual sex is 15 years.

MAPS

Official maps produced by Foiben Taosarintanin'i Madagasikara (FTM) are available at bookshops in Antananarivo and major towns for about FMg40,000. The maps are fairly dated but generally accurate, and more than adequate for visiting the country. FTM also produces street maps of the provincial capitals, although these are increasingly hard to find.

Edicom and Carambole both publish detailed maps of Antananarivo, which are widely available at bookshops and cost about FMg30,000.

A detailed map and compass is essential when hiking without a guide.

In Malagasy, *lalana* means street; *arabe* or *araben* means avenue; and *kianja* or *kianjan* means place or square. In this book, street names are given in either French or Malagasy, depending on local usage. One street often has several names depending on what map you look at, and locals basically don't use street names at all.

MONEY
Madagascar

Madagascar is currently in the first stage of its plan to change its currency from the Malagasy franc to the pre-colonial ariary, which will be worth five Malagasy francs. At the time of writing both old-style Malagasy francs banknotes and the new ariary notes were legal tender, although prices (particularly those given to tourists) were still quoted in francs. The old Malagasy franc will remain exchangeable up to 2009. Euros are also widely accepted. US dollars are sometimes accepted in Antananarivo, major cities and tourist areas.

Taxi drivers and market vendors often cannot change large bills, so keep a selection of small change with you.

ATMS

BMOI, BNI-CL and BFV-SG all have ATMs at some branches in Antananarivo and other major towns. However, the amount you can take out is only around €150, and the machines often don't have enough cash to support multiple withdrawals. Many ATMs are only open a couple of hours later than the bank's normal opening hours. At the time of research, ATMs in Madagascar only accepted Visa cards.

BLACK MARKET & MONEYCHANGERS

There is no black market in Madagascar. Moneychangers may approach you on the street, but are best avoided.

CREDIT CARDS

Credit cards are accepted at some upmarket hotels, at Air Madagascar, and at some larger travel agencies. Some places levy a commission of about 5% for credit-card payments. The most useful card is Visa, with MasterCard also accepted in a minority of places.

Visa and MasterCard can also be used at some banks to obtain cash advances (in Malagasy francs). BFV-SG, BNI-CL and BMOI all provide cash advances against Visa cards, while BOA gives advances for MasterCard. UCB in Antananarivo accepts both Visa and MasterCard. Authorisation can take several hours, and commission rates are up to about 2%, depending on the bank.

EXCHANGE RATES

Exchange rates fluctuate daily, so it is generally best only to change what you need as you go along. At the time of writing average exchange rates were as follows.

country	unit		Malagasy francs
Australia	A$1	=	FMg4240
Canada	C$1	=	FMg4385
euro zone	€1	=	FMg7115
Japan	¥100	=	FMg55
New Zealand	NZ$1	=	FMg3702
South Africa	R1	=	FMg858
Switzerland	Sfr1	=	FMg4566
United Kingdom	UK£1	=	FMg10,147
United States	US$1	=	FMg5730

EXCHANGING MONEY

The best foreign currencies to carry are euros, followed by US dollars. Otherwise UK pounds, Swiss francs, Japanese yen and South African rand can be changed in Antananarivo and, sometimes, in other major cities.

The major banks in Madagascar, with branches in Antananarivo and all major towns, are the Bank of Africa (BOA), Banky Fampandrosoana'ny Varotra-Société Générale (BFV-SG), Banque Malgache de l'Océan Indien (BMOI) and Bankin'ny Indostria-Crédit Lyonnais (BNI-CL). These banks change travellers cheques and cash in major currencies. In Antananarivo, the Union Commercial Bank (UCB) will also change cash and travellers cheques. Exchange rates for travellers cheques are usually slightly lower than those for cash.

Exchange rates and commissions vary from bank to bank, so it is worth shopping around.

Some upmarket hotels will change US dollars and euros in travellers cheques and cash for guests (but rarely for the public) at rates about 10% lower than at the bank.

The foreign-exchange counter at Ivato airport has exchange rates that are just as good as those at the banks, and is usually open for international flight arrivals. Madagascar's other airports do not have exchange facilities. The bureau de change at Ivato airport will change Malagasy currency back into euros or dollars, but requires a minimum of €42.

The Comoros

The currency of the Union des Comores (the official name of the Comoros, excluding Mayotte) is the Comorian franc (CF), which is tied to the euro.

You can pay for major items such as accommodation, air tickets and boat fares in either Comorian francs or euros. For smaller purchases the local currency is usually preferable.

You can re-convert Comorian francs into euros at the bank if you have the original bank receipt. In Mayotte, the official currency is the euro, and Comorian or Malagasy francs are entirely useless.

CREDIT CARDS

Credit cards (Visa and MasterCard) are accepted by many hotels and restaurants in Mayotte, but in the other Comoros islands only the most upmarket establishments accept cards, and all charge high rates of commission.

EXCHANGE RATES

country	unit		Comorian francs
Australia	A$1	=	CF294
Canada	C$1	=	CF303
euro zone	€1	=	CF492
Japan	¥100	=	CF369
New Zealand	NZ$1	=	CF256
South Africa	R1	=	CF58
Switzerland	Sfr1	=	CF316
United Kingdom	UK£1	=	CF702
United States	US$1	=	CF396

EXCHANGING MONEY

The best foreign currency to carry in the Union des Comores is the euro, although you can in theory also change US dollars, British pounds, Swiss francs and Japanese yen in the Banque pour l'Industrie et le Commerce (BIC), which has branches on the islands of Grande Comore and Anjouan. The BIC, which is the only bank to change foreign cash or travellers cheques, can also do advances on Visa cards for a hefty commission.

In Mayotte, only one bank, Banque Française Commerciale Ocean Indien (BFC-OI), will change cash or travellers cheques. BFC-OI's ATMs theoretically should advance you money on a Visa card.

You cannot change Comorian or Malagasy francs anywhere on Mayotte. There are no money-changing facilities at the airport.

PHOTOGRAPHY & VIDEO

Print and slide film, batteries and a limited range of camera accessories are available in all major towns. Processing a roll of 36 exposures costs €2.50 to €4. Whatever camera you bring, a dust- and waterproof bag is essential.

Don't take photos of airports, ports, government buildings or anything that may be police or military property.

Always ask permission before photographing people, and don't snap a photo anyway if permission has been denied. Locals may ask a fee for being photographed. Don't promise to send someone a photo unless you will definitely be able to do it.

For the most comprehensive guide to travel photography, get a copy of Lonely Planet's *Travel Photography: A Guide to Taking Better Pictures* by internationally renowned photographer Richard I'Anson.

POST

There are post offices in all major towns of Madagascar and the Comoros. The postal service is generally reliable, although postcards frequently go missing.

To send a letter it costs FMg7500 to Europe, FMg11,500 to Australia, and FMg10,500 to the United States. In the Comoros, prices are CF300 to France, CF350 to Europe, and CF400 to the United States and Australia. Postcards are slightly cheaper.

SHOPPING

Madagascar offers a fantastic variety of handicrafts and souvenirs, so most of the visitors queuing in the departure hall of Ivato airport in Antananarivo are laden down with newspaper-wrapped bundles and bulging carrier bags. There is something for everyone – chess and solitaire sets made from semiprecious stones; musical instruments; sandals and belts; leather bags; chic brightly coloured raffia baskets; woodcarvings and wood-inlay boxes; embroidered tablecloths; hand-made Antaimoro paper; and tin model Citroëns and *pousse-pousse* (rickshaws).

Most souvenirs in the Comoros are simply everyday items, and can be bought at markets on all the islands – embroidered skullcaps, carved lecterns for the Quran, brass-inlaid wooden chests, silver and gold jewellery and colourful lengths of cloth known as *chiromani*.

In both countries, locally grown spices – white or black peppercorns, cinnamon sticks, cloves, saffron or vanilla – are widely available, but some countries, such as Australia, may not allow you to bring them in.

If you can cope with carrying your souvenirs until you get back to the airport, Ambositra in the central highlands (p87) is the shopping capital of Madagascar, with dozens of shops selling carvings and *marqueterie* (objects inlaid with coloured woods). Ambalavao is also known for its silk and hand-made Antaimoro paper (p96).

If you want to leave your purchasing until you're a taxi ride away from the airport, the best place for shopping is the Marché Artisanale de La Digue in Antananarivo (p74). Bargaining hard is expected – start from 50% of the price and work upwards.

When shopping, bear in mind that embroidery and raffia do far less environmental damage than wooden products, which are often carved from endangered tropical hardwoods. If you do want to buy wooden products, try to find something made of eucalyptus, which is not endangered. Don't buy anything made from tortoiseshell or seashells, which are both illegal.

SOLO TRAVELLERS

Travelling alone in Madagascar or the Comoros poses few safety problems, provided you use commonsense, such as avoiding unlit streets in bigger cities after dark.

The main disadvantages of travelling solo are financial – single rooms in hotels or guesthouses are uncommon, and you will invariably end up paying for a double room. You can expect to pay very high rates for organised tours if you're on your own, so it's best to find fellow travellers to share costs.

Speaking French will make a huge difference to your travels in Madagascar or the Comoros. If you are travelling independently, a grasp of at least the basics of the French language will enable you to communicate far more effectively. If you don't speak any French, consider hiring an English-speaking guide (p265) for at least part of your trip.

TELEPHONE & FAX
Fax

In Madagascar, the Comoros and Mayotte, faxes can be sent from telephone offices, post offices and from upmarket hotels. Some Internet cafés also offer fax services.

Madagascar

The country code for Madagascar is ☎ 261, followed by 20 if you are dialling a land line, then the seven-digit number. To call out of Madagascar, dial ☎ 00 before the country code.

International telephone lines are fairly good in Madagascar, but the internal telephone service, particularly away from the major towns, is less so.

The best way to dial internationally is with a *telecarte* (phonecard). Cardphones are scattered around all larger towns. Cards are sold at post offices, at Agence d'Accueil Telecom (Agate) offices and at some shops and hotels. For international calls you will need at least 100 units. Calls can also be made from more upmarket hotels (although rates will be much higher). Rates for international calls are FMg13,500 per minute to France, FMg13,500 to the Comoros, and about FMg20,250 per minute to Europe, the USA and Canada. Calls are 30% cheaper between 10pm and 6am, all day Sunday and on holidays. The international operator can be reached by dialling ☎ 10.

Numbers in Madagascar consist of a two-digit area prefix followed by a five-digit local number (usually given in the form of a three-digit then a two-digit number). The two-digit prefix must be dialled whether you are calling locally, from elsewhere in Madagascar or from abroad. These prefixes are listed throughout this book as part of each telephone number. If you are quoted a five-digit number, add the two-digit area prefix.

To reach remote areas that do not have direct-dialling facilities (all those telephone numbers that have only two digits), dial ☎ 15 for the local operator, then request the number.

MOBILE PHONES
These days, mobile (cell) phones are in common usage in Madagascar. Mobile phone prefixes are 030, 031, 032 and 033. If dialling a mobile phone number from abroad, omit the zero and the 20 prefix, but add the country code.

For calls to mobile numbers from within Madagascar, you will need to dial the zero. When calling landline numbers from a mobile phone, dial ☎ 020 before the seven-digit number.

The Comoros
The country code for the Comoros, including Mayotte, is ☎ 269, followed by the six-digit local number. To call out of the Comoros, dial 00 followed by the country code. If you need any help with international calls, dial the **operator** (☎ 10). To dial from Mayotte to the Comoros or vice versa, dial ☎ 0269 followed by the number.

Calls can be made on all the islands from phone booths and hotels. In the Union des Comores, calls can also be made from Telecom offices (known as SNPT), usually located near the post office. In both the Union des Comores and Mayotte the easiest way to make a call is to buy a phonecard and use it in a phone box. Some bars in Mayotte also have coin-operated phones. In Mayotte, phonecards are sold in kiosks, shops and supermarkets. In the other Comoros, you can get a card from one of the eager touts who hang around outside phone booths, proffering cards. Simply make your call, pay for the units you've used, and give the card back.

International calls cost CF1275 per minute to Europe and the US, and CF1500 per minute to Australia.

TIME
Madagascar and the Comoros are three hours ahead of GMT/UTC. There is no daylight savings.

TOILETS
Public toilets are pretty much unheard of in Madagascar and the Comoros. Facilities range from gleaming porcelain thrones in more upmarket hotels and restaurants, to squalid holes in the ground in less developed locations. Toilet paper is not generally used in the Comoros, so bring some with you when you feel the call of nature. For additional information on both countries, see p29.

TOURIST INFORMATION
The tourist offices in Madagascar, the Union des Comoros and Mayotte can all provide lists of hotels and guesthouses. See individual chapters for details. Tourist office contact details for each place are:

Comité du Tourisme du Mayotte (Map p237; ☎ 61 09 09; ctm@mayotte.tourisme.com; Rue de la Pompe, Mamoudzou, Mayotte; ⏰ 7.30am-4.30pm Mon-Fri) Also has a branch at the airport.

Direction Generale du Tourisme (Map p216; ☎ 74 42 43; dg.tourisme@snpt.km; Ave des Ministères; Moroni, Grande Comore, Union des Comores; ⏰ 7.30am-2.30pm Mon-Thu, 7.30-11.30am Fri, 7.30am-noon Sat)

Maison de Tourisme de Madagascar (Map pp64-5; ☎ 22 351 78; www.madagascar-tourisme.com in French; 3 Lalana Elysée Ravelomanantsoa, Antananarivo, Madagascar; ⏰ 8.30am-noon & 2-7pm Mon-Fri)

VISAS
Madagascar
All visitors must have a visa to enter Madagascar. Visas can be arranged in advance at any Malagasy embassy or consulate, or on arrival at the Ivato airport in Antananarivo – but get an update on the situation before making your plans. Visas are valid for up to three months from the date of entry and must be used within six months of the date of issue. It's best to request a three-month visa from the start if there is any chance that you may need one, as visa extensions can be time-consuming and expensive.

At most Malagasy embassies and consulates, visas cost the equivalent of about €29/34 for single/multiple entry. At most places you will need to provide a copy of your ticket or an itinerary from your travel agent and two to four photos.

One-month single-entry visas are available on arrival at Antananarivo and Mahajanga airports for about €30.

As long as you have not exceeded the normal three-month maximum, visas can be extended at the immigration office in Antananarivo or any provincial capital. You will need between two and four passport-size photos and a copy of your return air or boat ticket. A one-month extension costs about €21 and can take several days to process.

The Comoros

All visitors need a visa to enter the Union des Comores. If you're coming from Madagascar you can obtain a visa prior to departure from the Comorian consulate in Antananarivo or Mahajanga (p249).

Visas are also available on arrival in Grande Comore, Anjouan and Mohéli. They cost €5 for up to 45 days, and €9 for 90 days. Visas must be bought at the immigration offices in Moroni, Mutsamudu or Fomboni. If you arrive after the close of business on Friday and will be leaving before the following Monday, you will be issued with a free two-day weekend visa on arrival.

Only nationals of countries that need a visa to enter France will require a visa for Mayotte. These can be obtained at your nearest French consulate before arrival.

WOMEN TRAVELLERS

Most women do not feel threatened or insecure in any way when travelling in either Madagascar or the Comoros. Hospitality and kindness to strangers are firmly entrenched in both cultures and extend in equal measure to female travellers. The most you can expect – especially in the Muslim Comoros – is some mild curiosity about your situation, especially if you are single and/or don't have children. Meeting Malagasy or Comorian women is relatively easy – many are well educated and confident and hold responsible jobs in government-related offices, especially the offices of national parks.

That said, around holiday resorts, where most of the local girls are snapped up by male tourists, you may encounter a low level of verbal pestering from local men. Compared with similar attention in say, North Africa, it's positively lacklustre, and a polite refusal nearly always suffices. Travelling in a group, saying you are married and dressing modestly (essential anyhow in the Comoros) are all ways to minimise problems. Physical harassment and violent crime are very rare, and in fact male travellers face far more pestering from the hordes of prostitutes who frequent almost every disco.

Women shouldn't enter mosques unless specifically told they can do so.

A limited selection of tampons is available in Antananarivo and some of the larger towns, but it's best to bring your own supply, especially in the Comoros.

Transport

CONTENTS

GETTING THERE & AWAY

ENTERING THE COUNTRY

Getting into Madagascar entails nothing more onerous than a bit of queuing. Immigration officials generally just check or issue your visa before letting you go on your way. Landing cards are all printed in English as well as French. If you've come from a country where yellow fever is present you may be asked for a yellow-fever certificate.

Arriving in Mayotte and the Union des Comoros is also relatively hassle-free. There's a simple form to fill in (printed in English and French) and you're on your way.

If you need a visa on arrival in the Union des Comores, these are not issued at the airport but at the immigration offices in each island's capital.

See p254 for more information about visa requirements.

AIR
Airports & Airlines

Inter-continental flights come into Ivato airport, just north of Antananarivo. The airports in Mahajanga and Toamasina both handle flights from Réunion, Mauritius and the Comoros. International flights come into Moroni airport on Grande Comore, and Dzaoudzi on Mayotte.

Air Madagascar is the national carrier of Madagascar. In the past, its frequent and illogical cancellations and delays earned it the derogatory nickname 'Air Mad'. While occasional upsets still occur, service now is relatively good.

Air Madagascar, Air France and Corsair, all operating flights from France, are the only scheduled carriers that fly directly to Madagascar. There are no direct flights from outside the East African and Indian Ocean region to the Comoros. To fly to the Comoros from anywhere else, your best bet is to fly to Réunion, Mauritius, Antananarivo, Nairobi or Dar es Salaam and get an onward flight from there.

The main regional airline linking Madagascar and the Comoros with the Indian Ocean region is Air Austral (working in partnership with Air France and Air Mauritius).

In the Comoros, two airlines are currently operating – Comores Aviation and Comores Air Service. They both fly between the three islands of the Union des Comoros. Comores Aviation also flies to Mayotte, while Comores Air Service has flights to Mombasa, Dar es Salaam and Zanzibar in East Africa.

AIRLINES FLYING TO & FROM MADAGASCAR
Air Austral (UU; ☎ 22 359 90; www.airaustral.com in French) Hub Saint-Dénis, Réunion. Flies in conjunction with Air Mauritius.

Air France (AF; ☎ 23 230 23; www.airfrance.com) Hub Paris Charles de Gaulle.
Air Madagascar (MD; ☎ 22 222 22; www.airmadagascar .mg) Hub Antananarivo.
Air Mauritius (MK; ☎ 22 359 90; www.airmauritius.com) Hub St Maurice.
Corsair (SS; ☎ 22 633 36; www.corsair.fr in French) Hub Paris Orly.
Interair (D6; ☎ 22 224 06; www.interair.co.za) Hub Johannesburg.

AIRLINES FLYING TO & FROM THE COMOROS

African Express Airways (XU; ☎ 61 64 20) Hub Nairobi.
Air Austral (UU; ☎ 73 31 44; www.air-austral.com in French) Hub Saint-Dénis, Réunion. Flies in conjunction with Air Mauritius.
Air France (AF; ☎ 61 10 52; www.airfrance.com) Hub Paris Charles de Gaulle.
Air Madagascar (MD; ☎ 60 10 52; www.airmadagascar .mg) Hub Antananarivo.
Air Mozambique (LAM) (TM; ☎ 61 61 85; www.lam.co.mz) Hub Maputo.
Air Seychelles (HM; ☎ 73 31 44; www.airseychelles .net) Hub Malé, Seychelles.
Air Tanzania (TC; ☎ 73 54 26; www.airtanzania.com) Hub Dar es Salaam.
Sudan Airways (SD; ☎ 73 23 10; www.sudanair.com) Hub Khartoum, Sudan.
Yemenia (IY; ☎ 73 14 00/3; www.yemenairways.net) Hub San'aa, Yemen.

Tickets

Since there is so little competition, there are few specials for travel to Madagascar and the Comoros. Booking online for either destination is rarely possible or cheaper – your best bet is to approach a local tour operator. Even in this case, many tour operators don't deal with either destination and you may have to approach the airline office (if there is one) in your country directly.

Air Madagascar, Corsair and Air France occasionally offer some good deals to Madagascar, especially during the low season. The high season for air travel to Madagascar and the Comoros is June to August, December to January and around Easter.

Air Madagascar offers 30% discounts on domestic flights to anyone who has arrived in Madagascar on an Air Madagascar flight from Europe.

Air Austral offers an Indian Ocean pass, which allows passengers who have bought long-distance tickets on Air Austral, Air Mauritius and Air Seychelles to receive discounts of up to 30% on routes within the Indian Ocean region on all three airlines.

All ticket prices quoted in this book include international departure tax.

Africa & the Indian Ocean

Both Madagascar and the Comoros are well connected with the Indian Ocean islands of Mauritius and Réunion, and reasonably easy to reach from mainland Africa.

Once you're in Madagascar, **Dodo Travel & Tours** (Map pp64-5; ☎ 22 690 36; www.dodotraveltour .com; Lalana Elysée Ravelomanantsoa), in Antananarivo, is a useful place to seek information about flights within this region.

MADAGASCAR

The main hubs for flights to Madagascar are Johannesburg in South Africa and Nairobi in Kenya. There are flights several times weekly between Johannesburg and Antananarivo (about €400 return) on Interair, and twice weekly on Air Madagascar. Travel between Madagascar and Nairobi (about €500 return) generally works better if you purchase your ticket directly from Air Madagascar in Kenya or Madagascar.

Air Austral has regular flights between Réunion and Mauritius and Antananarivo (from €330), Toamasina (from €330), Mahajanga (from €420) and Nosy Be (from €400).

THE COMOROS

Air Austral has regular flights from Réunion and Mauritius to Mayotte and Moroni on Grande Comore. There are also regular flights from Mahajanga in Madagascar to Mayotte (€200).

Air Tanzania has a weekly flight from Moroni on Grande Comore to Dar es Salaam (about €284 return). Air Mozambique flies weekly between Mayotte and Pemba in northern Mozambique (€180 return), with connections to Maputo. Comores Air Service has flights to Mombasa in Kenya (about €270 one way) and Zanzibar in Tanzania (about €156 one way). African Express Airlines flies weekly from Mayotte to Nairobi (about €370 return). It's also possible to fly to Moroni from Khartoum in Sudan.

Bear in mind that Comores Air Service flights won't show up on travel agency booking systems in the rest of the world, so

TRANSPORT

if you want to use these flights, you'll have to book them yourself on the spot when you arrive in **Mombasa** (☎ 00254 41 404265) or **Zanzibar** (☎ 00255 54 2230029). It's definitely best to allow a few days' leeway if you're travelling to the Comoros via this route.

Asia
Since Air Madagascar stopped its service between Singapore and Antananarivo (which may resume again in the future) the best way to reach Madagascar or the Comoros from Asia is via Mauritius or Johannesburg. Air Mauritius has flights several times a week from Singapore and Hong Kong to Mauritius, and South African Airlines flies regularly to Johannesburg from both cities.

It's also easy to get flights on Kenya Airways or Air India from Bombay to Nairobi, from where you can connect to Madagascar or Mayotte.

Australia & New Zealand
There are no direct flights from Australia to Madagascar or the Comoros. The best routes are generally via Mauritius or Johannesburg. Air Mauritius has weekly flights connecting both Melbourne and Perth with Mauritius from about A$2000. From Mauritius there are regular connections on Air Austral to Antananarivo, Mayotte and Moroni on Grande Comore.

Alternatively, Qantas and SAA both have flights connecting Sydney with Johannesburg starting from A$1600 in the low season. From Johannesburg, you can connect with an Air Madagascar or Interair flight to Antananarivo. Try these agencies:

Flight Centre Australia (☎ 133 133; www.flightcentre .com.au); New Zealand (☎ 0800 233 544; www.flightcentre .co.nz)

STA Travel Australia (☎ 1300 733 035; www.statravel .com.au); New Zealand (☎ 0508 782 872; www.statravel .co.nz)

Europe
The main European hub for flights to/from Madagascar or the Comoros is Paris. Air Madagascar and Air France fly three to four times a week between Paris and Antananarivo. Prices from Paris on both airlines usually start from about €1270. There are also some good deals available with the scheduled airline Corsair, although prices are broadly similar on all three airlines.

It's also possible to fly from many European capitals to Johannesburg, Nairobi, St-Denis (Réunion) or Port Louis (Mauritius), and from one of these cities to Antananarivo. The best connections are usually via Réunion or Mauritius, which are linked by Air Austral flights to Antananarivo (from €330), as well as by several flights weekly to other places in Madagascar and to the Comoros. To the Comoros, you can take a flight from Europe to Mombasa in Kenya or Dar es Salaam in Tanzania and connect to Moroni (Grande Comore) from there (p257). Contact one of the following agents to get you started:

Air Fare (☎ 020 620 5121; www.airfair.nl in Dutch) A well-respected Dutch travel agent.

Nouvelles Frontières (☎ 08 03 33 33 33; www.nouvelles-frontieres.fr) A good French option with group tours to Madagascar.

OTU Voyages (☎ 0825 004 027; www.otu.fr in French) Has branches across France.

STA Travel UK (☎ 0870 1600 599; www.statravel.co.uk); Germany (☎ 01805-456 422; www.statravel.de in German) Also has plenty of other offices across Europe.

Trailfinders (☎ 020-7938 3939; www.trailfinders.com) Excellent, reliable UK travel agent with huge experience.

The USA & Canada
The cheapest way to fly from North America to Madagascar or the Comoros is generally via Paris. It may work out cheaper to get two separate tickets – one from North America to Europe, and then a second ticket from Europe to Madagascar.

Another option is to fly from Atlanta or New York to Johannesburg, with a connection to Antananarivo. In the USA, the main travel agency specialising in Madagascar is Cortez Travel & Expeditions (p265). It has information on good-value airfares and can book Air Madagascar flights. The following companies might also be able to help:

Cheaptickets (www.cheaptickets.com) A good source of online fares.

Flight Centre Canada (☎ 1 888 967 5355; www.flight centre.ca); USA (☎ 1866 WORLD 51; www.flightcentre.us) Contact it directly for fares.

STA Travel (☎ 800 329 9537; www.statravel.com) Good deals to Paris.

SEA
It's possible to travel to and from Madagascar and the Comoros by boat, but for most destinations you will need plenty of time and determination. Travel is likely to be on cargo

ships – unless you find a ride on a yacht as a crew member – so sleeping and eating conditions, combined with sometimes turbulent seas, can make it a rough trip.

Mombasa (Kenya) and the island of Zanzibar (Tanzania) are the main places to look for cargo boats to Madagascar or the Comoros. It's also sometimes possible to find passage on a yacht heading from South Africa, Réunion or Mauritius – or maybe even from France to Nosy Be or Mayotte.

See p171 for more information on ships between Madagascar, Mauritius and Réunion.

TOURS

For a list of organised tour companies within Madagascar, see p265. Following are a few companies operating general interest tours to, and around, Madagascar.

Australia

Adventure Associates (☎ 02-9389 7466; www.adventureassociates.com) Runs tours to Madagascar, combined with Réunion and Mauritius.

France

Comptoir de Madagascar (☎ 01 42 60 93 00; www.comptoirdemadagascar.com in French) Tours and air tickets to Madagascar.

Terre Malgache (☎ 01 44 32 12 80; www.terre-malgache.com in French) A wide range of tours to Madagascar, plus one to Mayotte.

Germany

Madagaskar Travel (☎ 08233-75341; www.madagaskar-travel.de in German) General and specialist wildlife itineraries.

Trauminsel Reisen (☎ 08152-9319-0; www.trauminselreisen.de in German) Itineraries all over Madagascar.

Italy

Zig Zag Viaggi (☎ 0341 284154; www.zigzag.it in Italian) Escorted group tours.

The Netherlands

Baobab Travel (☎ 020-6275129; www.baobab.nl in Dutch) Longer itineraries in Madagascar. Also has a branch in Belgium.

Summum Reisen (☎ 020-4215555; www.summum.nl in Dutch) Group tours.

Switzerland

Priori (☎ 041 922 18 45; www.priori.ch) Cultural and wildlife tours.

Zingg (☎ 01 709 2010; www.zinggsafaris.com) Kayak and trekking trips.

United Kingdom

Rainbow Tours (☎ 020 7226 1004; www.madagascar-travel.net) Specialist and general-interest guided trips to Madagascar.

Reef & Rainforest Tours (☎ 01803 866965; www.reefandrainforest.co.uk) Focuses on wildlife viewing.

Wildlife Worldwide (☎ 020 8667 9158; www.wildlifeworldwide.com) Wildlife tours.

United States

Cortez Travel & Expeditions (☎ 800-854 1029; www.air-mad.com) Well-established operator for Air Madagascar flights and tours.

Lemur Tours (☎ 1-415-695-8880; www.lemurtours.com) Focuses on lemur sightings.

Manaca (☎ 866 362 6222; www.manaca.com) Specialists in ecotourism and responsible travel.

For the Comoros, the only tour possibilities are the trips to Mayotte organised by one or two tour operators in France.

GETTING AROUND

AIR
Madagascar

Air Madagascar, Madagascar's national carrier, has an impressive network of domestic routes. While fares have leapt dramatically in recent years, tickets on 'Air Mad' flights are still relatively inexpensive, and provide a useful way of covering large distances and avoiding long road journeys. While cancellations, schedule changes and delays occur (especially during the low season, in stormy weather or on flights to more remote destinations) the airline is generally efficient.

A handy free booklet detailing timetables and routes (but not fares) is available from Air Madagascar's head office in Antananarivo and from some travel agents.

You can pay for tickets in Malagasy francs, euros or US dollars at the head office in Antananarivo and Air Madagascar offices in larger towns, but smaller offices may only accept francs. The office in Antananarivo also accepts travellers cheques and credit cards.

The baggage allowance for most internal flights is 20kg. On Twin Otter (small plane) flights baggage is limited strictly to 10kg.

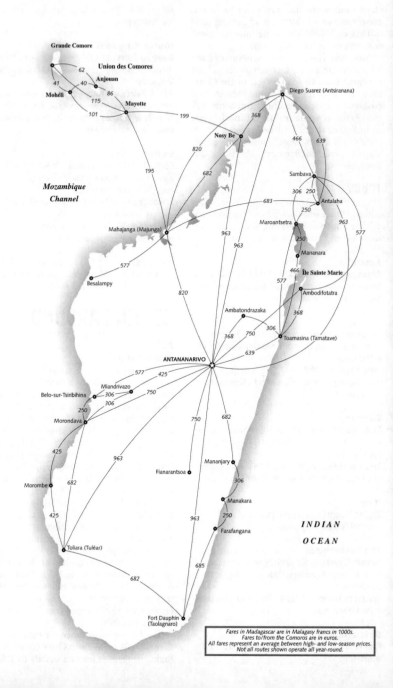

Grande Comore

Union des Comores

62

Anjouan

41   40   86

Mohéli   115

101   Mayotte

199   Diego Suarez (Antsiranana)

368

466   639

Nosy Be   820

682   Sambava

306   250

683   250   Antalaha

Mozambique
Channel

195   250   963   577

Maroantsetra

Mahajanga (Majunga)   963   250

Mananara

963   Île Sainte Marie

577   466

577   Ambodifotatra

Besalampy

820   Ambatondrazaka   368

368   750   306   Toamasina (Tamatave)

639

ANTANANARIVO

577   425

Miandrivazo   750

Belo-sur-Tsiribihina   306

250

Morondava   750   682

425

Mananjary

963   306

Morombe   682   Fianarantsoa   Manakara

250

425   Farafangana   INDIAN

OCEAN

Toliara (Tuléar)   963

685

682

Fort Dauphin
(Taolagnaro)

Fares in Madagascar are in Malagasy francs in 1000s.
Fares to/from the Comoros are in euros.
All fares represent an average between high- and low-season prices.
Not all routes shown operate all year-round.

The Comoros

The Comoros is served by two reasonably efficient internal airlines, Comores Air Service and Comores Aviation. See the Comoros chapter on p214, for information on routes and fares.

The Comores Aviation office in Mayotte may take credit cards (but sometimes it simply can't be bothered). The offices in the Union des Comores generally only accept Comorian francs or, at a pinch, euros, so come prepared with the right currency.

Reservations & Check-in

Air Madagascar flights are frequently full, so it's always worth booking as far in advance as possible.

While it's now officially not necessary to reconfirm your Air Madagascar tickets, it's always best to check with the airline a few days in advance and again on the day of departure, as there are frequent last-minute schedule changes. The same goes for flights on Comores Aviation and Comores Air Service, although these flights aren't usually full. In fact, the reverse is often true, so it's best to check the day before that your flight hasn't been cancelled due to lack of interest...

If you have checked in baggage, be sure to keep your baggage-claim ticket until you are reunited with your luggage at your destination.

BICYCLE

It may often be just as fast to travel by bicycle as by *taxi-brousse* (bush taxi). A mountain bike is normally essential. Carry spare parts, although inner tubes and other basic parts are sometimes available in larger towns. The terrain varies from very sandy to muddy or rough and rocky.

It's usually no problem to transport your bicycle on taxis-brousse or on the train if you want to take a break en route.

Although you are able to hire mountain bikes in many larger towns, including Toamasina, Antsirabe and Ambodifotatra on Île Sainte Marie, for around FMg30,000 per day, these are not normally in good enough condition for longer journeys. The Comoros are also theoretically good for mountain biking, but mountain bikes aren't available for hire, so you will have to bring your own.

BOAT
Cargo Boat

In certain parts of Madagascar, notably the northeast coast and Canal des Pangalanes, cargo boats (sometimes called *boutres*) are the primary means of transport. There are also frequent boats between the four Comoros islands, and between the Comoros and Madagascar.

When choosing a cargo boat, keep in mind that there have been several accidents involving capsized vessels (the ferry *Samsonette*, which used to run scheduled services between Île Sainte Marie and the mainland of Madagascar, sank killing over 20 people in 2000). Always check for life-jackets and don't get in if the seas are rough or if the boat is overcrowded.

Boat travel on the east coast is generally not safe, and theoretically it's illegal, during the rainy season between May and September.

While some cargo boats in Madagascar and the Comoros have passenger cabins, most have deck space only. Departure delays are common.

For cargo boat prices, consult the relevant regional chapters.

Pirogue

Engineless pirogues or *lakanas* (dugout canoes), whether on rivers or the sea, are the primary means of local transport for shorter journeys in many areas of Madagascar and the Comoros (where they are known as *galawas*).

Pirogues can easily be hired, along with a boatman, but bear in mind there are no amenities on board.

BUS & BUXI

In a few parts of Madagascar (such as the route between Antananarivo and Toamasina in the east) routes in and around major cities are served by bus. These usually use the same stations as the taxis-brousse (p263) and are generally slightly less expensive. However, taxis-brousse remain the main form of public road transport in Madagascar and the Comoros.

In Antananarivo, Fianarantsoa and some other towns, *buxis* (minibuses) are also used for local destinations. There is usually one fixed fare for all destinations, generally between FMg500 and FMg750.

TRANSPORT

TRANSPORT

THE RENAULT 4

The first thing many visitors notice on arrival in Antananarivo are the ubiquitous Renault 4 cars – known in French as *quatrelles*. The compact little tin boxes, with their appealing, eye-like round headlights, bounce over the cobbled streets of the capital, and are found absolutely everywhere in Madagascar. A *quatrelle* seems to be able to go anywhere, and it's not unusual to hear that a certain road or track needs 'a 4WD – or a *quatrelle*'. All other vehicles will be defeated.

The resounding success of the Renault 4 in Madagascar owes a lot to the separate chassis, and the body construction and soft suspension invented by postwar French designers. Today Madagascar's *quatrelles* take on mud, sand, potholes, forest tracks and even beaches with equal aplomb, often while carrying a family of 10 plus luggage!

CAR & MOTORCYCLE
Driving License
To drive in Madagascar or the Comoros, you will need to have an International Driving Permit.

Fuel & Spare Parts
You'll find petrol stations of some kind in all cities and in most major towns. Not all have pumps – particularly in the Comoros, petrol stations usually consist of a filthy youth stationed at the roadside with an array of old Coke bottles full of cloudy fuel. For longer trips, and for travel in remote areas, you will need to carry extra fuel with you.

Spare parts and repairs of varying quality are available in most towns. Make sure to check the spare tyre of any car you rent before setting out.

Hire
CAR
To rent a car in Madagascar or the Comoros, you must generally be at least 23 years old and have held a driving license for at least one year. Rental costs include insurance.

Due to the often difficult driving conditions and road hazards most rental agencies make hiring a driver obligatory with their vehicles. For a listing of car-rental agencies in the capital see p74. See the individual destination chapters for more information. Prices average between FMg500,000 and FMg700,000 per day for a 4WD including fuel. For almost all destinations off the main routes you will need a 4WD.

CHARTER TAXI
As an alternative to high car-rental prices, it's also possible to hire a taxi on the street. Make inquiries first at the taxi-brousse stand or nearby hotels to get an idea of the going rate for your destination. Be sure to clarify such things as petrol and waiting time, and try to check that the vehicle is in decent shape before departing.

For longer multiday journeys, you'll need to be more careful. In addition to the standard vehicle papers and a valid driving licence, the driver should have a special charter permit (indicated by a diagonal green stripe). It's not a bad idea to have a written contract signed by you and the driver stipulating insurance issues, the agreed-upon fee (including whether or not petrol is included) and your itinerary.

MOTORCYCLE
Motorcycles can be hired by the half day or full day at various places in Madagascar, including Toliara, Nosy Be, and Île Sainte Marie (for use on the islands only). At most places, they range from a Honda or Yamaha 125cc or 250cc to a tiny Peugeot *mobylette*. Some places also rent motorcycles suitable for longer, rougher journeys, and provide support vehicles as well. For more details on motorcycling in Madagascar, see p244.

ROAD VOCABULARY

When inquiring about local road conditions in Madagascar (taxi-brousse stations are a good place to start), the following French terms might come in handy:

Nids-de-poule Potholes.

Piste (or piste de sable) Sand or earth road.

Piste amenagée Sand road with some level of surfacing.

Piste de rocaille Road or track with loose stones.

Route goudronnée Tarmac road.

Route saisonnière Seasonal road.

Road Conditions

Of Madagascar's approximately 40,000km of roads, less than 15% are paved, and many of those that are paved are badly deteriorated. Nonpaved roads are often exceptionally muddy, sandy or rocky. Roads in the far northeast from Soanierana-Ivongo to Antsiranana, and in a few other areas of the country, are prone to flooding and often have broken bridges. Routes in many areas are impassable or very difficult during the rainy season. Madagascar's new government has, however, pledged to improve road conditions, and already some routes have been resurfaced, with the promise of more road improvements to come.

The designation *route nationale* (RN) is sadly no guarantee of quality. Most accidents, however, are caused by human failing (especially drunkenness) rather than by dangerous vehicles and roads. Delays are more common than accidents, so always factor in a few extra hours to allow for breakdowns or social calls en route.

Road conditions in the Comoros vary, but are generally good, and distances are so short that it's easy to get around on foot or by bicycle.

Road Rules

Driving in Madagascar and the Comoros is on the right-hand side. The police occasionally stop vehicles and carry out random checks, in the hope of detecting any of the 1001 possible (and probable) infractions of the vehicle code. Occasionally foreigners will be asked for their passport, but as long as your visa is in order there should be no problem.

If you aren't used to local driving conditions, watch out for pedestrians, animals, broken-down cars and slow-moving zebu carts on the road. It is particularly hazardous to drive at night, as there is no lighting, so try to avoid it.

HITCHING

Hitching is never entirely safe in any country in the world, and we don't recommend it. Travellers who do decide to hitch should understand that they are taking a small but potentially serious risk. People who do choose to hitch will be safer if they travel in pairs and let someone know where they are planning to go.

In Madagascar, traffic between towns and cities is thin, and most passing vehicles are likely to be taxis-brousse or trucks, which are often full. If you do find a ride, you will likely have to pay about the equivalent of the taxi-brousse fare. Along well-travelled routes or around popular tourist destinations, you can often find lifts with privately rented 4WDs or with hotel supply trucks. In the Comoros, hitching may be possible with tourists, but with most other vehicles you'll probably have to pay for a ride.

LOCAL TRANSPORT

Charette

In more rural parts of Madagascar and the Comoros, the *charette*, a wooden cart drawn by a pair of zebu cattle, is a common form of local transport. They're most useful for carting your luggage when you're trekking, so that you can forge ahead and leave the *charette* to bring up the rear. Fares are entirely negotiable, and breakdowns are frequent.

Pousse-Pousse

The brightly coloured *pousse-pousses* (rickshaws) seen in hordes in various Malagasy towns supposedly got their name when drivers yelled '*pousse, pousse*' ('push, push') at passers-by for aid as they were going uphill.

Many travellers have scruples about using them, perceiving an association with slave labour or finding the prospect of being pulled around by another human offensive. This sympathy may wane after a few days of relentless hounding by *pousse-pousse* drivers, who seem to regard the sight of a tourist on foot as a personal slight. In any case, the *pousse-pousse* men need work, not sympathy, as they rent their rickshaws and have to pay a daily amount to the owners. If you have heavy luggage, it's polite to hire two. In most places, locals pay between FMg500 and FMg2000 for a ride. Tourist rates are higher, and always negotiable, so agree to a fare before you climb aboard. When it's raining, the price sometimes doubles.

For more details about *pousse-pousses*, see p86.

Taxi-brousse

Taxis-brousse are slow, unreliable, uncomfortable and sometimes unsafe. But they are as much a part of daily life in Madagascar as

TRANSPORT

a the sight of a humped cow or a raffia hat, and you'll find it hard to travel independently around the country without wedging yourself into one at some point. Taxis-brousse are used in the Comoros, too, but distances are mercifully shorter.

COSTS

Fares for all trips are set by the government and are based on distance, duration and route conditions. Prices are the same for locals and foreigners. However, fares vary among vehicle types, with minibuses (which tend to be somewhat quicker) or *taxis-be* (which are more comfortable, and hold fewer people) being slightly more expensive than larger trucks.

Dishonest taxi-brousse touts occasionally overcharge foreigners but this is relatively rare. If you think you are being overcharged, ask to see the list of official fares, which is sometimes posted in the ticket office. If you want to keep your backpack with you in the vehicle you'll need to pay for an extra seat.

RESERVATIONS

If you want one of the more comfortable seats on a less-frequented route, it's advisable to book a seat the day before you want to travel. This can be done at the transport company offices located at taxi-brousse stations. Prices are generally fixed and non-negotiable.

TAXI-BROUSSE STATIONS

All towns have one or more *gares routières* or *stationnements des taxis-brousse* (bus or taxi-brousse stations). Despite the general appearance of anarchy, the taxi-brousse system is a relatively well-organised one once you get the hang of it. Upon arrival to a town, you may well be besieged by pushy but harmless touts, tugging at your luggage and yelling in your ear to try and win your custom.

TAXIS-BROUSSE GLOSSARY

The term *taxi-brousse* (literally 'bush taxi') is used generically in Madagascar and the Comoros to refer to any vehicle providing public transport. When you buy your taxi-brousse ticket, therefore, you could be about to climb into anything from a tiny Renault 4 packed with 10 passengers to a rumbling juggernaut with entire suites of furniture tied to its roof. Most taxis-brousse, however, are 24-seater Japanese minibuses in varying states of dilapidation. Most of the time, simply the term taxi-brousse will suffice to describe any form of motorised public transport, but you might come across some of the following terms in the course of your road adventures. It goes without saying that all the vehicles (described below in order of size) will be carrying at least four times the number of passengers that you thought was anatomically possible, and that they will break down regularly.

The *camion-brousse* is a huge 4WD army-style truck, fitted with a bench or seats down each side, although the majority of passengers wind up sitting on the floor or each other. They are used for particularly long or rough journeys, which you may well wish you had never begun.

A *familiale* or *taxi-be* (literally, 'big taxi') – usually a Peugeot 504 or 505 – is a big jump up in comfort and generally in speed as well. In theory, *taxis-be* accommodate nine passengers – two in the front with the driver, four in the middle and three in the back – although drivers frequently manage to fit in a few more. The price for a *taxi-be* is generally about 25% higher than for the same route in a *bâché* or *camion-brousse*, and they fill up and leave much faster than minibuses.

A *bâché* is a small, converted pick-up, which usually has some sort of covering over the back and a bench down each side. *Bâché* are used on shorter, rural routes and are hideously uncomfortable.

A *taxi-ville* (town taxi) is a small car, usually an old Renault 4 or Citroën 2CV, used for transport within towns on a jump-in-and-ride basis. Fares are per person and fixed according to the distance you go, and the taxi will stop to pick up new passengers along the way. *Taxis-ville* can also be hired to take you to spots further outside the town for a negotiable fee.

A *taxi-spécial* is any kind of taxi-brousse rented by a person or group exclusively.

Vehicles display the destination in white paint on their windscreen, and fares are pinned up in the transport company offices that line the edges of the station. The choice will often come down to simply joining the next vehicle to leave, which will be packed to the roof, or holding out for a decent seat in a later taxi-brousse. If you want to speed up departure, it's sometimes effective to pay for the remaining empty seats, which will also provide more comfort for everyone (although keep in mind that other passengers are often picked up along the way regardless).

TAXI-BROUSSE TIPS

No matter what type of vehicle you are in, the two front seats beside the driver are usually the most comfortable and most sought after. To get these seats you'll need to arrive early at the station, buy a ticket the day before, or do some serious pleading, bribing, hustling or flirting.

Rear seats are designed for the more compacted Malagasy physique and can be uncomfortable or simply impossible for long-legged Westerners. In desperate situations, it may be better to pay for an extra seat.

Luggage goes on the roof, so make sure your rucksack is waterproof and not liable to burst open under stress.

If at all possible, avoid travelling on a taxi-brousse after dark. Unlit roads, driver fatigue and less security for your luggage all contribute to make the journey riskier. You'll also miss the scenery en route, which is often spectacular.

TOURS

Madagascar's many tour operators and freelance guides offer mountain-bike excursions, 4WD circuits, walking tours, wildlife-viewing trips and cultural and historic tours.

An organised tour can be particularly valuable if you don't speak much French, as it can otherwise be hard to break the communication barrier with the fairly reserved Malagasy people, who rarely speak English.

The general rule of thumb for organised tours is to check as much as possible beforehand – this includes vehicles, camping equipment and even menu plans. Try to

get all the details, agreed by both parties in advance, in writing.

For details of the very few organised tour companies in the Comoros, see p217 and p235.

Following is a list of some of the reliable Antananarivo-based companies that can arrange excursions throughout Madagascar. For details about foreign travel agencies, see p259.

Boogie Pilgrim (☎ 22 530 70; www.boogie-pilgrim .net; Île des Oiseaux, Tsarasaotra, Alarobia) Adventurous ecotours and camps in several places in Madagascar, including the Parc National d'Andringitra and the Canal des Pangalanes. English and German speaking.

Cortez Travel & Expeditions (Map pp60-1; ☎ 22 219 74; cortezmd@dts.mg; 25 Lalana Ny Zafindriandiky, Antanimena) American-based agency offering a wide range of itineraries for individuals and groups.

Espace Mada (Map pp64-5; ☎ 22 262 97; www .madagascar-circuits.com; 50 Arabe Ramanantsoa, Isoraka) Vehicles, guides and off-road excursions, including Tsiribihina River and Parc National de Tsingy de Bemaraha trips.

Mad Cameleon (☎ 22 344 20; madcam@dts.mg; Lot 11-K, Lalana Rasamoely, Ankadivato-Ambony) Tours focusing on western Madagascar, including the Tsiribihina River descent, Parc National Tsingy de Bemaraha, and pirogue trips down the Manambolo River.

Malagasy Tours (☎ 22 356 07; www.malagasy -tours.com; Avaradrova) Inside the Grill du Rova restaurant this is a reliable, upmarket operator offering tours in all areas of the country, with trekking and trips along the Tsiribihina River and the Canal des Pangalanes.

Setam (Map pp64-5; ☎ 22 324 31; www.setam -mg.com; 56 Ave du 26 Juin, Analakely) Bicycle expeditions, orchid tours and visits to *Famadihana* ceremonies, along with the usual circuits.

Tany Mena Tours (Map pp64-5; ☎ 22 326 27; tanym enatours@simicro.mg; Ave de L'Indépendance) Specialist cultural tours led by botanists, herbalists, anthropologists and historians.

Tropic Tours & Travel (☎ 22 580 75; www.tropic -tours.net; 1 Bis, Rte de l'Aéroport, Ivato) Tours within Madagascar; can also help with trips to the Comoros.

Tropika Touring (☎ 22 222 30, 22 276 80; tropika@ dts.mg; 41 Lalana Ratsimilaho, Ambatanakanga) Offers various tours throughout the country, including descents of the Tsiribihina River.

Transcontinents (Map pp64-5; ☎ 22 223 98; transco@dts.mg; 10 Ave de L'Indépendance) Tours and car hire.

Za Tours (☎ 22 656 48; za.tour@dts.mg; Lot ID 33 Lalana Printsy, Ratsimamanga) Well-regarded English-speaking tour company.

TRAIN

The Malagasy rail system, known as the Réseau National des Chemins de Fer Malgaches (RNCFM), is made up of over 1000km of tracks and was built during the colonial period. At the time of writing, the only sections operating were the Fianarantsoa to Manakara line, which passes through some beautiful forest scenery. For departure and fare information see p94.

Plans are, however, afoot to restore the Antananarivo to Toamasina and Antananarivo to Andasibe services. The best place to get the latest information on this is at the station in Antananarivo.

There are no trains in the Comoros.

Health Dr Caroline Evans

CONTENTS

As long as you stay up to date with your vaccinations and take some basic preventive measures, you'd have to be pretty unlucky to succumb to most of the health hazards covered in this chapter. Madagascar and the Comoros certainly have an impressive selection of tropical diseases on offer, but you're much more likely to get a bout of diarrhoea (in fact, you should bank on it), a cold or an infected mosquito bite than an exotic disease such as sleeping sickness. When it comes to injuries (as opposed to illness), the most likely reason for needing medical help is as a result of road accidents – vehicles are rarely well maintained, some roads are potholed and poorly lit, and drink-driving is common.

BEFORE YOU GO

A little planning before departure, particularly for pre-existing illnesses, will save you a lot of trouble later on. Before a long trip, get a check-up from your dentist and your doctor if you require any regular medication or have a chronic illness, eg high blood pressure or asthma.

You should also: organise spare contact lenses and glasses (and take your optical prescription with you); get a first-aid and medical kit together; and arrange necessary vaccinations.

Travellers can register online with the **International Association for Medical Assistance to Travellers** (IAMAT; www.iamat.org). Its website can help travellers to find a doctor who has recognised training in the country they are travelling to. You might like to consider doing a first-aid course (contact the Red Cross or St John's Ambulance) or attending a remote medicine first-aid course, such as that offered by the **Royal Geographical Society** (www.wildernessmedicaltraining.co.uk).

If you are bringing medications with you, carry them in their original containers, clearly labelled. A signed and dated letter from your physician (ideally translated into French) describing all medical conditions and medications, including generic names, is also a good idea. If carrying syringes or needles, be sure to have a physician's letter documenting their medical necessity.

INSURANCE

Find out in advance whether your insurance plan will make payments directly to providers or will reimburse you later for overseas health expenditures (in many countries, doctors expect payment in cash). It's vital to ensure that your travel insurance will cover the emergency transport required to get you to a good hospital, or all the way home, by air and with a medical attendant if necessary. Not all insurance covers this, so check the contract carefully. If you need medical help, your insurance company might be able to help locate the nearest hospital or clinic, or you can ask at your hotel. In an emergency, contact your embassy or consulate.

Membership of the **African Medical and Research Foundation** (Amref; www.amref.org) provides an air-evacuation service in medical emergencies in some African countries, sometimes including Madagascar, as well as air-ambulance transfers between medical facilities. Money paid by members for this service goes into providing grass-roots medical assistance for local people.

HEALTH

RECOMMENDED VACCINATIONS

The **World Health Organization** (WHO; www.who .int/en/) recommends that all travellers are covered for tetanus, polio, measles, rubella, mumps and diphtheria, as well as for hepatitis B, regardless of the destination they are travelling to.

According to the **Centers for Disease Control and Prevention** (www.cdc.gov), the following vaccinations are recommended for Madagascar and the Comoros: hepatitis A, hepatitis B, rabies and typhoid, and boosters for tetanus, diphtheria and measles. Yellow fever is not a risk in the region, but the certificate of yellow-fever vaccination is an entry requirement if travelling from an infected region (see p272).

MEDICAL CHECKLIST

It is a very good idea to carry a medical and first-aid kit with you, to help yourself in the case of minor illness or injury. Following is a list of items you should consider packing.

- Acetaminophen (paracetamol) or aspirin
- Adhesive or paper tape
- Antibacterial ointment (eg Bactroban) for cuts and abrasions (prescription only)
- Antibiotics (prescription only), eg ciprofloxacin (Ciproxin) or norfloxacin (Utinor)
- Antidiarrhoeal drugs (eg loperamide)
- Antihistamines (for hayfever and allergic reactions)
- Anti-inflammatory drugs (eg ibuprofen)
- Antimalaria pills
- Bandages, gauze and gauze rolls
- DEET-containing insect repellent for the skin
- Fluids (if travelling to remote areas)
- Iodine tablets (for water purification)
- Oral rehydration salts
- Permethrin-containing insect spray for clothing, tents and bed nets
- Pocket knife
- Scissors, safety pins and tweezers
- Steroid cream or hydrocortisone cream (for allergic rashes)
- Sun block
- Syringes and sterile needles
- Thermometer

Given the prevalence of malaria, consider taking a self-diagnostic kit that can identify malaria in the blood from a finger prick.

INTERNET RESOURCES

There is a wealth of travel health advice on the Internet. **Lonely Planet** (www.lonelyplanet.com) is a good place to start. The **World Health Organization** (www.who.int/ith/) publishes a superb book called *International Travel and Health*, revised annually and is available online at no cost. Other websites of interest are **MD Travel Health** (www.mdtravelhealth.com), the **Centers for Disease Control and Prevention** (www.cdc.gov) and **Fit for Travel** (www.fitfortravel.scot.nhs.uk).

You may also like to consult your government's travel health website, if one is available:

Australia (www.dfat.gov.au/travel/)
Canada (www.hc-sc.gc.ca/pphb-dgspsp/tmp-pmv/pub_e.html)
United Kingdom (www.doh.gov.uk/traveladvice/index.htm)
United States (www.cdc.gov/travel/)

FURTHER READING

- *A Comprehensive Guide to Wilderness and Travel Medicine* by Eric A Weiss (1998)
- *Healthy Travel* by Jane Wilson-Howarth (1999)
- *Healthy Travel Africa* by Isabelle Young (2000)
- *How to Stay Healthy Abroad* by Richard Dawood (2002)
- *Travel in Health* by Graham Fry (1994)
- *Travel with Children* by Cathy Lanigan (2004)

IN TRANSIT

DEEP VEIN THROMBOSIS (DVT)

Blood clots can form in the legs during flights, chiefly because of prolonged immobility. This formation of clots is known as deep vein thrombosis (DVT). Although most blood clots are reabsorbed uneventfully, some might break off and travel through the blood vessels to the lungs, where they could cause life-threatening complications.

The chief symptom of DVT is swelling or pain of the foot, ankle or calf. When a blood clot travels to the lungs, it may cause chest pain and breathing difficulty. Travellers with any of these symptoms should immediately seek medical attention.

To prevent DVT, walk about the cabin, perform isometric compressions of the leg muscles (ie contract the leg muscles while sitting), drink plenty of fluids and avoid alcohol.

JET LAG & MOTION SICKNESS
If you're crossing more than five time zones you could suffer jet lag, resulting in insomnia, fatigue, malaise or nausea. To avoid jet lag, try drinking plenty of nonalcoholic fluids and eating light meals. Upon arrival, get exposure to natural sunlight and readjust your schedule (for meals, sleep etc) as soon as possible.

Antihistamines such as dimenhydrinate (Dramamine) and meclizine (Antivert, Bonine) are usually the first choice for treating motion sickness. The main side effect of these drugs is drowsiness. A herbal alternative is ginger (ginger tea, biscuits or crystallized ginger).

IN MADAGASCAR & THE COMOROS

AVAILABILITY & COST OF HEALTH CARE
Health care in the area is varied: there are excellent private hospitals in Antananarivo, but health care can be pretty patchy in both countries, although Mayotte – as part of France – has a European standard of health care. The public health system is underfunded and overcrowded. Medicine and even sterile dressings and intravenous fluids might need to be purchased from a local pharmacy by patients or their relatives. The standard of dental care is equally variable, and there is an increased risk of hepatitis B and HIV transmission via poorly sterilised equipment. By and large, public hospitals offer the cheapest service, but will have the least up-to-date equipment and medications; private hospitals and clinics are more expensive but tend to have more advanced drugs and equipment and better-trained medical staff.

Most drugs can be purchased over the counter, without a prescription. Many drugs for sale might be ineffective: they might be counterfeit or might not have been stored under the right conditions. It is strongly recommended that all drugs for chronic diseases be brought from home.

Also, the availability and efficacy of condoms cannot be relied upon – bring all the contraception you'll need as condoms bought in the region might not have been correctly stored.

There is a high risk of contracting HIV from infected blood if you receive a blood transfusion. The **BloodCare Foundation** (www.bloodcare.org.uk) is a useful source of safe, screened blood, which can be transported to any part of the world within 24 hours.

Unfortunately, adequate – let alone good – health care is available to very few Malagasy.

INFECTIOUS DISEASES
It's a formidable list but, as we say, a few precautions go a long way...

Cholera
Cholera is usually only a problem during natural or artificial disasters, eg cyclones, war, floods or earthquakes, although small outbreaks can also occur at other times. Travellers are rarely affected. It is caused by a bacteria and spread via contaminated drinking water. The main symptom is profuse watery diarrhoea, which causes debilitation if fluids are not replaced quickly. An oral cholera vaccine is available in the USA, but it is not particularly effective. Most cases of cholera can be avoided by seeking out good drinking water and by keeping away from potentially contaminated food. Treatment is by fluid replacement (orally or via a drip), but sometimes antibiotics are needed. Self-treatment is not advised.

Dengue Fever (Breakbone Fever)
Dengue fever is spread through mosquito bites. It causes a feverish illness with headache and muscle pains similar to those experienced with a bad, prolonged, attack of influenza. There might be a rash. Mosquito bites should be avoided whenever possible. Self-treatment: paracetamol and rest.

Diphtheria
Diphtheria is spread through close respiratory contact. It usually causes a temperature and a severe sore throat. Sometimes a membrane forms across the throat, and a tracheostomy is needed to prevent suffocation. Vaccination is recommended for those likely to be in close contact with the local

population in infected areas, although this is more important for long stays than for short-term trips. The vaccine is given as an injection alone or with tetanus, and lasts 10 years. Self-treatment: none.

Filariasis

Found in most parts of West, Central, East and Southern Africa, and in Sudan in North Africa. Tiny worms migrating in the lymphatic system cause filariasis. The bite from an infected mosquito spreads the infection. Symptoms include localised itching and swelling of the legs and/or genitalia. Treatment is available. Self-treatment: none.

Hepatitis A

Hepatitis A is spread through contaminated food (particularly shellfish) and water. It causes jaundice and, although it is rarely fatal, it can cause prolonged lethargy and delayed recovery. If you've had hepatitis A, you shouldn't drink alcohol for up to six months afterwards, but once you've recovered, there won't be any long-term problems. The first symptoms include dark urine and a yellow colour to the whites of the eyes. Sometimes a fever and abdominal pain might be present. Hepatitis A vaccine (Avaxim, Vaqta, Havrix) is given as an injection: a single dose will give protection for up to a year, and a booster after a year gives 10-year protection. Hepatitis A and typhoid vaccines can also be given as a single dose vaccine, hepatyrix or viatim. Self-treatment: none.

Hepatitis B

Hepatitis B is spread through infected blood, contaminated needles and sexual intercourse. It can also be spread from an infected mother to the baby during childbirth. It affects the liver, causing jaundice and occasionally liver failure. Most people recover completely, but some people might be chronic carriers of the virus, which could eventually lead to cirrhosis or liver cancer. Those visiting high-risk areas for long periods or those with increased social or occupational risk should be immunised. Many countries now give hepatitis B as part of the routine childhood vaccination. It is given by itself or at the same time as hepatitis A (hepatyrix).

A course will give protection for at least five years. It can be given over four weeks or six months. Self-treatment: none.

HIV

Human immunodeficiency virus (HIV), the virus that causes acquired immune deficiency syndrome (AIDS), is an enormous problem throughout Africa, but is most acutely felt in sub-Saharan Africa. The virus is spread through infected blood and blood products, by sexual intercourse with an infected partner and from an infected mother to her baby during childbirth and breastfeeding. It can be spread through 'blood-to-blood' contacts, such as with contaminated instruments during medical, dental, acupuncture and other body-piercing procedures, and through sharing used intravenous needles. At present there is no cure; medication that might keep the disease under control is available, but these drugs are too expensive for the overwhelming majority of Africans, and are not readily available for travellers either. If you think you might have been infected with HIV, a blood test is necessary; a three-month gap after exposure and before testing is required to allow antibodies to appear in the blood. Self-treatment: none.

Leptospirosis

This disease is spread through the excreta of infected rodents, especially rats. It can cause hepatitis and renal failure, which might be fatal. It is unusual for travellers to be affected unless living in poor sanitary conditions. It causes a fever and sometimes jaundice. Self-treatment: none.

Malaria

Malaria is present throughout Madagascar, particularly in the coastal areas; it is less common in the central highlands and Antananarivo, but outbreaks can occur. It is found throughout the Comoros. The disease is caused by a parasite in the bloodstream spread via the bite of the female *Anopheles* mosquito. There are several types of malaria, falciparum malaria being the most dangerous type. Infection rates vary with the seasons and climate, so check out the situation before departure. Several different drugs are used to prevent malaria and new ones are in the pipeline. Up-to-date advice from a travel health clinic is essential as some medication is more suitable for some travellers than others (eg people with epilepsy should avoid mefloquine, and doxycycline should not be taken by pregnant women or children younger than 12).

The early stages of malaria include headaches, fevers, generalised aches and pains, and malaise, which could be mistaken for flu. Other symptoms can include abdominal pain, diarrhoea and a cough. Anyone who develops a fever in a malarial area should assume malarial infection until a blood test proves negative, even if you have been taking antimalarial medication. If not treated, the next stage could develop within 24 hours, particularly if falciparum malaria is the parasite: jaundice, then reduced consciousness and coma (also known as cerebral malaria), followed by death. Treatment in hospital is essential, and the death rate might still be as high as 10% even in the best intensive-care facilities.

Many travellers are under the impression that malaria is a mild illness, and that taking antimalarial drugs causes more illness through side effects than actually getting malaria. This is unfortunately not true. If you decide that you really do not wish to take antimalarial drugs, you must understand the risks, and be obsessive about avoiding mosquito bites. Use nets and insect repellent, and report any fever or flu-like symptoms to a doctor as soon as possible. Some people advocate homeopathic preparations against malaria, such as Demal200, but as yet there is no conclusive evidence that this is effective, and many homeopaths do not recommend their use.

Adults who have survived childhood malaria have developed immunity and usually only develop mild cases of malaria; most Western travellers have no immunity at all. Immunity wanes after 18 months of non-exposure, so even if you have had malaria in the past and used to live in a malaria-prone area, you might no longer be immune.

Malaria in pregnancy frequently results in miscarriage or premature labour. The risks from malaria to both mother and foetus during pregnancy are considerable. Travel throughout the region when your pregnant should be carefully considered.

Meningococcal Meningitis

Meningococcal infection is spread through close respiratory contact and is more likely in crowded situations, such as dormitories, buses and clubs. Infection is uncommon in travellers. Vaccination is recommended for long stays and is especially important towards the end of the dry season. Symptoms include a fever, severe headache, neck stiffness and a red rash. Immediate medical treatment is necessary.

The ACWY vaccine is recommended for all travellers to the region. This vaccine is different from the meningococcal meningitis C vaccine given to children and adolescents in some countries; it is safe to be given both types of vaccine. Self-treatment: none.

Poliomyelitis

Polio is generally spread through contaminated food and water. It is one of the vaccines given in childhood and should be

HEALTH

THE ANTIMALARIAL A TO D

- **A** Awareness of the risk. No medication is totally effective, but protection of up to 95% is achievable with most drugs, as long as other measures have been taken.

- **B** Bites – avoid at all costs. Sleep in a screened room, use a mosquito spray or coils and sleep under a permethrin-impregnated net at night. Cover up at night with long trousers and long sleeves, preferably with permethrin-treated clothing. Apply appropriate repellent to all areas of exposed skin in the evenings.

- **C** Chemical prevention (ie antimalarial drugs) is usually required in malarial areas. Expert advice is needed as resistance patterns can change, and new drugs are in development. Not all antimalarial drugs are suitable for everyone. Most antimalarial drugs need to be started at least a week in advance and continued for four weeks after the last possible exposure to malaria.

- **D** Diagnosis – if you have a fever or flu-like illness within a year of travel to a malarial area, malaria is a possibility, and immediate medical attention is necessary.

boosted every 10 years, either orally (a drop on the tongue) or as an injection. Polio can be carried asymptomatically (ie showing no symptoms) and could cause a transient fever. In rare cases it causes weakness or paralysis of one or more muscles, which might be permanent. Self-treatment: none.

Rabies

Rabies is spread by being bitten or licked on broken skin by an infected animal. It is always fatal once the clinical symptoms start (which might be up to several months after an infected bite), so post-bite vaccination should be given as soon as possible. Post-bite vaccination (whether or not you've been vaccinated before the bite) prevents the virus from spreading to the central nervous system. Animal handlers should be vaccinated, as should those travelling to remote areas where a reliable source of post-bite vaccine is not available within 24 hours. Three preventive injections are needed over a month. If you have not been vaccinated you will need a course of five injections starting 24 hours or as soon as possible after the injury. If you have been vaccinated, you will need fewer post-bite injections, and have more time to seek medical help. Self-treatment: none.

Schistosomiasis (Bilharzia)

This disease is spread by flukes (minute worms) that are carried by a species of freshwater snail. The flukes are found inside the snail, which then sheds them into slow-moving or still water. The parasites penetrate human skin during paddling or swimming and then migrate to the bladder or bowel. They are passed out via stool or urine and could contaminate fresh water, where the cycle starts again. Paddling or swimming in suspect freshwater lakes or slow-running rivers should be avoided. There might be no symptoms. There might be a transient fever and rash, and advanced cases might have blood in the stool or in the urine. A blood test can detect antibodies if you suspect you have been exposed, and treatment is then possible in specialist travel or infectious disease clinics. If not treated, the infection can cause kidney failure or permanent bowel damage. It is not possible for you to infect others. Self-treatment: none.

Trypanosomiasis (Sleeping Sickness)

Spread via the bite of the tsetse fly, this disease causes a headache, fever and eventually coma. There is an effective treatment. Self-treatment: none.

Tuberculosis (TB)

TB is spread via close respiratory contact and occasionally through infected milk or milk products. BCG vaccination is recommended for those mixing closely with the local population, although it gives only moderate protection against TB. It's more important for long stays than for short-term stays. Inoculation with the BCG vaccine is not available in all countries. It is given routinely to many children in developing countries. The vaccination causes a small permanent scar at the site of injection, and is usually given in a specialised chest clinic. It is a live vaccine and shouldn't be given to pregnant women or immunocompromised individuals.

TB can be asymptomatic, only being picked up on a routine chest X-ray. Alternatively, it can cause a cough, weight loss or fever, sometimes months or even years after exposure. Self-treatment: none.

Typhoid

This is spread through food or water contaminated by infected human faeces. The first symptom is usually a fever or a pink rash on the abdomen. Sometimes septicaemia (blood poisoning) can occur. A typhoid vaccine (typhim Vi, typherix) will give protection for three years. In some countries, the oral vaccine Vivotif is also available. Antibiotics are usually given as treatment, and death is rare unless septicaemia occurs. Self-treatment: none.

Yellow Fever

Yellow fever is not a problem in Madagascar or the Comoros, but travellers should still carry a certificate as evidence of vaccination if they've recently been in an infected country, to avoid any possible difficulties with immigration. For a full list of these countries visit the websites of the **World Health Organization** (www.who.int/wer/) or the **Centers for Disease Control and Prevention** (www.cdc.gov/travel/blusheet.htm). A traveller without a legally required, up-to-date certificate may be vaccinated and detained in isolation at the port of arrival for up to 10 days or possibly repatriated.

TRAVELLER'S DIARRHOEA

Although it's not inevitable that you will get diarrhoea while travelling in Madagascar and the Comoros, it's certainly very likely. Diarrhoea is the most common travel-related illness – figures suggest that at least half of all travellers to Africa will get diarrhoea at some stage. Sometimes dietary changes, such as increased spices or oils, are the cause. To avoid diarrhoea, only eat fresh fruits or vegetables if cooked or peeled, and be wary of dairy products that might contain unpasteurised milk. Although freshly cooked food can often be a safe option, plates or serving utensils might be dirty, so you should be highly selective when eating food from street vendors (make sure that cooked food is piping hot all the way through).

If you develop diarrhoea, be sure to drink plenty of fluids, preferably an oral rehydration solution containing lots of salt and sugar. A few loose stools don't require treatment, but if you start having more than four or five loose stools a day, you should start taking an antibiotic (usually a quinoline drug, such as ciprofloxacin or norfloxacin) and an antidiarrhoeal agent (such as loperamide) if you are not within easy reach of a toilet. If diarrhoea is bloody, persists for more than 72 hours or is accompanied by fever, shaking chills or severe abdominal pain, you should seek medical attention.

Amoebic Dysentery

Contracted by eating contaminated food and water, amoebic dysentery causes blood and mucus in the faeces. It can be relatively mild and tends to come on gradually, but seek medical advice if you think you have the illness as it won't clear up without treatment (which is with specific antibiotics).

Giardiasis

This illness, like amoebic dysentery, is also caused by ingesting contaminated food or water. The illness usually appears a week or more after you have been exposed to the offending parasite. Giardiasis might cause only a short-lived bout of typical traveller's diarrhoea, but it can also cause persistent diarrhoea. Ideally, seek medical advice if you suspect you have giardiasis, but if you are in a remote area you could start a course of antibiotics.

ENVIRONMENTAL HAZARDS

Heat Exhaustion

This condition occurs following heavy sweating and excessive fluid loss with inadequate replacement of fluids and salt, and is particularly common in hot climates when taking unaccustomed exercise before full acclimatisation. Symptoms include headache, dizziness and tiredness. Dehydration is already happening by the time you feel thirsty – aim to drink sufficient water to produce pale, diluted urine. Self-treatment: fluid replacement with water and/or fruit juice, and cooling by cold water and fans. The treatment of the salt-loss component consists of consuming salty fluids (as in soup) and adding a little more table salt to foods than usual.

Heatstroke

Heat exhaustion is a precursor to the much more serious condition of heatstroke. In this case there is damage to the sweating mechanism, with an excessive rise in body temperature; irrational and hyperactive behaviour; and eventually loss of consciousness and death. Rapid cooling by spraying the body with water and fanning is ideal. Emergency fluid and electrolyte replacement is usually also required by intravenous drip.

Insect Bites & Stings

Mosquitoes might not always carry malaria or dengue fever, but they (and other insects) can cause irritation and infected bites. To avoid these, take the same precautions as you would for avoiding malaria (see p270). Bee and wasp stings cause real problems only to those who have a severe allergy to the stings (anaphylaxis), in which case, carry an adrenaline (epinephrine) injection.

Scorpions are frequently found in arid or dry climates. They can cause a painful bite that is sometimes life-threatening. If bitten by a scorpion, try taking a painkiller. Medical treatment should be sought if collapse occurs.

Bed bugs are often found in hostels and cheap hotels. They lead to very itchy, lumpy bites. Spraying the mattress with crawling insect killer after changing bedding will get rid of them.

Scabies is also frequently found in cheap accommodation. These tiny mites live in

HEALTH

the skin, particularly between the fingers. They cause an intensely itchy rash. The itch is easily treated with malathion and permethrin lotion from a pharmacy.

Water

High-quality water is available almost everywhere, and you need not fear drinking from taps. Drinking from streams might put you at risk of waterborne diseases.

TRADITIONAL MEDICINE

Although Western medicine is available in larger cities and towns, *fanafody* (traditional medicine or herbal healing) plays an important role in Madagascar. Many urban dwellers prefer traditional methods, visiting market kiosks to procure age-old remedies. *Ombiasy* (healers) hold considerable social status in many parts of the country, particularly in more remote areas where traditional practices are still strong. They are often consulted for a variety of ailments.

It remains unlikely in the short term that even a basic level of conventional Western-style medicine will be made available to all the people of Madagascar and the Comoros. Traditional medicine, on the other hand, will almost certainly continue to be practised widely.

HEALTH

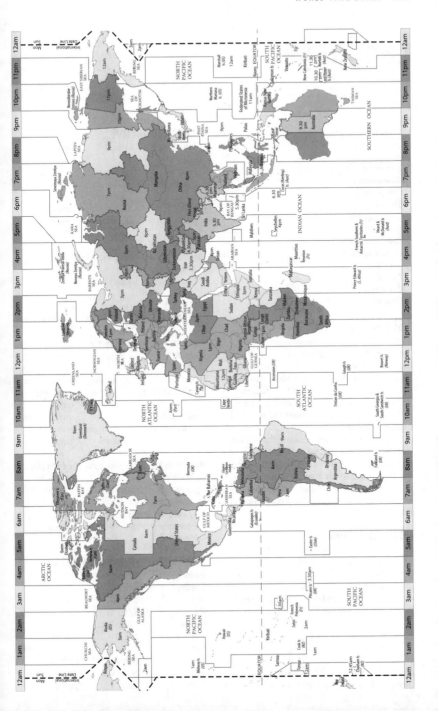

Language

CONTENTS

FRENCH

An important distinction is made in French between *tu* and *vous*, both of which mean 'you'; *tu* is only used when addressing people you know well, children or animals. If you're addressing an adult who isn't a personal friend, *vous* should be used unless the person invites you to use *tu*. In general, younger people insist less on this distinction between polite and informal, and you will find that in many cases they use *tu* from the beginning of an acquaintance.

For a more comprehensive guide to the language, pick up a copy of Lonely Planet's *French phrasebook*.

PRONUNCIATION

j as the 's' in 'leisure' (**zh** in our pronunciation guides)

c before **e** and **i**, as the 's' in 'sit'; before **a**, **o** and **u**, it's pronounced as English 'k'. When undescored with a 'cedilla' (**ç**), it's always pronounced as the 's' in 'sit'.

r pronounced from the back of the throat while restricting the flow of air

Most other letters in French are pronounced more or less the same as they would be in English. In any case, the pronunciation guides we've included should help make things a lot easier.

ACCOMMODATION

I'm looking for	*Je cherche ...*	zher shersh ...
a ...		
camping ground	*un camping*	un kom·peeng
guesthouse	*une pension (de famille)*	ewn pon·syon (der fa·mee·ler)
hotel	*un hôtel*	un o·tel
youth hostel	*une auberge de jeunesse*	ewn o·berzh der zher·nes

Do you have any rooms available?
Est-ce que vous avez des chambres libres?
e·sker voo·za·vay day shom·brer lee·brer

I'd like (a) ...	*Je voudrais ...*	zher voo·dray ...
single room	*une chambre à un lit*	ewn shom·brer a un lee
double-bed room	*une chambre avec un grand lit*	ewn shom·brer a·vek un gron lee
twin room with two beds	*une chambre avec des lits jumeaux*	ewn shom·brer a·vek day lee zhew·mo
room with a bathroom	*une chambre avec une salle de bains*	ewn shom·brer a·vek ewn sal der bun

How much is it ...?	*Quel est le prix ...?*	kel e ler pree ...
per night	*par nuit*	par nwee
per person	*par personne*	par per·son

May I see the room?
Est-ce que je peux voir la chambre?
es·ker zher per vwa la shom·brer

CONVERSATION & ESSENTIALS

Hello.	*Bonjour.*	bon·zhoor
Goodbye.	*Au revoir.*	o·rer·vwa
Yes.	*Oui.*	wee
No.	*Non.*	no
Please.	*S'il vous plaît.*	seel voo play
Thank you.	*Merci.*	mair·see
You're welcome.	*Je vous en prie.*	zher voo·zon pree
	De rien. (inf)	der ree·en
Excuse me.	*Excuse-moi.*	ek·skew·zay·mwa
Sorry. (forgive me)	*Pardon.*	par·don

EMERGENCIES

Help!
Au secours!   o skoor
There's been an accident!
Il y a eu un accident!   eel ya ew un ak·see·don
I'm lost.
Je me suis égaré/e. (m/f)   zhe me swee·zay·ga·ray
Leave me alone!
Fichez-moi la paix!   fee·shay·mwa la pay

Call ...!   Appelez ...!   a·play ...
  a doctor   un médecin   un mayd·sun
  the police   la police   la po·lees

What's your name?
Comment vous   ko·mon voo·za·pay·lay voo
appelez-vous? (pol)
Comment tu   ko·mon tew ta·pel
t'appelles? (inf)
My name is ...
Je m'appelle ...   zher ma·pel ...
Where are you from?
De quel pays êtes-vous?   der kel pay·ee et·voo
De quel pays es-tu? (inf)   der kel pay·ee e·tew
I'm from ...
Je viens de ...   zher vyen der ...
I like ...
J'aime ...   zhem ...
I don't like ...
Je n'aime pas ...   zher nem pa ...
Just a minute.
Une minute.   ewn mee·newt

DIRECTIONS

Where is ...?
Où est ...?   oo e ...
Go straight ahead.
Continuez tout droit.   kon·teen·way too drwa
Turn left.
Tournez à gauche.   toor·nay a gosh
Turn right.
Tournez à droite.   toor·nay a drwat
at the corner
au coin   o kwun

behind	derrière	dair·ryair
in front of	devant	der·von
far (from)	loin (de)	lwun (der)
near (to)	près (de)	pray (der)
opposite	en face de	on fas der
island	l'île	leel
lake	le lac	ler lak

museum	le musée	ler mew·zay
old city (town)	la vieille ville	la vyay veel
sea	la mer	la mair
square	la place	la plas
tourist office	l'office de	lo·fees der
	tourisme	too·rees·mer

HEALTH

I'm ill.   Je suis malade.   zher swee ma·lad
It hurts here.   J'ai une douleur   zhay ewn doo·ler
    ici.   ee·see

I'm allergic   Je suis   zher swee
to ...   allergique ...   za·lair·zheek ...
  antibiotics   aux antibiotiques   o zon·tee·byo·teek
  aspirin   à l'aspirine   a las·pee·reen
  bees   aux abeilles   o za·bay·yer
  nuts   aux noix   o nwa
  peanuts   aux cacahuètes   o ka·ka·wet
  penicillin   à la pénicilline   a la pay·nee·
    see·leen

antiseptic	l'antiseptique	lon·tee·sep·teek
aspirin	l'aspirine	las·pee·reen
condoms	des préservatifs	day pray·zair·va·teef
contraceptive	le contraceptif	ler kon·tra·sep·teef
diarrhoea	la diarrhée	la dya·ray
medicine	le médicament	ler may·dee·ka·mon
nausea	la nausée	la no·zay
sunblock cream	la crème solaire	la krem so·lair
tampons	des tampons	day tom·pon
	hygiéniques	ee·zhen·eek

LANGUAGE DIFFICULTIES

Do you speak English?
Parlez-vous anglais?   par·lay·voo ong·lay
Does anyone here speak English?
Y a-t-il quelqu'un qui   ya·teel kel·kung kee
parle anglais?   par long·glay
How do you say ... in French?
Comment est-ce qu'on   ko·mon es·kon
dit ... en français?   dee ... on fron·say
What does ... mean?
Que veut dire ...?   ker ver deer ...
I understand.
Je comprends.   zher kom·pron
I don't understand.
Je ne comprends pas.   zher ner kom·pron pa
Could you write it down, please?
Est-ce que vous pouvez   es·ker voo poo·vay
l'écrire?   lay·kreer
Can you show me (on the map)?
Pouvez-vous m'indiquer   poo·vay·voo mun·dee·kay
(sur la carte)?   (sewr la kart)

LANGUAGE

NUMBERS

0	*zero*	zay·ro
1	*un*	un
2	*deux*	der
3	*trois*	trwa
4	*quatre*	ka·trer
5	*cinq*	sungk
6	*six*	sees
7	*sept*	set
8	*huit*	weet
9	*neuf*	nerf
10	*dix*	dees
11	*onze*	onz
12	*douze*	dooz
13	*treize*	trez
14	*quatorze*	ka·torz
15	*quinze*	kunz
16	*seize*	sez
17	*dix-sept*	dee·set
18	*dix-huit*	dee·zweet
19	*dix-neuf*	deez·nerf
20	*vingt*	vung
21	*vingt et un*	vung tay un
22	*vingt-deux*	vung·der
30	*trente*	tront
40	*quarante*	ka·ront
50	*cinquante*	sung·kont
60	*soixante*	swa·sont
70	*soixante-dix*	swa·son·dees
80	*quatre-vingts*	ka·trer·vung
90	*quatre-vingt-dix*	ka·trer·vung·dees
100	*cent*	son
1000	*mille*	meel

QUESTION WORDS

Who?	*Qui?*	kee
What?	*Quoi?*	kwa
What is it?	*Qu'est-ce que c'est?*	kes·ker say
When?	*Quand?*	kon
Where?	*Où?*	oo
Which?	*Quel/Quelle?*	kel
Why?	*Pourquoi?*	poor·kwa
How?	*Comment?*	ko·mon

SHOPPING & SERVICES

I'd like to buy ...
  Je voudrais acheter ...   zher voo·dray ash·tay ...
How much is it?
  C'est combien?   say kom·byun
I don't like it.
  Cela ne me plaît pas.   ser·la ner mer play pa
May I look at it?
  Est-ce que je peux le voir?   es·ker zher per ler vwar

I'm just looking.
  Je regarde.   zher rer·gard
It's cheap.
  Ce n'est pas cher.   ser nay pa shair
It's too expensive.
  C'est trop cher.   say tro shair
I'll take it.
  Je le prends.   zher ler pron

Can I pay by ...?	*Est-ce que je peux payer avec ...?*	es·ker zher per pay·yay a·vek ...
credit card	*ma carte de crédit*	ma kart der kray·dee
travellers cheques	*des chèques de voyage*	day shek der vwa·yazh

more	*plus*	plew
less	*moins*	mwa
smaller	*plus petit*	plew per·tee
bigger	*plus grand*	plew gron

I'm looking for ...	*Je cherche ...*	zhe shersh ...
a bank	*une banque*	ewn bonk
the hospital	*l'hôpital*	lo·pee·tal
the market	*le marché*	ler mar·shay
the police	*la police*	la po·lees
the post office	*le bureau de poste*	ler bew·ro der post
a public phone	*une cabine téléphonique*	ewn ka·been tay·lay·fo·neek
a public toilet	*les toilettes*	lay twa·let

TIME & DATES

What time is it?	*Quelle heure est-il?*	kel er e til
It's (8) o'clock.	*Il est (huit) heures.*	il e (weet) er
It's half past ...	*Il est (...) heures et demie.*	il e (...) er e day·mee
in the morning	*du matin*	dew ma·tun
in the afternoon	*de l'après-midi*	der la·pray·mee·dee
in the evening	*du soir*	dew swar
today	*aujourd'hui*	o·zhoor·dwee
tomorrow	*demain*	der·mun
yesterday	*hier*	yair

Monday	*lundi*	lun·dee
Tuesday	*mardi*	mar·dee
Wednesday	*mercredi*	mair·krer·dee
Thursday	*jeudi*	zher·dee
Friday	*vendredi*	von·drer·dee
Saturday	*samedi*	sam·dee
Sunday	*dimanche*	dee·monsh

January	*janvier*	zhon·vyay
February	*février*	fayv·ryay

March	mars	mars
April	avril	a·vreel
May	mai	may
June	juin	zhwun
July	juillet	zhwee·yay
August	août	oot
September	septembre	sep·tom·brer
October	octobre	ok·to·brer
November	novembre	no·vom·brer
December	décembre	day·som·brer

TRANSPORT
Public Transport
I want to go to ...

	Je voudrais aller à ...	zher voo·dray a·lay a ...

What time does	À quelle heure	a kel er
... leave/arrive?	part/arrive ...?	par/a·reev ...
the boat	le bateau	ler ba·to
the bus	le bus	ler bews
the minibus taxi	le taxi-brousse	le tak·see broos
the plane	l'avion	la·vyon

I'd like a ...	Je voudrais	zher voo·dray
ticket.	un billet ...	un bee·yay ...
one-way	simple	sum·pler
return	aller et retour	a·lay ay rer·toor

the first	le premier (m)	ler prer·myay
	la première (f)	la prer·myair
the last	le dernier (m)	ler dair·nyay
	la dernière (f)	la dair·nyair
ticket office	le guichet	ler gee·shay
timetable	l'horaire	lo·rair

Private Transport
I'd like to hire	Je voudrais	zher voo·dray
a/an...	louer ...	loo·way ...
car	une voiture	ewn vwa·tewr
4WD	un quatre-quatre	un kat·kat
motorbike	une moto	ewn mo·to
bicycle	un vélo	un vay·lo

Is this the road to ...?
C'est la route pour ...? say la root poor ...
Where's a service station?
Où est-ce qu'il y a oo es·keel ya
une station-service? ewn sta·syon·ser·vees
Please fill it up.
Le plein, s'il vous plaît. ler plun seel voo play
I'd like ... litres.
Je voudrais ... litres. zher voo·dray ... lee·trer

petrol/gas	essence	ay·sons
unleaded	sans plomb	son plom
leaded	au plomb	o plom
diesel	diesel	dyay·zel

I need a mechanic.
J'ai besoin d'un zhay ber·zwun dun
mécanicien. may·ka·nee·syun
The car/motorbike has broken down (at ...)
La voiture/moto est la vwa·tewr/mo·to ay
tombée en panne (à ...) tom·bay on pan (a ...)
The car/motorbike won't start.
La voiture/moto ne veut la vwa·tewr/mo·to ner ver
pas démarrer. pa day·ma·ray
I have a flat tyre.
Mon pneu est à plat. mom pner ay ta pla
I've run out of petrol.
Je suis en panne zher swee zon pan
d'essence. day·sons
I had an accident.
J'ai eu un accident. zhay ew un ak·see·don

MALAGASY

Madagascar has two official languages: Malagasy and French. Malagasy is the everyday spoken language while French is often used for literary, business and administrative purposes, and in many of the more upmarket sectors of the tourism industry. Unless you travel on an organised tour, stick to big hotels in major towns or speak Malagasy, it'll be essential to speak at least basic French in order to get by comfortably in cities and towns. In rural areas, where knowledge of French is less widespread, you'll almost always find someone who speaks enough French to allow communication, but you may need to learn a bit of Malagasy also.

Although more Malagasy are learning English, relatively few people speak it and you shouldn't rely on English unless you are using middle- to top-range hotels and restaurants in Antananarivo, Nosy Be and Île Sainte Marie. If your French is poor, it isn't difficult to find someone in the major towns who is willing to try out whatever English words they might have picked up at school or elsewhere.

Malagasy belongs to the Austronesian family of languages; its closest linguistic relative is a language spoken in southern Borneo. Over the centuries it has incorporated numerous other influences, including Bantu (particularly in some of the west

DIALECTS

Despite the linguistic unity of Malagasy, regional differences do exist, and in some coastal areas, standard Malagasy is shunned. The three broad language groups are those of the highlands; the north and east; and the south and west. However, even within these areas there are local variations. The following table indicates a few of the lexical and phonetic differences between standard Malagasy and some of the regional dialects.

English	Highlands	North & East	South & West
Greetings.	*Manao ahoana.*	*Mbola tsara anarô.*	*Akore aby nareo.*
(reply)	*Tsara.*	*Mbola tsara.*	*Tsara/Soa.*
What's new?	*Inona no vaovao?*	*Ino vaovaonao?*	*Talilio?*
Nothing much.	*Tsy misy.*	*Ehe, tsisy fô manginginy.*	*Mbe soa.*
Where?	*Aiza?*	*Aia?*	*Aia?*
Who?	*Iza?*	*La?*	*La?*
spouse	*vady*	*vady*	*valy*
ancestor	*razana*	*raza*	*raza*

coast dialects) and Arabic. The influence of Arabic is most evident in the names of the days of the week.

Malagasy was first written using a form of Arabic script (see the 'Sorabe' box on p281), and then only in very limited areas in southeastern coastal Madagascar. It wasn't until the early 19th century during the reign of Radama I that Malagasy developed its current written form when missionaries from the London Missionary Society began devising the modern Latin-based alphabet. This 'standard Malagasy', which is based on the Merina dialect, has since served as the national language.

If you're serious about learning Malagasy, it'll be worth investing in one of the dictionaries or instructional textbooks that are available in Antananarivo bookshops.

PRONUNCIATION

When King Radama I sent out a request for missionaries from the London Missionary Society to help with the education and development of Madagascar, two of those sent were Welshmen David Jones and David Griffiths. Together with the king himself, they set about romanising and transliterating the Malagasy language. Despite this early effort, written Malagasy bears remarkably little resemblance to today's spoken language. Syllables seem to evaporate and vowels aren't pronounced the way English (or even French) speakers might anticipate. The general advice is to 'swallow as many syllables as you can and drop the last one'

– vowels at the end of most words are dropped in pronunciation.

The Malagasy alphabet has 21 letters; the English letters 'c', 'q', 'u', 'w' and 'x' don't exist in Malagasy. In words borrowed from English, French or other languages, the 'c' is replaced by an **s** or **k**, the 'q' is replaced by **k** and the 'x' by **ks**. When **k** or a **g** are preceded by an **i** or a **y** (which are pronounced more or less the same), the **i** is pronounced both before and after the **k** or **g**.

The letter **o** is usually pronounced like a double **o**; thus *veloma* (goodbye) emerges as 've-*loom*'. The letter **a** is pronounced as the 'u' in 'cut'.

You only have to glance at a map of the country and you'll notice that Malagasy place names generally contain lots of letters. Similarly, people's surnames can be a mouthful. In the interests of avoiding embarrassment or possible offence through mispronouncing family names, you may want to accept invitations to address people by their Christian names, which are often biblical.

CONVERSATION & USEFUL WORDS

Greetings/Good day.	*Salama.*
Welcome!	*Tonga soa!*
Come in.	*Midira.*
How are you?	*Manao ahoana ianao.*
I'm fine.	*Salama tsara aho.*
Very well, thank you.	*Tsara fa misaotra.*
What's new?	*Inona no vaovao?*
Nothing much.	*Tsy misy.*
Goodbye.	*Veloma/Manorapihaona.*

SORABE

The Sorabe (Great Writings) are sacred manuscripts written in Malagasy using a form of Arabic script. The earliest of these were made sometime after the 8th century under the influence of stranded Arab traders who wanted to reproduce pages of the Quran. The Sorabe were later expanded to include histories and genealogies, astrologers' predictions and various works on traditional medicine. Knowledge of the script used in writing the Sorabe was primarily the preserve of specially trained scribes known as *katibo*. Most Sorabe are in the possession of the Antaimoro and Antambohoaka tribes in southeastern Madagascar.

See you soon.	*Vetivety.*
See you later.	*Mandram pihaona.*
Yes.	*Eny/Eka.*
No.	*Tsia.*
Please/Excuse me.	*Azafady.*
Thank you (very much).	*Misaotra (indrindra).*
You're welcome.	*Tsy misy fisaorana.*
My name is ...	*... no anarako.*
Bon apetit!	*Mazoto a homana!*
Bon voyage!	*Tongava soa!*
Cheers!	*Ho ela velona!*
Sir/Madam	*Tompoko*

I don't understand.	*Tsy azoka.*
Alright/OK.	*Ekena.*
Show me.	*Atoroy ahy.*
How much is it?	*Ohatrinona?*
It's too expensive.	*Lafo loatra, lafo be.*
It's very cheap.	*Tena mora be.*
Please give me some.	*Mmba omeo aho.*
Where is ...?	*Aiza ...?*

chief	*lehibe*
driver	*mpamily*
father/mother	*ray/reny*
friend	*sakaiza*
man/woman	*lehilahy/vehivavy*
name	*anarana*
traveller	*mpandeha*

bad	*ratsy*
beautiful	*mahafinaritra/tsara tarehy*
big	*be*
deep	*lalina*
dirty	*maloto*

CITY & TOWN NAMES

Although most people continue to use French place names, since the time of independence, cities, towns and places have been officially known by their Malagasy names. The following list may help alleviate some of the confusion:

Malagasy	French
Ambohitra	Joffreville
Andasibe	Périnet
Andoany	Hell-Ville
Antananarivo	Tananarive
Antsiranana	Diego Suarez
Fenoarivo	Fénérive
Iharana	Vohémar
Mahajanga	Majunga
Mahavelona	Foulpointe
Nosy Boraha	Île Sainte Marie
Anantsogno	St Augustin
Taolagnaro	Fort Dauphin
Toamasina	Tamatave
Toliara	Tuléar

Pronunciation can be difficult; one general rule for Malagasy names is to drop word-final vowels.

easy	*mora*
good	*tsara*
interesting	*mahasondriana*
little	*kely*
lost	*very*
more	*mihoatra*
slow	*votsa*

accommodation	*zavatra ilaina*
bed	*fandriana*
breakfast	*sakafo maraina*
food	*hanina*
kitchen	*lakozia*
lunch	*sakafo antoandro*
room	*efitra*
tariff	*tarify*
water	*rano*

time	*fotoana*
today	*androany*
tomorrow	*rahampitso*
yesterday	*omaly*
beach	*morona*
beside	*akaiky*
boulevard	*arabe, araben*
to buy	*mividy*

danger	*loza*
entry/exit	*fidirana/fivoahana*
forest	*ala*
guide	*mpitarika*
help	*fanampiana*
island	*nosy*
lake	*farihy*
left/right	*havia/havanana*
map	*sarin tany*
market	*tsena*
sea	*ranomasina*
station	*gara*
street	*làlana*
to swim	*milomano*
to walk	*mandeha*
town/village	*tanana/vohitra*
waterfall	*riana*

COMORIAN

Arabic and French are both official languages of the Comoros, but the most commonly spoken language is Shimasiwa (Comorian), a dialect of Swahili. There are several variations, but they are all mutually understood. The local language on Anjouan is known as Shinzuani; on Mohéli, it's Shimwali; on Grande Comore, it's known as Shingadzija; and on Mayotte, it's called Mahorais. Very little English is spoken and visitors without at least a smattering of French may find themselves at a loss in the Comoros.

The following is a list of useful Comorian words and phrases. Unfortunately, Comorian spelling isn't standardised so you may see several different transliterations for these words.

CONVERSATION & USEFUL WORDS

Hello.	*Salama.*
Good day.	*Bariza.* (Grand Comore)
Good day. (in response)	*M'bona.*
Welcome.	*Karibu.*
How's it going?	*Njeje?* (Anjouan)
	Ndje? or *Habare sa?* (Mohéli & Mayotte)
Fine. (in response)	*Ndjema/Sijouha.*
Goodbye.	*Kwaheri.*
Good night.	*Lala ha unono.*
Please.	*Tafatvali.*
Thank you.	*Marahaba.*
Yes.	*Aiwa.*
No.	*Uh uh.*
I don't understand.	*Ntsu elewa.*

I don't speak Comorian.	*Mimi tsidji ourogowa shimasiwa.*
My name is ...	*Mi opara ...*
I'm from ...	*Mi tsila ...*
How much is this?	*Ryali nga?* or *Beyi hindri?*
That's expensive/ inexpensive.	*Ngohouzo anli/Rahisi.*
It's beautiful.	*Udjisa*
I'd like to go to ...	*Ngamwandzo nende ...*
Where?	*Ndahu?*
shady dealings	*makarakara*
Sir	*monye*
Madam	*bueni*
mother	*mama*
father	*baba*
grandmother/ elderly woman	*koko*
grandfather/ elderly man	*bakoko*
European/foreigner	*mzungu*

road/street	*pare*
beach	*mtsangani*
to drink	*hunua*
to swim	*huyeleya*
boat	*markabu*
to fish	*mulowa*
fisherman	*mulozi*
mosque	*mukiri*
the top or the peak	*liju*
town	*mjini*
post office	*poste*
paradise	*pevoni*
mosquito	*dundi*

It's hot.	*Ina moro.*
It's cold.	*Ina baridi.*
night	*uku*
day	*mtsana*
today	*leo*
tomorrow	*meso*
yesterday	*jana*

FOOD & DRINK

I'm hungry/thirsty.	*Ngamina ndzaya/nyora.*
Do you have anything to eat?	*Kamtsina bahidrou ya houla?*
I'm looking for a place to eat/sleep.	*Tamtsaho pvahanou nililye/nilale.*
Do you have ...?	*Ngagina ...?*
It's good.	*Ya djema*
to eat	*houla*
market	*shindoni* or *bazari*
banana	*masindza* or *ndrovi*
coconut (fresh/dried)	*idjavou/nadzi*

orange	*trundra*	**3**	*ndraru*
sugar	*muwa*	**4**	*nne*
coffee	*kafe*	**5**	*ntsanu*
milk	*dziwa*	**6**	*sita*
rice	*tsohole* or *mayele*	**7**	*nfukare*
bread	*mkatre*	**8**	*nane*
meat	*nyama*	**9**	*shenda*
tea	*kayi*	**10**	*kume*
chicken	*kuhu*	**11**	*kume na mwedja*
shark	*papa*	**12**	*kume na mbili*
lobster	*kamba diva*	**20**	*shirini*
water	*madji*	**30**	*mengo-mi-raru*
fish	*fi*	**40**	*mengo-mi-ne*
		100	*djana*

NUMBERS

1	*montsi, moja*	**200**	*majana mbili*
2	*mbili*	**300**	*majana mi-raru*
		1000	*shihwhi*

Also available from Lonely Planet:
French Phrasebook

Glossary

For a glossary of food and drink terms, see p41.

Agate – Agence d'Acceuil Télécom; telephone office
aloalo – elaborate woodcarvings used to adorn tombs
andevo – traditional underclass
andriana – noble
Angap – Association Nationale pour la Gestion des Aires Protégées (National Association for the Management of Protected Areas), the organisation that administers most of Madagascar's parks and reserves
Antaimoro – east coast tribe from the region around Manakara; also the name given to a type of handmade paper
Antakàrana – tribe from northern Madagascar
arabe/araben – avenue
ariary – Madagascar's new unit of currency; one ariary will equal five Malagasy francs
aye-aye – rare nocturnal lemur

bâché – small, converted pick-up truck
baie – bay
banga – colourful temporary dwelling built by bachelors in the Comoros
bangwe – village or town square
bao – a popular game in the Comoros and elsewhere in Africa, played by dropping polished seeds into a series of holes in a wooden board
baraza – stone bench found in the Comoros
Basse-Ville – lower town
bazary – market; often designated Bazary Kely (small market) or Bazary Be (big market)
be – 'big' in Malagasy; denotes larger parts of a town
betsa-betsa – an alcoholic drink made from fermented sugar-cane juice
Betsileo – Madagascar's third-largest tribe after the Merina and the Betsimisaraka
Betsimisaraka – Madagascar's second-largest tribe
Boina – Sakalava territory in the area around Mahajanga
boutre – single-masted dhow used for cargo
buxi – local term for minibus in Fianarantsoa and some other areas of Madagascar

camion-brousse – large truck used for passengers
cassava – root vegetable also known as manioc, or *mhogo* in Comorian
CFPF – Centre de Formation Professionnelle Forestière (Centre of Professional Forestry Training)
chambre d'hôtes – B&B-style accommodation, often in a family home

chiromani – cloth wrap worn by Comorian women
coelacanth – prehistoric fish, still living off the Comoros and southern Madagascar
collectivité territoriale – French overseas territory; status of Mayotte
Comorian – the English term for a person from the Comoros; also spelt Comorien or Comoran
côtier – literally 'person from the coast'; the term is usually used to describe someone who is not a member of the Merina tribe
coua – bird belonging to one of nine species of coucou

fady – taboo, forbidden
Famadihana – exhumation and reburial; literally 'the turning of the bones'
familiale – a synonym for *taxi-be* (big taxi)
Fihavanana – conciliation or brotherhood
fijoroana – a ceremony invoking the ancestors
fosa – a puma-like animal and the largest of Madagascar's carnivores (not to be confused with the *fossa*)
fossa – local name for the striped civet

galawa – Comorian dugout canoe
gare routière – bus station
gargote – cheap restaurant
gasy – Malagasy (pronounced 'gash')
gîte – rustic shelter
Grands Mariages – Comorian wedding ceremonies

Hajj – pilgrimage to Mecca
hasina – a force that flows from the land through the ancestors into the society of the living
Haute-Ville – upper town
hauts plateaux – highlands; the term is often used to refer to Madagascar's central plateau region
hira gasy – music, dancing and storytelling spectacles
hôtel de ville – town hall
hotely – small roadside place that serves basic meals
hova – commoners

Id-ul-Fitr – Muslim festival at the end of the fast of Ramadan; also spelt Eid-el-Fitr
Imerina – region ruled by the Merina
immeuble – building
indri – largest of Madagascar's lemur species

kabary – discourse performed by a highly skilled orator
kely – 'small' in Malagasy; often used to denote a township or satellite town

kianja – place or square; also known as *kianjan*

lac – lake
lakana – dugout canoe; synonym for *pirogue*
lalana – street
lamba – white cotton or silk scarf
lamba mena – literally 'red cloth'; used as a burial shroud, but is rarely red

Mahafaly – southern tribe
maki – Malagasy and Comorian term for a lemur
malabary – long gowns worn by dancers
masonjoany – face pack made from ground wood and water
medina – old Arab quarter of a Comorian town
Merina – Madagascar's largest tribe, centred in Antananarivo
metropole – continental France (as opposed to French overseas possessions)
mihrab – niche in a mosque indicating the direction of Mecca
minaret – tower of a mosque, from where the call to prayer is issued
mofo – bread, usually baked as baguettes
mora mora – 'slowly, slowly' or 'wait a minute'; often used to mean the Malagasy pace of life
Mosquée de Vendredi – Friday mosque
mzungu – foreigner or white person; mostly used in the Comoros

nosy – island
Nouvelle-Ville – new town

ombiasy – highly respected healers who not only prescribe herbal cures, but also carry out rituals to secure assistance from the ancestors, to balance out negative *vintana*, or to communicate with a *tromba* that has possessed a person

paositra – post office
parc marin – marine national park
parc national – national park
petit marché – small market
pic – peak
pirogue – dugout canoe
pisteur – untrained guide, often speaking Malagasy only
pousse-pousse – rickshaw

Ramadan – Muslim month of fasting from sunrise to sunset
rangani – marijuana; pronounced 'roungoun'
ranovola – a drink made by adding boiling water to the residue left in the pot used to cook rice; also known as *ranon'apango*
ravinala – literally 'forest leaves'; also known as travellers' palm, the most distinctive of Madagascar's palm trees
Réseau National des Chemins de Fer Malgaches (RNCFM) – Madagascar's rail system

réserve forestière – forest reserve
réserve spéciale – special reserve (often similar to a national park)
rhumerie – bar selling varieties of rum
RN – route nationale; national road (often still no more than a track)
rova – palace

Sakalava – western tribe
salegy – Kenyan-influenced music of the Sakalava tribe
salon de thé – tea room
sambatra – mass circumcision ceremony
sambos – samosas
Sava – region comprising Sambava, Andapa, Vohémar (Iharana) and Antalaha
sifaka – a type of lemur, known in French as a *propithèque*
sigaoma – a type of music similar to black South African popular music
stationnement de taxi-brousse – bush-taxi station

table d'hôtes – fixed menu or set meal
tapia – small red berries that taste similar to dates
tavy – Malagasy term for the slash-and-burn method of agriculture
taxi-be – literally 'big taxi'; also known as a *familiale*
taxi-brousse – bush taxi; generic term for any kind of public passenger truck, car or minibus
taxi-spécial – charter taxi
taxi-ville – literally 'town taxis'; used for shorter distances
tenrec – small mammal resembling a hedgehog or shrew
THB – Three Horses Beer, Madagascar's most popular beer
tilapia – freshwater perch (fish)
tromba – spirit
tsapika – a form of music that originated in the south
tsingy – limestone pinnacle formations; also known as karst

valiha – a stringed instrument that is played like a harp
vary – Malagasy for rice
vazaha – foreigner or white person
Vezo – nomadic fishing subtribe of the Sakalava, found in the southwest
vintana – destiny
voay – crocodile

WWF – World Wide Fund for Nature

ylang-ylang – bush with sweet-smelling white flowers used to make perfume

Zafimaniry – a subgroup of the Betsileo people who live in the area east of Ambositra, and are renowned for their woodcarving skills
zebu – a type of domesticated ox found throughout Madagascar; it has a prominent hump on its back and loose skin under its throat

Behind the Scenes

THIS BOOK

This is the 5th edition of *Madagascar & Comoros*. The 1st edition of this book was researched and written by Robert Willcox, the 2nd edition by Deanna Swaney, the 3rd by Paul Greenway and the 4th by Mary Fitzpatrick. This edition was written and researched by Gemma Pitcher; Patricia Wright contributed the Environment chapter.

THANKS from the Author

Firstly, a big thanks to all the anonymous Malagasy and Comorian people who helped me out in a million small ways during my stay – from saving me a seat on a *taxi-brousse* (bush taxi) to giving me directions as I wandered around various towns with my clipboard! Secondly, huge thanks to the following people who helped me so much with my research: Joanna from Durrell Wildlife Trust, Sally from Conservation International, Sonia from Boogie Pilgrim, Robert in Nosy Be, the tourism offices in Grand Comore and Mayotte, Paolo from the EU in Mohéli, Christian and Giselle, Rakoto and Olivier in Maroantsetra, Tom in Mananara, Angelin the demon motorbike rider on Île Sainte Marie, Henri in Anjouan, all the staff of Angap, Harry from Za Tours, James Ingham from BBC World TV, Brett and the Azafady volunteers in Fort Dauphin, Alain and Gilles in Toliara and Franćcois in Andringitra.

Thanks also to Federico, Christine, Adrien, Fabien, Daniel and Anne-Hélène, and Christian and Iris for sharing their travel experiences with me while on the road, and all the Lonely Planet book and website readers who wrote in with feedback. Finally, thanks as always to Mut, Noster, Dof – and Marc Douma.

CREDITS

This edition of *Madagascar & Comoros* 5 was commissioned and developed in Lonely Planet's Melbourne office by Hilary Rogers. The manuscript was assessed by Cathy Lanigan, and Will Gourlay steered the book through production. Cartography for this guild was developed by Shahara Ahmed. The book was coordinated by Nancy Ianni (editorial) and James Ellis (cartography). Holly Alexander, Susannah Farfor, Carly Hall and Lara Morcombe assisted with editing and proofing. Chris Crook, Jack Gavran and Jenny Jones assisted with cartography. Sally Darmody and Laura Jane laid the book out. Wendy Wright designed the cover and Maria Vallianos did the artwork. Quentin Frayne prepared the Language chapter. Overseeing production were Ray Thomson (Project Manager); Kerryn Burgess and Danielle North (Managing Editors), with assistance from Darren O'Connell and Melanie Dankel; and Shahara Ahmed (Managing Cartographer). Thanks to Fiona Siseman, Gerard Walker and Glenn Beanland from LPI.

THANKS from Lonely Planet

Many thanks to the travellers who used the last edition and wrote to us with helpful hints, useful advice and interesting anecdotes:

A Kelyn Akuna, Martine & Gérard Aymonnier **B** Bierta Barfod, Inge Bartsch, Kathryn Baskerville, Patricia Bernard, Martin Bohnstedt, Andrea Brugnoli, Meti Buh, Terence Burgers, Alexis Burke, Martin J Byrne **C** Dan Cavanagh, Rita Chambers, Flavio Ciferri, Nat Ciferri, Lisa Cliff, Ofir Cohen, Richard Cooper, Ortwin Costenoble, Marie Cousens, Zsolt Cseke **D** Andrea de Laurentiis, Ivo Domburg **E** Na'ama Eilat, Alink Ellen **F** Bianca Frei **G** Witek Gdowski, Sheena M Gibson, Arend

Goens **H** Johan Hedve, Cherifa Hendriks, Miriam Henze, Hilmar Jobst Herzberg, Julian Hewitt, Simon Hill, Gill Hoggard, Nardy Hudson, Charlie Humble, Krista Humble **J** Volkmar E Janicke **K** Alan Keeble, Michael Keller, Metka Koren, Elena Kostoglodova, David Kromka **L** Bruno Laforge, Menno & Angela Lanting, Jo Leech, Laura Lefkowitz, Adam Levine, David Lewis, Margaret Lorang **M** Bianka Madej, Monika & Alex Marion, Silvia Merli, Nick Morphet, Stephen Muecke, Strother Murray **N** Frick Nadja, Fabrizio Nicoletti, Jochen Nicolini, Suzanne Nuttall **O** Gustaf Ossmer **P** Nicki Parnell, Ilan Peri, Ann M Pescatello, Hans Pflug, Mark Pickens, Jean-Pierre Pignard, John Pitterle, Apurv Puri **R** Helen Randle, Sarah Ravaioli, Sue Rees, Paula Jane Reid, John Robertson, Andrew Robson, Ayliffe Rose **S** Andrea Michele Sacripanti, Oyvind Sathre, Beth Schaeffer, Kyley Schmidt, Derek Schuurman, Mark Shahinian, Rieky Slenders, Vernon & Susanne Steward, Mark Sutcliffe **T** Benita Tapster, Mara Tattarletti, Brock Thiessen, Lesuthu Tshepo **V** Ingrid Van de Ven, Vincent van Reenen, Dominique & Anond Viki **W** Iain Walker, Thomas Werner, Richard H Wiersema, John Wilson, Manfred Wolfensberger **Y** Rodger Young **Z** Maya Zeller

ACKNOWLEDGMENTS

Many thanks to the following for the use of their content:

Mark Eveleigh for allowing us to reproduce material from his book, *Maverick in Madagascar*.

Globe on back cover © Mountain High Maps 1993 Digital Wisdom, Inc.

SEND US YOUR FEEDBACK

We love to hear from travellers – your comments keep us on our toes and help make our books better. Our well-travelled team reads every word on what you loved or loathed about this book. Although we cannot reply individually to postal submissions, we always guarantee that your feedback goes straight to the appropriate authors, in time for the next edition. Each person who sends us information is thanked in the next edition – and the most useful submissions are rewarded with a free book.

To send us your updates – and find out about LP events, newsletters and travel news – visit our award-winning website: **www.lonelyplanet.com**.

Index

MAP LEGEND

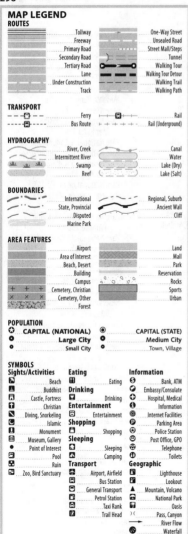

LONELY PLANET OFFICES

Australia
Head Office
Locked Bag 1, Footscray, Victoria 3011
☎ 03 8379 8000, fax 03 8379 8111
talk2us@lonelyplanet.com.au

USA
150 Linden St, Oakland, CA 94607
☎ 510 893 8555, toll free 800 275 8555
fax 510 893 8572, info@lonelyplanet.com

UK
72–82 Rosebery Ave,
Clerkenwell, London EC1R 4RW
☎ 020 7841 9000, fax 020 7841 9001
go@lonelyplanet.co.uk

France
1 rue du Dahomey, 75011 Paris
☎ 01 55 25 33 00, fax 01 55 25 33 01
bip@lonelyplanet.fr, www.lonelyplanet.fr

Published by Lonely Planet Publications Pty Ltd
ABN 36 005 607 983

© Lonely Planet 2004

© photographers as indicated 2004

Cover photographs: Verreaux's sifaka, Kevin Schafer/Corbis (front);
Outrigger on Nosy Komba, Carol Polich/Lonely Planet Images (back).
Many of the images in this guide are available for licensing from
Lonely Planet Images: www.lonelyplanetimages.com.

Printed through SNP SPrint Singapore Pte Ltd at
KHL Printing Co Sdn Bhd Malaysia